Quentin Bell is Emeritus Professor of the H
University. Born in 1910, he is a painter, a s
art critic. He has held a number of academ
in Art Education, King's College, Newca
University; Slade Professor of Fine Art, Oxford University, and Ferens
rofessor of Fine Art, Hull University. His works include: *On Human Finery*,
Those Impossible English (with Helmut Gernsheim), *Roger Montané*, *The
Schools of Design*, *Ruskin*, *Victorian Artists* and *Bloomsbury*.

biography of Virginia Woolf won both the James Tait Black Memorial
e and the Duff Cooper Memorial Prize.

Quentin Bell

Virginia Woolf

A Biography

VOLUME TWO
Mrs Woolf
1912 – 1941

**TRIAD
GRANADA**

Published by Triad/Granada in 1976
Reprinted 1979, 1982

0 586 08354 5

Triad Paperbacks Ltd is an imprint of
Chatto, Bodley Head & Jonathan Cape Ltd and
Granada Publishing Ltd

First published in Great Britain by The Hogarth
Press Ltd 1972
Copyright © 1972 Quentin Bell

Made and printed in Great Britain by
Richard Clay (The Chaucer Press) Ltd
Bungay, Suffolk
Set in Monotype Bembo

CONTENTS

ILLUSTRATIONS

Virginia Woolf.

Margaret Llewelyn Davies and Leonard Woolf, 1916. Virginia walking in Cornwall, 1916. Vanessa Bell in 1914. Ka Cox at Asham, 1914.

Duncan Grant, Maynard Keynes and Clive Bell at Charleston, 1919. Barbara Bagenal, 1921. Katherine Mansfield, 1920 (*reproduced by courtesy of Miss I. C. Baker*).

Virginia Woolf, c. 1925. V. Sackville-West, 1926 (*reproduced by courtesy of Nigel Nicolson*). Lydia Lopokova, c. 1920. Lady Ottoline Morrell by Simon Bussy (*The National Portrait Gallery, London*).

Carrington and Ralph Partridge with Lytton Strachey at Ham Spray, 1930. Roger Fry, Desmond MacCarthy and Clive Bell at Charleston, 1933. Angus Davidson. George Rylands.

T. S. Eliot. E. M. Forster. Julian Bell, 1932. Leonard and Virginia at Cassis, 1928.

Hugh Walpole. Leonard Woolf at Monk's House, c. 1933. Virginia with John Lehmann, c. 1931.

Virginia with Angelica Bell, 1932. (*Photograph by Lettice Ramsey.*) Virginia with V. Sackville-West at Monk's House. Virginia with Ethel Smyth at Monk's House.

Head of Virginia Woolf by Stephen Tomlin, 1931 (*The National Portrait Gallery, London*).

ACKNOWLEDGMENTS

In the first volume of this Biography I expressed my gratitude to those individuals and corporate bodies without whose aid or encouragement it would not have been undertaken at all; and to those others whose help in one way or another advanced its progress. With the completion of this volume my obligations are further extended. I should like to express or repeat my thanks to the following for the help that they have given and the permissions they have granted:

Christabel Lady Aberconway; Lord Annan; Dr Igor Anrep; Mr Mark Arnold-Forster; Mrs Barbara Bagenal; Mrs Mary Bennett; Miss Mary Bennett of the Walker Art Gallery, Liverpool; Professor John W. Bicknell of Drew University; Miss Elizabeth Bowen; Mr Gerald Brenan and Messrs Hamish Hamilton Ltd; the British Broadcasting Corporation; Mr Noel Carrington; Mr John Carter; Lord David Cecil; Mr Angus Davidson; Mrs Pamela Diamand; Mrs Beata Duncan; Mrs David Garnett; Mr Duncan Grant; Professor Leon Edel; Mrs T. S. Eliot; the late E. M. Forster and King's College, Cambridge; Mr Nicholas Furbank; Mr Philip Gaskell, Librarian of Trinity College, Cambridge; Miss Winifred Gill; Dr and Mrs A. D. Harris; Lady Hills; Mr Michael Holroyd; the staff of the India Office Records; Mr Julian Jebb; Lady Roderick Jones; Mr David Jolley; Sir Geoffrey Keynes; Miss Jacqueline Latham; Mr John Lehmann; Mrs Su Hua Ling; Longman Group Ltd for permission to quote from *Ethel Smyth, A Biography* by Christopher St John; Mr Michael MacCarthy; M. Georges Mevil-Blanche; the late Charles Mauron; Mrs Louie Mayer; the late Mrs Robin Mayor; Dr A. N. L. Munby, Librarian of King's College, Cambridge; Mrs Lyn Newman; Mr Benedict Nicolson; Mr Nigel Nicolson; Miss Lucy Norton; Mr Stanley B. Olson; Mrs Ian Parsons; Mrs Ralph Partridge; Mr Kenneth Phelps; Sir Edward Playfair; Mr William Plomer; Mrs Sophie Pryor; Miss Berta Ruck; Mr George Rylands; Miss Daphne Sanger; The Society of Authors as the Literary Representative of the Estate of Katherine Mansfield; Mr George A. Spater; Mr Stephen Spender; the late Sebastian Sprott; Mrs James Strachey; Mrs Lola Szladits, Curator of the Berg Collection, New York Public Library; Mr Barry Till of Morley College; Mr Julian Trevelyan; Dame Janet Vaughan; Mrs Julian Vinogradoff; and Mr C. J. White.

A Dinner Party at 46:

Here we have the first entertainment: which comprised, reading from left to right, Mr Bell, Lytton Strachey, Lord Robert Cecil, Mrs Humphry Ward, the Quaker, & the poet Yeats. Such an assembly had rarely got together, & seldom sprung apart. Now they did both. "Ha" said Mrs Ward.

"Hum" said the Quaker.

"Huh!" said Lord Robert

& "Tosh!" said Lytton.

The Poet Yeats was not observed to make a single remark, but grinding his teeth, & stamping his feet produced a sound which was expressive of considerable mental engagement in a congealed condition.

Virginia Woolf's handwriting, 1925

Chapter One

1912–1915

Virginia and Leonard are engaged. They appeared this morning to tell me so and seemed very happy. It happened some days ago but they kept it secret till we returned.

(Vanessa Bell to Roger Fry, 2 June, 1912)

IT was not a very well kept secret nor in any way a surprise for their friends, who had been discussing the possibility of such an engagement for a long time. Vanessa had undoubtedly been hoping for it; she saw well enough that Leonard was the only one of Virginia's suitors whom she could respect both as a man and as an intelligence. For their friends the marriage had the double advantage of keeping him in England while giving her a husband whom they liked. Of these, one, Lytton, received the news in the form of a postcard bearing the words:

Ha! Ha!
Virginia Stephen
Leonard Woolf

One may suppose that he was both amused and relieved.

Clive was the only person whose feelings were in some measure to be pitied. His passion for Virginia was much less acute than it had been two years earlier, and his infidelities had taken a new direction; but he still felt, and was always to feel, that he had a special relationship with and a special claim upon her. He wrote to her to say that he would always cheat himself into believing that he appreciated and loved her better than did her husband. This, it would appear, was not unkindly received; but unfortunately Clive's feelings for Virginia were equally compounded of love and of exasperation. This, if it was not clear to her already, was certainly made so when Adrian showed her letters in which Clive, giving vent to his frustrations, had said some very bitter things indeed. Virginia and Leonard were incensed and there was the devil to pay in Brunswick Square and Gordon Square where everyone seemed to be cross with everyone else. Vanessa had the thankless role of peacemaker and in the end succeeded in her task; Leonard and Virginia were too happy to remain angry for long and there was a general reconciliation. But, as Vanessa remarked: "an engagement seems an exhausting and bewildering thing even to the bystanders."

The principals certainly found it so. There were a great many people whom Leonard had to meet: George and Gerald Duckworth, Aunt Minna, Aunt Mary, Aunt Anny, Jack Hills, Nelly Cecil. All these belonged to the past and their disapproval might be endured with philosophy. But there were others of greater consequence; above all there was Violet Dickinson. At one time Virginia had felt that Violet's good opinion of her was essential to her happiness; this was no longer the case; but it was still necessary that Violet should be informed and her approbation solicited. Virginia wrote to her, almost in a spirit of bravado:

> 38 Brunswick Square W.C.
> June 4, 1912

My Violet,

I've got a confession to make. I'm going to marry Leonard Woolf. He's a penniless Jew. I'm more happy than anyone ever said was possible—but I *insist* upon your liking him too. May we both come on Tuesday? Would you rather I come alone? He was a great friend of Thoby's, went out to India—came back last summer when I saw him, and he has been living here since the winter. You have always been such a splendid and delightful creature, whom I've loved ever since I was a mere chit, that I couldn't bear it if you disapproved of my husband. We've been talking a great deal about you. I tell him you're 6 ft 8″, and that you love me.

My novel's just upon finished. L. thinks my writing the best part of me. We're going to work very hard. Is this too incoherent? The one thing that must be made plain is my intense feeling of affection for you. How I've bothered you—and what a lot you've always given me

> your Sp[arroy]

Fortunately Leonard and Violet were ready enough to like each other, although Virginia's marriage could not but increase a separation which was already becoming evident.

The case of Madge Vaughan was different; Leonard could not understand what Virginia had ever found to admire in such over-scented sensibility. But Madge no longer counted for much in Virginia's life and her husband, Will Vaughan, whom Leonard frankly disliked, counted for even less. Then there were the Vaughan sisters, Emma and Marny; the meeting with Emma was no more than a formality; but Marny, working for the Care Committee amongst the poor of Hoxton, became, in her way, influential. Leonard, who had returned to England with a considerable sense of social duty, was sufficiently interested in Marny's efforts to offer to take a part in them. He paid several visits to the East End; what he saw of the horrors of urban poverty and of the futile charities to which poor Marny devoted her life made him a socialist. Another of Virginia's acquaintances whom he now met for the first time was to give a more precise direction to his developing political understanding. This was Margaret Llewelyn Davies, a woman of enormous energy and intelligence which she devoted largely to the organisation of the Women's Co-operative Guild, of which she was Secretary. Virginia had come to know her through Janet Case, her Greek teacher, and these two, Margaret and Janet, not only remained her loyal friends for life but were to prove amongst Leonard's best allies in the calamities of the ensuing years.

Virginia for her part had to meet the Woolf family. It was a daunting experience. Leonard himself was sufficiently Jewish to seem to her disquietingly foreign; but in him the trait was qualified. He had become so very much a citizen of her world that, unless she had married Lytton, she could hardly have remained more completely in Bloomsbury. But Leonard's widowed mother, a matriarchal figure living with her large family in Colinette Road, Putney, seemed very alien to Virginia. No place could have been less like home than her future mother-in-law's house.

And how did the Woolfs regard her? Did they perceive that she thought their furniture hideous? Did she seem to them a haughty goy thinking herself too good for the family of their brilliant son? I am afraid that probably they did.

When in *Night and Day* Ralph Denham brings Katherine Hilbery to visit his family in Highgate, Virginia is surely remembering that first visit to the Woolf family. Whether the situation was saved, as in the novel it was saved, must be doubted. Virginia seems to have disgraced herself.

"A sandwich, Miss Stephen–or may I call you Virginia?"
"What? Ham sandwiches for tea?"
"Not *Ham*: potted meat. We don't eat Ham or bacon or Shellfish in this house."
"Not Shell fish? Why not shell fish?"
"Because it says in the Scriptures that they are unclean creatures & our Mr Josephs at the Synagogue–&–"
It was queer.

Virginia was ready to allow that Mrs Woolf had some very good qualities, but her heart must have sunk as she considered what large opportunities she would have for discovering them.

"Work and love and Jews in Putney take it out of me," she wrote, and it was certainly true. She and Leonard undertook many excursions that were purely delightful: walking, riding, listening to the Opera or watching the Russian dancers, but she still had her novel to finish: it was always about to be finished. It is not surprising that she was at times unwell.

The wedding had been planned for 12 August, but it was moved forward to suit the Bells. It therefore took place on Saturday, 10 August, the official business being conducted at St Pancras Registry Office. (It was perhaps for this reason that Mrs Woolf did not attend.) To Virginia it seemed a very good way of getting married, very simple and soon done. Nevertheless the Registrar found it trying, partly because he was, or so it seemed to Virginia, half blind, partly because a violent thunderstorm was raging and partly because, when it came to witnessing the marriage, he got muddled by names which were, to him, unfamiliar: Virginia and, still worse, Vanessa. And then, in her vague but deliberate way, Vanessa interrupted the proceedings. She wanted to change the name of her younger son; how should she set about it?

George and Gerald, in frock coats and everything else that the occasion could demand, attended the wedding breakfast given by the Bells at 46 Gordon Square. They must have been somewhat distressed by the appearance of Duncan Grant which, in intention, was equally ceremonious but somehow failed in its effect, and by a conversation which turned upon the best manner of pawning clothes. Those which Duncan wore could not have been pawned; he could never have redeemed them. They were, only too evidently, borrowed from wearers of very different sizes. The other guests were Roger Fry, Saxon Sydney-Turner, Aunt Mary Fisher (carrying a crutch) and Frederick Etchells, who came bearded, bespectacled and uncouth, to lend a final touch of oddity to the scene.

Although she had been agitated earlier in the morning, Virginia enjoyed both the ceremony and the party. When this was over she and Leonard left for Asham in high spirits. They spent the night there and then went to stay for a few days in the Quantocks before going abroad. They had had the idea of taking their honeymoon in Iceland; but it was too late in the season and they set off from Somerset in a more orthodox direction, to Avignon and Vaucluse and thence to Spain.

In Barcelona the food was bad, in Madrid the heat was overpowering; they went on to Toledo and Saragossa. They were desperately hot and often tired; but the bareness and the beauty of the country amazed them. They rode on mules and took dilatory trains. Virginia read Dostoievsky and Charlotte M. Yonge. Presently they found themselves in Valencia and by now she was reading *Le Rouge et le Noir*. From Valencia a boat took them to Marseilles; they travelled on into northern Italy and Venice, which, after Spain, seemed comfortable but decidedly tame. At last on 3 October* they returned to London. They had, so they declared, talked incessantly and become "chronically nomadic and monogamic."

They were wrong in thinking of themselves as nomads. Never again were they to travel so far or for so long; but certainly they were, in comparison with most of their friends, monogamous. In two months of wandering they had discovered that their personalities were complementary, their sympathies extraordinarily close. Their love and admiration for each other, based as it was upon a real understanding of the good qualities in each, was strong enough to withstand the major and the minor punishments of fortune, the common vexations of matrimony and, presently, the horrors of madness. It is a proof of their deep and unvarying affection that it was not dependent upon the intenser joys of physical love. Even before her marriage, they must have suspected that Virginia would not be physically responsive, but probably they hoped that Leonard, whose passionate nature was never in question, could effect a change. A letter written from Saragossa to Ka Cox shows clearly enough that, if this hope was entertained, it was also disappointed.

> Why do you think people make such a fuss about marriage & copulation? Why do some of our friends change upon losing chastity? Possibly my great age makes it less of a catastrophe; but certainly I find the climax immensely exaggerated. Except for a sustained good humour (Leonard shan't see this) due to the fact that every twinge of anger is at once visited upon my husband, I might still be Miss S.

Thus, with placid conversational ease, Virginia alludes to her frigidity. It was, nevertheless, a cause of worry to both of them, and when they were back in England they sought Vanessa's advice.

* "... at the end of November ..."–Leonard Woolf (*Beginning Again*, p. 83). For once he is at fault, perhaps owing to the fact that he kept no diary during the autumn of 1912. See VB/VW, 19 August 1912 and VW/VD, 11 October 1912.

They seemed very happy, but are evidently both a little exercised in their minds on the subject of the Goat's coldness. I think I perhaps annoyed her but may have consoled him by saying that I thought she never had understood or sympathised with sexual passion in men. Apparently she still gets no pleasure at all from the act, which I think is curious. They were very anxious to know when I first had an orgasm. I couldnt remember. Do you? But no doubt I sympathised with such things if I didnt have them from the time I was 2.

Vanessa, Leonard and, I think, Virginia herself were inclined to blame George Duckworth. George certainly had left Virginia with a deep aversion to lust; but perhaps he did no more than inflame a deeper wound and confirm Virginia in her disposition to shrink from the crudities of sex, a disposition which resulted from some profound and perhaps congenital inhibition. I think that the erotic element in her personality was faint and tenuous. Of the two women who knew her best, one, as we have seen, said that she had no understanding of sexual passion in men, the other – Vita Sackville-West – was to note many years later that "She dislikes the possessiveness and love of domination in men. In fact she dislikes the quality of masculinity." I would go further and suggest that she regarded sex, not so much with horror, as with incomprehension; there was, both in her personality and in her art, a disconcertingly aetherial quality and, when the necessities of literature compel her to consider lust, she either turns away or presents us with something as remote from the gropings and grapplings of the bed as is the flame of a candle from its tallow.

But although Virginia was sexually frigid, in other respects she seems to have entertained all the hopes and fears of any normal bride. About a week after her return to London she wrote:

> 38 Brunswick Square, W.C.
> Oct 11 1912

My Violet,
    Yesterday, happening to go into one of the bachelor sitting rooms, I discovered a cradle, fit for the illegitimate son of an Empress. When I brought forth my theory, however, they fathered the cradle on me. I blushed, disclaimed any intention, and so on: and blushing leant my elbow on a table. "What a beautiful table this is anyhow!" I exclaimed, thinking to lead the conversation away from my lost virginity and the probable fruits of it. The table was disclaimed too. Bit by bit I pieced together the story–how a great packing case had arrived, how Miss Dickinson etc etc. Nobody but Miss Dickinson could deal with the facts of life so boldly of course. Nobody else ever routed old shops to

such effect. My baby shall sleep in the cradle. I'm going to eat my dinner off the table tonight.

At this time, Virginia was still cheerfully expecting to have children. Leonard already had his misgivings but I do not think that Virginia became aware of them until the beginning of 1913. Before that time the Woolfs (to use a term which passed into common use amongst their friends) had moved out of Brunswick Square, their place being taken by Maynard Keynes's brother Geoffrey, and had found rooms in Clifford's Inn, just off Fleet Street. This took them out of Bloomsbury, and had the double advantage that they were more exclusively in each other's company and that they had more time for work.

There was plenty of work to be done. Leonard on his return had accepted a part-time job at the Grafton Galleries until the end of the year; here Roger Fry was showing his Second Post-Impressionist Exhibition. It was Leonard's duty to deal with the indignant artlovers who exploded with mirth or with rage before the works of Picasso and Matisse. It must have been an exasperating and a depressing job. Virginia was irritated on Leonard's behalf and also because, as sometimes happened, she found herself out of patience with the art of painting. Artists, she declared, "are an abominable race. The furious excitement of these people all the winter over their pieces of canvas coloured green and blue, is odious." I think she resented the fact that Leonard should be engaged in the service of "an inferior art." By this time she must surely have realised that he might excel in a more serious art form: the novel. *The Village in the Jungle* was finished before their marriage. At what point Virginia read it we cannot tell (it was accepted for publication by Edward Arnold in November); when she did see it she admired it very much. In fact they both intended to make their living by writing. They entertained the idea of starting a magazine of their own, but this, like all such notions, required money; they hoped but failed to raise £2000 for it. In addition Leonard had certainly decided that he must be politically active and was, by the beginning of 1913, strenuously undertaking his own political education. At the same time, when the job at the Grafton Galleries came to an end, he began to look for some other equivalent employment.

Virginia's own work continued to present formidable difficulties. Leonard has described her as writing with "a kind of tortured intensity" during the months of January and February, when *The Voyage Out* was almost completed. Already, by the time of their return from the honeymoon, he was worrying about her health. She needed rest and quiet and clearly there was more chance of these in the country. They went to Asham for Christmas and discussed the possibility of living there altogether, of buying horses and a cow, chickens and some pigs. These plans resulted in nothing more than a little strenuous gardening; the Woolfs had, as they were always to have, too many interests drawing them back to London.

In January they were joined at Asham by Vanessa; she also was unwell:

> Virginia has been very nice to me. She saw that I was depressed yesterday & was very good–& cheered me up a great deal. Do you think I sometimes laugh at her too much? I dont think it matters, but really I am sometimes overcome by the finest qualities in her. When she chooses she can give one the most extraordinary sense of bigness of point of view. I think she has in reality amazing courage & sanity about life. I have seen so little of her lately that it has struck me here.

And yet, at the very time when Vanessa was remarking on Virginia's "sanity about life," Leonard was anxiously noting in his diary the variations in her health, and although I think that Vanessa was not altogether wrong in what she said and that there was a kind of sanity about Virginia, it was certainly a quality which could be submerged by other internal forces and these, as the year advanced, grew stronger.

At the end of January Virginia and Vanessa were discussing the question of whether Virginia should have children. Leonard talked to Dr (now Sir George) Savage, and Sir George, in his breezy way, had exclaimed that it would do her a world of good; but Leonard mistrusted Sir George; he consulted other people: Maurice Craig, Vanessa's specialist, T. B. Hyslop, and Jean Thomas, who kept a nursing home and knew Virginia well; their views differed but in the end Leonard decided and persuaded Virginia to agree that, although they both wanted children, it would be too dangerous for her to have them. In this I imagine that Leonard was right. It is hard to imagine Virginia as a mother. But it was to be a permanent source of grief to her and, in later years, she could never think of Vanessa's fruitful state without misery and envy.

Perhaps comparison between Vanessa and herself may occasionally have soured a relationship which, at most other times, was very happy and which could no longer be damaged by Clive. There were some sisterly bickerings in the Spring of 1913. Adrian and Leonard got on badly and Vanessa tended to take Adrian's side. The feelings of jealousy which had hurt Virginia so much when Vanessa married may have sounded a tiny echo when Virginia found a husband.

Neither sister could really think that anyone was quite good enough for the other. "I wish Woolf didn't irritate me so," Vanessa once observed, and Leonard might have said the same about her. They were both strong characters; neither was easily convinced that he or she might be mistaken. And if there were a difference of opinion between Vanessa and Leonard, Virginia would side with her husband. Marriage, so Vanessa discovered, had made Virginia part of an alliance. Leonard had his own particular moral and intellectual position and this she accepted. She was perfectly in sympathy with the high seriousness of Cambridge which Leonard, in the arid climate of an eastern exile, had fragrantly preserved but which others, in the softer and more corruptive atmosphere of London–the London of Clive and Lytton, Lady Ottoline and Maynard Keynes–had half lost. The difference between him and them was a slight one. Leonard accepted the irreverent scepticism of his friends but he did not quite accept their frivolity or their worldliness. Having finished *The Village in the Jungle* he set to work upon a novel which he called *The Wise Virgins*.* The story is that of a young man (Leonard himself) who oscillates between two young women; they come from very different social backgrounds; one belongs–more or less–to the same milieu as the Woolf family in Putney, the other is more or less Virginia. She is carefully described and there are fairly recognisable portraits of Vanessa and Clive. The hero brings the ideas of Bloomsbury to the young woman in Putney and without being himself really in earnest, gets her with child and is obliged, although it is really Virginia whom he loves, to marry without affection. "The whole moral significance of the book," as Leonard put it to his publisher, was that his hero was "living in a circle of somewhat unnatural cultured persons and like them he indulges in a habit of wild exaggerated talk which he believes that he believes." The effect of such talk is disastrous for all concerned.

The novel obviously does not represent Leonard's considered opinion of people who were, after all, to be his closest friends for

---

* *The Wise Virgins/A Story of Words, Opinions and a few Emotions*, by L. S. Woolf, Edward Arnold, 1914. According to Leonard it appeared at the very beginning of the war and was one of the first casualties. Vanessa deprecated the resemblance of the characters in this novel to Leonard's friends (VB/LW, 14 January 1914) and Morgan Forster seems to have felt similar misgivings (EMF/LW, 7 November 1914). ". . . it's a remarkable book: very bad in parts; first rate in others. A writer's book, I think, because only a writer perhaps can see why the good parts are so very good and why the very bad parts aren't very bad . . . I like the poetic side of L[eonard] and it gets a little smothered in Blue Books and organisations." *AWD (Berg)*, 31 January 1915.

the greater part of his life; but it does accurately reflect his mood in 1913, his impatience with a certain amount of brittle talk in Gordon Square and, above all, his attitude towards Clive.

Leonard was of course perfectly aware of Virginia's long flirtation with Clive and although, in later years, he would not defend her part in it, at that time, ardent, impatient and in love, he might have found it hard to blame her and easy to find fault with his brother-in-law. When he went to Ceylon he had left Clive in a peripheral situation on the fringes of intellectual Cambridge; he returned to find him a central figure in Bloomsbury and, as such, a rather unwelcome newcomer. He thought that Clive was not disinterested, that he was altogether too preoccupied by the social decorations of life, by little questions of vanity and decorum; and like Virginia he felt that Clive was not really good enough for Vanessa. Probably he was aware that Clive, on his side, felt that Leonard was not nearly good enough for Virginia. Leonard was, in Clive's opinion, provincial and puritanical, an enemy to all that was charming and amusing in life. Moreover, his effect on Virginia was disastrous. She was, he declared, losing her looks, drifting away from her old friends and being led into the dreary routines of politics. He didn't object to her being a Socialist—at that time he was not far from being a Socialist himself; but he didn't like a beautiful woman to be anything but charming. He was vexed to see her carried into Committee rooms and Co-operative halls, wearing 'sensible' clothes and stout boots. And of course he might object, with a fair show of reason, that she had neither the abilities nor the stamina for such work.

Virginia did indeed go with Leonard on the first of his political tours of investigation, although she confessed that economic problems were beyond her, and for ten days in March 1913 they travelled through the industrial north, visiting Liverpool, Manchester, Leeds, York, Carlisle and Leicester. So far as I know, this strenuous journey did her no harm. Later in the year a further political excursion was accompanied by a sudden deterioration in her health, but for this there may well have been another cause.

In March *The Voyage Out* was at last finished. Leonard read it through and on 9 March, before setting out on their Northern tour, he took the manuscript to Gerald Duckworth, Virginia's half-brother, who had his own publishing house. "I expect to have it rejected," wrote Virginia to Violet Dickinson, adding that this might "not be in all ways a bad thing." However, Gerald's reader, Edward Garnett, gave an extremely favourable report upon it, and on the morning of 12 April Virginia went herself to Henrietta Street to hear from Gerald how pleased he would be to publish her novel.

It is fair to suppose that she immediately had misgivings. Almost anyone who has attempted to create a work of art will have an inkling of what she then felt. A book is so much a part of oneself that in delivering it to the public one feels as if one were pushing one's own child out into the traffic. If it be killed or hurt the injury is done to oneself, and if it be one's first-born, the product of seven years' gestation, if it be awkward and vulnerable and needing all the tenderness and all the understanding that no critic will ever give, anxiety for its fate becomes acute.

Virginia already knew whither such anxieties might lead her. She knew that she had to be sensible and to exert self-control if the horrors of 1895 and 1904 and 1910 were not to be repeated. But how does one learn to be sensible? How, when one longs for sleep, does one command the brain to lie still and lose consciousness? Most people have experienced this inhibition. Quite a little thing—a social blunder, the prospect of an unpleasant interview—can keep one awake at night. The topic that one orders oneself to forget returns again and again into the mind which, at one level, desires only to dismiss the unwelcome trifle, but at another insists on bringing it back again and again so that, for a time, the spirit is at war with itself and, while the unhappy body begs for oblivion, insists that there shall be no respite until at last exhaustion brings a truce or the clock turns the mind to the business of the day. But Virginia was not tormented with a trifle; her sleepless nights were spent in wondering whether her art, the whole meaning and purpose of her life, was fatuous, whether it might not be torn to shreds by a discharge of cruel laughter.

After such nights the days brought headaches, drilling the occiput as though it were a rotten tooth; and then came worse nights, nights made terrible by the increasing weight of anxiety and depression, "those interminable nights which do not end at twelve, but go on into the double figures—thirteen, fourteen, and so on until they reach the twenties, and then the thirties, and then the forties . . . there is nothing to prevent nights from doing this it they choose."*

---

* *The Voyage Out*, p. 403. Here, and in subsequent passages, I have attempted to describe Virginia's madness from her point of view; such an attempt seems necessary if one is to write her biography but, obviously, it must be very largely a matter of conjecture. I have used *The Voyage Out*, *Mrs Dalloway* and also Leonard Woolf's description of her symptoms in *Beginning Again*.

Something of this sort is, I suppose, concealed beneath the laconic daily record of Virginia's condition in Leonard's diary for 1913: V.f.w., V.sl.h., g.n., f.g.n., b.n. and so on: Virginia fairly well, Virginia slight headache, good night, fairly good night, bad night. Clearly he was increasingly worried. They remained prudently at Asham for the greater part of April and May, but went back to London to attend the *Ring* at Covent Garden, which Virginia then vowed she would never do again: "My eyes are bruised, my ears dulled, my brain a mere pudding of pulp–O the noise, the heat, & the bawling sentimentality, which used once to carry me away, & now leaves me sitting perfectly still." But once in London, the social pressures were irresistible: their friends called, they dined out, went to concerts, ballets, theatres. Again they retreated to Asham and again were seduced by London. During the summer days of late June and early July their friends joined them in Sussex and shared their country pleasures: riding, walking, talking and gardening. Oliver and Ray Strachey, Lytton and Norton, Morgan Forster and Molly MacCarthy–all these came to stay at Asham. Each day Leonard noted down his wife's state: fairly well, fair night, good night, fairly good night. On 1 July she was thrown from her horse which bolted and was brought back in the evening. On 7 July they were again in London, going to Ottoline's after dinner, to Gordon Square, to the Russian Ballet, to *Don Giovanni*. They returned to Asham, and by now Leonard was very seriously alarmed: Virginia's headaches, her sleeplessness, her depression and sense of guilt, her aversion to food, had all increased to a frightening degree, and he began to realise that the danger of suicide was now very real.

Leonard, who by this time had been enlisted by Sidney and Beatrice Webb, was committed to speaking at a Fabian Society conference at Keswick on 22 July. Virginia insisted that there was nothing the matter with her and that she should go with him; but when they reached the Lodore Hotel she was barely able to leave her bed. Leonard took her back to London on the 24th and, convinced that she was on the brink of disaster, sought the advice of the specialist who knew her entire history, Sir George Savage.

. . . he seems to have thought Virginia rather bad [wrote Vanessa to Roger Fry.] . . . He said it was just the same thing as usual & she would get all right but must have the rest. So she was going off to Jean [Thomas] at Twickenham yesterday afternoon. Its too wretched I'm afraid. . . . Please be *very* careful not to say a word to *anyone* about her worrying over what people will think of her novel, which seems really to be the entire cause of her breakdown. I told Duncan simply that she had been worried about her proofs, which seems the easiest thing to say & that Asheham hadn't been very successful. I suppose she must be in a state where anything which made her think about herself in this way would get on her nerves. Oh God, I cant help being rather worried lest I ought to have done more, but after all one cant do much with married people.

Savage could see, as Leonard saw, that Virginia was very ill indeed, but I doubt whether he had more understanding of the causes or cure of her illness than Leonard. For him it was the same thing as usual, and the same remedy was prescribed. A few weeks in bed in Jean Thomas's Twickenham nursing home appeared to have cured her in 1910; it therefore seemed best, in spite of her own remonstrances, to repeat this treatment. And since on that previous occasion the rest cure had been fortified by a holiday in Cornwall, Savage promised, if she now would do as he ordered, she might afterwards go with Leonard to Somerset on the holiday they had already planned.

In retrospect both these recommendations seem disastrous. The rest cure proved worse than useless; it separated Virginia from the one person who could now help her; the holiday in Somerset made it more difficult to restrain the suicidal impulse fostered by her seclusion in Twickenham.

And yet at this distance one cannot but wonder whether there *was* a better remedy—then at all events. The doctors with their prescriptions of rest and food, "Robin's Hypophosphate," and mulled wine at night, could at least relieve the symptoms of Virginia's disorder. It was something of which they understood almost as little as did their great-grandfathers. The disease was in control: it struck when its hour had come.

Virginia went to Twickenham on 25 July and remained there until 11 August. A few miserable shaky pencil-written notes to Leonard survive from that time. They make one think of a child sent away by its parents to some cruel school. Everything, she complained, seemed so cold, so unreal. Childlike, she burst out against the husband who had put her away in this awful place. But then, seeing his worn and distressed face, she was overcome with guilt and misery. Again and again they expressed to each other the hope that somehow the cure would work, that somehow they would yet be able to make a happy life together.

But this time, although she tried to think otherwise, it did not work. She left Twickenham shaky, desperate, and so intolerably driven that the temptation to end it all by suicide became acute.

They returned to Asham, and during the ten days they were there Leonard introduced two new terms into his abbreviated records of Virginia's daily health: *worry*—"Virginia good deal worried," "less worry,"—and *cheerful*, which word indeed occurs but rarely among the worries and the good and bad nights—nights when he had to give her veronal for her sleeplessness. From 20 August he kept his diary in cypher; he had invented a code composed of a mixture of Sinhalese and Tamil characters which he had employed on occasions before his marriage when he wished to be discreet (not that it concealed anything very scandalous); now however he used it regularly to note Virginia's state.

On the morning of 22 August the Woolfs returned to London, where they were to spend the night with Vanessa at Gordon Square. Leonard was by this time thoroughly frightened by the prospect of taking Virginia alone to Somerset and, when he saw Savage, he expressed his fears. Sir George pooh-poohed them, and insisted that, since this holiday had been promised as a reward, the promise must be kept; to break it would be psychologically disastrous. Meanwhile Virginia had been at 46 Gordon Square with Vanessa. "Virginia," she reported to Clive, "seems to me pretty bad. She worries constantly and one gets rid of one worry only to find that another crops up in a few minutes. Then she definitely has illusions about people." After his interview with Savage, Leonard was able to talk things over with Vanessa, and also with Roger Fry, who being himself a man of science and the husband of a mad wife, was able at least to suggest an alternative to Savage, in whom Leonard had now lost all faith. Henry Head, a very distinguished scientist and a man of culture (he had translated Heine), seemed altogether a more suitable consultant. Leonard arranged to see him at once. But there was little that Head could do at this juncture. He had to agree with Savage that the promised holiday must be undertaken; it might possibly work a cure. If it did not, and Virginia's condition deteriorated, Leonard should summon help and, if it got worse still, they must return to London.

This in fact was the sequence of events. On 23 August Leonard and Virginia took the train to Bridgewater and motored out to the Plough Inn at Holford in the Quantock Hills, where they had stayed just after their wedding. It was a lovely and peaceful place, and the people who kept the Inn showed the utmost consideration to their uneasy guests; but Virginia was by now oblivious to such attentions. The entries in Leonard's diary suggest an alternation of moods; bad mornings and good evenings, delusions by day and peaceful nights, bad nights and cheerful days; but the worries, the delusions, the arguments about food, the necessity for sleeping-draughts, increased, and on 1 September Leonard telegraphed for Ka Cox. That warm, sensible and kindly woman arrived at Holford on 2 September and could at least relieve the strain on him.

But the pressures on Virginia did not relax: she thought people were laughing at her; she was the cause of everyone's troubles; she felt overwhelmed with a sense of guilt for which she should be punished. She became convinced that her body was in some way monstrous, the sordid mouth and sordid belly demanding food–repulsive matter which must then be excreted in a disgusting fashion; the only course was to refuse to eat. Material things assumed sinister and unpredictable aspects, beastly and terrifying or–sometimes–of fearful beauty.

And yet, dimly, like things seen through a dirty window pane, ordinary life was going on. It was one of the horrors of Virginia's madness that she was sane enough to recognise her own insanity, just as one knows that one is dreaming when one begins to wake. But she could not wake.

At length Leonard determined that they really must go back and see a doctor. At first Virginia demurred, too afraid to go; but then, to his astonishment, suggested that they might see Dr Head, which was what he had secretly wanted. She had not been a party to the discussion concerning Head at Gordon Square, but no doubt she had been affected, as most people were affected, by the conversation of Roger Fry. So, on the afternoon of 8 September they travelled back with Ka to London; by now his wife's condition was such that Leonard expected her at any moment to try to throw herself from the train. They arrived however at Brunswick Square, where they spent the night in Adrian's rooms. The next morning they went to see Dr Maurice Wright, whom Leonard had more than once consulted on his own account and in whom he had considerable faith. Dr Wright told Virginia that she must accept the fact that she really was ill; and in the afternoon Dr Head repeated this opinion, saying that she would get perfectly well again if she followed advice and re-entered a nursing home.

Virginia, believing that there was nothing wrong with her, that her anxieties and insomnia were due simply to her own faults, faults which she ought to overcome without medical assistance, was silent. They returned to Brunswick Square; Vanessa came and had tea with them; Virginia seemed more cheerful, and presently lay down to rest. Then Leonard, who had committed the indiscretion of consulting Dr Head without the prior agreement of Sir George Savage, went off with Vanessa to make his excuses. He was with Savage when at 6.30 Ka telephoned to tell him that she had found Virginia unconscious on her bed.

He ran for a taxi and, arriving at Brunswick Square realised what had happened. Virginia had found the case in which he kept drugs. It was unlocked. She had taken 100 grains of veronal—a mortal dose.

Dr Head, nurses, Vanessa, were sent for; Ka stood by. Lodging on the top floor was Maynard Keynes's younger brother Geoffrey, a house surgeon at St Bartholomew's. He drove Leonard at high speed through the London traffic shouting: "Urgent! Doctor!" got a stomach-pump from his hospital and raced back. The doctors and nurses pumped the veronal out of Virginia and then watched through the night. At 12.30 Leonard went exhausted to bed and slept. At 1.30 Virginia nearly died; at six in the morning Vanessa woke Leonard to tell him that she was better; at nine Dr Head returned and was able to say that she was practically out of danger. She remained unconscious all that day.*

But the nightmare did not end with her return to consciousness. "She is" wrote Ka Cox to Janet Case, "a little quieter and eating more, but the symptoms continue very bad." As her strength returned so did her manias, and Leonard had now to face the question whether she should be certified and put into an asylum. He looked at some "homes" only to dismiss the idea. The doctors agreed that if she could be cared for by Leonard and trained nurses she need not be certified. But for this their rooms at Clifford's Inn were out of the question. Here George Duckworth intervened, and with great kindness offered them Dalingridge Place, his large and well-appointed house near East Grinstead in Sussex, where there

---

* "It is the novel which has broken her up. She finished it and got the proof back for correction . . . couldnt sleep & thought everyone would jeer at her. Then they did the wrong thing & teased her about it and she got desperate—and came here a wreck. It was all heart rending. . . . They will blame Sir George [Savage] probably, but they have never really done what he advised, except get married. And the marriage brought more good than anything else till the collapse came from the book—and as the doctors say, it might have come to such a delicate brilliant brain after such an effort *however* much care and wisdom had been shown." Jean Thomas to Violet Dickinson, 14 September 1913 (*Berg*).

According to Leonard, one of the difficulties of the situation was that Jean Thomas felt an unconscious but violent homosexual passion for Virginia and was also devoted to Sir George Savage; this made her awkward and quarrelsome. (p.i. LW)

was plenty of room, a staff of servants, and every material comfort.

On 20 September Ka and a nurse went ahead to Dalingridge, followed by Leonard and Virginia and a second nurse in a motor-car. Virginia was worse than ever; she could not sleep, she would not eat, she was by turns deeply depressed and violently excited.* The faithful Ka remained for a week, and while she was there, Leonard took a day off and went over to Asham, where he found Clive and Vanessa. Clive wrote to Molly MacCarthy:

Woolfe bicycled over to lunch yesterday, looking ill and very much tired, I thought, and in very low spirits. Virginia seems to have been even worse since the veronal affair and is intractable about food–the key to the situation so they say. The nurses they took with them seem to be powerless to persuade her to do anything; they are seeking others; meanwhile the bulk of the really hard work falls on Woolfe. One begins to wonder whether she will ever get really sound again.

Very slowly Virginia began to improve. The days of "excitement" became rather less numerous, she was gradually persuaded to eat a little. There were more quiet days and more good nights until at last, after two months, her doctors agreed that she might be moved, still with two attendant nurses, to Asham. Here the Woolfs settled, giving up their rooms at Clifford's Inn, here they remained almost continuously from 18 November 1913 until August 1914; and here, despite numerous setbacks, Virginia seemed to recover.

In his autobiography Leonard describes Virginia's state of mind;

---

* The entries concerning Virginia in Leonard's diary at this time suggest but do not describe the day-to-day strain under which he was living:

Sept 10: V. unconscious all day. Sept 11: Saw V. morn. Spoke to me. Saw V. even. more consc. Sept 12: V fully conscious. V. fairly happy even. Sept 13: V. fairly cheerful. V. very cheerful even. Sept 14: V. fairly calm & cheerful. Sat w V. 6–7.30. Very worried at first. Sept 15: W. V. morn. Talked V. aftn. Sat w V. aft dinner cheerful. Sept 16: W V. even. rather cheerful Not good night. Sept 17: W V. aft tea much worry. V. had bad night. Sept 18: Tea w V. walked w her in sq. V. depressed & much worry V. slept v badly. Sept 19: W V. morn. V. much worry bad night. Sept 20: Motor w nurse & V. to Dalingridge. V. v bad night. Sept 21: V. very excited & worried. Gr trouble w food bad night. Sept 22: V. v depressed, continual trouble w food v. bad night. Sept 23: V. v depressed great trouble w all meals 5 hrs sl. paraldahide. Sept 24: V. fair day. diff. lunch, great diff. dinner. 5 hours sl. w sl. dr. paral. Sept 25: V. v excited all day 2 hrs over each meal. Did not sleep at all. Sept 26: Some diff w br. None w 11.30 milk. Ka left 11.47 trn. V. v queer on walk, cd hardly walk for a moment, & then jumpy. Lay down. Nurse got her eat 1½ courses lunch, I did rest without diff. Walk w me aftn. much calmer. Ate good tea. Nurse got her eat dinner 2½ hours sleep Adalin. Sept 27: Some diff w br. None w 11.30 milk. Marg [Llewelyn] D[avies]. arrived lunch. V. v excited. Nurse succeeded w ½ lunch I w rest Ditto dinner. V. violent w nurses at times 5½ hrs nat sl. asperine. [And so on.]

he does not describe his own. He does not pause in order to indulge in self-pity nor—and this would have been much more in character—does he pause to shake an angry fist at Jehovah, just in case Jehovah should be there to take notice. All complainings and whinings were omitted from his book as they were from his life. And yet he might well have complained of those who, unlike Jehovah, could be called to account.

Leonard had undertaken the care of a woman who had twice been mad and had once attempted suicide without—as far as I can discover—any serious and wholly unequivocal warning of what he was letting himself in for. Neither Vanessa nor Adrian gave him a detailed and explicit account of Virginia's illnesses or told him how deadly serious they might be, until this greatest and worst crisis occurred. Her insanity was clothed, like some other painful things in that family, in a jest.

"Oh you know very well the Goat's mad." That was easily said and easily disregarded. Virginia herself, then and later on, would cheerfully allude to the times when she was "off her head." Thus, in effect if not in intention, Leonard was allowed to think of Virginia's illnesses as something not desperately serious, and he was allowed to marry her without knowing how fearful a care such a union might be. In fairness to all parties it must be said that, even if Virginia's brother and sister had been as explicit and circumstantial as they ought to have been, Leonard certainly would not have been deflected from his purpose of marrying Virginia; but his subsequent treatment of one who was, in fact, already dangerously ill might well have been different. As it was, he learnt the hard way and one can only wonder, seeing how hard it was, and that he had for so long to endure the constant threat of her suicide, to exert continual vigilance, to exercise endless persuasive tact at meal-times and to suffer the perpetual alternations of hope and disappointment, that he too did not go mad.

In fact he nearly did, although he does not mention it. The strain upon him was intense and continuous. Now and then he had been able to escape for a day or a night to London, to see his friends or his family, to visit a theatre or to attend a meeting. But after almost six months of unremitting vigilance the burden became too great. During the early part of 1914 he was troubled by bad headaches; they became so violent and disabling that, early in March, it was arranged that Ka Cox and Janet Case should come by turns to Asham to be with Virginia so that Leonard might have ten days' holiday. He went to Wiltshire to stay in an uncomfortable cottage with Lytton, who read him his *Cardinal Manning* and argued about Ulster–a strange cure, but it seems to have worked.*

By April 1914 the Woolfs felt well enough to venture upon a change of scene, and Maurice Craig, whom they now consulted and whose opinions and advice Leonard respected (Savage was by now only referred to as a matter of courtesy), agreed that Virginia was sufficiently improved to justify the undoubted risk of removing her from her familiar surroundings. They went for three weeks to Cornwall–to Lelant, St Ives and Carbis Bay. Leonard found the excursion a pretty nerve-wracking affair; Virginia was very fearful of strangers, still difficult over food, and liable to bursts of excitement or bouts of despair. But on the whole the holiday did her good; her nostalgic delight in the scenes of her childhood soothed her overwrought nerves, and her progress towards recovery, though erratic, was maintained during the summer months at Asham.

In mid-June Leonard, who had to some extent been able to continue his political studies and interests, went to Birmingham to attend a Women's Co-operative Guild meeting. Before going, he drew up a kind of treaty, comic in form but serious in intention, the articles of which bound Virginia to rest on her back with her head on the cushions for a full half-hour after luncheon, to eat exactly as much as if he were there, to be in bed by 10.25 each night and settle off to sleep at once, to have her breakfast in bed, to drink a whole glass of milk during the morning, in certain contingencies to rest on the sofa and not walk about the house or garden, to be wise and to be happy. These injunctions were to be observed on the 16th, 17th and 18th of June 1914. Virginia signed with a flourish. And in fact, though she was still liable to bad days or bad nights, the empirical method, which consisted of rest, food, calm, and the avoidance of intellectual excitement, was yielding good results.†

* "Leonard *is* better . . . I think if only I can behave now, he will soon be quite right. . . . By occupying myself with typewriting & Co-operative manuals, I keep cheerful, which I see does more to inspirit L. than anything else." VW/Janet Case, March 1914.

Leonard and Virginia's friends did what they could to help them; Lytton Strachey showed his sympathy and concern by offering hospitality and conversation to Leonard, and the menial tasks of her own profession to Virginia. She was typing his short story, *Ermyntrude and Esmeralda*. We do not know *how* she occupied herself with the Co-operative manuals.

† In May 1914, Leonard was reading Freud's *Interpretation of Dreams* as a preliminary to reviewing his *Psychopathology of Everyday Life* for *The New Weekly*. He was a good deal impressed and it is possible that, if he had read Freud two years earlier, Virginia's medical history might have been different. It is however doubtful whether she could have been analysed or whether analysis would have

She was able to read and to write short letters, to sew, to some extent to manage her household of cook and housemaid (the nurses were gone), and to go for long walks with her two dogs Shot and Mike. Vanessa reported from Asham at the end of July that Virginia was certainly very much better and was indeed bent upon returning to London. This idea filled Leonard with despair. London would certainly be bad for her and would lead, inevitably, to another breakdown.

Shortly after the declaration of war he did take Virginia to London, but only for a night on their way to Northumberland. They stayed at Wooler in the Cheviots. From thence Virginia wrote to Ka Cox:

> It is thought that you are probably doing service somewhere, either as a nurse, or part of the military. I never felt anything like the general insecurity. We left Asheham a week ago, & it was practically under martial law. There were soldiers marching up and down the line, & men digging trenches, & it was said that Asheham barn was to be used as a hospital. All the people expected an invasion–Then we went through London–& oh Lord! what a lot of talk there was! Roger, of course, had private information from the Admiralty, & had been seeing the German Ambassadress, & Clive was having tea with Ottoline, & they talked & talked, & said it was the end of civilisation, & the rest of our lives was worthless. I do wish you would write & tell me what you hear–They say there must be a great battle, & here, where we are 15 miles from the North Sea, they expect to be in the midst of it, but then so they did at Seaford.
>
> Your future is practically blasted, because you will be on 20 different committees. The very earnest & competent are already coming to town, with their practical habits–but I never could see the use of committees.
>
> We have struck about the most beautiful country I've ever seen here.

---

been an appropriate treatment. Analysts are usually reluctant to treat patients who have actually been mad and Virginia's first breakdown could hardly have been treated even by Freud himself: it was contemporaneous with his *Studien über Hysterie* (1895). The Freudian techniques of analysis would barely have been heard of in this country at the time of her second breakdown (1904), and even in 1913 cannot have been at all well known. (Ernest Jones began to practice in London in 1913.) The Japanese psychiatrist Mme Miyeko Kamiya is, I believe, preparing a pathography of Virginia Woolf and this may enable us to know whether psychiatry could have helped her. To a lay observer it would appear, as to Leonard himself it appeared, that her symptoms were of a manic-depressive character, which would not have responded to analysis. In her later years she showed little interest in and less enthusiasm for the discoveries of Freud and could not have been persuaded to consult a psychiatrist.

Except that it has no sea, I think that it is better than Cornwall–great moors & flat meadows with very quick rivers. We are in an Inn full of north country people, who are very grim to look at, but so up to date that one blushes with shame. They discuss Thomson's poetry, & post impressionism, & have read everything, & at the same time control all the trade in Hides, & can sing comic songs & do music hall turns–in fact the Bloomsbury group was stunted in the chrysalis compared with them. But why did you never prepare me for the Scotch dialect, & the melodious voice which makes me laugh whenever I hear it?

This northern holiday was undoubtedly a success. Leonard's diary records their expeditions and an almost unbroken series of good nights. They returned to London on 15 September and Virginia remained in excellent health, so much so that, in the month of October, his daily record ceases.

This marked improvement in her condition made it easier for Virginia to insist that they should live in London. She and Leonard spent much of that autumn looking for a house. They tried Hampstead and Highgate, Westminster, Holborn, Chelsea and Twickenham; finally they decided that Richmond would suit them best of all. Richmond was near enough to London for Leonard's political work and far enough out to prevent the social distractions of town from becoming too much of a threat to Virginia's health. They took lodgings there in October with a Belgian lady, Mrs le Grys, at 17 The Green, and sent for their own furniture and books which had been in storage since Clifford's Inn was given up. While house-hunting in Richmond they came across a beautiful eighteenth-century mansion, Suffield House, which had been divided into two, one half keeping the original name, the other now called Hogarth House. This they liked very much; they tried to get a lease of it; but there were difficulties and delays, so that they alternated between hope and resignation, and continued their search elsewhere.

Virginia could again be active and she felt, as the wife of a poor man, that she ought to have some domestic skills; she began to attend a school of cookery in Victoria Street:

At one end of the room are sailors & then there are a few greyheaded ladies of great culture & refinement, dabbling in the insides of chickens, & some very smart, come to improve their knowledge of dinner-party soup. I distinguished myself by cooking my wedding ring into a suet pudding!

She found it all great fun, but it is doubtful whether she put her training to much practical use at that time, since their meals were provided by their landlady.

She began again to enjoy a little social life, having friends to tea or dinner, and sometimes going up to London to see people, to get books from a library, or to hear a concert or a play. Bloomsbury had been scattered by the onset of the war, though its remnants were being gathered up and reinforced by Lady Ottoline Morrell; her brilliant and hectic parties in Bedford Square were exactly the kind of social event which Leonard was anxious that Virginia should avoid. The Woolfs did not look for excitement; their visitors came singly or perhaps in pairs—Janet Case, Margaret Llewelyn Davies, Saxon or Ka, Leonard's family, Sydney Waterlow and Walter Lamb; he was now Secretary to the Royal Academy, lived near them at Kew and was regarded as a figure of fun.

By the end of the year Virginia was writing again—a novel or a story which has been lost; she also began to keep a diary. It is the record of a perfectly sane woman leading a quiet but normal life:

Saturday, January 2nd [1915]
This is the kind of day which, if it were possible to choose an altogether average sample of our life, I should select. We breakfast: I interview Mrs Le Grys. She complains of the huge Belgian appetites and their preference for food fried in butter. "They never *give* one anything" she remarked. The Count, taking Xmas dinner with them, insisted, after pork and turkey, that he wanted a third meat. Therefore Mrs Le G. hopes that the war will soon be over. If they eat thus in their exile, how must they eat at home, she wonders? After this, L. and I both settle down to our scribbling. He finishes his Folk Story review and I do about four pages of poor Effie's story; we lunch and read the papers; agree that there is no news. I read Guy Mannering upstairs for 20 minutes and then we take Max for a walk. Halfway up to the Bridge, we found ourselves cut off by the river, which rose visibly, with a little ebb and flow, like the pulse of a heart. Indeed, the road we had come along was crossed, after five minutes, by a stream several inches deep. One of the queer things about the suburbs is that the vilest little red villas are always let and that not one of them has an open window or an uncurtained window. I expect that people take a pride in their curtains and there is great rivalry among neighbours. One house had curtains of yellow silk, striped with lace insertion. The rooms inside must be in semi-darkness and I suppose dank with the smell of meat and human beings. I believe that being curtained is a mark of respectability. Sophie used to insist upon it. And then I did my marketing. Saturday night is the great buying night and some counters are besieged by three rows of women. I always choose the empty shops, where I suppose one pays

½d a lb. more. And then we had tea and honey and cream; and now L. is typewriting his article; and we shall read all the evening and go to bed.

Mrs le Grys complained a good deal of her refugee lodgers. The Count spat in his bath (a fact which was to be remembered in *The Years*). Her servants were also a source of interest, distress and amusement to Virginia. Lizzy, the house-maid, nearly set the house on fire and on another occasion made the boiler, which had no water in it, red hot; also she broke the crockery. Maud, her successor, claimed that she was a Colonel's daughter; she attempted genteel talk when she brought in the coals. Visitors are recorded: Sydney Waterlow came and talked about philosophy; Walter Lamb came and talked about royalty; Margery Strachey came and talked about herself. Molly MacCarthy brought gossip from Bloomsbury, described Clive's latest love affair, Desmond's resolve to live in the country and, at last, to write his novel.

Leonard was now able to devote considerably more time to his own writing and other activities; he was increasingly in demand on committees and as a speaker on Co-operative and International subjects. "The Sidney Webbs ask us to dinner about once a week, & Leonard has got to go tomorrow, though it sounds too dismal. They've clawed him for a huge job*. . ." wrote Virginia in December. She went with him to political meetings and much admired his speeches, his clarity, and the complete lack of condescension with which he addressed himself to working men and women. She herself now became a member of the Fabian Society. Interest in the progress of the war is barely manifested in her diary, though she noted the sinkings of the *Formidable* and of the *Blücher*.

On 25 January, her 33rd birthday, Leonard gave her a green purse and a brown parcel containing the 3-volume first edition of *The Abbot*. In the afternoon they went for a treat to a Picture Palace, and to tea at Buszards; and that evening they decided that if they possibly could they would live at Hogarth House; they would buy a printing press; and a bulldog. Virginia was delighted by her birthday and greatly excited by the idea of having their own press.

Two days later Virginia noted in her diary that she and Janet Case had discussed the novel "which everyone, so I predict, will assure me is the most brilliant thing they've ever read: and privately condemn, as indeed it deserves to be condemned." It is her only reference to *The Voyage Out* and if, as I suspect, the diary

* Leonard was asked by the Fabian Society to prepare a report on International Relations, which was the germ of the League of Nations.

was at this time intended partly as a sedative, a way of proving to herself how normal she now was, then this reticence, so unlike the anxious speculations of later years, is not astonishing. The novel was to appear at the end of March; in the middle of February Leonard took Virginia to the dentist, and afterwards to look at printing presses in Farringdon Street; the following day he came home to find her with a bad headache. He began the usual treatment; rest, seclusion, veronal at night; and, as before, recorded her progress in his diary.

But one morning, while she was breakfasting in bed, Virginia began to talk to her mother; she became very distressed and more and more excited and incoherent. A day or two later she seemed–to herself at any rate–to have stepped back from the abyss and, re-membering the nightmare of the previous year, tried to express something of what she felt she owed to Margaret Llewelyn Davies:

> 17, The Green, Richmond.
> Thursday [25 February 1915]

My dear Margaret

Thank you so much for troubling about the Morris. [She had asked if Margaret could lend her *The Pilgrims of Hope*.] I shd. very much like to see it.

I want just to tell you how wonderfully things have changed in the last few days. I am now all right though rather tired. It is so wonderful that I can hardly believe it. And I wanted to say that all through that terrible time I thought of you, & wanted to look at a picture of you, but was afraid to ask! You saved Leonard I think, for which I shall always bless you, by giving him things to do. It seems odd, for I know you so little, but I felt you had a grasp on me, & I could not utterly sink. I write this because I do not want to say it, & yet I think you will like to know it. Our happiness now is something I cannot even think about.

Please come. We have given up the Shaws, & Saturday afternoon about 4 would suit me. I can't do much but lie still, but I should like immensely to see you & gossip about Madame Tournier and other friends.

Dear Margaret, I so often think of you, & thank you for what you have done for us both, & one cd do nothing to show what it meant.

> Yrs V.W.

I wanted to tell Janet [Case] what I have told you but Leonard thought better not. Her goodness was so great

This letter, rather hurriedly, rather wildly but quite firmly written in pencil, may possibly express a sentiment of rational guilt and remorse resulting from agonies of irrational fury, and the reason why Margaret Llewelyn Davies should inspire such feelings need to be explored. She had indeed saved Leonard and, during the past two years had become, after Virginia, the most important woman in his life. She was, as Leonard has said, a born leader, energetic, enthusiastic, likeable and handsome; she brought Leonard into the work of her own particular organisation–the Women's Co-operative Guild; Virginia came too and was indeed very much impressed. Nevertheless it must have been clear from the outset that Leonard would move further and faster on this excursion than Virginia. With Margaret as his guide, Leonard had soon adventured deep into politics and, as Virginia realised, this was what he needed at a time when her illness would otherwise have driven him to despair.

But the influence of this wholly benevolent, altogether virtuous, 50-year-old Egeria cannot have been altogether welcome. Virginia was never drawn to female politicians and Margaret, with all her fine qualities, was something of a bore.* That Leonard should be so dependent upon her–and Virginia too, for Margaret's kindness was such during Virginia's illness that Leonard found his gratitude too deep to express–was not altogether a recommendation.

Virginia believed that she had recovered when she wrote to Margaret on 25 February, but it was no more than a respite. Two letters which followed, both oddly frivolous, were dictated to Leonard, who added postscripts saying that he thought her a little better; but in fact she grew rapidly worse. It was quite unlike the first phase of her madness when she was depressed, languid and, though sometimes violent, more often quietly suicidal. Now she entered into a state of garrulous mania, speaking ever more wildly, incoherently and incessantly, until she lapsed into gibberish and sank into a coma. Doctors and nurses were sent for. It was clear that the Woolfs couldn't remain indefinitely in their lodgings. Mrs le Grys was a nice woman but she could hardly be expected to cater for a raving lunatic and her attendants. The negotiations for the lease of Hogarth House were completed, and on 25 March, the day before the publication of *The Voyage Out*, Virginia was taken to a nursing home; she remained there for a week while Leonard made the move to their new home, and was then installed under the

---

* Leonard compares Margaret Llewelyn Davies with Robert Owen, the founder of the Co-operative Movement (*Beginning Again*, pp. 104/5) and in so doing quotes Leslie Stephen's description of that great man: "one of those intolerable bores who are the salt of the earth"–but Leonard omits the word "intolerable".

care of four mental nurses. Life at Hogarth House began with the dreary and all too familiar alternation of good days and bad days, exasperating mealtimes and sleepless nights, but with even more harrowing symptoms, for now Virginia was violent and screaming, and her madness culminated in virulent animosity towards Leonard himself. On 20 May Leonard's diary reads: "Exc. & irritable all day but not as bad as yest Marg. came tea. Nurse Missenden came. Did not see V." For almost two months he scarcely saw her. Vanessa reported to Roger Fry:

> I saw Woolf yesterday. He too was very dismal. Virginia seems to go up & down, at times being pretty reasonable & at others very violent & difficult. The only thing to do is to hang on as long as possible he thinks in the hope that she may get well enough to be able to go to some nursing home & not have to go to an asylum which he thinks might have a disastrous effect on her. The question is whether the nurses will stand it. Woolf himself seemed to have reached a state when he didnt much care what happened which was rather dreadful; & one couldn't say anything much.

Very, very slowly Virginia began to improve. That is to say there were fewer moments of violence and excitement. She became more lucid and more rational. But it seemed that there would be no real recovery from this second bout of the disease; it had inflicted a wound which appeared to be incurable. In April, Jean Thomas told Violet Dickinson that Virginia's mind seemed "played out" and that it was not only her mind but her entire personality which had deteriorated. At the end of June Vanessa wrote:

> Ka had been to see Virginia & thinks she's really getting better slowly, but it sounds most depressing as she seems to have changed into a most unpleasant character. She won't see Leonard at all & has taken against all men. She says the most malicious & cutting things she can think of to everyone & they are so clever that they always hurt. But what was almost the worst thing to me was a small book of new poems by Frances Cornford which has just come out which Virginia has annotated with what are meant to be stinging sarcasms & illustrations. They are simply like rather nasty schoolboy wit, not even amusing. I had just been reading a lot of her old letters & it is really terrible. The early ones are so brilliant, better than her novel—perhaps I told you about them before—& the later ones during the last year or two are so dull by comparison—it looks as if she had simply worn out her brains.

Thus by the summer of 1915 it was clear that Virginia, however completely she might seem to recover from her insanity, could easily relapse into madness, and each attack seemed worse than its predecessor. After two years of intermittent lunacy it appeared that her mind and her character were permanently affected.

Chapter Two

1915–1918

WHEN *The Voyage Out* appeared in March 1915 it was greeted cordially by Virginia's friends and, on the whole, by the Press. E. M. Forster (and there was no one whose opinion mattered more to her) published his criticism in the *Daily News*.

"Here at last is a book which attains unity as surely as *Wuthering Heights*, though by a different path."

Other reviewers were equally enthusiastic. Several used the word "genius."

> That is not a word [wrote the critic of the *Observer*] to use inadvisedly, but there is something greater than talent that colours the cleverness of this book. Its perpetual effort to say the real thing and not the expected thing, its humour and its sense of irony, the occasional poignancy of its emotions, its profound originality—well, one does not wish to lose the critical faculty over any book, and its hold may be a personal and subjective matter, but among ordinary novels it is a wild swan among good grey geese to one reviewer, to whom its author's name is entirely new and unknown.

At what point in the summer of 1915 Virginia was able to read these words I do not know; but when she did read them they must have given her lively pleasure and, what was more important, reassurance.

In December 1914, she had told Molly MacCarthy that she was relieved to find that one sentence "more or less followed another"; that her book "though long and dull" was not, as she sometimes feared, pure gibberish. I do not think that this was simply false modesty. Her novels were very close to her own private imaginings; she was always conscious that, to the outside world, they might simply appear to be mad, or, worse still, that they really were mad. Her dread of the ruthless mockery of the world contained within it the deeper fear that her art, and therefore her self, was a kind of sham, an idiot's dream of no value to anyone.* For her, therefore, a

---

* "Suppose one woke and found oneself a fraud? It was part of my madness that horror." *AWD (Berg)*, 16 May 1927.

favourable notice was more valuable than mere praise; it was a kind of certificate of sanity. The point is one that should be borne in mind when we consider her extreme sensitivity to criticism, a sensitivity which may be considered morbid and which indeed in a sense *was* morbid, in that it arose from a diseased condition. The critical thrusts and buffets which could easily have been resisted by a more robust organism might, in her case, reopen wounds that had never quite healed and had never ceased to be acutely tender.

I believe then that Virginia's gradual return to health in 1915 was helped by the favourable notices given to her first novel. But it was a very slow and unsteady recovery; in whatever other ways it may have been assisted it would not have been possible without a long regime of tedious inertia on her part and Leonard's infinite patience. His success was such that in August he no longer felt it necessary to keep a daily record of her health. In that month he began to take her for drives or wheel her out in a Bath chair; she was seeing one or two friends, and beginning to be allowed to read more and write a little; a postcard to Margaret Llewelyn Davies postmarked 31 August is much in her old style:

> Your letter still delights me. I take it up at intervals to get into closer touch with Madame T. [presumably Margaret had passed on a compliment about *The Voyage Out*]. But my dear Margaret, what's the use of *my* writing novels? You've got the whole thing at your fingers ends–& it will be envy not boredom that alienates my affections. I saw Forster, who is timid as a mouse, but when he creeps out of his hole very charming. He spends his time in rowing old ladies upon the river, & is not able to get on with his novel. Also I saw Ray Strachey, but, alas, she makes me feel like a faint autumnal mist, she's so effective & thinks me such a goose.

In September she was well enough to be moved, still with an attendant nurse, to Asham, where she lived very quietly. They had few visitors–Vanessa, the Waterlows, her cousin Fredegond with her husband Gerald Shove*–and this regime was so beneficial that by the middle of October she was writing to Lytton: "I think it is about time we took up our correspondence again. . . . I am really all right again, and weigh 12 stone!–three more than I've ever had, and the consequence is I can hardly toil uphill."

On 4 November the Woolfs returned to Hogarth House, and a

---

* Gerald Shove, a Cambridge economist and pacifist, married Fredegond Maitland in 1915; she was a daughter of Florence, *née* Fisher, Virginia's first cousin, and F. W. Maitland, the Cambridge historian and biographer of Leslie Stephen.

few days later the last nurse left. Now, very cautiously, they began once more to lead a normal life. This they spent mainly at Richmond, but they kept Asham and went there usually for Christmas and Easter, with perhaps a week or so in May and, always, a prolonged summer holiday, lasting sometimes from late July until October. I am speaking here of the war years and a time when publishing had not put a limit to their holidays.

At Hogarth House, during the years 1915 and 1916, Virginia was very much isolated from London—one cannot say from Bloomsbury for Bloomsbury hardly existed. "It has vanished like the morning mist," wrote Virginia to Ka Cox. In so far as it revived at all its reassembly was due to the development of the war. The year 1915 had been inconclusive and bloody (Rupert Brooke died in that year) and so, in order to continue the *jeu de massacre* fresh soldiers had to be found. In January 1916 a Conscription Bill was introduced. Nearly all Virginia's friends were in one way or another affected by it; most of them were conscientious objectors, all of them reacted against the chauvinism and the hysteria of the home front and many of them faced the alternatives of fighting for a cause in which they did not believe or of facing a Tribunal which, having passed judgement on their sincerity, might send them to do war work, or to prison, or into the armed services where there was always the possibility that they might be court-martialled and shot. In the face of this common peril Bloomsbury was reunited.

Leonard had decided that he was not a conscientious objector; he was therefore in immediate danger of being called to the colours. This would undoubtedly have meant the end of all hopes of permanent recovery for Virginia. He suffered from a trembling of the hands which prevented him from filling tea cups with any ease or, on occasions, from signing his own name. Dr Maurice Wright,* whom Leonard had consulted about this ailment and on Virginia's behalf, must have known very well that the health of both his patients depended upon Leonard's ability to stay at home. He provided Leonard with a certificate which secured exemption by the medical board.

Lytton's obvious debility made it impossible that he could be

* Although Leonard says (*Beginning Again*, p. 178) that it was Dr Maurice Wright who gave him the certificate, Virginia wrote on 14 May 1916 to Vanessa: "Leonard went to Craig who said that he would give him a certificate of unfitness on his own account, as well as mine. He has written a very strong letter, saying that L. is highly nervous, suffers from permanent tremor, & would probably break down if in the army. Also that I am still in a very shaky state, & would very likely have a bad mental breakdown if they took him."

effectively pursued by the military and he used the Tribunal as a platform on which to tease the tribunes. Clive, whose opinions had hardened more rapidly than those of his friends,* slipped through the official net without too much difficulty; he agreed to do agricultural work and found employment on Philip Morrell's farm at Garsington. Philip Morrell, one of the few Members of Parliament to be openly opposed to the war, employed a number of pacifists as farm workers on his estate without, one imagines, much profit to his land.

Adrian, who early in the war had married Karin Costelloe (Virginia and Vanessa thought her not nearly good enough for their brother), was the most convinced and the most active of the Bloomsbury pacifists and defended conscientious objectors before the Tribunals. Maynard Keynes's position was the most equivocal; he held a position of major responsibility in the Treasury and was out of reach of the Tribunals; his sympathies were given to the pacifists, his efforts to the war.

Virginia's chief concern was, of course, for Leonard. But she had other cares. During her madness there had been a change in the affairs of the Bells. Clive lived his own life at 46 Gordon Square and at Garsington; Vanessa lived with Duncan Grant, and when the local Tribunal refused him exemption, she turned to Virginia for assistance. In her efforts to get the verdict set aside Vanessa did not hesitate to ask her sister to use improper influence. She hoped that Virginia might be able to persuade Lady Robert Cecil to speak on Duncan's behalf to Lord Salisbury, who in his turn could sway the judgement of the Tribunals. Nor might Virginia–who could not be insensible to anything that touched Vanessa so deeply–refuse to act in the matter. Representations *were* made to Lady Robert and Lady Robert *did* write to her brother-in-law; but he could not intervene and the matter went no further.

It was soon after the failure of this intrigue, in July 1916, that Leonard and Virginia went to stay with Duncan, David Garnett and Vanessa, who were then attempting to manage a farm at Wissett in Suffolk. For Virginia the visit was important, for it had an effect upon her next novel.

She was again able to write but it would appear that her writing was very strictly rationed. After her visit to Wissett she told Lytton:

* *Peace at Once*, a pamphlet in which Clive urged the necessity of a negotiated settlement, was published during the spring of 1915 by the National Labour Press. In the summer of 1915 it was destroyed by order of the Lord Mayor of London (see Clive Bell, *Warmongers*, published by the Peace Pledge Union [1938], p. 1).

My industry has the most minute results, and I begin to despair of finishing a book on this method–I write one sentence–the clock strikes–Leonard appears with a glass of milk. However, I daresay it don't much matter. Wissett seems to lull asleep all ambition–Don't you think they have discovered the secret of life? I thought it wonderfully harmonious.

This may probably be translated into the statement that she was allotted one, or perhaps two, hours for work every morning. At all events her mind was certainly active and on returning home from Wissett she wrote to Vanessa:

I am very much interested in your life, which I think of writing another novel about. Its fatal staying with you–you start so many new ideas.

And in fact the new ideas which Vanessa started were to develop into *Night and Day*.

Despite the failure of Virginia's *démarche* with the Cecil family, Duncan Grant and David Garnett, who was in a similar predicament, were granted exemption from military service on condition that they undertook full-time agricultural work. For a variety of reasons it seemed best to leave Suffolk and they thought, naturally enough, of Sussex. Already in May Virginia had written to Vanessa:

I wish you'd leave Wissett and take Charleston. Leonard . . . says it is a most delightful house & strongly advises you to take it. . . . It is about a mile from Firle . . . under the Downs. It has a charming garden, with a pond, & fruit trees, & vegetables, all now rather wild, but you could make it lovely. The house is very nice with large rooms . . . There is a w.c. & a bathroom, but the bath only has cold water . . . It sounds a most attractive place–& 4 miles from us, so you wouldn't be badgered by us.

This was premature. But in July when the question of the future of Vanessa's household again arose in more urgent form, Virginia was active in making enquiries on her behalf. In September Vanessa herself came to Sussex and settled the matter, rented Charleston, found work on a neighbouring farm for Duncan and David Garnett, and in October moved in. It seemed an eminently convenient disposition and it meant that the sisters would be able to see much more of each other. If this was desirable then the propriety of the arrangement was obvious. But was it desirable? Vanessa obviously thought that it was or she would hardly have applied to Virginia in the first place; Virginia, in letter after letter, had urged Vanessa to leave Suffolk and come to Sussex. Nevertheless a doubt persists.

I think the Woolves have a morbid terror of us all [wrote Vanessa to Lytton]—I can't think why. They seem to think we should contaminate the atmosphere & bring wicked gaieties into Virginia's life. If they could only see the quiet lives we lead! Surely the downs are wide enough for us all & they needn't fear a constant flow in & out of Asheham as long as Woolf is in it–of course it might provide useful spare rooms when they were away.

To Lytton, Leonard explained that his objection to Vanessa's presence in the neighbourhood was that Virginia was sure to insist on walking over to see Vanessa every Sunday, four miles there and four miles back, which would be bad for her health. But although that was what Leonard said there was, in Lytton's view, "some pollution theory in the background."

Lytton may have been making mischief; but he may also have been right–up to a point. Virginia and Leonard would hardly have objected to having Duncan and Vanessa as neighbours had they been the only neighbours; but they were not coming by themselves. They were bringing children and they were bringing David Garnett.

David Garnett's first visit to Asham had been, to put it mildly, unfortunate. When he came to Sussex to interview the farmer who was to employ him and Duncan he brought with him two young women art students, Barbara Hiles and Dora Carrington. The party was overtaken by nightfall somewhere near Asham and, the Woolfs being away, they broke into the house and slept the night there. They were observed leaving in the early morning and this burglarious exploit was reported before David Garnett's explanation, or rather the explanation which he asked Vanessa to concoct for him, could be received.

There are people who don't mind having their houses broken into by friends or even by intruders such as these, who were hardly more than acquaintances; but the Woolfs did not like it. Virginia was upset. The case was made worse by Garnett's explanation, which was, as Vanessa herself said, disingenuous, and by the fact that he had taken the Oxford Book of poetry which Virginia kept by her bedside.*

* "Carrington has been asked to dine with Virginia who wants to hear all about Asheham! I expect she'll worm every detail out of her so Bunny's letter will be exposed. I don't believe Carrington will be a match for Mrs Woolf as one knows her powers if she wants to find out something. However I told Carrington she must stick to Bunny's account, which may be true in the letter but hardly in the spirit." VB/DG, [?17 October 1916]. ". . . I went yesterday evening to

Were these then the kind of neighbours whom Vanessa intended to bring with her? The "cropheads," the "Bloomsbury Bunnies," the semi-intellectual underworld? "We are not at all anxious," said Virginia, "to have neighbours (unless you)." Was Charleston to become another Garsington filled with casual, carefree Slade students, amoral, anti-social and noisy?

Vanessa would probably have allowed that, under the circumstances, Leonard and Virginia had a case. Virginia was in no condition to be bothered by such people and Leonard would not in any case much want to see them. In fact the menace was imaginary; David Garnett was too discreet to offend in future and it was, in the event, the Woolfs themselves who were to encourage Barbara Hiles as a visitor. But there was another objection that Vanessa could not see and which was real enough; it was impossible for Virginia to resist or for Leonard not to resent the visits of Vanessa's children and their nurse and these, for some years, were to be a real menace to the peace of Asham.

Leonard was cast in the ungrateful role of family dragon. He had to make sure that Virginia did not have too many visitors, to keep her from exhausting excursions, to see to it if she were away from home that she should leave early, or if she received a guest that the guest should not stay too long. In 1916, with Virginia still slowly recovering, he could take no chances and neglect no precautions. This made him seem fussy, and indeed curmudgeonly. Usually it was hard to believe–hard for the visitor and hard for Virginia herself–that there was anything wrong with her. But a few days in company, a party or two or an excursion to London, might bring back headaches and sleepless nights which could be cured only by long periods of rest and seclusion.

But there was more to it than this; even if Virginia had been in good health, Leonard would still have been more domestic and more serious-minded than the younger members of Ottoline's circle. His temper was more severe, his habits more sober than theirs and, in that the inhabitants of Charleston were more tolerant of the kind of frivolity that verges on silliness, there was also a difference between

<hr />

Virginia. What an examination!!! But I was rigid and denied everything. Even to Bunny taking a book which of course was true. But she asked me if Bunny did take a book, which I denied. So you *must* say you borrowed it the weekend before, & give it to her back. She asked if we spent the night at Firle. So I supported Bunny's story and said yes. I thought her indeed charming and also the grissily wolf." Carrington to VB, n.d. [? October 1916]; see also VW/VB, [24 October 1916]. See also Carrington, *Letters*, p. 45.

him and them. He would hardly have condemned his sister-in-law's 'way of life,' but he might have considered it a trifle ramshackle, a little desperate. His attitude, I surmise, was marked by an almost imperceptible shade of disapproval and in a way this sentiment was shared by Virginia–but not entirely.

Virginia believed that she was quite capable of bicycling over to Charleston and back; she was pretty sure that a visit to Vanessa could do nothing but good, and she may even have accepted her nephews at their mother's valuation–for an afternoon at all events; if she curtailed her visits and put off the children it was (in writing to Vanessa at all events) out of deference to a husband who got into unreasonable 'states' when she lived a reasonably social life. In fact she was not quite consistent in these matters; she liked to be (from Leonard's point of view) naughty, and yet she respected his views. In all serious matters they were united, and even in small things she would usually allow, on reflection, that he was in the right.

These considerations have taken me somewhat beyond the year 1916, for in fact Vanessa did not settle at Charleston until October of that year (after David Garnett's blunderings at Asham), while the subsequent social transactions belong rather to the years 1917 and 1918. In fact the autumn and winter months of 1916 were quiet and uneventful, and Leonard and Virginia evolved a pattern of life at Hogarth House to which they adhered more or less all their lives. They wrote in the morning, they walked in the afternoon, they read in the evening; once or twice a week political or publishing business would take Leonard up to London; once or twice a week Virginia would accompany him and visit libraries, shops, concerts or friends. They would meet again at tea time and dine out or go home together. Their friends came out to Richmond to tea or to dine and often to spend the night. On Sundays their afternoon walk would very likely turn into a rather more ambitious expedition and they would take a bus or train and go further afield–it might well end in a visit to Leonard's family.

In the autumn Virginia became an active member of the Richmond Branch of the Women's Co-Operative Guild, and presided once a month at a meeting held in her own house, at which she was responsible for providing the speaker.

This function she continued to fulfil for the next four years, after which she rather thankfully resigned. In that time she prevailed upon Leonard and upon many of her friends ("we have had nothing but brilliancy and charm the last 3 months–Morgan Forster on India, Bob Trevelyan on China, Mary Sheepshanks on Peru")–to speak. The Guild members liked a change of subject, but at times the subject was too much for them. On 23 January 1917, they were addressed by Mrs Bessie Ward from the Council of Civil Liberties. She spoke on the subject of Conscription and, in particular, of the possible conscription of women. Noting the presence in the audience of two quite young girls she said that she was going to touch on "moral" questions and asked whether she should continue? No one objected, so she proceeded to describe, in some detail, the dangers of venereal disease, the risks to young soldiers of infection and so on. There was a queer silence when the talk ended and Virginia had thanked Mrs Ward. Two ladies left immediately, one very fat woman sat and wept; the company dispersed except for a Mrs Langston, an active and valuable member, who expressed her sense of outrage. Only a childless woman, she said, could have made such a speech, "for we mothers try to forget what our sons have to go through." She then burst into tears.

Virginia was quite unrepentant. Writing an account of the whole affair to Margaret Llewelyn Davies, she said she had never heard such nonsense; poor Mrs Ward on the other hand was well used to it—she had gone up and down the country provoking tears and indignation wherever she went. Margaret seems to have replied that the women's anxiety for their sons was quite natural and with this, in a second letter, Virginia agreed, although she still found it surprising that working women should choose to remain ignorant of a matter which might well concern them closely. Her cook, Nelly Boxall, who admitted that she had been shocked, acknowledged that it was right that women should know about such things. And indeed, in time, the other members did too, and told her so; they even asked for a lecture on Sex Education—all of which Virginia thought did them great credit.*

It cannot have been very long before Mrs Ward's lecture that Virginia made a new and important friend. It was Lytton who had suggested that she might like to meet Katherine Mansfield—

* ". . . I went to the Guild, which pleased me by its good sense, and the evidence that it does somehow stand for something real to these women. In spite of their solemn passivity they have a deeply hidden and inarticulate desire for something beyond the daily life. I believe they relish all the pomp of officers and elections because in some way it symbolises this other thing. They recanted their abuse of the woman on syphilis, which I think to their credit. Since then they have learnt, they said, that she only spoke the truth. They wish me to get them a speaker on Sex Education, Mrs Hiscoke telling us that she had had to get a friend to explain the period to her own daughter, and she still feels shy if the daughter is in the room when sexual subjects are discussed. She's 23 years old." *AWD* (*Berg*), 18 April 1918.

" . . . decidedly an interesting creature, I thought–very amusing and sufficiently mysterious. She spoke with great enthusiasm about *The Voyage Out*, and said she wanted to make your acquaintance more than anyone else's. So I said I thought it might be managed. Was I rash?" The lady was said to be in Cornwall. "If," said Virginia, who was to spend a fortnight near St Ives at the end of September, "I see anyone answering to your account on a rock or in the sea I shall accost her." She did not, and presumably their meeting took place in London later in the year.* By this time Katherine Mansfield and John Middleton Murry were living, with Carrington and Dorothy Brett, at 3 Gower Street, a house rented from Maynard Keynes, who himself had taken over the Bells' house at 46 Gordon Square. By February 1917 they were on such terms that Virginia could write to Vanessa: "I have had a slight rapprochement with Katherine Mansfield; who seems to me an unpleasant but forcible & utterly unscrupulous character."

They were always to disagree and never to disagree finally. United by their devotion to literature and divided by their rivalry as writers, they found each other immensely attractive and yet profoundly irritating. Or at least these were certainly Virginia's sentiments. She admired Katherine; she was also fascinated by that side of Katherine's life which was beyond her own emotional capacity. Katherine had knocked about the world and had been hurt by it; she had given rein to all the female instincts, slept with all kinds of men; she was an object of admiration–and of pity. She was interesting, vulnerable, gifted and charming. But also she dressed like a tart and behaved like a bitch. Or so it sometimes seemed to Virginia and in rather the same way she admired her stories, so sharply observed, so perceptive, at times so tragic and yet, at others, so cheap and so obvious. Katherine Mansfield, I think, returned Virginia's admiration and also her animosity. Probably she was rather frightened and at the same time half amused by her, and not displeased to discover that she could give Virginia not only pleasure but pain. Their doubts and reservations about each other were considerable; but in each other's company they were at ease and felt themselves to be fellow-workers.

Virginia certainly thought well enough of Katherine's talents to

---

* Leonard Woolf (*Beginning Again*, p. 203) says that it was at Garsington that they first came across Katherine Mansfield and Middleton Murry; but the Woolfs' first visit to Garsington was in November 1917. They are first mentioned in Leonard's *Diary* on 12 January 1917: "Katherine Mansfield, Murry & S. Waterlow to dinner."

want to print one of her stories. It will be remembered that, in 1915, before Virginia's collapse, the Woolfs were thinking of buying a printing press. Now that she was better the idea was revived. Leonard's purpose in this was to some extent therapeutic: it would be good for Virginia to have some manual occupation; but of course they were both of them writers, and the idea of printing and publishing their own works, even on the small scale dictated by a hand press, was very seductive. In October 1916 Virginia was again talking of getting a press, and she and Leonard began to consider whether they ought not to take lessons in printing. It was not easy, for Schools of Printing would not take middle-aged amateurs, and in the end they had to learn from a book. Then another difficulty arose; they had not enough money to buy a press.

It has been said, and the story has been repeated more than once, that the Hogarth Press was founded upon Leonard's winnings in the Calcutta Sweepstake. It sounds a pleasantly substantial foundation on which to build a business; but those winnings had been gained long before Leonard married Virginia and in fact the Press started on a capital outlay of £41. 15s. 3d—and this was not easily raised.

When, in 1912, Virginia told Violet Dickinson that she was marrying a penniless Jew she was not, if we understand the word penniless as Violet's friends would have understood it, overstating the case. For they would have considered an income of less than £600 a year as something like penury and Leonard, who had been earning £260 a year from the Colonial Office was, as a result of his resignation, reduced to something very much less. His mother, at the time of her husband's death, had been left with just enough money to keep herself and her nine children and to give the sons a good education. Once educated they had to fend for themselves. With his salary, and no doubt his sweepstake winnings, Leonard was able to save some money and this he increased by speculation. According to his diary his investments on 1 January 1912 amounted to £517. 15s. 2d, which would yield—but here I have no exact figures—something like £30 a year—not affluence, even by the standards of 1912. He and Virginia had hoped to make money by writing, but their novels in 1916 were bringing in less than £25 a year, and although Leonard was earning something by journalism, Virginia since 1913 had been unable to earn anything at all, while her illnesses were extremely expensive.

Fortunately Virginia had money of her own. It is not easy to know how much. When Sir Leslie Stephen died in 1904 and his children set up house together at 46 Gordon Square Vanessa, who looked after the money, was asked by an old family friend what their income amounted to.

When I said I thought about £300 a year each she said all was well–£200 would have been too little but with £1,200 between us we need not worry. Nor did we–but in fact our income was largely imaginary, depending on the successful letting of the Hyde Park Gate house, which remained obstinately empty for years owing to Duckworth mismanagement: not only that but Adrian was still at Cambridge, Thoby reading for the Bar, neither Virginia nor I earning anything. Then there were our old family servants who took it for granted all should go on as before, as did we ourselves. Sometimes I had a vague suspicion we were heading for bankruptcy, but all my life I had heard my father say gloomily that we should soon be in the workhouse & I had got used to not taking it seriously.

Virginia, who had inherited some money from Thoby and some from her aunt Caroline Emelia Stephen, had–"theoretically," as Leonard puts it–an invested capital of some £9,000; and this yielded less than £400 a year.*

In 1914 the Woolfs were living just within their income; doctors' bills were no doubt high in that year and, when they took a holiday in Northumberland, Virginia had to ask Vanessa for an advance of £15 on her share of the rent of Asham. In 1915 Leonard cast the following account of his and Virginia's expenses:

	£
Rooms	130
Food	156
Pocket Money	52
Doctors (this includes patent foods and medicaments for Virginia)	25
Dress	50
Miscellaneous	30
TOTAL	443

The payments to doctors, which seem comparatively reasonable, were probably largely postponed until 1916. By this time the Woolfs were established with their own servants at Asham and

---

* After their half-sister Stella's death in 1897 her husband Jack Hills made over the income on her marriage settlement to Vanessa and Virginia, and continued this until his second marriage (in 1931). Virginia inherited one-third of Thoby's estate (valued at £6,681) in 1906, and £2,500 from Caroline Emelia in 1909. She tried to persuade Adrian to take a half of this legacy, but I think without success.

Hogarth House, and the pattern of spending had changed; at the same time Virginia was beginning to earn money once more while Leonard's takings decreased a little.

	Estimate £	Expenditure £		
Houses	140	129.	5.	8.
Misc. House. (including fuel, furniture, etc.)	50	69.	0.	8.
Food	220	220.	5.	2.
Servants	60	67.	2.	2.
Doctors	25	81.	3.	3.
Dress (Virginia)	36	30.	8.	7.
Dress (Leonard)	14	14.	1.	5.
Miscellaneous	50	66.	17.	9.
TOTAL	595	678.	4.	8.

Leonard's estimate was made at the beginning of the year 1916, and as will be seen was exceeded by £83. 4s. 8d, largely owing to the unexpectedly heavy bills from the doctors. For the rest the Woolfs seem to have practised economies with some care; that Leonard exceeded his estimate of £14 for dress by 1s. 5d shows, I think, that it was exiguous. The servants were a new item; it will be noted that their joint wages came to less than the doctors' fees or the rent of the two houses, but of course, the increased expenditure on food must have been largely on their account. In that year, realising that the Woolfs were in difficulties, Violet Dickinson tried, but failed, to lend them money. The highly detailed accounts that Leonard kept (Virginia attempted to keep them but soon gave up) show that he counted every penny. Expenditure on newspapers and cigarettes was carefully entered and continued to be noted long after there was any need for such strict accounting; undoubtedly Leonard took pleasure in such exactitude and it became an end in itself; but in the early years of their married life such care was necessary. It is not easy to find items that can be classed as luxuries; in fact I think that there must have been some separate fund for the rare visits to music halls and cinemas, indulgences which they did occasionally allow themselves but which I cannot find mentioned. The nearest to luxuries that I can discover in the year 1916 are a total of 5s. 1d on cigarettes, 1s. 7d on flowers, £2. 5s. 6d on tips and presents, 3s. 4d on coloured papers (for which Virginia had a passion) and 1s.9d on a dog collar. They spent £5.3s.5d on books and library subscriptions but these can hardly be classed as luxuries. There is no mention of wines and spirits, gramophone records, cigars, taxis or concerts—all things that they were to enjoy in later years.

Keeping two houses and two servants the Woolfs cannot be described as poor; but neither, by the standards of their class, were they prosperous. In 1914, 1915 and 1916 they were what their friends would have called very hard up. The printing press could no doubt have been purchased by selling securities,* but clearly they were reluctant to do this. Their intention was to use an income tax rebate of £35 which they expected in December 1916. But the rebate amounted to only £15. More money had to be found and they thought that it could be raised by selling some inherited Thackeray manuscripts to the Pierpont Morgan Library. Adrian was to manage this business but before the sale was completed they found the capital elsewhere. On 23 March Leonard and Virginia went to the Farringdon Road and ordered a press.

It arrived a month later. They unpacked it with enormous excitement and carried it up to the drawing-room, only to discover that an essential part was broken. Leonard sent for a replacement. With all the excitement of children on Christmas morning, they began to divide the blocks of type into separate letters. Some got lost in the drawing-room carpet and Virginia managed, almost at once, to get the lower case h's mixed with the n's.

"I see that real printing will devour one's entire life. I am going to see Katherine Mansfield, to get a story from her, perhaps," wrote Virginia to Vanessa, and after a week Leonard was telling Margaret Llewelyn Davies that he wished he had never bought the cursed thing for now he would do nothing else but print. They decided that their first publication should be a joint effort and by 7 May they were able to post off to likely subscribers the hand-printed announcement: "It is proposed to issue shortly a pamphlet containing two short stories by Leonard Woolf and Virginia Woolf (price, including postage 1s. 2d)."

Virginia was by this time working hard for *The Times Literary Supplement*;† at the same time the idea which she had conceived at Wissett in July 1916 was sprouting into a novel which increasingly

---

* The Woolfs may have sold securities in order to pay the doctors. There is no evidence of this and it appears that they had other resources: ". . . it meant selling my few earrings and necklaces." VW/ES, 1 May 1931.

† Kirkpatrick (*A Bibliography of Virginia Woolf*, 1967) lists 12 contributions in 1916, 32 in 1917.

occupied her mind. On Easter Day 1917 Duncan and Vanessa came over from Charleston to tea at Asham, and Virginia was able to have a comfortable, intimate talk with her sister and tell her "all about her new novel."

> I am the principal character in it & I expect I'm a very priggish & severe young woman but perhaps you'll see what I was like at 18–I think the most interesting character is evidently my mother who is made exactly like Lady Ritchie down to every detail apparently. Everyone will know who it is of course.

Night and Day was, and was intended to be, a fairly pedestrian affair. Virginia wanted to see if she could achieve a perfectly orthodox and conventional novel. Also she wanted to do something which would not bring her too close to the abyss from which she had so recently emerged. In the final chapters of *The Voyage Out* she had been playing with fire. She had succeeded in bringing some of the devils who dwelt within her mind hugely and gruesomely from the depths, and she had gone too far for comfort. That novel and the final effort of giving it to the world had taken her over the edge of sanity and she could not yet risk a repetition of that appalling operation. Deliberately therefore she embarked upon something sane, quiet and undisturbing. She was to use this expedient again and to follow a particularly exacting novel with something lighter and easier; thus *Orlando* follows *To the Lighthouse*, *Flush* follows *The Waves* and *Three Guineas* follows *The Years*; the heavyweight novel is succeeded by a lightweight book–what she called "a joke." *Night and Day* was more than a joke, but despite its ambitious proportions it was a recuperative work. She did not altogether enjoy working on it. She compared it, writing to Ethel Smyth many years later, to drawing from the cast–an academic exercise. She began to promise herself a holiday–a kind of trip into those perilous areas that were forbidden.

> . . . they were the treats I allowed myself when I had done my exercise in the conventional style. I shall never forget the day I wrote the *Mark on the Wall*–all in a flash, as if flying, after being kept stone-breaking for months. The *Unwritten Novel* was the great discovery however. That–again in one second–showed me how I could embody all my deposit of experience in a shape that fitted it . . . *Jacob's Room* . . . *Mrs Dalloway* &c. How I trembled with excitement–& then Leonard came in & I drank my milk, concealed my excitement, & wrote I suppose another page of that interminable *Night & Day*.

In the summer of 1917 *Night and Day* was not nearly finished and, even if it had been, it would have been far too large an undertaking for the Woolfs' little hand press. It was *The Mark on the Wall* which, together with Leonard's *Three Jews*, appeared in July from the Hogarth Press under the title *Publication No. 1. Two Stories.*

This publication and its favourable reception* (by a very small public, for only 150 copies were printed) were both the result of and a contribution to Virginia's steady return to health. By this time she was leading almost as normal a life as she was ever to do, seeing a good many people in London and Richmond and, in August and September, at Asham. Henceforward it became a habit of many of their friends to spend a few days with the Woolfs at Asham and then proceed to Charleston to stay with Vanessa–or *vice versa*, and there was a continual to-ing and fro-ing between the households. This summer Virginia's guests at Asham were Roger Fry, Lytton Strachey and Desmond MacCarthy, who came from, or went on to Charleston, as well as Katherine Mansfield, Sidney Waterlow, G. Lowes Dickinson, Pernel Strachey and Philip Morrell, whom Leonard had insisted upon inviting on the grounds that he was never asked away on his own account without Lady Ottoline. "And then," as Virginia wrote to Margaret Llewelyn Davies,

> we've seen a lot of the younger generation, who seem to me the essence of good sense, honesty, sobriety & kindliness . . . [they] walk across the downs in brown corduroy trousers, blue shirts, grey socks, & no hats on their heads, which are cropped, so that as I sit on the terrace, I really don't know Barbara Hiles from Nick Bagenal, who is in the Irish Guards.

Leonard's invitation to Philip Morrell may be considered a sort of reply to one of Virginia's more reckless social adventures. This summer, for the first time since her marriage, she met Ottoline again–a reunion which seems to have been highly gratifying to both ladies. Virginia wrote to Vanessa:

> I was so much overcome by her beauty that I really felt as if I'd suddenly got into the sea, & heard the mermaids fluting on their rocks. How it was done I can't think; but she had red-gold hair in masses, cheeks as soft as cushions with a lovely deep crimson on the crest of them, & a body really shaped more after my notion of a mermaid's than I've ever

---

* "The *Two Stories* was a most cheering production. I could never have believed it possible. My only criticism is that there doesn't seem to be quite enough ink. Virginia's is, I consider, a work of genius. The liquidity of the style fills me with envy: really some of the sentences!–How on earth does she make the English language float and float? And then the wonderful way in which the modern point of view is suggested. *Tiens!*" Lytton Strachey to Leonard Woolf, 17 July 1917.

seen; not a wrinkle or blemish, swelling, but smooth.

Our conversation was rather on those lines, so I'm not surprised that I made a good impression. She didn't seem so much of a fool as I'd been led to think; she was quite shrewd, though vapid in the intervals. I begged her to revive Bedford Sqre. & the salon, which she said she would, if anyone missed her. Then came protestations, invitations – in fact I don't see how we can get out of going there, though Leonard says he wont, & I know it will be a disillusionment. However, my tack is to tell her she is nothing but an illusion, which is true & then perhaps she'll live up to it. She was full of your praises . . .

She & Virginia [wrote Roger Fry] have fallen into each others arms and each flatters t'other to the top of their bents. What a lot of contemporary mischief it'll brew, that liaison – I suppose it'll cut me off Virginia, & Ott. will get in some fine whacks at you too. But it wont last long.

Roger was perhaps writing to please Vanessa, who was not sorry to hear him speak ill of Ottoline and, at an earlier period, seems to have caused a breach between them. He took Virginia's infatuation a little too seriously; she never fell into Ottoline's arms so violently as to lose her balance. Certainly she was delighted to renew the acquaintance and certainly she was inclined to disregard the protests of Leonard and the aspersions of Vanessa, Clive and Roger. But this didn't prevent her from making fun of Ottoline and perhaps something that was not quite fun. Ottoline appealed to the snob in her; she had the grand manner and she was also one of the grand entertainments. Virginia liked to think that anything so improbable existed.

Their meeting in May did result in an invitation to Garsington. The visit had to be postponed because Ottoline caught the measles and, for one reason or another – perhaps Leonard managed to defer the evil day – it did not take place until November.

Meanwhile there had been a change, if not exactly in Virginia's life, at least in the manner in which that life was henceforth to be recorded. Returning from Asham on 5 October she discovered the diary she had written during her interval of sanity in 1915; it made her laugh and she was pleased enough by what she read to begin again. The record which she now kept was often to be neglected for days, for weeks, or indeed for months; but she never abandoned it altogether. She found in it an outlet for her immediate feelings, a source which she hoped, one day, when she had grown old, might enable her to write an autobiography. She fell into the habit of opening her book after tea and writing perfectly freely: she believed that this practice of spontaneous composition helped to give her more pondered works greater force and directness. This spontaneity makes her diary biographically interesting; it also makes it hard to publish. She wrote with the passion of the moment in her heart and at times she relieved her feelings with bitter ferocity. But despite their uncalculating sincerity I do not believe that these volumes give an entirely true picture of their author. There were times when she wrote in her diary because she could not read, and when she could not read it was usually because she was nervous, cross, or in some way disturbed and wanted, as she put it, "to write out the pain." Thus she often shows herself in a rather sad light, catching anxious and fearful moods rather than the gaiety and fantasy (which was equally a part of her character) which becomes more evident in her letters. Nevertheless, with the aid of these volumes it should be possible to give an accurate idea of her life.

Here are three entries from October 1917:

Wednesday, October 10th
No air raid; no further disturbance by our country's needs [Leonard had again been summoned for a medical inspection]; in fact L. made out in his bath that he deserved some good fortune, and opening his letters found a cheque for £12 from a Swedish paper which never was born and yet pays its debts. And I had 4/- for myself. Late last night, I was told to have my Henry James [review for *The Times Literary Supplement*] done if possible on Friday, so that I had to make way with it this morning and as I rather grudge time spent on articles, and yet can't help spending it if I have it, I am rather glad that this is now out of my power. And another article upon the country in Hardy and E. Brontë is suggested. We walked down the river, through the park and back to an early tea. At this moment L. is bringing the [19]17 Club into existence. I am sitting over the fire, and we have the prospect of K. Mansfield to dinner, when many delicate things fall to be discussed. We notice how backward the leaves are in falling and yellowing here as compared with Asheham. It might still be August, save for the acorns scattered on the path–suggesting to us the mysterious dispensation which causes them to perish, or we should be a forest of oaks.

Thursday, October 11th
The dinner last night went off: the delicate things were discussed. We could both wish that our first impression of K. M. was not that she stinks like a–well, civet cat that had taken to street walking. In truth, I'm a little shocked by her commonness at first sight; lines so hard and cheap. However, when this diminishes, she is so intelligent and inscrutable that she repays friendship. ... We discussed Henry James, and K. M. was illuminating, I thought. A munition worker called Leslie Moor came to fetch her–another of these females on the border land of propriety and naturally inhabiting the underworld–rather vivacious,

sallow skinned, without any attachment to one place rather than another. Today poor L. had to go the round of Drs. and committees, with a visit to Squire thrown in. His certificates are repeated. He weighs only 9 [stone].6 [lbs]. I bought my winter store of gloves, got a reference in the London Library, and met L. at Spikings for tea. Heaven blessed us by sending a quick train and we came home very glad to be home, over our fire, though we had to light it and cook up our dinner, owing to the servants' off day.

Sunday, October 14th
That is an awful confession, and seems to show the signs of death already spreading in this book. I have excuses though. We were rung up and asked to dine with the Bells in Soho, and this, I regret to say, led to much argument; we put off going to Kingston [i.e. to see Leonard's mother]; the night was wet, and L. didn't want–old arguments in short were brought out, with an edge to them. So we went dolefully enough, found the place, behind the palace, dined with Roger, Nina Hamnett, Saxon, Barbara [Hiles] and a party such as might figure in a Wells novel: I enjoyed it though, and L. was a model of self control. . . . Saturday was entirely given over to the military. We are safe again and, so they say, for ever. Our appearance smoothed every obstacle; and by walking across Kingston we got to the doctor about 12, and all was over by half past. I waited in a great square, surrounded by barrack buildings and was reminded of a Cambridge College–soldiers crossing, coming out of staircases and going into others; but gravel and no grass. A disagreeable impression of control and senseless determination; a great boarhound, emblem of military dignity, I suppose, strolled across by himself. L. was a good deal insulted: the doctors referred to him as the "chap with the senile tremor", through a curtain. Mercifully the impression slowly vanished as we went about Richmond. Herbert [Woolf, Leonard's brother] came to tea, bringing the dog, Tinker, a stout, active, bold brute, brown and white with large humourous eyes, reminding me a little of Dominic Spring-Rice. We have taken him for a walk, but directly he is loosed he leaps walls, dashes into open doors and behaves like a spirit in quest of something not to be found. We doubt rather if we can cope with him. Have I put down our Manx cat, also presented to us, one day this week?

These three entries may serve to announce those themes which in 1917 and 1918 recur most frequently in her diary: the air raids, Katherine Mansfield, the "Underworld" and the 1917 Club. The fact that she frequently adverts to them does not mean that they were, for her, of supreme importance. Virginia's mind was so constituted that it is very hard to know what would have been supremely important to her and, although it may sound ludicrous, her acquisition, at a rather later date, of a green glass jar from a chemist–one of those great flagons that glow or used to glow in pharmacy windows–was for her, it having been coveted perhaps since childhood, an event possibly as important as Katherine Mansfield's friendship or the German air raids. The point is not one that can be decided or, in any exhaustive way, discussed, but it should be borne in mind. More obviously important than either Katherine Mansfield or the chemist's jar was the continual progress of *Night and Day*. But during the autumn of 1917 she says nothing about it.

On the other hand she says a good deal about her journalism; at this time her book reviews were appearing in *The Times Literary Supplement* almost every week. This journalism was a source of mixed pleasure and vexation. If the Editor stopped sending her books she complained that she had been dismissed; if on the other hand he gave her a great deal of work then of course it took time from her novel. Virginia's ephemeral writing, if one may use such a word of contributions to *The Times Literary Supplement*, was never easily accomplished; she made several drafts, sometimes a great many drafts, before she was satisfied with a review.

. . . this sort of writing is always done against time; however much time I may have. For example here I have spent the week (but I was interrupted 2 days, & one cut short by a lunch with Roger) over Hakluyt: who turns out on mature inspection to justify over & over again my youthful discrimination. I write & write; I am rung up & told to stop writing: review must be had on Friday; I typewrite till the messenger from the Times appears; I correct the pages in my bedroom with him sitting over the fire here.

"A Christmas number not at all to Mr Richmond's taste, he said. Very unlike the Supplement style."

"Gift books, I suppose?" I suggested.

"O no, Mrs Woolf, its done for the advertisers."

But to retrace. On Thursday I lunched with Roger in order to hear the following story.

Mrs MacColl to Mr Cox of the London Library:

"Have you *The Voyage Out* by Virginia Woolf?"

"Virginia Woolf? Let me see; she was a Miss Stephen, daughter of Sir Leslie–her sister is Mrs Clive Bell I think. Ah, strange to see what's become of those two girls. Brought up in such a nice home too. But then, they were never *baptised*."

If she were to write reviews it was of course necessary to use the London Library, a good hour's journey from Hogarth House, and having gone so far she might go further and buy herself a pen or a pair of gloves or stockings, or take tea with Vanessa (if she happened to be in London), and thus an entire afternoon would be expended. Afternoons at home were now almost entirely devoted to printing. The Woolfs had started work on Katherine Mansfield's *Prelude*, Virginia setting up type–it came to 68 pages–Leonard doing the heavier work of machining. Printing was a constant source of delight and of misery; the actual processes and operations frequently perplexed them. Leonard consulted a local jobbing printer, who convinced him that he needed a larger press; they also began to look for an assistant. They thought that one of those sensible and well-disposed young women whom Virginia had noticed might help them.

On 10 October Virginia had written in her diary: "At this moment L. is bringing the 17 club into existence." This club* had a local habitation in Gerrard Street, Soho. Leonard and other socialist intellectuals thought that it might provide a congenial meeting place. It very soon became a centre, not only for the politically-minded, but for a kind of second-generation Bloomsbury. The old pre-war Bloomsbury was already beginning to acquire a sort of mythical existence, to be admired and imitated or denigrated by younger people who were, for the most part, non-conformists in a nation at war. Many in fact were not seriously interested in politics, but they were all deeply and decidedly hostile to the faith and morals of those Victorians and Edwardians who, they thought, had led their generation to catastrophe. When *Eminent Victorians* appeared in June 1918 it found in them a ready and responsive audience. There was in fact what Leonard was to call an "element of unadulterated culture" amongst the members of the 1917 club. In the visual arts they were naturally on the side of the *avant-garde*; but painting had had its great explosive flowering in 1910. It was the writers who seemed to be just within sight of new possibilities. Ezra Pound, James Joyce, T. S. Eliot and Katherine Mansfield were beginning to be read and discussed; and Roger Fry came back from France with news of an undoubted literary genius; admittedly he was rather apt to return from France with news of this kind, but on this occasion the genius was Marcel Proust.

The writer of *The Voyage Out* also had her place among the nascent stars–stars, it must be borne in mind, visible only to a very few. She was half pleased, half irritated by the attention shown her in the 1917 club. She found it a convenient place at which to meet Leonard. After delivering her article to *The Times* she would collect books from Mudie's, or Day's or the London Library,

* The Club took its name from the Russian Revolution, presumably the February Revolution.

drink tea in Gerrard Street and find company to engage her interest. Many of the people whom Virginia met at the club were already known or half known to her; there were some whom she referred to as: "Cropheads" or "Bloomsbury Bunnies;" others she referred to as "the Underworld." * It was among the former that she sought a helper in the quite considerable task of printing and binding *Prelude*. Their first assistant, a tall and grave young woman called Alix Sargant-Florence, came to start work on 16 October 1917. After showing her what to do, Leonard and Virginia left her on her high stool and took their dog for a walk. When they returned Alix said that she found the work totally without interest and saw no point in continuing. Their next apprentice was much less critical and considerably more persevering. Barbara Hiles had been one of the thoughtless trio who had broken into Asham and spent the night there. She came, trotting like a little pony, into the lives of the Bells and the Woolfs (sometimes, it must be said, on the wrong side of the road), pretty, practical and sensible, eager to be of service to everyone; she was ready and willing to be helpful in the Hogarth Press and turned up on a bicycle, bright as a button, on 21 November.

She set to work with more enthusiasm than competence, so that often enough Leonard had to take down and re-set the formes after she had gone home. She chattered, she was lively and decorative and never grumbled—as well she might have, for her wages amounted only to a meat meal on the days when she worked, an assurance of shelter in case of air raids and a proportion of the profits, which proportion she received after two months' work, when Leonard pressed half a crown into her hand. The real wages, one imagines, were Virginia's company and the opportunity of talking about her rather agitated life to a sympathetic listener.

Virginia had plenty of opportunity for getting to know Barbara fairly well during the next weeks. She and her friend Carrington –both ex-Slade students, with their bobbed hair and thick fringes, their free and independent ways, their healthy high spirits and bright sensible clothes, their passion for culture–represented Virginia's archetypal Cropheads. "The Bloomsbury hypnotism," she wrote to Vanessa, "is rank, & threatens the sanity of all the poor Bunnies, who are perpetually feeling their hind legs to see if they haven't turned into hares." Carrington fell in love with

---

* These terms were of course extremely imprecise. "Bloomsbury Bunnies" was invented by Mrs Desmond MacCarthy, "Cropheads" was Virginia's own word.

Lytton Strachey and devoted her life to serving him. Barbara's artless charms touched some chord in Saxon's heart and disturbed his deeply entrenched celibacy; his devotion–which was to be lifelong –promised access to the imagined Empyrean of Bloomsbury, though when it came to marriage she settled for a younger and more human admirer, Nicholas Bagenal. The movements of this *pas de trois*, as described by Barbara herself and by her friends, were for Virginia a source of endless fascination and speculation. Nick Bagenal's sister Faith, the austere and melancholy Alix (desperately, but in the end successfully, engaged in the pursuit of James Strachey), and her own cousin Fredegond, a very intense and poetic young woman, helped also to provide the company and the youthful indiscretions which enlivened Virginia's visits to the 1917 club. There too she was able to observe many examples of what she called "the Under-world." She used this term with malicious intent and certainly with a kind of snobbery, sometimes with a purely social meaning, but also to classify those who were not so much creative artists as critics and commentators–people who could write a clever essay or a smart review; people who were more interested in reputations than in talents. For them the important thing was success; they would know who was on the way up or the way down; they could measure one author against another in terms of copies sold and retail the latest scandal in the world of journalism or of publishing. Their ambition was to be on the winning side. Thus, to anticipate a little, when Conrad published *Victory* Virginia found it hailed by the Underworld as a masterpiece: Conrad was very much 'the thing.' But when she expressed her doubts, finding the book below his best level, there was a kind of uneasy shift of opinion–perhaps Conrad was going out, perhaps the moment had come to disparage him. One must tack, shift, reinsure, turn and come again.

Grub Street, I suppose, has always been like this, and the Squires and Lynds, Sullivans or Swinnertons of Virginia's Underworld were no worse and probably better than most. But for her the perpetual president and oracle of the Underworld was John Middleton Murry, for he added another ingredient–a high moral tone, a pretentious philosophy borrowed in part from his friend D. H. Lawrence– which allowed the game to be played under the cover of deep, manly, visceral feelings and virtuous protestations. I think that most of Virginia's generalisations about the Underworld are really based upon Murry; he was so very much 'the coming man.' She and Lytton agreed that he would probably end as Professor of English Literature at Oxford or Cambridge.

The Cropheads and the Underworld met and to some extent fused at the 1917 Club; some of them were also to be found at Garsington Manor near Oxford, where Philip and Ottoline Morrell kept open house and whither, it may be remembered, the Woolfs were invited during the summer of 1917.

Long before she finally persuaded Leonard to accompany her there, Virginia had gained a pretty accurate notion of what Garsington was like. Here, since the introduction of conscription, Philip Morrell had offered easy employment on his farm to pacifists and conscientious objectors, and here there was in consequence a resident population which included at different times Clive Bell, Gerald and Fredegond Shove, Middleton Murry's younger brother, and the painter Mark Gertler; this was reinforced by the visits for longer or shorter periods of Middleton Murry and Katherine Mansfield, Carrington and her friend Brett,* Lytton Strachey and relays of young men who came out from the University to extend their education. The atmosphere was not a happy one and may be illustrated by one story which was told by Clive Bell and in the truth of which he firmly believed.

On one occasion he had had to go unexpectedly to London on a Sunday leaving on the hall table several letters to be posted on Monday morning. Gertler and Carrington thought that it would entertain a dull Sunday evening if they were to steam these letters open and read the contents aloud. Ottoline protested too little or not at all, which was unwise of her, for the company was entertained by an account, no doubt in Clive's best Walpolian manner, of all that was mean, base or ridiculous in her Ladyship. There was, in particular, the story of a peacock which, having died of old age complicated by various disgusting maladies, reappeared pompously accoutred on the dining-room table. There was, not unnaturally, an awkward coolness when Clive returned from London, all the more awkward in that its cause could not be avowed.

True or false, the story is significant in that it gives a notion of the moral atmosphere of Garsington at that time.

When, on 19 November 1917, Virginia returned from her first visit there she wrote:

> We came back from that adventure two hours ago. It's difficult to give the whole impression, save that it wasn't much unlike my imagination. People strewn about in a sealingwax coloured room. Aldous Huxley

* The painter Mark Gertler, unhappily in love with Carrington, watched with bitter jealousy her infatuation for Lytton; Brett (the Hon. Dorothy Brett) had been at the Slade with Carrington and Gertler.

toying with great round disks of ivory and green marble–the draughts of Garsington: Brett in trousers: Philip tremendously encased in the best leather: Ottoline, as usual, velvet and pearls: two pug dogs: Lytton semi-recumbent in a vast chair. Too many nicknacks for real beauty, too many scents and silks and a warm air which was a little heavy. Droves of people moved about from room to room–from drawing room to dining room, from dining room to Ottoline's room–all Sunday. At moments the sense of it seemed to flag; and the day certainly lasted very long by these means. Fredegond was admitted in the morning; and then after tea I had perhaps an hour over a log fire with Ottoline. . . . On the whole I liked Ottoline better than her friends have prepared me for liking her. Her vitality seemed to me a credit to her and in private talk her vapours give way to some quite clear bursts of shrewdness. The horror of the Garsington situation is great of course, but to the outsider the obvious view is that O. and P. and Garsington house provide a good deal, which isn't accepted very graciously. However to deal blame rightly in such a situation is beyond the wit of a human being: they've brought themselves to such a pass of intrigue and general intricacy of relationship that they're hardly sane about each other. In such conditions I think Ott. deserves some credit for keeping her ship in full sail, as she certainly does. We were made immensely comfortable, a good deal of food; the talk had frequent bare patches, but then the particular carpet had been used fairly often. By talking severely to Philip, L. made him come up to Parliament today. He is a weak amiable long-suffering man who seems generally to be making the best of things, and seeing the best of people whom by nature he dislikes.

The "horror" of Garsington lay in the fact that it was a refuge. The angular and difficult characters whom Ottoline entertained were bound–or should have been bound–to their hostess by a sentiment of gratitude. But the consciousness of an obligation does not engender affection. The refugees quarrelled with her and with each other; having done so, they could not go away but had to stay and live with the objects of their discontent. They could not leave Garsington precisely because it offered a refuge from the war, and for the same reason they could not be happy while they remained there. Visitors, like Virginia, could enjoy the pleasures of what one may almost call "neutral territory," and like it the better by reason of the fact that they returned to the abominable moral atmosphere, the increasing hardships, and the dangers of a capital at war.

Air raids came–or were expected–each month with the full moon, and when they did, they drove the inhabitants of Hogarth House into the basement. On these occasions bedding and blankets were brought down and disposed in passages and pantries; Leonard would lie like a funerary image upon the kitchen table, Virginia lay beneath it. The servants had regular bunks, preferring to sleep below ground every night; they chattered and giggled at Virginia's jokes until Leonard called for silence. Then they all slept as best they might while Zeppelins or aeroplanes cruised overhead dropping bombs on what they no doubt supposed to be Slough or Staines, and the anti-aircraft guns added to the general noise and discomfort of the night. On one occasion however, when their dinner party had to adjourn to the cellar, their friend R. C. Trevelyan continued his discourse in so loud a voice that friend and foe were alike inaudible.*

The Woolfs went to Asham for Christmas and on their return to town at the New Year found that a great many people were talking about the possibility of peace. "This talk...," Virginia noted, "comes to the surface with a kind of tremor of hope once in three months: then subsides: then swells again." It was a regularly renewed disappointment and this time Virginia found no great consolation in the knowledge that she had been given a vote. Despite her efforts on behalf of Women's Suffrage in the years before the war the triumph, now that it had come, did not appear very considerable. It was altogether a rather gloomy time. She was, however, working fast and had written over 100,000 words of *Night and Day* by March 1918; but she felt depressed, and in February she fell ill with influenza. When she was well enough Leonard took her to Asham for ten days to recuperate, and they seriously discussed the possibility of remaining there until the war was over. They returned to Hogarth House but were back again at Asham three weeks later for an Easter holiday. The late March days were blazing hot, and the sound of artillery fire in Flanders was clearly audible upon the hill as the Germans pushed the Allies back towards Amiens. One of Leonard's brothers had been killed over there before Christmas, and now Barbara's new husband was in the fighting;† Virginia felt uneasy and unhappy and it seemed to her there was an odd and unhealthy pallor in those days of spring sunshine.

* "We had a raid last night–Bob was dining with us & talked so loud that we couldn't hear the guns; but Saxon says it was rather bad in London. We ate most of our dinner in the coal cellar." VW/VB, 19 December 1917 (Berg).

When I first read this it seemed typical of Virginia's exaggerated style; but compare it with Leonard's diary entry for 18 December 1917: "Aft. tea Bob Trevelyan came to spend night. At 6.45 air raid began but Bob's raucous voice never stopped & drowned the sound of guns. Dined between dining room & cellar. But it went on so long that we got tired & settled upstairs. Played & won a game of chess. Raid over at 10."

† He was in fact seriously wounded on Easter Saturday, 30 March 1918.

Lytton came to Asham and perhaps did something to relieve her melancholy, but Lytton presented problems. *Eminent Victorians*, much of which had been read to her (to her shame she fell asleep during the reading of one chapter), was now in the press. It would soon appear, and Lytton tactfully but repeatedly suggested that she should review it for *The Times Literary Supplement*, until at length, much against her better judgement, she consented and wrote to Bruce Richmond. He replied that she could review the book if she could keep her authorship secret; but this she felt that she could not do and the book fell into other hands.

A rather different literary transaction began on 14 April, by which time the Woolfs had returned to Richmond. Miss Harriet Weaver, owner and editor of the *Egoist Press*, came bearing the manuscript of *Ulysses*; she hoped that the Hogarth Press might publish it.*
It was a work which Virginia could neither dismiss nor accept. Its power and subtlety were sufficiently evident to arouse her admiration and, no doubt, her envy. It seemed to her to have a kind of beauty but also a kind of cheap, smart, smoking-room coarseness. Joyce made use of instruments not dissimilar to her own and this was painful, for it was as though the pen, her very own pen, had been seized from her hands so that someone might scrawl the word *fuck* on the seat of a privy. Also she felt that Joyce wrote for a clique; and when she refers to him she writes of "these people," classing him perhaps with Ezra Pound and I know not what other figures of the "Underworld." Her reaction is perhaps significant; the gratuitous and impudent coarseness of Joyce made her feel suddenly desperately lady-like. Nevertheless she was quite perceptive enough to see that this was clearly something well worth publishing; equally clearly it was wholly beyond the technical capacity of the Hogarth Press. Professional printers would have to be employed; and it was the impossibility of finding one to undertake such a task—for those whom Leonard consulted insisted that they would court certain prosecution—which obliged the Woolfs to give up the attempt.

Eminent Victorians appeared in June. Lytton's friends were in

---

* According to Leonard Woolf Miss Harriet Weaver came to Hogarth House on the recommendation of T. S. Eliot (*Beginning Again*, p. 247). This is no doubt the case; but when he says: "He told us at the end of 1917 or the beginning of 1918 that Miss Harriet Weaver . . . was much concerned about a MS by James Joyce . . ." he suggests a degree of intimacy between Virginia and T. S. Eliot which did not then exist. A diary entry in November 1918 makes it hard to believe that she had ever met Mr Eliot before the 15th of that month.

some ways disappointed. It was, of course, brilliant – it had always been taken for granted that Lytton would achieve brilliance. But was it quite worthy of him? Vanessa and Virginia thought not. Clive was more enthusiastic; he also declared that Virginia was jealous – absurdly and disgracefully jealous – of Lytton's success. If she was, she didn't tell her diary, but probably she did feel a pang. Inevitably when a friend, one's obvious rival in the literary game, with whom one has, so to speak, run neck and neck for years, all at once draws ahead – even though it only be in public estimation, so that people say "Do you really know Lytton Strachey?" rather than "Are you *the* Virginia Woolf?" – a superhuman degree of detachment and a quite exceptional degree of moral superiority – qualities no-one could possibly claim for Virginia – would be required if the distanced runner were to remain entirely calm. And Clive, it must be said, would not have hesitated to rub salt into the wound. He still enjoyed teasing Virginia and relations between them were strained that autumn, so much so that there was, as we shall see, a rather violent break. For a time, too, relations with Vanessa were little better; but in order to explain their embroilment it is necessary to enter a rather long digression, for it arose from what Vanessa called "the servant problem."

It was a practical problem, a moral problem, a personal problem and it was of agonising importance to Vanessa, Virginia and, I suppose, to a great mass of people like them. In order to understand it I must remind the reader of some very obvious facts which we tend to forget. If you can afford to buy this book it is probable that when you take it home with you in the evening you can make a light with which to read it by pressing a switch. The room is warmed by central heating, you turn a tap and hot water pours into your bath or into your sink, you pull a plug and cold water gushes into your lavatory. You may do your own cooking and your own housework, but you are probably assisted by dozens of mechanical devices, tins and tin-openers, frozen foods, refrigerators and plastic containers. Heaven knows how many thousand horses give their power every day at the touch of your fingers. No very serious effort is demanded of you when ovens have to be heated, foods ground and mixed, floors swept, rooms lighted and fires made.

Now, when Virginia Woolf went to Asham she found none of these commodities. To get there at all she had to walk or to bicycle for several miles or to go to the expense of a taxi or a fly. To make a light she had candles which dropped grease on the carpet, or lamps which smoked and had to be refilled with oil and trimmed every morning; heat was supplied by wood or coal—and coal was in short supply from 1916 to 1919; the coal had to be carried about in scuttles, grates had to be cleaned, fires laid, and if they were not competently managed they would fill the room with smoke or die miserably. In the country you got hot water by boiling it over a stove. Cold water had to be pumped up into a tank every day and Asham was furnished only with an earth closet. There were no refrigerators or frozen foods, a tin-opener was a kind of heavy dagger with which you attacked the tin hoping to win a jagged victory. All the processes of cooking and cleaning were incredibly laborious, messy and slow. There are still plenty of people who live in conditions of this kind or worse—far worse—but obviously in these circumstances someone must be perpetually at work if any kind of comfort or cleanliness is to be maintained.

Before 1914 a surprisingly large number of people could employ, at all events, one indoor servant. Labour was plentiful and girls would accept places for their keep and a pittance. The rich, who might afford a ratio of say six servants to one master, probably found them more efficient than we our mechanical appliances.

The Woolfs before the war kept two servants, the Bells four—the minimum for a household in which the wife had a full-time occupation and, as in the case of the Bells, two children. During the war the condition of the market changed radically. There were good wages to be earned in factories and female labour became scarce. Younger women were unwilling to go into service; the isolation of domestic work in the country was very discouraging.

At the same time there was a moral problem. In Hyde Park Gate, with its army of servants, the situation had been frankly patriarchal. Leslie Stephen was the head of the house. Minny, Julia, Stella or Vanessa were his deputies and the servants were immediately responsible to them. Everyone knew their respective place. The system had the faults and the virtues of benevolent despotism. During the years between 1904 and 1914 that system began to break down; the Stephen sisters lacked the social assurance of their parents; they disliked the servant/mistress relationship, but they did not know how to avoid it. Paternalism only works when both sides accept it as proper and natural. When it breaks down, injustices may be removed, but the moral situation becomes extremely uncomfortable. Mrs Bell and Mrs Woolf looked for, felt for, some other and more equal form of contract between employer and employed. With Sophia Farrell—a family treasure if ever there was one—they were particularly uneasy. It was hard either to take her or to leave her. They could neither live up to her standards nor play the matriarchal part which she expected of them. On the other hand, if she needed employment, clearly the family had to provide it. She went from one household to another, ending at last with the George Duckworths who still played the game in the old way.

Her successors did not have the same traditional background and in that sense were easier, but the personal relationship was if anything more difficult than before. In Bloomsbury the domestic servants were not offered the servile status of the Victorian age, but neither had they the businesslike employer/employee relationship which can be established today between the "daily" woman who "helps" and the woman who is "helped." They were part of the household, in a sense a part of the family, but they were also independent human beings, equals with feelings to be respected. Ideally, hopefully, they were friends. But how many of one's friends are there whom one can see daily, who are dependent on one for a livelihood, who hold one's comforts in their hands, and with whom one is never bored or cross? And how hard to base a friendship on a written character, an interview, and no similarity of upbringing, of interests, of education or of class. Class is today almost a dirty word, and one hopes represents less than it did fifty years ago in English society, but to imagine that anybody at that time was not class-conscious would be crazy.

Class divisions produce incomprehension on both sides. In Bloomsbury the servants had to deal with neurotic and unusual people who wore the wrong clothes, hung the wrong pictures, held the wrong views and had the most peculiar friends. (Thus in 1917 Vanessa's cook found herself having to discuss with her mistress the relationship between one of the guests in the house and a particularly seductive stable-boy on the adjacent farm. The guest, of course, was Lytton Strachey.)

Virginia's household did not present quite the problems that Vanessa's did, but undoubtedly she puzzled and at times infuriated her servants.

Early in 1916, when Virginia was recovering, Leonard had engaged Nelly Boxall and her lifelong friend Lottie Hope as cook and housemaid. They had previously been in the service of Roger Fry at Guildford. The two girls were very devoted to one another. Lottie, a foundling, was a simple character, generous, impulsive, untruthful and passionate. She passed easily from high spirits to rage. Nelly was quieter, gentler and, at bottom, even more passionate than her friend.

Nelly was to recall her first interview in 1916, when she came into the drawing-room at Hogarth House and found Virginia lying on the sofa in an old dressing-gown and thought her "so sweet" and knew that she would like working for her. What she didn't know, poor Nelly, was that she would be so enchanted by Virginia and so aggravated by her that, for the next eighteen years, she could neither live with her nor live without her, nor that Virginia was to be so exasperated and at the same time so touched by *her* changing moods that she could neither endure her nor dismiss her. Nelly and Lottie quarrelled and were reconciled, sulked and were mollified, complained and gave notice, over and over again. They were torn between an extreme terror of air raids in town and despair at the tedium of living in the country. They provided a constant source of drama. Virginia was fascinated but infuriated by them; they brought out the best and the worst in her.

In April 1918, Vanessa found that she was pregnant. There were then living at Charleston Vanessa, Duncan, David Garnett, a governess and her lover, four children, including the governess's daughter and nephew, a cook and a kitchen-maid. Clearly the burden of work in this household was heavy. Then the cook gave notice. It seemed almost impossible to get another. In this crisis, Virginia, not for the first time, made herself useful by visiting domestic agencies, while Vanessa made enquiries in her immediate district, all to no avail. Then Virginia had the idea that Nelly and Lottie should go to her sister, at all events for two weeks. Privately she thought that they might remain there, for the Woolfs were getting so short of money that it seemed impossible to go on keeping servants; there was, however, the chance that Leonard might be offered an editorship, in which case, of course, they would want to have Nelly and Lottie back. At all events the possibility that they might not return was concealed from them. The negotiations between Vanessa and Virginia and between Virginia and her servants and between the servants and Vanessa, in which the suspicions of Nelly and Lottie that they might be leaving for good, Vanessa's hesitations about coming to an agreement which might not be permanent, with the added complication of a Miss Ford, a local gir who would obviously not be as good as Nelly and Lottie, but was momentarily available, fill page after page of the almost daily correspondence between the sisters in May and June 1918. In the end Vanessa, being unwell, had to send Trissie, the cook who was leaving her, to Richmond to conclude negotiations, and she managed matters so ill that Nelly and Lottie declared that nothing would induce them to leave the Woolfs or go to Charleston at all. This *dénouement* came just too late for Vanessa to secure Miss Ford; she was snatched up by somebody else. In her anxious and exasperated state Vanessa asked whether it was not Leonard who all along had been opposed to her having Nelly and Lottie? This brought a rather stiff rejoinder from Leonard, followed by explanatory peace-making letters from both sides.

Virginia could always make her peace with Vanessa easily enough. But not with Clive; and during the autumn of 1918 she was again at odds with him.

Clive always accused Virginia of being a mischief-maker and he believed, perhaps rightly, that the unkind remarks which he and Desmond MacCarthy had made about Katherine Mansfield at Hogarth House were repeated to Katherine by his hostess. This of course led to some trouble; but there was worse to come.

At this time the most important person in Clive's life was neither Virginia nor Vanessa, but Mrs St John Hutchinson, and this of course meant that she became, if not a "member," at least a very frequent visitor in Bloomsbury. Both Vanessa and Virginia admired her; but Clive demanded more of his friends than that they should like Mary. In his enthusiasm he insisted that they should recognise in her the most infinitely subtle and civilised being in their society—a du Deffand with the charms of a Pompadour. She herself had no such pretensions and probably realised that, in making these claims, Clive injured rather than advanced her cause and succeeded only in spoiling what would otherwise have been a sufficiently warm welcome. In fact Virginia's feelings about Clive's friend varied a great deal. There was no-one whose stock did not rise and fall in the uncertain market of her regard; but if this issue sometimes crashed to fearful depths it was because Clive had drawn up a wholly misleading prospectus.

It is within this context that we should consider Virginia's mischief-making (if it was she who made it) in the autumn of 1918.

It was at this time that Mrs Hutchinson was told—by whom it is not clear—that Clive's friends, and Vanessa in particular, thought her a great bore and only tolerated her for his sake. Naturally this ill-natured report distressed her very much. Clive and Vanessa jumped to the conclusion that this story must have come from Virginia and have been repeated by Mark Gertler, who had been at Asham in September. "Whatever you may have said to Gertler was at once repeated by him . . ." wrote Vanessa, adding: "Do be careful what you say . . . & please dont let him or in fact anyone think that I don't like Mary for as you know I do."

Virginia replied with some heat: yes, Mary had once been the subject of conversation between her and Gertler at Asham–Leonard was there, and could testify that all she had said was that she scarcely knew Mary, who always seemed very silent in her company, and that yes, she supposed she was equally silent with Vanessa. As for Gertler, he had been neither inquisitive nor malicious, being ("as usual") entirely absorbed in himself and in his own affairs.* Some of Mary's friends might have a motive for making mischief; she certainly had none. She objected very strongly to "being made the victim of this infernal spy system" and resolved in future to steer clear of Clive and his new set.

A letter from Clive to Vanessa suggests that Virginia's indignation was justified:

> I just want to put you right on one point. It was not I who said that Virginia had been telling Gertler tales. I merely said that tales had been told and it was someone else–you I rather think–who suggested Virginia as the *fons et origo*. We all agreed that this was probable and I think so still, but I'm quite sure I didn't say the tales came from Virginia because to this day I don't know how they reached Mary. I will find out. It isnt that I in the least mind being embroiled with Virginia. I am well used to it and rather like it, but let it be on a real issue.

She had been accused on suspicion, and not on evidence, and the evidence, as far as it goes, tends to exonerate her. It may however be argued that Vanessa (if it was Vanessa) would not have suspected her if she had not already earned a bad reputation. Certainly she was indiscreet. She herself recalls an occasion on which she told secrets, not realising they would be blurted out in company, so that, as she puts it, she found herself in "hot water." On another occasion Vanessa thought it necessary to warn her when she was going to see Lady Strachey, "Do, for God's sake, be careful about what you say. . . . Remember, she's *not* up to date in morals–has never heard of buggery–at any rate not in her own family. You have the wildest ideas about such things." Indeed she had an alarming

---

* In her diary Virginia records that she was at Charleston on 17 September when Clive and Mrs Hutchinson arrived by car. "She was," she wrote on the 23rd, "as usual, mute as a trout–I say trout because of her spotted dress–also because, though silent, she has the swift composure of a fish." And on the same day she writes: "We have been talking about Gertler to Gertler for some 30 hours; it is like putting a microscope to your eye. One molehill is wonderfully clear; the surrounding world ceases to exist." *AWD* (*Berg*).

tendency to say whatever came into her head. But this is not the same thing as the kind of deliberate, pointlessly cruel mischief-making of which she was here accused.

These private dramas must be imagined against a background of large public events, events towards which Virginia's attention was increasingly directed. For the Gertler-Mary Hutchinson row took place in mid-October 1918 and by then it had become clear that the war really was at last coming to an end. Leonard was much occupied by the political struggles that resulted from the search for an international peace-keeping organisation to be established after the war, and something of these efforts is recorded in Virginia's diary. When Beatrice and Sidney Webb had come to stay at Asham in September, a visit which for Virginia involved a considerable social effort, their incessant talk was largely concerned with reconstruction and the new social order that would be established.

"The work of government," declared Sidney Webb, "will be enormously increased in the future."

"Shall I have a finger in the pie?" asked Virginia.

"Oh yes, you will have some small office no doubt. My wife and I always say that a railway guard is the most enviable of men. He has authority and is responsible to a government. That should be the state of each one of us."

As the weeks passed these fair visions of the future became brighter.

"Whatever we have done this week," wrote Virginia on 12 October, "has had this extraordinary background of hope; a tremendously enlarged version of the feeling I can remember as a child as Christmas approached." The following Sunday her cousin, H. A. L. Fisher, then a Cabinet Minister, appeared unheralded at Hogarth House at tea-time and announced: "We've won the war today."

In fact there was still a month to wait, and Virginia noted, not without anger, Lord Northcliffe's anxiety to prolong the slaughter. She wrote in her diary:

Wednesday, October 30
Just in from a walk in the Park on this incredibly lovely autumn day. Various houses have orange berries growing upon them; the beech trees are so bright that everything looks pale after you have looked at them. (How I dislike writing directly after reading Mrs. H. Ward!–she is as great a menace to health of mind as influenza to the body). We talked of peace: how the sausage balloons will be hauled down and gold coins dribble in; and how people will soon forget all about the

war and the fruits of our victory will grow as dusty as ornaments under glass cases in lodging house drawing rooms. How often will the good people of Richmond rejoice to think that liberty has been won for the good people of Potsdam? I can believe though that we shall be more arrogant about our own virtues. The Times still talks of the possibility of another season, in order to carry the war into Germany and there imprint a respect for liberty in the German peasants. I think the distance of the average person from feelings of this sort is the only safeguard and assurance that we shall settle down again neither better nor worse.

And later:

Monday, November 11th.
Twentyfive minutes ago the guns went off, announcing peace. A siren hooted on the river. They are hooting still. A few people ran to look out of windows. The rooks wheeled round and wore for a moment the symbolic look of creatures performing some ceremony, partly of thanksgiving, partly of valediction over the grave. A very cloudy still day, the smoke toppling over heavily towards the east; and that too wearing for a moment a look of something floating, waving, drooping. We looked out of the window; saw the housepainter give one look at the sky and go on with his job; the old man toddling along the street carrying a bag out of which a large loaf protruded, closely followed by his mongrel dog. So far neither bells nor flags, but the wailing of sirens and intermittent guns.

Chapter Three

November 1918 – December 1922

NOVEMBER 1918, which brought the armistice, brought also the end of *Night and Day*–the last words were written on 21 November; it also brought Virginia a new friend, T. S. Eliot. He came to Hogarth House on 15 November bringing with him three or four poems. Mr Eliot himself appeared to Virginia a polished, cultivated, elaborate young American, and almost too decorous; but very intelligent and very much a poet. He was very firm in his opinions, which were not Virginia's, for he thought Ezra Pound and Wyndham Lewis great men, and admired James Joyce immensely. Leonard and Virginia agreed that the Hogarth Press should publish his latest poems and she began to set them up towards the end of January 1919.

But most of January Virginia spent in bed. She had a tooth extracted and then a headache; her nephews, whom she had undertaken to house during Vanessa's *accouchement*, had to be sent off to their father at Gordon Square. The armistice did not end but seemed rather to have intensified shortages of every sort. Life was made more difficult by a wave of industrial unrest. In a letter to Ka Cox, who had now become Mrs Arnold-Forster and had settled in Cornwall, she describes the inconveniences of that time:

. . . to be ill at the Lizard seems to me better than to be well here. You can't conceive what existence is like without trains or tubes, a heavy snow falling, no coal in the cellar, a leak in the roof which has already filled every possible receptacle, & probably no electric light tomorrow. We in Richmond can still get to Waterloo; but Hampstead is entirely cut off. Leonard's staff of course live upon the northern heights, & hardly get to the office at all, so the poor man has to go up himself, & here I sit waiting, & God knows, what with the snow & the fog, when he'll be back. Then the experts say that the working classes have behaved with such incredible stupidity that the Government will beat them; & this strike is only the beginning of others far worse to follow. They say we are in for such a year as has never been known. Sensible people like you go & live in Cornwall. I wish you'd go to Gurnards Head & see if there's a cottage there to let, as I've been told. We are faced with the appalling prospect of having to give up Asheham. It's wanted for the farm probably; there's still a ray of hope but I'm afraid not much. . . .

I'm quite well again, though slightly restricted in my jaunts to London, so I haven't a great deal of gossip . . . Have you heard of the catastrophes at Charleston? I cant go into them in any detail, since they would fill volumes. But imagine a country doctor ordering some medicine for the baby [Vanessa's daughter Angelica, born on Christmas Day, 1918] which made it ill by day and by night—Nessa commands him to stop—he refuses—he wont say what it is—the gamp has to obey him—child loses more & more pounds—Duncan goes over to Brighton & interviews Saxon's father about the quality of Nessa's milk—without result—Noel [Olivier] telegraphed for—lady doctor arrives secretly —finds the doctor is ordering some form of poison—Mrs. Brereton [the governess] thinks it her duty to inform the Dr. of his rival's presence—scenes, explosions, dismissal—triumph of Nessa & the lady doctor & partial recovery of the Baby. Just as this was over, the servants took to drink or worse, & had to be got rid of; frantic efforts of course to get others; none to be had; telegrams sent, interviews arranged, cook discovered, fails at the last moment—whole thing begins over again; more cooks discovered; just about to start when their father falls dead in the street, upon which both Nessa & I rush about in a fury, with the result that we each engage cooks without telling the other, and one has to be dismissed at enormous expense & terrific cost of energy. You can't think what a lot of time this has all taken up, or how sick I am of beginning my letters, "Jane Beale, I am writing for my sister –" For one thing I detest that style of sentence, & then the bold abrupt handwriting is what I can't compass.

The catastrophes at Charleston had in fact involved Virginia in a great deal of fatiguing exertion at a time when she was not at all well. She could not resist, but could not but be exasperated by the demands which her sister made (demands which were all the more eloquent for being unspoken). When things got too bad, Nelly was sent to Charleston to save the situation but, as usual, Leonard had to intervene in order to protect Virginia from the effects of her own generosity.

It was not until early March that Virginia was able to go to Sussex to inspect her new niece and see for herself how Vanessa was managing. Living, she noted, was rather bare at Charleston –"nothing but wind and rain and no coal in the cellar." All the same there was something attractive and soothing about that bleak interior. It was disorderly and might fairly be called disreputable; but the atmosphere was congenial and in some moods, comparing it with her own relatively well-regulated and completely irreproachable domesticity, Virginia could find it enviably romantic.

On the first of June Virginia again spent a night at Charleston. This visit was important, for reasons which must be explained by returning to the events of the spring.

It will be remembered that, in her letter to Ka, Virginia was deploring the probable loss of Asham, though there was then still a ray of hope. This hope was extinguished on 1 March when Mr Gunn the farmer gave them six months' notice. Leonard and Virginia at once began house-hunting–an occupation which she confessed was always a source of great pleasure to her–hoping to find something in the same district. From Katherine Mansfield however she heard of three adjacent cottages near Zennor to let at £5 a year each. D. H. Lawrence had lived in them, and this was the only occasion that the two novelists entered into any kind of correspondence. Virginia could not resist the temptation of Cornwall, and took them, but must soon have recognised that Higher Tregerthen was too far from London to be a practical proposition. I do not think the Woolfs ever went there, and no more was heard of this plan.

Meanwhile they had printed three small books: T. S. Eliot's *Poems*, Middleton Murry's *The Critic in Judgement*, and Virginia's *Kew Gardens*–and these were all published on 12 May. By 31 May only 49 copies of *Kew Gardens* had been sold, while business in Eliot and Murry was fairly brisk. Virginia blamed Leonard a little for having persuaded her that *Kew Gardens* was worth publishing.

Thus it was in a rather discontented frame of mind, her book unwanted, her house problem unsolved, that she returned to Charleston. The domestic situation there had by this time more or less resolved itself, but another sisterly dispute arose. This time it was aesthetic and concerned the production of *Kew Gardens*. Vanessa, who had made the woodcuts for this book, did not at all like the way in which they had been printed. According to Virginia, who was rather inclined to exaggerate the gravity of Vanessa's strictures, she went so far as to question the use of having a Press that could print so badly, and to say that for her part, if that was the best they could do, she would never work for it again. The effect of this conversation, to judge again by Virginia's account of the matter,* was strange. She went to Lewes, found a house for sale, and bought it outright.

* "Did you realise that it was your severity that plunged me into the recklessness of buying a house that day? Something I must do to redress the balance, to

It was an odd thing to do and an odd house to buy. It had once been a windmill and stood high upon Lewes Hill near the Castle Wall. Being in the middle of the town it was not really what they wanted at all. She returned to London in a rather defiant mood; she was always upset by a quarrel with Vanessa and by this time it is likely that the purchase, for £300, of a small cylindrical edifice in the middle of Lewes had begun to appear a less crushing reply to her sister's criticisms of the printing techniques of the Hogarth Press than she had first supposed; nevertheless it was a course of action which had to be defended.

That evening, when the Woolfs opened the front door of Hogarth House, they found a snowdrift of mail. It consisted of orders for *Kew Gardens*: orders from distributors, from shops and from private people. Suddenly everybody wanted it; there had been a very favourable review in *The Times Literary Supplement*.

It should have been a wholly joyful occasion; but the repercussions of the Charleston visit made a cantankerous evening; and then, what was Leonard going to say about the house?

He was in fact magnanimous, but they both realised that it was a mistake when Leonard was able to look at it a few weeks later. What they really wanted was a house in the country. On their way through Lewes to inspect the Round House they had noticed a poster which announced the forthcoming sale of a property at Rodmell, a village lying about three miles south of Lewes. "That would have suited us exactly," said Leonard, ruefully.

Monk's House lay at the bottom of the village street that winds down from the high road between Lewes and Newhaven and on which nearly all of Rodmell has been built. It was a modest brick and flint dwelling, weather-boarded on the street side, two stories high with a high-pitched slate roof; inside, many low small rooms opened one from another; the ground floors were paved with brick, the stairs were narrow with worn treads; there was of course neither bath nor hot water nor W.C. Rising behind the house was a profuse and untidy garden, with flint walls and many out-houses, and beyond the garden was an orchard and beyond the

---

give myself value in my eyes, I said: & so I bought a house; the blood will there-fore be upon your head. Did anyone ever suffer as I did? You might have seen my soul shrivelling like a —— I cannot remember the image exactly, but its something one does by rubbing a piece of sealing wax & then everything curls up–as if in agony. Not that there was any imagery about it in my case. But the immanent greatness of my soul formed, as it were, a cream upon the surface. I survived." VW/VB, [18 June 1919], Berg.

orchard the walled churchyard. The more Leonard and Virginia looked at the place, the more they liked it. They tried their best to find faults, but only succeeded in liking it better. They decided they must try to buy it and sell the Round House. The sale by auction of Monk's House took place in Lewes on 1 July. They gave their agent, Mr Wycherley, a limit of £800, which he thought should give them a good chance of success.

> I don't suppose many spaces of five minutes in the course of my life have been so close packed with sensation. Was I somehow waiting to hear the result, while I watched the process, of an operation? The room at the White Hart was crowded. I looked at every face and in particular at every coat and skirt, for signs of opulence, and was cheered to discover none. But then, I thought, getting L. into line, does *he* look as if he had £800 in his pocket? Some of the substantial farmers might well have their rolls of notes stuffed inside their stockings. Bidding began. Someone offered £300 . . . Six hundred was reached too quick for me.

After this figure, there were only two competitors; they were allowed to bid in twenties; then in tens; then in fives; at £700 there was a pause; an appeal from the auctioneer. The hammer fell. The Woolfs had bought Monk's House.

Of the two remaining months before they need make the move to Rodmell, they managed to spend the whole of August at Asham. It was a mournful interval, particularly for Virginia. Asham, so beautiful, so melancholy and so haunted, had a quality which suited her exactly. She had celebrated its gentle ghosts in words which, for one who has lived there, are almost painfully evocative. It was no doubt exciting to move into a new home, but really, compared to Asham, Monk's House was only a pleasant cottage with some nice views and a pretty garden.

She wrote her last letter from Asham on 29 August 1919 to Vanessa:

Asheham,
Friday.

Dearest,

Many thanks for the cheque. Leonard quite agrees with you that I shall be merely in the way during the move. I, on the other hand, think myself indispensable. I don't see how they could manage without me. But I am very grateful for the offer. Perhaps I might come over one day later in my shay, if you have any horse accommodation at Charleston.

The move begins on Monday; we are already strewn with old boxes full of the most interesting letters – yours & Madge's & Walter Lambs, & I see a very tart one from Maynard about my arrangements at Brunswick Square. We shall be in by Wednesday; but I'm afraid I shant be able to ask Lytton to stay, as the servants will be distracted, and I suppose, giving notice. Tell him I'm much disappointed.

When will you come over & see Monks? If you took train to Lewes my shay would meet you & bring you out; & then take you back. I shall be doing a good deal of brush work on the house, but without any false shame.

Every one felt that Mrs. Dolphin [i.e. Vanessa] was the soul of the party the other night. Morgan said he was going to tell you that he thought you beautiful & charming, but he might be too shy. What struck me most was the farewell – every one feeling a little sentimental about Asheham – old mother Bell hurrying about the Terrace looking for her Badmington set. "It's no good being sentimental on these occasions. Now Leonard, wasn't there a bit of old carpet —?" Immortal woman!

Yr.

B.

Monk's House was only two or three miles from Asham. On 1 September the two waggons on which the Woolfs' possessions were loaded might easily cross the river Ouse and discharge all their business within the space of a morning; and that night Leonard and Virginia were able to sleep in their own home.

Being thus translated Virginia did her best to dwell upon the advantages of her new situation. In addition to the superiority of the garden, the views were more extensive and offered greater variety; but she was obliged to admit to herself that she was depressed. Whether this melancholy arose from the comparative imperfections of her new house or from the fact that Duckworth was about to publish *Night and Day* is not easily determined.

As always, she found publication an agitating business, and, as usual, tried to be philosophic about it. When on 20 October she received her own six copies, she at once sent five of them off – to Vanessa, Clive, Lytton, Morgan Forster and Violet Dickinson. She waited anxiously for their comments. Clive immediately declared it a work of the highest genius, Violet and Vanessa were eulogistic, Lytton enthusiastic. She accepted their praise with great pleasure if a little dubiously. But Morgan wrote to say that he preferred *The Voyage Out*; he couldn't really sympathise with her characters; *Night and Day* seemed to him (as it seems to most subsequent critics) less successful than its predecessor. But his verdict was delivered with such discernment and so much kindness that she was only momentarily cast down.

Katherine Mansfield hated *Night and Day*. Her private opinion was that it was "a lie in the soul." "The war never has been: that is what its message is. . . . I feel in the *profoundest* sense that nothing can ever be the same—that, as artists, we are traitors if we feel otherwise: we have to take it into account and find new expressions, new moulds for our new thoughts and feelings." Thus Katherine to Middleton Murry; and, three days later: "Talk about intellectual snobbery—her book *reeks* of it. (But I can't say so). You would dislike it. You'd never read it. It's so long and so tahsome." Writing in the *Athenaeum* Katherine Mansfield was discreet; but she said enough to inflict pain. Virginia thought it a spiteful review; so did Leonard. "He could see her looking about for a loophole of escape. 'I'm not going to call this a success—or if I must, I'll call it the wrong kind of success.'"

And yet this review was in many ways perceptive. In that *Night and Day* was a deliberate evocation of the past it might seem unreasonable to complain that it lacked actuality; but it belonged to the past in another way: it was a very orthodox performance and Katherine Mansfield does no more than anticipate the bewilderment of many later critics at finding in it none of the audacity of *The Voyage Out* or of *Kew Gardens*. "We had thought that this world was vanished for ever, that it was impossible to find on the great ocean of literature a ship that was unaware of what has been happening; yet there is *Night and Day*, new, exquisite—a novel in the tradition of the English novel. In the midst of our admiration it makes us feel old and chill. We had not thought to look upon its like again."

Virginia's feelings about Katherine Mansfield were as always mixed, and the question of their relationship continued to interest her very much:

> . . . I should need to write a long description of her before I arrived at my queer balance of interest, amusement and annoyance. The truth is, I suppose, that one of the conditions, unexpressed but understood, of our friendship has been precisely that it was almost entirely founded on quicksands. It has been marked by curious slides and arrests; for months I've heard nothing of her; then we have met again upon what has the appearance of solid ground. We have been intimate, intense perhaps rather than open; but to me at any rate our intercourse has been always interesting and mingled with quite enough of the agreeable personal element to make one fond—if that is the word—as well as curious.

This Virginia had written in her diary in February 1919 in a rather chagrined mood, because Katherine, whom she had visited almost weekly in Hampstead before Christmas, had since fallen totally silent. She was in fact ill, and when they did again meet Virginia noted:

> The inscrutable woman remains inscrutable–I'm glad to say; no apologies or sense of apologies due. At once she flung down her pen and plunged, as if we'd been parted for 10 minutes, into the question of Dorothy Richardson; . . . as usual, I find with Katherine what I don't find with the other clever women–a sense of ease and interest, which is, I suppose, due to her caring so genuinely if so differently from the way I care, about our precious art.

Through the summer of 1919 they had continued to meet, though often enough Murry was there too; his presence inhibited them both. But Murry was then editing *The Athenaeum*; Virginia was pleased to be asked for contributions; she wrote some seventeen articles for it in the next two years. Katherine was in France when her review of *Night and Day* appeared; returning to England in the summer of 1920 she made no attempt to see Virginia and it was Virginia who made the first move. When at last they did meet there was

> a steady discomposing formality and coldness at first. Enquiries about house and so on. No pleasure or excitement at seeing me. It struck me that she is of the cat kind; alien, composed, always solitary–observant. And then we talked about solitude and I found her expressing my feelings as I never hear them expressed. Whereupon we fell into step, and as usual talked as easily as though 8 months were minutes–till Murry came in. . . . A queer effect she produces of someone apart, entirely self-centred; altogether concentrated upon her 'art': almost fierce to me about it.

Virginia was unable to refrain from mentioning *Night and Day*. "An amazing achievement," declared Katherine, with pardonable disingenuity. "Why, we've not had such a thing since I don't know when——"
"But I thought you didn't like it?"

> Then she said she could pass an examination in it. Would I come and talk about it–lunch–so I'm going to lunch; but what does her reviewing mean then? Or is she emotional with me? Anyhow, once more as keenly as ever I feel a common understanding between us–a queer sense

of being 'like', not only about literature and I think its independent of gratified vanity. I can talk straight out to her.

For the rest of Katherine's life, and indeed for long after her death, Virginia was to regard her with feelings nicely compounded of sympathy and jealousy. Their last meeting was in August 1920. Virginia went from Rodmell to London in order to say goodbye, for Katherine was going abroad again. Virginia wondered how much she really minded losing her; and came to the conclusion that she did mind a good deal.

The year 1919 ended in vexation. Nelly and Lottie gave notice, as they so often did, only to withdraw it; Leonard returned from a meeting of the Oxford University Socialist Society with a fever, and this, which proved to be malarial, made him unwell for about three weeks. Before he had recovered Virginia went down with influenza. She was still in bed on Christmas Day, when Adrian and Karin (not the guests whom Leonard would have most wished to see) came to tea and dinner at Hogarth House. When, at the end of December, the Woolfs were able to get to Rodmell the weather was atrocious and Leonard, who went out to prune the fruit trees, very nearly pruned off a finger.

"We think we now deserve some good luck," wrote Virginia at the end of her diary for 1919. "Yet I daresay we are the happiest couple in England."

1920, which was to be a momentous year, began with no grand stroke of good luck, but it began well. The Woolfs stayed on at Monk's House for some days and on 7 January Virginia wrote:

This is our last evening. We sit over the fire, waiting for the post–the cream of the day, I think. Yet every part of the day has its merits–even the breakfast without toast. That, however it begins, ends with Pippins; most mornings the sun comes in; we finish in good temper; and I go off to the romantic chamber [one of the garden buildings which she used as a work-room] over grass rough with frost and ground hard as brick. Then Mrs. Dedman comes to receive orders–to give them, really, for she has planned our meals to suit her day's cooking before she comes. We share her oven. The result is always savoury–stews and mashes and deep many coloured dishes swimming in gravy thick with carrots and onions. Elsie aged 18 can be spoken to as though she had a head on her shoulders. The house is empty by half past eleven, empty now at five o'clock. We tend our fire, cook coffee, read, I find, luxuriously, peacefully, at length.

This is but a little part of an entry that is almost entirely devoted to the pleasures of country life: Leonard's activities in the garden and her own walks–Monk's House offered a greater variety of walks than Asham–through landscapes of astonishing beauty. Here, and in succeeding passages, she sounds a rare note of contented serenity.

She has very little, in these early days of 1920, to say about her writing. After finishing *Night and Day* she must have been mainly occupied by those short stories which were to be published for the first time in *Monday or Tuesday* and by *An Unwritten Novel* which appeared in *The London Mercury* in July. Also she was extremely active as a journalist*; but she seems to have had no full-scale work in mind, or at least in her conscious mind.

In November 1919 she had written:

It is true that I have never been so neglectful of this work of mine [her Diary]. I think I can foresee in my reluctance to trace a sentence, not merely a lack of time and a mind tired by writing, but also one of those slight distastes which betoken a change of style. So an animal must feel at the approach of spring when his coat changes.

By the end of January the spring to which Virginia refers began to approach. By that time the Woolfs were back in Richmond and Virginia celebrated her birthday by listening to Mozart and Beethoven, and on the following day, Monday, 26 January, she wrote:

The day after my birthday; in fact, I'm 38. Well, I've no doubt I'm a great deal happier than I was at 28; and happier today than I was yesterday, having this afternoon arrived at some idea of a new form for a new novel. Suppose one thing should open out of another–as in an unwritten novel–only not for 10 pages but 200 or so–doesn't that give the looseness and lightness I want; doesn't that get closer and yet keep form and speed, and enclose everything, everything? My doubt is how far it will enclose the human heart–Am I sufficiently mistress of my dialogue to net it there? For I figure that the approach will be entirely different this time: no scaffolding; scarcely a brick to be seen; all crepuscular, but the heart, the passion, humour, everything as bright as fire in the mist. Then I'll find room for so much–a gaiety–an inconsequence–a light spirited stepping at my sweet will. Whether I'm sufficiently mistress of things–that's the doubt; but conceive *Mark on the Wall*, *K. G.* and *Unwritten Novel* taking hands and dancing in unity. What the unity shall be I have yet to discover; the theme is a

---

* Not since 1905 or 1906 had her book reviews appeared so frequently as in the years 1918 to 1920. In 1920 she had articles in *The Times Literary Supplement*, the *Athenaeum* or the *New Statesman* every month except September.

blank to me; but I see immense possibilities in the form I hit upon more or less by chance two weeks ago. I suppose the danger is the damned egotistical self; which ruins Joyce and Richardson to my mind: is one pliant and rich enough to provide a wall for the book from oneself without its becoming, as in Joyce and Richardson, narrowing and restricting? My hope is that I've learnt my business sufficiently now to provide all sorts of entertainments. Anyhow, I must still grope and experiment but this afternoon I had a gleam of light. Indeed, I think from the ease with which I'm developing the unwritten novel there must be a path for me there.

It is rare to find an author who sees so clearly and suddenly, not the plot, or indeed the method, of a particular novel, but the whole programme for a decade.

During the spring of 1920 *Jacob's Room* began to take shape, and although in May, after the initial rush had spent its force, the novel proceeded more steadily, still she was enjoying it, feeling her renewed strength and noting that it was the most amusing novel-writing that she had ever done.

June brought one of those psychologically charged sequences of events which for her were of capital importance, not so much by reason of their intrinsic character as because she received their impression with a heightened power of perception.

She had what she called one of her "field days": took an afternoon train into town from Richmond, went to the National Gallery and there met Clive, who, as his habit was, took her to eat ices at Gunter's, where she observed her fellow patrons with fascinated interest. Then she dined with Vanessa at Gordon Square and heard the whole story of Mary. Mary was one of the servants, a girl of some beauty and very great charm. Misfortunes had fallen upon her with dreadful suddenness; first her father, then her brother, then her fiancé, were killed in accidents. Her grief was frightening in its intensity and naturally with each blow it increased. The tale of her misfortunes became more and more appalling and more and more highly complicated until at length, after some quite startling peripeteia, it was discovered that she had invented her own calamities, and that the relatives and friends who left messages of bad news for her at Gordon Square or who wrote to advise or to admonish her, were herself, using a disguised hand or voice. After a dramatic flight, she was brought back raving and then removed to St Pancras Infirmary. The sight of her being taken away, watched from every window by all the other servants in the Square, made a most sinister impression upon Virginia.

This made my drive to Waterloo on top of a bus very vivid. A bright night, with a fresh breeze. An old beggarwoman, blind, sat against a stone wall in Kingsway holding a brown mongrel in her arms and sang aloud. There was a recklessness about her; much in the spirit of London. Defiant–almost gay, clasping her dog as if for warmth. How many Junes has she sat there, in the heart of London? How she came to be there, what scenes she can go through, I can't imagine. O damn it all, I say, why can't I know all that too? Perhaps it was the song at night that seemed strange; she was singing shrilly, but for her own amusement, not begging. Then the fire engines came by–shrill too; with their helmets pale yellow in the moonlight. Sometimes everything gets into the same mood; how to define this one I don't know. It was gay and yet terrible and fearfully vivid. Nowadays I'm often overcome by London; even think of the dead who have walked in the city. Perhaps one might visit the churches. The view of the grey white spires from Hungerford Bridge brings it to me; and yet I can't say what 'it' is.

That old blind woman appears in *Jacob's Room*; and perhaps it is she who sings "Lay by my side a bunch of purple heather" in *Mrs Dalloway*.

On that memorable evening in 1919 when the Woolfs found the front hall at Hogarth House littered with demands for *Kew Gardens*, the Hogarth Press began to change from a hobby into a business. In some ways they found its rapid growth alarming and they wondered whether they should allow it to expand. But at the same time it offered large opportunities and substantial advantages which they could not easily disregard. Virginia, who hated submitting her novels to Gerald Duckworth–he had what she called "a clubman's view of literature"–began to think what a comfort it would be to publish her own books. Friends who had been amused and sceptical at the time of their first amateurish efforts made suggestions or sent them manuscripts. They attracted some remarkable authors. Katherine Mansfield, T. S. Eliot, Middleton Murry, E. M. Foster, Logan Pearsall Smith, and Maxim Gorki had all appeared, or were soon to appear, beneath their imprint. The possibilities were interesting, and the Press continued to grow. They began to farm out some of the setting and printing, although they continued to do a great deal themselves at Hogarth House.

But the Press made work, and as the volume of work increased the time available for it diminished. Virginia, as we have seen, was occupied not only by her novel but by a great deal of journalism. Leonard, who in 1919 had finished his book *Empire and Commerce in Africa*–a book which Virginia greatly admired–was now busy with another (*Socialism and Co-operation*); he was also editing a monthly paper, *The International Review*, and in May 1920 was adopted as a parliamentary candidate for one of the two Combined University seats. It was clear that they needed an assistant who could undertake more responsibility and do more business than had been required of Barbara Hiles. They needed an intelligent young man, and there were surely a number of intelligent young men to whom an apprenticeship leading perhaps to an eventual partnership in the Hogarth Press would seem a most attractive proposition–an ideal arrangement for all parties.

It was, in fact, a trap into which all parties fell headlong. For the aspiring young men, publishing was above all a matter of discrimination, of choosing the right authors and presenting them beautifully to the world. For Leonard–and Leonard was necessarily the effective power in the management of the Press–it was a matter of setting and distributing type, of printing page after page after page, of cleaning up the machinery, of binding and pasting, of doing up and addressing parcels and delivering messages and writing letters; and although this was no doubt explained to the applicants when they came to the Hogarth Press, somehow they continued to hope that all this menial business was but a purgatory leading to the heaven of aesthetic direction. Presently, however, they would discover that such hopes were vain. Leonard had his own idea about the literary policy of the Press and if he was in any doubt he would turn to Virginia. Leonard was an excellent man of business and drove a hard bargain–a cruelly hard bargain it seemed to some–and of course there was plenty of work for the assistant to do. Leonard and even more Virginia regarded publishing as a part-time business, but for the assistant it was to be very much more than that. He was, in fact, expected to do everything except the few things that he wanted to do. Thus the situation was, in its nature, difficult. It was made worse by the fact that, as Leonard himself says, he was a perfectionist, and still young enough to be hot-tempered. The Press was his child and as time went on he was not perfectly rational about it. Perhaps it might be more true to say that it was his mistress. He could at a pinch share it with a woman but not with a man. Leonard and the succession of young men who came to work at the Hogarth Press did not usually get on well together, while the women assistants were, I think, much more easily and happily accommodated.

The first of the young men whose difficult passage through the Press Virginia was to observe with sympathy, amusement, and some irritation was Lytton's friend Ralph Partridge. It was arranged that he was to work at Hogarth House three days a week. Ralph Partridge was an engaging and vigorous person, handsome, intelligent, with considerable drive and a marked talent for business.

In October 1920 Virginia noted that he was "putting his ox's shoulder to the wheel, and intends to do "hurricane" business." Clearly great things were hoped of him. By the end of the year Virginia's enthusiasm had waned a little; he was indomitable, but he was also rather domineering and increasingly there was friction with Leonard. It was only at moments of crisis, or in matters that concerned the fate of her own books, that Virginia made an effort fully to understand the disputes between Leonard and his collaborators in the press; there was much that she did not notice or did not bother to examine; but whatever the dispute and whatever the degree of attention that she brought to it, she never had any doubt that Leonard was in the right.

Friday, February 18th [1921]

I have been long meaning to write a historical disquisition on the return of peace; for old Virginia will be ashamed to think what a chatterbox she was, always talking about people, never about politics. Moreover, she will say, the times you lived through were so extraordinary. They must have appeared so, even to quiet women living in the suburbs. But indeed nothing happens at one moment rather than another. The history books will make it much more definite than it is. The most significant sign of peace this year is the sales; just over. The shops have been flooded with cheap clothes. A coat and skirt that cost £14 in November went for 7 perhaps 5. People had ceased to buy and the shops had to dispose of things somehow. Margery Strachey who has been teaching at Debenhams foretells bankruptcy for most of the shopkeepers this very month. Still they go on selling cheaply. Pre-war prices, so they say. And I have found a street market in Soho where I buy stockings at 1/- a pair, silk ones (flawed slightly) at 1/10. A hundred yards down the road they ask 5/6 to 10/6 for the same things, or so they seem. Food has fallen a penny here, a penny there, but our books scarcely show a change. Milk is high—11d a quart. Butter fallen to 3/- but this is Danish butter. Eggs—I don't know what eggs are. Servant girls aged 20 get £45 wages. And the Times pays me 3 guineas instead of 2 guineas for a column. But I think you'll find all this written more accurately in other books, my dear Virginia; for instance in Mrs. Gosse's diary and Mrs. Webb's. I think it is true to say that during the past two months we have perceptibly moved towards cheapness—*just* perceptibly. It is just perceptible too that there are very few wounded soldiers abroad in blue, though stiff legs, single legs, sticks shod with rubber, and empty sleeves are common enough. Also at Waterloo I sometimes see dreadful looking spiders propelling themselves along the platform–men all body–legs trimmed off close to the body. There are few soldiers about.

It is true that in her diary she was "always talking about people, never about politics," or at least when she does talk about politics –as for instance when she mentions the great railway strike of 1919 and her active support of the strikers–it was an exceptional effort. In the same way it was an interruption of her life, a life which in the spring of 1921 was mainly devoted to *Jacob's Room*, *Monday or Tuesday* and an abortive effort to learn Russian, when she went electioneering with Leonard in March of that year. They went together to Manchester and Virginia, as usual, admired Leonard's masterly way of dealing with public meetings. But the socialist academics of Manchester filled her with despair. She saw, clearly enough, that they were good, brave and earnest people, fighting against fearful odds, against strong, blind and wicked forces. But they were dreadfully dull; she despised them and was ashamed of her own snobbery in doing so, and she was depressed by Manchester itself. She did not accompany Leonard on his other electoral excursions.

Monday or Tuesday* appeared at the beginning of March, but owing, as Virginia believed, to a blunder by Ralph, who made a mistake about the date of publication, the book was inadequately reviewed by *The Times*, Doran (the American publisher of *The Voyage Out*) refused it, and altogether it seemed to have fallen very flat. Meanwhile Lytton's *Queen Victoria* was received everywhere with deafening applause. Ralph Partridge gave a celebration dinner party for him and the Woolfs in Gordon Square at which Lytton never so much as mentioned *Monday or Tuesday*, so that from Virginia's point of view the evening would have been a total failure had they not gone on to the Old Bedford Music Hall and seen Marie Lloyd:–"a mass of corruption–long front teeth–a crapulous way of saying 'desire', and yet a born artist."

Virginia's depression, though severe, was not of long duration for soon praise started to arrive. She began again at once to feel "important"–"and its that that one wants"–and by the middle of April she was able to consider Lytton's continued success–he was

* *Monday or Tuesday* was a book of Virginia's stories which included *An Unwritten Novel*, *Kew Gardens*, and *The Mark on the Wall*, and five new pieces, as well as four woodcuts by Vanessa.

said to have sold 5,000 copies in a week while she had sold 300 in all–with decent philosophy. Moreover Lytton might be forgiven for a great deal; Ralph had repeated to her what he had said about *The String Quartet* (one of the stories in *Monday or Tuesday*)–he thought it marvellous. This did for a moment flood her every nerve with pleasure.*

With Ralph Partridge at the Hogarth Press, Virginia became involved in the affairs of the ménage at The Mill House, the country home which had been established for Lytton at Tidmarsh in Berkshire. Since her role in one of the dramas which distracted that household has been rather harshly described, it requires particular attention.

Life at Tidmarsh was, as Lytton told Virginia, "very complex"; it was conducted by a nearly incomprehensible trinity consisting of Ralph Partridge, Dora Carrington and Lytton himself, three persons who were all more or less in love with each other but each in a rather different way. Carrington was deeply and devotedly in love with Lytton and, at this period, sufficiently fond of Ralph Partridge to sleep with him and be, at all events, unwilling to lose him. But when he pursued her she fled from him, sometimes into the arms of other gentlemen. When he retired, she advanced. Partridge, although he could see her faults well enough, was obsessed by her and wished, passionately, to marry her; he was also very attached to Lytton, and Lytton, who in his turn was in love with Ralph, felt a tender, almost paternal, regard for Carrington–upon whom, moreover, he entirely depended for the domestic comforts of his life at Tidmarsh.

I do not think that Virginia knew, or perhaps she did not want to know, how important Carrington really was to Lytton. Carrington had good qualities–a kind of debauched innocence which was at once entertaining and touching–and in fact Virginia liked her; but at the same time she was very ignorant and rather silly; her charm was the charm of youth. "Carrington grows older," Virginia noted in her diary, "and her doings are of the sort that age." She felt, I suspect, that Lytton deserved and needed the companionship of a more informed and a more powerful intellect than you would find in a Crophead. Carrington, it appeared, was not altogether good

---

* "And Eliot astounded me by praising *Monday or Tuesday*! This really delighted me. He picked out the String Quartet, especially the end of it. 'Very good' he said, and meant it, I think. The Unwritten Novel he thought not successful; Haunted House 'extremely interesting.'" *AWD (Berg),* 7 June 1921.

for Lytton.* Lytton himself, perhaps in deference to the ghost of an old attachment, perhaps half agreeing with Virginia's views, encouraged her to under-estimate the strength of his affections.† In December 1920, meeting by chance in Gordon Square, they spoke of the possibility of a marriage between Ralph and Carrington.

"Well," Virginia observed, "I wouldn't marry Ralph. A despot."

"True. But what's to happen to C[arrington]? She can't live indefinitely with me–perhaps with him?"

And again, when Lytton dedicated *Queen Victoria* to Virginia, a compliment which delighted her, she objected nevertheless that it should have been dedicated to Carrington.

"Oh dear no," he replied, "we're not on those terms at all."

In May 1921 Ralph Partridge, now desperate and made positively ill by Carrington's evasions and equivocations, laid all his troubles and perplexities before Leonard and Virginia.

He was very shrewd and bitter about C[arrington]. "She thinks herself one of the little friends of all the world" he said. Then he said she was selfish, untruthful, and quite indifferent to his suffering. So people in love always turn and rend the loved, with considerable insight too. He was speaking the truth largely. But I expect he was biassed; and also I expect–and indeed told him–that he is a bit of an ogre and tyrant. He wants more control than I should care to give–control I mean of the body and mind and time and thoughts of his loved. There's his danger and her risk; so I don't much envy her making up her mind this wet Whit Sunday.

This in fact was what Carrington had now to do, for Ralph's state of mind was such that Leonard and Virginia told him that he must, as Leonard said: "put a pistol to Carrington's head"–that is to say, tell her that if she would not marry him he would break with her altogether and go abroad.

Faced by the alternatives of marrying Ralph or, as she felt, of

* In 1928, commenting upon *Elizabeth and Essex*, Virginia remarks: "So feeble, so shallow; and yet Lytton himself is neither. So one next accuses the public; and then the Carringtons and the young men?" *AWD* (*Berg*), 28 November 1928. Vanessa, in the same year, wrote: "Carrington has a funereal effect on Lytton who loses all interest in her presence." VB/CB, 23 May 1928.

† "He [Lytton] spoke of her [Carrington] . . . with a candour not flattering, though not at all malicious. 'That woman will dog me,' he remarked. 'She won't let me write I daresay.' 'Ottoline was saying you would end by marrying her.' 'God! The mere notion is enough. One thing I know–I'll never marry anyone.' 'But if she's in love with you?' 'Well, then she must take her chance.'" *AWD* (*Berg*), 12 December 1917.

being parted from Lytton altogether–for she knew that her life with Lytton was inextricably bound up with his affection for Ralph, Carrington capitulated. They were in fact married ten days later. In a moment of unreserve Ralph revealed to her that his resolve had been strengthened by the Woolfs' advice. Virginia had told him that Lytton was afraid that Carrington might feel she had some claim on him; everyone was surprised that he could have stood her for so long, for obviously she had nothing in common with him, either intellectually or physically. Carrington, in a very moving and unhappy letter to Lytton, described the feelings and motives that had led her to marry; she also gave Ralph's version of what the Woolfs had told him. In a postscript she added: "You musn't think I was hurt by hearing what you said to Virginia and Leonard and *that* made me cry. For I'd faced that long ago with Alix in the first years of my love for you." Lytton answered:

> You must not believe, too readily, repeated conversations. I think that possibly some bitterness of disappointment makes you tend to exaggerate the black side of what you are told. . . . Certainly, I thought that it was generally agreed that one didn't believe quite everything that came through Virginia!

Virginia's part in this affair has been misunderstood and misrepresented. She has been credited with the most odious motives and to Lytton has been ascribed a denunciation of her conduct which is almost pure invention. When Ralph told the Woolfs of his feelings for Carrington, Virginia, it is said, "with her love of stirring up trouble, and knowing only too well that everything she said would be repeated, interposed a few poisonous comments of her own." Lytton's gentle and perhaps slightly guilty disclaimer (for, after all, it was he who had given Virginia the impression that Carrington might bore him) has been altered out of all recognition: "He told her that Virginia, with characteristic neurotic malevolence, had lied about his feelings and intentions."

Virginia *did* have some qualms of conscience; but they were not related to any remarks of hers that Ralph might have repeated. What disturbed her was the thought that she could have helped to promote an imprudent marriage.

> So Carrington did make up her mind to become Partridge–no, that is precisely what she is determined not to do; and signs herself aggressively Carrington for ever. If people ever took advice I should feel a little responsible for making up Ralph's mind. I mean I am not sure that this marriage is not more risky than most.

Her doubts were well-founded; within a year there were violent rows and recriminations, and Virginia then found herself very much on Carrington's side.

Although at first, no doubt, she had been a little piqued and puzzled by Lytton's attachment, Virginia was fond of Carrington for her own sake. And when it became clear how important that attachment was to Lytton, she loved Carrington for his sake too. In all these transactions – in which she was certainly unwise to become involved – Virginia's and Leonard's concern was with Lytton; he was, after all, one of their oldest and dearest friends, and it was his happiness that was their chief object.

Three days before Ralph Partridge married Dora Carrington at St Pancras Registry Office, Virginia and Leonard conducted an experiment, the subject of which was Desmond MacCarthy. In 1919 Virginia had written of him:

I'm not sure he hasn't the nicest nature of any of us – the nature one would soonest have chosen for one's own. I don't think that he possesses any faults as a friend, save that his friendship is so often sunk under a cloud of vagueness; a sort of drifting vapour composed of times and seasons separates us and effectively prevents us from meeting. Perhaps such indolence implies a slackness of fibre in his affections too – but I scarcely feel that. It arises from the consciousness which I find imaginative and attractive that things don't altogether *matter*. Somehow he is fundamentally sceptical. Yet which of us, after all, takes more trouble to do the sort of kindnesses that come his way? Who is more tolerant, more appreciative, more understanding of human nature? It goes without saying that he is not an heroic character. He finds pleasure too pleasant, cushions too soft, dallying too seductive and then, as I sometimes feel now, he has ceased to be ambitious. His "great Work" (it may be philosophy or biography now, and is certainly to be begun, after a series of long walks, this very spring) only takes shape, I believe, in that hour between tea and dinner, when so many things appear not merely possible but achieved. Comes the daylight, and Desmond is contented to begin his article; and plies his pen with a half humorous half melancholy recognition that such is his appointed life. Yet it is true, and no one can deny it, that he has the floating elements of something brilliant, beautiful – some book of stories, reflections, studies, scattered about in him, for they show themselves indisputably in his talk. I'm told he wants power; that these fragments never combine into an argument; that the disconnection of talk is kind to them; but in a book they would drift hopelessly apart. Consciousness of this, no doubt, led him in his one finished book to drudge and sweat until his fragments were clamped together in an indissoluble stodge. I can see myself, however, going through his desk one of these days.

shaking out unfinished pages from between sheets of blotting paper, and deposits of old bills, and making up a small book of table talk, which shall appear as a proof to the younger generation that Desmond was the most gifted of us all. But why did he never do anything? they will ask.

Those who knew him may still ask themselves that question. Desmond, in the imagination of his friends, was going to be the successor of Henry James. Hearing him talk you could believe that. Even when he had sunk beneath repeated failures to float magazines, to produce copy on time, to meet the demands of bailiffs, to cope with life at all, still he had only to speak in order to command, not so much attention as affection, to fill one with delight, and, when he was in the vein, to convince one that he was the master of some prodigious treasury. He had only to put his hand into his pocket and draw out whatever you might wish–subtlety, brilliance or deep imaginative richness. It was "ask and have," for he was the most carelessly generous, the most intellectually spendthrift of men. How few plays have ever enchanted one half so much as Desmond's small talk.

Conversation was his art, and for him the tragedy was that he should have chosen so ephemeral a medium. For Virginia there was an inconvenience of another kind; he would turn up at Richmond for dinner, uninvited very probably, and probably committed to a dinner elsewhere, charm his way out of his social crimes on the telephone, talk enchantingly until the small hours, insist that he be called early so that he might attend to urgent business on the morrow, wake up a trifle late, dawdle somewhat over breakfast, find a passage in The Times to excite his ridicule, enter into a lively discussion of Ibsen, declare he must be off, pick up a book which reminded him of something which, in short, would keep him talking until about 12.45, when he would have to ring up and charm the person who had been waiting in an office for him since 10, and at the same time deal with the complications arising from the fact that he had engaged himself to two different hostesses for lunch, and that it was now 1 o'clock and it would take forty minutes to get from Richmond to the West End. In all this Desmond had been practising his art– the art of conversation. Unfortunately, in order to do so he had to prevent Virginia from practising hers, and there would be occasions when she looked back on a wasted morning with some bitterness of spirit.

And yet, it was impossible to think of Desmond without affection or without a lively regret that his words could not be given a permanent form. A great many efforts had been made to persuade him to achieve something more serious than journalism. It is said that he was once locked into a room in an attempt to make him at least start his novel. More subtly, his wife invented the Novel Club, which was to lure him into literature, and in 1920 the Memoir Club* was devised with a similar purpose. This club lasted for many years without ever extracting from Desmond that masterpiece which it was still hoped that he might produce.

The Woolfs' experiment was different in its means but similar in its general purpose. The aim was, quite simply, to record Desmond's conversation. Desmond was invited to dine at Hogarth House. Roger Fry was asked too. Miss Green, Leonard's secretary at *The International Review*, whom Virginia unkindly, but accurately, likened to a chest of drawers, was posted in a convenient place with paper and pencils and Desmond, ignorant of the plot and fortified with two bottles of Chablis, was encouraged to talk. He talked magnificently and Miss Green set down every word. There was only one flaw in the scheme: the record of Desmond's conversation was completely uninteresting.

On 10 June Virginia went to a concert and that night she could not sleep. On the next day she kept her bed and it soon became depressingly clear that she was in for one of her bouts of illness. The next two months she spent more or less in bed. Leonard took her to Monk's House for a time, but she did not improve, and it was not until 8 August, again at Rodmell, that she was well enough to write in her diary.

These, this morning, the first words I have written–to call writing–for 60 days; and those days spent in wearisome headache, jumping pulse, aching back, frets, fidgets, lying awake, sleeping draughts, sedatives, digitalis, going for a little walk, and plunging back into bed again–all

* The Memoir Club met for the first time on 4 March 1920. The members were: Desmond and Molly MacCarthy, Leonard and Virginia Woolf, Saxon Sydney-Turner, Maynard Keynes, Lytton Strachey, Duncan Grant, Clive and Vanessa Bell, Morgan Forster, Sydney Waterlow and Roger Fry. David Garnett became a member fairly soon afterwards. The club had no rules, save that there was an understanding that members were free to say anything they pleased, nor did it keep any records. Leonard Woolf suggests (*Downhill . . .*, p. 114) that the membership was identical with the original thirteen members of Bloomsbury. But it is arguable that if the club had been started in 1912 it would have included Adrian Stephen, and I am not sure that Sydney Waterlow can really be considered a member of Bloomsbury. The Novel Club, so far as I can find out, existed only briefly in 1913.

the horrors of the dark cupboard of illness once more displayed for my diversion. Let me make a vow that this shall never, never, happen again; and *then* confess that there are some compensations. To be tired and authorised to lie in bed is pleasant; . . . I feel that I can take stock of things in a leisurely way. Then the dark underworld has its fascinations as well as its terrors.

She recovered slowly, but she was irritable. Rodmell, she declared, was becoming a colony for Georgian poets, and the village children made a hideous noise playing in the meadow beyond their orchard. She began to think that they had better look for a new house. For the first time she thought of making a will.

Finding that she could write again her morale improved and she returned to Richmond with her equanimity restored; Ralph and the new printing machine were working well, Nelly and Lottie were at peace and even a visit by her cousin Dorothea Stephen, stamping and trumpeting across the carpet of Hogarth House like some obscene relic of the Ice Age, did not disturb her too much. Moreover Dorothea intended to spend the next five years improving the moral sense of the Indians. On Friday, 4 November Virginia wrote the last words of *Jacob's Room*, noting that she had begun it on 16 April of the previous year.

At the beginning of the new year she decided that she would do no more reviewing; it consumed altogether too much time and energy, Bruce Richmond tampered with her copy, and she felt that she was now able to make as much money by other forms of writing. Also, as Leonard must have observed, she was by no means really recovered.

Putting the revision of *Jacob* aside she began a new work which she had for some time been meditating and which she called *Reading*. She began it with the greatest enjoyment but almost at once she was struck down with influenza and was back in bed for a fortnight. Dr Fergusson forbade her to work for another two or three weeks. Dr Fergusson was their General Practitioner at Richmond and clearly a man of sense. He needed to be, for now Virginia's erratic pulse "had passed the limits of reason and was in fact insane." Her temperature too behaved very abnormally. She was sent to two specialists, one of whom pronounced that her heart was affected and that she had not long to live; the other said it was her lungs. Dr Fergusson decided to disregard them and Leonard did likewise. But the first three months of 1922 were spent as an invalid. She had her bed moved into the drawing-room beside the fire, and there wrote a little and read a great deal, received her visitors, and observed the worsening relationship between Leonard and Ralph over the Hogarth Press.

Virginia, however, was not such an invalid that she could not again undertake a mild flirtation with Clive.

> . . . I am seeing Clive rather frequently. He comes on Wednesdays; jolly, and rosy, and squab; a man of the world; and enough of my old friend, and enough of my old lover, to make the afternoons hum. Once a week is probably enough. His letters suggest doubts. But, oh dear me, after 9 weeks of claustration, I want to vault the wall and pick a few flowers.

> . . . We talked from 4.30 to 10.15 the other day. It is clear that I am to rub up his wits; and in return I get my manners polished. I hear of supper parties; elicit facts about drink and talk and goings on. . . . He enjoys *everything*–even the old hag in the doorway. There is no truth about life, he says, except what we feel. It is good if you enjoy it; and so forth. Obviously we reach no heights of reason. Nor do we become completely intimate. A little colour is added to taste. We have our embrace; our frill of sentiment,–impossible, as Nessa says, to talk without it. But I perceive . . . that once a fortnight is the pitch of our relationship.

Clive for his part had written to Vanessa to say that "as usual" he had fallen slightly in love with Virginia and, ten days later: "I hope I shan't fall more deeply in love. However its a great compliment for a woman of forty don't you think?"

Neither of them was in much danger. Clive's affections were at this time engaged elsewhere; as for Virginia, her feelings for him fluctuated, but the pendulum of her heart never swung anywhere near to passion. Dining with him and Vanessa, she reflected that they had all become happier, more tolerant, more secure, since those days when meals *à trois* at Gordon Square had been a habit and Clive had been the most important man in her life. Now she could enjoy his company and his gallantries, which stemmed from a natural kindness and a genuine desire to please; even his absurdities, which only the year before she had severely condemned, she now could laugh at. At that time his mundane life, his dinings-out and little luncheon parties, his duchesses and his fine French phrases, his name-dropping, his fancy waistcoats, his bawling voice and his balding head, had exasperated and slightly shocked her. Now she still disapproved of him, but liked him better.

The variations in Virginia's comments upon Clive are in themselves an indication that her strictures should not be taken too seriously. But it was true that, since the war, Clive had become more worldly, and at the same time she herself had become both more interested in and more critical of worldliness. Being herself a snob she was able to understand the subtle corruption of values which she discerned in Clive and which she herself was to describe with some particularity in *Mrs Dalloway*.

In June 1922 T. S. Eliot came to Hogarth House and read a new work.

> He sang it and chanted it and rhythmed it. It has great beauty and force of phrase; symmetry; and tensity. What connects it together, I'm not so sure. But he read till he had to rush—letters to write about the London Magazine—and discussion thus was curtailed. One was left, however, with some strong emotion. The Waste Land, it is called; and Mary Hutch[inson], who has heard it more quietly, interprets it to be Tom's autobiography—a melancholy one.

To Virginia, as to many others, it seemed wrong that so serious and original a poet should have to spend his days working for his livelihood in a bank, and she became involved in one of the periodic attempts that were made to release Eliot from this necessity. An Eliot Fellowship Fund was set up, the intention being to raise £300 a year for him for five years. An account was opened in the names of E. G. Aldington, Lady Ottoline Morrell and Mrs Virginia Woolf at Lloyds Bank and Ottoline, who was a prime mover in the matter, prepared a circular inviting regular contributions from likely supporters. It fell to Virginia to discuss the matter with Mr Eliot; he was invited to Monk's House, together with E. M. Forster, for the week-end of 23 September 1922. Their talk was largely about *Ulysses*; and Virginia was both impressed and illuminated by Eliot's analytical defence of the book, which she summarised in her diary.

> After Joyce, however, we came to ticklish matters—the Eliot Fund; the upshot of it was (and we were elliptical, tactful, nervous) that Tom won't leave the Bank under £500 and must have securities, not pledges. So next morning, when Ott.'s letter & circular arrived, aiming at £300, on a 5 year basis of pledges, I had to wire her to stop and then to draft a long letter giving my reasons; and another to Tom, asking him to confirm my information. I shall be scalded in two separate baths of hot water no doubt.

Subscriptions did come in; but the poet's reticence, his reservations and embarrassment, made benefaction an uphill task. As a gesture the Fund sent him £50 for Christmas, but even that Virginia expected him to refuse.*

* After some five years the subscribers were re-imbursed; Eliot had by then liberated himself from the Bank by other means.

T. S. Eliot and his finances have taken me too far into the year 1922. The pleasures and embarrassments of knowing Mr Eliot were but a minor incident in the events of that year. It began badly with the coldest spring on record and Virginia's health was not good; she had trouble with her teeth–three were extracted–she had trouble also with her heart and her persistent high temperature. But she managed to work hard and by June she was making a fair copy of *Jacob's Room* for Miss Green to type out: Harcourt, Brace, who had published *Monday or Tuesday* in America, asked to read it, and the copy was promised for July. On the 23rd of that month Leonard read it, and declared it to be her best work–"amazingly well written" and unlike any other novel. Virginia was excited and grew increasingly anxious as the prospect of publication approached. She speculated as to other people's reactions and began the usual soliloquy in her diary. The book would fail, it would be abused by the critics, and she told herself that she would not mind, or would not mind very much.

She devised a plan to guard herself against the expected wounds of criticism: she would go on with *Reading* and write a story or two for magazines; if people disliked her fiction, they could read her criticism; if they thought *Jacob* merely a clever experiment she would produce *Mrs Dalloway in Bond Street*.

Mrs Dalloway had made a brief appearance on board the *Euphrosyne* in *The Voyage Out*; now she re-emerged from the shadows of Virginia's imagination. She was connected with several short stories which Virginia invented at Rodmell that summer. To some extent she may be identified with Kitty Maxse, and Kitty's sudden death in October 1922–she fell from the top of a flight of stairs and Virginia believed that she had committed suicide–almost certainly helped to transform the stories into a book and to give that book its final character.

By the time the Woolfs came back to Richmond early in October the future of the Hogarth Press had become a matter of critical concern. It had become obvious that Leonard and Ralph could not work together–but Ralph would not leave. The whole question was complicated by Lytton's interest in Ralph and Ralph's career. At one time he had thought of purchasing, with Maynard Keynes, the *English Review*, largely so that Ralph might manage it. Lytton let it be known that if Ralph were able to stay on at the Hogarth Press they might publish his, Lytton's, books. This bait, which could not be ignored, created a certain awkwardness in the continual discussions which took place; and so too did Lytton's next idea of establishing a rival Tidmarsh Press for Ralph. Roger produced a rich and cultured young man who would put money into, and make money for, the Press; Logan Pearsall Smith tried to negotiate an arrangement between the Woolfs and Constable; Heinemann made a most tempting takeover offer. The uncertainty was said by Lytton to be trying to Ralph's nerves and yet, Virginia burst out, "this nervous man makes no attempt to do the most ordinary things for us. L. has to tie parcels every morning. Ralph catches no earlier or later trains. Monday morning he spent at the tailor's."

After endless and wearing discussions they opted for freedom— freedom from commercial publishers, freedom from Ralph, and freedom from the perpetual strain of hurting Lytton's feelings. By pure chance they came upon a young woman who longed to become a printer and would work full time for a salary; she came in January, and, in March 1923, Ralph Partridge left.

Jacob's Room was the first full-length book to be published by the Hogarth Press (it was printed by R. & R. Clark of Edinburgh). It was published on 27 October 1922. To Virginia it seemed at first that the press reviews were against her and the private people enthusiastic. Of these, one, T. S. Eliot, shall be quoted:

> You have freed yourself from any compromise between the traditional novel and your original gift. It seems to me that you have bridged a certain gap which existed between your other novels and the experimental prose of *Monday or Tuesday* and that you have made a remarkable success.

And this, it seemed presently, was the opinion both of the reviewers and of the public. Virginia was satisfied; *Jacob's Room* marks the beginning of her maturity and her fame.

Chapter Four

1923–1925

VIRGINIA began the new year in a mood of depression and of introspection. She imagined herself, rather in the style of Mr Ramsay,

> . . . forging ahead, alone, through the night . . . suffering inwardly, stoically; . . . blazing my way through to the end–and so forth. The truth is that the sails flap about me for a day or two on coming back; and not being at full stretch I ponder and loiter. And it is all temporary; yet let me be quite clear about that. Let me have one confessional where I need not boast. Years and years ago, after the Lytton affair, I said to myself, walking up the hill at Bayreuth, never pretend that the things you haven't got are not worth having; good advice, I think. At least it often comes back to me. Never pretend that children, for instance, can be replaced by other things. And then I went on . . . to say to myself that one must (how am I to convey it?) like things for themselves; or rather, rid them of their bearing upon one's personal life. One must throw that aside; and venture on to the things that exist independently of oneself. Now this is very hard for young women to do. Yet I got satisfaction from it. And now, married to L., I never *have* to make the effort. I do it, if I enjoy doing it. Perhaps I have been too happy for my soul's good? Perhaps I have become cowardly and self-indulgent? And does some of my discontent come from feeling that? I could not stay at 46 [Gordon Square] last night, because L. on the telephone expressed displeasure. Late again. Very foolish. Your heart bad, and so my self reliance being sapped, I had no courage to venture against his will. Then I react. Of course it's a difficult question. For undoubtedly I get headaches or the jump in my heart; and then this spoils his pleasure and if one lives with a person, has one the right–So it goes on.

It is possible to disengage a number of connected elements from Virginia's melancholy reflections: a perennial and incurable regret that she had no children; a natural jealousy of Vanessa in this respect and–a further source of envy–Vanessa's ability, despite her parental commitments, to lead a freer, a more adventurous life than Virginia. This again was related to her feeling, as she approached her forty-first birthday, that life was slipping away and that it could in some manner be arrested, or more effectively detained in its flight, by one who lived in town than by an inhabitant of the suburbs. She wanted to return to London.

Her longing for social adventures was in part assuaged, but also in part exacerbated, by the acquisition of new friends. In December 1922 she had met Vita and Harold Nicolson at Clive's dinner table, a meeting which shall be discussed in a later chapter; at this time too she began to see a number of young and brilliant people: George Rylands and Angus Davidson (both of whom she was to know well), F. L. Lucas and Frank Ramsay from Cambridge, Raymond Mortimer and Lord David Cecil from Oxford. Most of them might be met at 46 Gordon Square, which, in 1916, had been taken over by Maynard Keynes. Maynard was a genial and energetic host, and he made Gordon Square the centre of an enlarged and altogether more amorphous "Bloomsbury" (the term is very loosely used). Here too one might be certain to find Lydia Lopokova.

Lydia had come to London as a principal dancer in Diaghilev's company in 1918, 1919 and 1921, and had danced very beautifully in *Boutique Fantasque*, *Les Sylphides* and *The Sleeping Beauty*. Maynard, like most of his friends, was a passionate devotee of the ballet; he became an equally passionate devotee of Lopokova. His devotion was very understandable. But supposing he were to marry her? Lydia as a friend, Lydia as a visiting bird hopping gaily from twig to twig was, Virginia thought, very delightful. She was pretty, high-spirited, a comic, a charmer and extremely well-disposed.* In that gay, peripatetic capacity she was altogether irreproachable. But how, without two solid ideas to rub together, could she fail to destroy the intellectual comforts of Maynard Keynes's friends, and indeed of Maynard himself?

> I can foresee only too well [wrote Virginia to Vanessa], Lydia stout, charming, exacting; Maynard in the Cabinet; 46 [Gordon Square] the resort of dukes and prime ministers. Maynard, being a simple man, not analytic as we are, would sink beyond recall long before he realised his state. Then he would awake, to find 3 children, & his life entirely and for ever controlled.

The nature of Bloomsbury was such that the fine web of intimate friendships upon which it depended for its existence could be snapped by any intruder. Thus Adrian had married himself away from his sisters and his friends, and thus Clive's mistresses formed a constantly

---

* On 11 September 1923 Virginia noted, after staying with Maynard Keynes and Lydia Lopokova at Studland: "I wanted to observe Lydia as a type for Rezia; and did observe one or two facts." *AWD* (*Berg*).

disturbing element. Eventually however Maynard decided, and decided wisely, that his happiness could best be secured by marrying Lydia. Friends must take the two of them together – and in fact they did.

But in January 1923 Lydia was still, so to speak, one of the decorations of Bloomsbury. Her dancing was one of the delights of Maynard's Twelfth Night party at Gordon Square; Marjorie Strachey gave her own obscenely comic renderings of nursery rhymes, Sickert acted Hamlet; Virginia found herself among all her friends and her spirits rose wonderfully. The evening was immensely enjoyable.

But it was no more than an interlude. She returned to her work, her cares, her depression and her suburb.

"Mrs. Murry's dead! It says so in the paper." Nelly made the announcement dramatically at breakfast on 12 January. Virginia's feelings were mixed and, on the whole, painful. It was a rival struck down; she could not repel that thought or refrain from recording it. But Katherine and Katherine's injunction "do not quite forget me" were remembered, and her loss – a loss genuinely felt despite all the vicissitudes and jealousies of their relationship – was one more unhappiness in an unhappy season.

Berta Ruck was also dead. She had been killed in *Jacob's Room*.

Yet even in this light the legends on the tombstones could be read, brief voices saying: 'I am Bertha Ruck, I am Tom Gage'. And they say which day of the year they died, and the New Testament says something for them, very proud, very emphatic or consoling.

Somewhere Virginia must have seen that odd name and unconsciously distorted it a little, adding an *h*, an addition which did not save her from a lawyer's letter pointing out that the real Berta Ruck was very much alive and inclined to be litigious on the subject of her literary extinction. She was, it appeared, in the same line of business as Virginia, the authoress of *The Lad with Wings*, *Sir or Madam* and *The Dancing Star*; but whereas Virginia might be content to sell a few hundred copies of *her* works, Miss Ruck, who very skilfully combined the qualities of the *feuilleton* writer with those of an authority on social behaviour, sold by the thousand and tens of thousands. Like Virginia, she was married to a literary man, Oliver Onions, and it was he, indignant on his wife's behalf, who refused to believe Virginia's disarming reply to their solicitors' letter: how could Mrs Woolf never have heard of Berta Ruck, whose name and fame were emblazoned even on the tops of London omnibuses? Fortunately his rage evaporated, and peace was made. The two authoresses exchanged letters, were reconciled, and later found that they had a common friend in Lydia. Virginia and Berta Ruck both found Mlle Lopokova amusing and, at times, disconcerting;* she formed a tenuous link between them. When a year or so later at a Bloomsbury party, Berta Ruck gave a most spirited rendering of "Never allow a Sailor an inch above your knee"–a performance which filled Virginia with amazement and delight–all differences over tombstones had long been forgotten.

There was a further annoyance in the early weeks of 1923. *The Nation* was changing hands. H. W. Massingham, the editor, had employed Leonard as a salaried contributor; but now Maynard Keynes had emerged as a major shareholder and Chairman of the new Board of Directors. He wanted to change the style and policy of the paper. The result might be injurious, in a financial sense, to the Woolfs, but it was not so much this as the feeling of uncertainty, and perhaps even more, the feeling of subordination which demoralised not only Virginia, but Leonard.

> Leonard thinks himself a failure. And what use is there in denying a depression which is irrational? Can't I always think myself one too? It is inevitable. But there was Maynard arrived and trim, yet our junior. The absurd unreality of this as a standard strikes me, but it is not easy to make these truths effective. It is unpleasant waiting in a dependent kind of way to know what Massingham will do.

The weather was wet and wan. The Hogarth Press was in a most

---

* Miss Ruck recalls a performance of *The Frogs* to which she and Virginia were taken by Lydia Lopokova. They sat in the front row of the stalls and the two novelists were greatly enjoying themselves.

"Lydia, however (invariably one to speak her mind in her enchantingly original English) said, 'This is so doll.'

'Lydia! It's *not* dull! It's very very *funny*.'

'It is doll. We will go out.'

'We can't' said your Aunt [Virginia] in a whisper, 'At least wait until the Interval.'

'We will go out *now*. It is too doll to bear. Now. Come.'

'We can't, possibly ——'

'No one will see.'

'Lydia, *everybody* will see us! We are all much too noticeable ——'

We were, you know. Your famous Aunt wore a very large black sombrero hat, I was as tall as she, and had fat black plaits done over my ears, Lydia between us was small, but always outstandingly striking in movement and manner, you might not see what she wore, but she drew every eye.

Fortunately she allowed herself to be persuaded to sit down and see it out before the audience joined in!"

Miss Berta Ruck to the author, 11 September 1971

uncomfortable condition; Ralph, who was not to leave until Easter, was defiant and argumentative; the drawling voice of the new aspirant, Marjorie Joad, grated on Virginia's ears. But they had to work together, they had to be given lunch and tea, and the need to maintain some kind of conversation between them all imposed a heavy burden upon her. Her melancholy mood was intensified by a fever and a violent cold and, to add to her anxieties, there seemed, in the remodelling of *The Nation*, to be a chance of solving Mr Eliot's financial problems by making him Literary Editor.

Virginia pulled strings, rang people up, exhorted and advised; but she found herself wishing that "poor dear Tom had more spunk in him, less need to let drop by drop of his agonised perplexities fall ever so finely through pure cambric." Finally *The Nation's* demand for a quick decision, and the fact that it could not guarantee more than six months' employment settled the matter. Eliot found that he could not take the risk of accepting. The job was offered to Leonard and he took it.

Virginia was a good deal taken aback by this surprising turn of events. She could see the disadvantages of such an employment, but at the same time it offered security and she was immensely relieved.

It was on Friday, 23 March that Maynard offered the post of Literary Editor of *The Nation* to Leonard; on 1 April the Woolfs were in Madrid. It was many years since they had crossed the Channel; the experience was exhilarating and therapeutic and I think that something of Virginia's delight in that holiday is preserved in a contribution (it is not easy to know whether one should describe it as a story or an article) to the refurbished *Nation* entitled *To Spain*. Their journey took them – partly on muleback – to Yegen in the mountains south of Granada, where they were entertained by Ralph Partridge's friend Gerald Brenan, at that time a rather earnest young man who was devoting himself very seriously to the art of writing. The Woolfs stayed with him for a fortnight and, according to Virginia, they discussed literature twelve hours a day. She called him a mad Englishman and liked him very much. Forty years later he remembered not only the beauty and distinction of her appearance and her voice, not only the brilliance, gaiety and irony of her conversation, but her real friendliness and her insatiable curiosity.

Perhaps because Virginia lacked the novelist's sense for the dramatic properties of character and was more interested in the texture of people's minds, she was much given to drawing them out and documenting herself upon them. She asked me a great many questions – why I had come to live here, what I felt about this and that, and what my ideas were about writing. I was conscious that I was being studied and even quizzed a little, and also that she and Leonard were trying to decide whether I showed any signs of having literary talent. If so, I must publish with them. Yet it must not for a moment be thought that she was patronizing. On the contrary her deference to the views of the callow and rather arrogant youth with whom she was staying was quite surprising. She argued with me about literature, defended Scott, Thackeray, and Conrad against my attacks, disagreed with my high opinion of *Ulysses* on the grounds that great works of art ought not to be so boring, and listened humbly to my criticisms of her own novels. That was the great thing about 'Bloomsbury'–they refused to stand on the pedestal of their own age and superiority. And her visit was followed by a succession of highly characteristic letters in which she continued the theme of our discussions.

The Woolfs returned by way of Paris, where Virginia hoped to meet Vanessa. She stayed for a few days, while Leonard went on alone to Richmond and *The Nation*.

Whenever they were apart, which was seldom enough, Leonard and Virginia wrote to each other every day. Her letters usually give a faithful account of her activities; they did so on this occasion. Vanessa did not come. Virginia saw Paris as a tourist might see it; she was lonely, and without her husband everything seemed pointless and second-rate; his absence was acutely felt. The tenderness of her feelings was well expressed in an earlier letter:

> I lie & think of my precious beast, who does make me more happy every day & instant of my life than I thought it possible to be. There's no doubt I'm terribly in love with you. I keep thinking what you're doing, & I have to stop–it makes me want to kiss you so.

Virginia's friends would hardly have been surprised by such an avowal. Seeing the Woolfs together the observer certainly received a very strong impression of happiness and unity in their marriage. Their affection, despite much teasing and some tiffs, was manifest; so too was Virginia's dependence upon Leonard in practical matters and all judgements requiring calculation and solid good sense. What was less generally apparent was *his* need of her, particularly in moments of disappointment and pain. Certainly in the early part of that year he had needed her sympathy and she his; they were united in their discouragement. But by May 1923, and in the following year, the solidarity that is born of misfortune was unnecessary.

Returning to England with the prospect of being a Literary Editor, of undergoing all the fatigues and exasperations incidental to an employment in which, as in a treadmill, the last step of the old week is but the first step of the new, Leonard required no sympathy; he was never in the least dismayed by the prospect of hard work. His discontents at this time, and they were not very serious, did not arise from calamities but from success.

Jacob's Room had been well received; Virginia felt a certain buoyancy in her situation; she was, as she herself put it, being "pushed up"; she had become, almost, a celebrity.

The growth of her reputation showed itself in social terms. Lady Colefax (a sensitive barometer of fame) began to issue invitations. At first Virginia refused them. She was still socially timid, she still felt that it took a good deal of courage to go into strange rooms "properly dressed"; she was still visited by horrid doubts as to whether she *was* properly dressed and, when she had mastered her fears well enough to enable her to go into Lady Colefax's dining-room, she might well find herself placed next to Sir Arthur, who always seemed to imagine that his neighbour took a passionate interest in the fate of the Dye-stuffs Bill. Nevertheless, Lady Colefax was persistent and Lady Colefax was persuasive, and of course Virginia half wanted to be persuaded. Moreover, although she thought that Lady Colefax was rather like a glossy artificial cherry stuck on a hat, she had her perceptions, she had her character. When she came to tea and left her umbrella, Virginia referred to it as "glowing and gleaming among my old gamps." She was taken up sharply. "Mrs. Woolf, I know what you think of my umbrella— a cheap, stubby, vulgar umbrella, you think my umbrella: and you think I have a bag like it—a cheap flashy bag covered with bad embroidery." Since this was precisely what Virginia did think, she considered Lady Colefax with a new respect.

Virginia's social adventures became part of a game which she used to play with Clive: the game of "boasts". Two examples give a notion of what Virginia's boasting was like. One: "My boast: 2 invitations: one to stay with Cecils & meet Lady Gwendolen; the other to spend 5 days at Easter playing Badmington & discussing fiction with H. G. Wells. Yes—this sort of thing *does* give me pleasure." Or, again to Clive: "Lady Londonderry gave a party and did ask me—at which my heart leapt up, as you can imagine, until I discovered that it was to meet 500 Colonial dentists and to hear Mr. Noyes read his own poetry aloud. Not a distinguished gathering." Virginia had certainly not outgrown her snobberies and, unlike her husband, succumbed easily to the blandishments of hostesses. She was welcomed by the world of fashion, and she enjoyed it. "Leonard," she wrote in her diary, "Leonard thinks less well of me for powdering my nose and spending money on dress. Never mind, I adore Leonard."

Writing to her old art student friend, Margery Snowden, in April 1923, Vanessa said that Virginia was now more like what she used to be, and in saying this I think that she meant that her sister was completely cured. She had regained her serenity, her moral and intellectual balance. Physically she showed signs of the ordeal of the past ten years. She had grown more angular, more bony, more austere; she had lost whatever prettiness she may have possessed; but certainly she continued to be very beautiful. In her dress, there was only a passing and reluctant acceptance of the demands of fashion, and not the least coquetry; those frivolities which, as she believed, were condemned by Leonard were certainly on a very minute scale.* Her powder was minimal, her dress allowance stringent. Looking for some analogy to the style of her appearance I come nearest to finding it in the art of the Sienese masters of the fourteenth century: in everything she was linear, elegant, dignified, graceful, with very little high renaissance bulk about her, no Raphaelesque sweetness or softness, no corregiescity. In her attitudes there was the oddest mixture of grandeur and clumsiness. Imagine a Simone Martini dismissing the annunciate angel to roll a cigarette or take a hearty four-mile walk over the hills, and you may perceive something of the fine incongruity that I am trying to suggest. The pictures and photographs of this period are unreliable; a ciné-camera could in ten seconds have caught the essential quality that is lacking in the still image; for it was in movement that she was most truly herself. Then she reminded one of some fantastic bird, abruptly throwing up her head and crowing with delighted amusement at some idea, some word, some paradox, that took her fancy. Her conversation was full of surprises, of unpredictable questions, of fantasy and of laughter – the happy laughter of a child who finds the world more strange, more absurd and more beautiful than any

* "Her hair was allowed to drift about in all directions, she never wore any make-up – she seemed quite devoid of personal vanity, and yet she never appeared anything but beautiful. Sometimes in the summer when I was working in the printing room she'd wander in and set up type or distribute it with her quick, sensitive fingers, looking like a dishevelled angel – her bare feet shuffling about in bedroom slippers, in a nightdress with a great tear down the side, and a dressing-gown vaguely thrown over it, but her mind far, far away from her mechanical task. . . ." Ralph Partridge, *Portrait of Virginia Woolf*, BBC Home Service, 29 August 1956.

one could have imagined possible; laughter seemed in those years to be her natural element.

For children she was a treat. The announcement: "Virginia is coming to tea" was like a warm capricious breeze blowing in from the south-west and bringing with it a kind of amazed joy. Of the miseries of her life, they were allowed to know nothing, nor did it seem, in their company, that she could be unhappy.

She could, though, inspire terror. Not that she ever set herself to terrify children; but I can remember listening to a conversation between her and Vanessa when Virginia described two old ladies—I don't know who—living quietly in one of those London streets which are closed at one end to traffic by means of solid iron posts. A house further up the street was burgled. The thieves were surprised; they slipped out of the front door, leapt into a fast car and crashed against the barrier. The old ladies heard this and heard the men shrieking in mortal pain until the ambulance arrived. The story was told simply but with such incredible power that my blood ran cold—it still does a little when I recall it and the way Virginia told it. But, of course, a child wants to be frightened. One would have liked to have heard more. I can't remember that I did. Usually it was all jokes and fun.

She seems to have had a natural sympathy with the young, accepting their fantasies, joining in their games without effort and without condescension, exercising a purely benevolent power of enchantment. But in speaking here of "the young" I refer to the inhabitants of the nursery rather than to those of the campus. If you were old enough to regard her as a celebrity (a role in which the nursery did not see her) her incantations might be of a different kind. She could charm and she could terrify; but her magic was not purely benevolent. It is said that she could behave with some ferocity, that she had claws and could bite, that several young men and women had been mauled.

. . . her social approach to young people was thoroughly intimidating. She was particularly hard on innocent young women with any intellectual pretensions; she would question them in a relentlessly encouraging way, get them to air all their high-minded views and then expose their utter ignorance and ineptitude to the assembled company in her low, mocking voice, without ever losing the benign expression on her face. Yet the relish with which she punctured their poor aspirations to partake in intelligent conversation was only too evident. Pretty girls, who only wanted to attract the men present physically, were spared these snubs—the silly nincompoops could flirt as much as they liked with impunity. But it was *lèse-majesté* for a girl to think herself clever enough to talk to Virginia as an equal. Aspiring young men weren't so obviously maltreated. They too were encouraged by her to speak what was in their callow, shallow minds, but they were not publicly humiliated; they were just left to go home with the uncomfortable sensation that in some inscrutable way they'd made utter fools of themselves.

Certainly there is an element of truth in this, although I think that, in a matter of this kind, Ralph Partridge cannot be considered a reliable witness. He was very much inclined to make large generalisations upon rather slender material and I strongly suspect that he was doing so in this instance. Nor do I think that his analysis of Virginia's motives is a correct one; indeed the evidence on which it is based is highly questionable, for of those who charged Virginia with cruelty to the young, there was one – Clive – who always took the view that it was young *men* who suffered at her hands and that she was indulgent, almost too indulgent, to the claims of young women. But having made these reservations the charge itself must be accepted. Like many people who have been socially terrified, Virginia could be and probably rather enjoyed being socially terrifying; as her reputation grew, as the success of *Jacob's Room* was followed by the acclaim of *Mrs Dalloway*, her ability and her opportunities for social misbehaviour of this kind increased.

As we have seen, in 1922 Virginia hit upon the plan of writing two books simultaneously: her novel and a work of criticism which she had at first called *Reading* and now *The Common Reader*. The one, she calculated, would provide relief from the other. *The Common Reader* was based, largely, upon articles which she had already published, but to this she added some new material and, notably, the long essay entitled *On Not Knowing Greek*. It was with this theme in mind that she planned, in October 1922, to read Sophocles, Euripides and the first five books of the *Odyssey*. (Her usual practice was to read the original Greek text, consulting a crib when she had to.) She was also intending to read the lives of Bentley and of Jebb, and a little later she decided that she must also read Zimmern and Aeschylus.*

* Sir Alfred Eckhard Zimmern, 1879–1957. Virginia probably read *The Greek Commonwealth – Politics and Economics in 5th Century Athens*, Oxford, 1911. *The Life and Letters of Sir R. C. Jebb*, by Caroline Jebb, Cambridge, 1907, contains an essay by A. W. Verrall which might have been useful; in other respects the book seems barely relevant to Virginia's topic and she may have had in mind Jebb's edition of the *Trachiniae* (1892) which belonged to Leonard (see Holleyman & Treacher Ltd., *Catalogue of important and association books from the Library of the late Leonard and*

That autumn of 1922 both books seem to have hung fire. In late October and in November Virginia was rethinking *Mrs Dalloway*. On 7 November she planned to tackle her Greek chapter before the end of the month, although she felt that she had not done half enough reading and had still to tackle Aeschylus, Bentley and the *Odyssey*. On 23 January she notes that she wants to get *Mrs Dalloway* into full talk. By the month of May the Greeks were still unwritten. Early in June she spent a week-end at Garsington and this visit showing her, as it must have done, a striking though singular vision of the British social apparatus, directed her mind to the main theme of her novel (which she now called *The Hours*).

"I am a great deal interested suddenly in my book," she wrote on 4 June. "I want to bring in the despicableness of people like Ott. I want to give the slipperiness of the soul. I have been too tolerant . . ." The reflection may have been unkind and unjust, but it was not unproductive. A fortnight later she examined herself and her novel with some care.

I took up this book with a kind of idea that I might say something about my writing – which was prompted by glancing at what K. M. said about her writing in *The Dove's Nest*. But I only glanced. She said a good deal about feeling things deeply: also about being pure, which I won't criticise, though of course I very well could. But now what do I feel about *my* writing? – this book, that is, *The Hours*, if that's its name? One must write from deep feeling, said Dostoievsky. And do I? Or do I fabricate with words, loving them as I do? No, I think not. In this book I have almost too many ideas. I want to give life and death, sanity and insanity; I want to criticise the social system, and to show it at work, at its most intense. But here I may be posing. . . . Am I writing *The Hours* from deep emotion? Of course the mad part tries me so much, makes my mind squirt so badly that I can hardly face spending the next weeks at it. It's a question though of these characters. People, like Arnold Bennett, say I can't create, or didn't in *Jacob's Room*, characters that survive. My answer is – but I leave that to the *Nation*: it's only the old argument that character is dissipated into shreds now; the old post-Dostoievsky argument. I daresay it's true, however, that I haven't that "reality" gift. I insubstantise, wilfully to some extent, distrusting reality – its cheapness. But to get further. Have I the power of conveying the true reality? Or do I write essays about myself? Answer

Virginia Woolf, May 1970, III, 12). The Woolfs also owned a copy of Monk's *Life of Bentley* (1883) (*ibid*. VII, 4) and this served not only Virginia's purposes in her essay *On Not Knowing Greek* but was used too in the writing of *Dr Bentley* (also in *The Common Reader*). It was lent to Lytton Strachey and was his main, perhaps his only, source, in *The Sad Story of Dr Colbatch*. (*Portraits in Miniature*, 1931; p. i.)

these questions as I may, in the uncomplimentary sense, and still there remains this excitement. To get to the bones, now I'm writing fiction again I feel my force glow straight from me at its fullest. After a dose of criticism I feel that I'm writing sideways, using only an angle of my mind. This is justification; for free use of the faculties means happiness. I'm better company, more of a human being. Nevertheless, I think it most important in this book to go for the central things. Even though they don't submit, as they should, however, to beautification in language. No, I don't nail my crest to the Murrys, who work in my flesh after the manner of the jigger insect. It's annoying, indeed degrading, to have these bitternesses. Still, think of the 18th Century. But then they were overt, not covert, as now.

I foresee, to return to *The Hours*, that this is going to be the devil of a struggle. The design is so queer and so masterful. I'm always having to wrench my substance to fit it. The design is certainly original and interests me hugely. I should like to write away and away at it, very quick and fierce. Needless to say, I can't. In three weeks from today, I shall be dried up.

In July she was still confronted by the unwritten Greek chapter of *The Common Reader*; but *Mrs Dalloway* was going well. At Monk's House she found herself in good health and able to work. But on 6 August she re-read what she had written. It seemed to her "sheer weak dribble." Middleton Murry had said that with *Jacob's Room* she had reached a dead end and could go no further. Was he perhaps right? His criticism had worried her a good deal and she adverts to it frequently in her diary. But the check was overcome; she had confidence enough to go on and began to discover new ways of doing so. At the end of August she drew up a systematic scheme for *The Common Reader*.

Then, on 18 September, she suffered a short but violent mental tremor.

And I meant to record for psychological purposes that strange night when I went to meet Leonard and did not meet him. What an intensity of feeling was pressed into those hours! It was a wet windy night; and as I walked back across the field I said Now I am meeting it; now the old devil has once more got his spine through the waves. (But I cannot re-capture reality). And such was the strength of my feeling that I became physically rigid. Reality, so I thought, was unveiled. And there was something noble in feeling like this; tragic, not at all petty. Then cold white lights went over the fields; and went out; and I stood under the great trees at Iford waiting for the lights of the bus. And that went by; and I felt lonelier. There was a man with a barrow walking into Lewes, who looked at me. But I could toy with, at least control, all this until suddenly, after the last likely train had come in, I felt it was intolerable to sit about, and must do the final thing, which was to go to London. Off I rode, without much time, against such a wind; and again I had a satisfaction in being matched with powerful things, like wind and dark. I battled, had to walk; got on; drove ahead; dropped the torch; picked it up; and so on again without any lights. Saw men and women walking together; thought you're safe and happy; I'm an outcast; took my ticket; had three minutes to spare, and then, turning the corner of the station stairs, saw Leonard, coming along, bending rather, like a person walking very quick, in his mackintosh. He was rather cold and angry (as perhaps was natural). And then, not to show my feelings, I went aside and did something to my bicycle. Also, I went back to the ticket office and said to the humane man there "It's all right. My husband caught the last train. Give me back my fare" which he did. And I got the money more to set myself right with Leonard than because I wanted it. All the way back we talked about a row (about reviewers) at the office; and all the time I was feeling My God, that's over. I'm out of that. It's over. Really, it was a physical feeling of lightness and relief and safety, and yet there was too something terrible behind it – the fact of this pain, I suppose; which continued for several days, and I think I should feel it again if I went over that road at night; and it became connected with the deaths of the miners and with Aubrey Herbert's death next day.* But I have not got it all in, by any means.

There were no ill effects – indeed no effects at all, unless it be that this odd experience had something to do with the work on which she was engaged during the weeks that followed it, for at that time she was describing the madness of Septimus Warren-Smith.

Thereafter there is no record of *Mrs Dalloway*'s progress for some months, but *The Common Reader* was not neglected and in November the necessities of the Greek chapter required that she should read Sophocles; the amount of reading and writing that went into the production of that essay, an essay of about 7,000 words, was remarkable.

On 23 January 1924 she wrote:

back again tomorrow to *The Hours*, which I was looking at disconsolately – oh the cold raw edges of one's relinquished pages – when the House business started this morning. But now I am going to write till we move – 6 weeks straight ahead. I think it's the design that's good this time – God knows.

* "the deaths of the miners." On 25 September 1923 the No. 23 Redding Pit near Falkirk was flooded and 41 men lost their lives. Lt.-Col. Aubrey Herbert, M.P. (b. 1880), died on 26 September 1923; he was a half-brother of Lady Margaret Duckworth.

The "move" to which Virginia refers was a move from Richmond to London, for, in the autumn of 1923, Virginia won her long struggle with Leonard. It had begun in the summer when she suggested that really the time had come to leave Hogarth House. She was, surely, well again. She found the incessant journeying to and from Richmond tiresome, time-consuming and exhausting. Leonard, however, was worried and made the old objections; London life was too rackety for her. He thought a move unwise – or at least, premature.

For a time Virginia was in despair. How could she argue against a husband to whom she owed so much, who had proved so wise in the past, who had devoted himself so greatly? I don't know, but she did – and she won her argument. In October she began house-hunting and eventually, on 7 January 1924, found what she wanted in No. 52 Tavistock Square, Bloomsbury. The Woolfs moved there on 13 March.

No. 52 was part of an early nineteenth-century block forming the southern side of Tavistock Square, a characteristic specimen of its district and period; its plain façade was of darkened brick rising four storeys above a railed area which illuminated the basement. When the Woolfs bought the ten-year lease from the Bedford Estate, they took on the sitting tenants on the ground and first floors; their relations with this firm of solicitors, Messrs Dollman and Pritchard, were so harmonious that when eventually they had to leave Tavistock Square on the expiry of their (extended) lease, old Mr Pritchard and his staff moved with them. The two floors above these offices became the Woolfs' London home for the next fifteen years. Their rooms were light and spacious and well-proportioned, and Virginia commissioned decorations by Vanessa and Duncan. The basement, originally the domestic offices – kitchen, scullery, pantries and so forth – housed the Hogarth Press. A long passage led to the back of the house where, in place of the garden, was a huge room with a skylight which had been a billiard room. This Virginia used as her workroom, and referred to as the Studio. It had also to serve as a storeroom and repository for Hogarth Press publications, and here, among the heaped-up parcels of books and piles of paper, in conditions of dirt and disorder, surrounded by what the Stracheys called "filth packets" – accumulations of old pen nibs, paper-clips, buttons and fluff, empty ink bottles and un-emptied ashtrays, used envelopes and galley proofs – Virginia could be found in the morning, seated beside the gas fire in an old arm-chair, the stuffing of which emerged in disembowelled confusion upon the floor, a board of three-ply on her lap, writing and re-writing her books.

Every now and again someone would creep in apologetically and remove what was needed from the store of books; but Virginia, sensitive though she normally was to noise of any kind, took no notice.

But she took a great interest in the Press and in the afternoons she would go and work there. She had become an able compositor and she enjoyed exercising her skill in the company of her fellow-workers. When they first came to Tavistock Square, only Marjorie Joad was working with them, but Leonard had already broken it to her that there was to be a new regime in the Hogarth Press. George Rylands was soon to leave Cambridge; he wanted to learn about printing and publishing from the Woolfs while working upon his Fellowship dissertation. The idea was that he might grad-ually relieve Leonard of the burden of management. (It was not the last time that they were to entertain this completely unrealistic idea.)

Rylands came to the Hogarth Press at the beginning of July 1924; his connection with the firm was comparatively short (he was awarded his Fellowship at the turn of the year). He and Virginia got on like a house on fire; she teased and questioned him, they chattered together about words and parties and people; when she was working there, the basement office was full of gaiety and laughter. There were times, however, when the new recruit found his duties less congenial; he had to tie up parcels, calculate discounts for waiting customers, oil, ink, operate and clean the machinery of the press itself. But the worst of his trials came when he had to go out and face booksellers and try to sell them modern poetry or the *Collected Works* of Freud, both of which were likely to be con-temptuously dismissed, the former as nonsense, the latter as por-nography. And Leonard seemed to take his efforts so much for granted; there seemed to be no praise for the struggling novice. Leonard who, with Virginia, was quite happy to take a holiday selling his publications to country bookshops, probably did not realise what agonies might be involved in such negotiations.

George Rylands returned to Cambridge and to a very distinguished academic career, and the Woolfs found another very charming young man, Angus Davidson, to take his place. The retiring assistant wrote with great tact and modesty: "Thank God, Angus is at once a soothing and a responsible person whose tranquil labours will do far more than my moments of frantic toil alternating with lackadaisical interims. I am terrified lest I shall not see a great deal of you and Leonard now I am out of the Press: I must. I depend upon you. A thousand thanks for the last six months." But in fact Angus was to have a much stormier passage.

In May 1924 Virginia went to Cambridge to speak on "Character in Modern Fiction" to a society called the Heretics. The result was *Mr Bennett and Mrs Brown*. It was as near as she came to an aesthetic manifesto. She speaks to the young and for the future–"we are trembling on the verge of one of the great ages of English literature." "We" means the *avant-garde*. As always happens in manifestos of this kind, it appears that the only way in which we can enter that great age is by pushing aside a certain number of human obstructions which clutter the road: the writers of "those sleek, smooth novels, those portentous and ridiculous biographies, that milk and watery criticism, those poems melodiously celebrating the innocence of roses and sheep which pass so plausibly for literature at the present time," as well as Bennett, Galsworthy and Wells. These indeed were the real enemies, for they obscured the true end of writing, which is the discovery of reality personified by the intriguing but obfusc person of Mrs Brown, the unknown lady in the railway carriage. Mr Bennett does no more than tell us about her rent; Mr Wells tells us rather what her rent ought to be; Mr Galsworthy, that she cannot possibly pay it. None of them captures the real Mrs Brown because none of them is interested in the real character of human beings–in the essential Mrs Brown, which is . . . At this point I hesitate, but so, I think, did Virginia, for she perceived that Mrs Brown was a chameleon, a creature which changes its colour according to its situations and the angle from which you look at it, so that in the end the best one can say is that Mrs Brown is a human being–an object largely composed I believe of water with certain added salts and so on–but also, and for Virginia, eminently a collection of memories, some ever present, others mysteriously varied, others capriciously available. The waking Mrs Brown knows very well she is Mrs Brown and can probably remember her age, certainly cannot remember her first meal, yet does recall the appearance of a teddy bear and more precisely the particular black buttons which served for its eyes when she smells a certain kind of furniture polish–this, I think, is the kind of Mrs Brown with whom Mr Bennett never comes to grips–a kind of awareness, sometimes luminous, sometimes intelligible, sometimes wholly awake, sometimes completely asleep. One day when the collection of water and salts is dissolved perhaps, who knows, this cloud, those memories, loosely tied by a wisp of semi-consciousness, may be the only Mrs Brown.

This, then, is the business of what Virginia calls the "Georgian novelists," to look past the circumstantial evidence of Bennett, the preaching and moralising of Wells and Galsworthy, and approach that central mystery, Mrs Brown herself. But having declared that this is the true battle, this the victory that has to be won, Virginia looks at the troops on her own side and, like Wellington, declares: "I don't know whether they will frighten the enemy but by God they frighten me." E. M. Forster and D. H. Lawrence were both of them brave and brilliant, but both spent much of their time marching in the wrong direction. Eliot and Joyce did not fall into that fault, but the former was guilty of indiscipline and the latter of atrocities. Strachey's heart was not really in the fight. Victory would be won and triumph was assured, but who would gain it? She never gives the answer but it is obvious, and indeed a manifesto, unless it be written at a time when there is a real coherent and unanimous doctrine amongst artists, is bound to be a personal confession and likely to be little else. *Mr Bennett and Mrs Brown* is, in fact, Virginia's own private manifesto. She outlines her programme for the next decade. To some extent she outlines her own life work.

In May 1924 she resolved to finish *Mrs Dalloway* in four months; then it would be done, or sufficiently done, to be put away for the next three months, which would be devoted to *The Common Reader*. The essays would be published in April 1925, the novel a month later. This she accomplished. That summer she worked swiftly and well; by 2 August she had reached the death of Septimus Warren Smith. It is true that, on the following day, she was contemplating what she supposed must be the eightieth systematic beginning of *The Common Reader* and was modestly proposing to read *Clarissa* as well as *The Pilgrim's Progress*, the *Medea* and Plato; but she returned to the novel and by September saw the end in sight. On 9 October just after her return to London, *Mrs Dalloway* was finished, and she congratulated herself on the speed with which it had been done. Already she could see the "Old Man"—and by this she almost certainly meant *To the Lighthouse*. But the last months of 1924 were spent in preparing *Mrs Dalloway* for the press (Leonard saw the typescript in January 1925) and in finishing *The Common Reader*. She does not seem to have done more than think about her next novel until the summer of 1925.

Virginia did not often discuss her own writing in letters; but she came near to doing so in a letter which she wrote to the French painter Jacques Raverat. He had asked her what she was writing. She, refusing to be drawn, replied:

> I don't think I shall tell you, because, as you know perfectly well, you don't care a straw. . . . I'm terrifically egotistic about my writing, think practically of nothing else, and so, partly from conceit, partly shyness, sensitiveness, what you choose, never mention it, unless someone draws it out with red hot pincers . . . (however, I've almost finished 2 books).

His reply, received at Rodmell while she was deeply absorbed in the writing of *Mrs Dalloway*, was of a kind to interest her greatly, for his ideas were to some extent congruous with those which she had tried to formulate in *Mr Bennett and Mrs Brown*. The difficulty about writing was that it has to be–as he put it–"essentially linear"–one can only write (or read) one thing at a time. Writing a word–the word 'Neo-Pagan' for instance, which Virginia had thrown at him–was like casting a pebble into a pond: "There are splashes in the outer air in every direction, and under the surface waves that follow one another into dark and forgotten corners. . . ." But this phenomenon was one which could only be represented by some graphic expedient such as placing the word in the middle of a page and surrounding it radially with associated ideas. Thus, in a fashion, a writer might achieve that simultaneity which the painter enjoys by reason of the nature of his art. Moreover, the mind cannot carry all the complexities of a literary design because such a design is, of necessity, sequential. "Surely, when you are writing you are not clearly conscious on Page 259 of what there was on Page 31? But perhaps that's only because I'm not a writer, & in fact do not naturally think in words."

"Certainly," Virginia replied, "the painters have a great gift of expression. A highly intelligent account you seem to me to give of the processes of your own mind when I throw Neo-Paganism in." But she would not allow that the circumstances of their art gave them a power of vision denied to an author; on the contrary: "I rather think you've broached some of the problems of the writers too, who are trying to catch and consolidate and consummate (whatever the word is for making literature) those splashes of yours." Indeed it was precisely the task of the writer–that is to say her task–to go beyond the "formal railway line of sentence" and to disregard the "falsity of the past (by which I mean Bennett, Galsworthy and so on)." The literary artist has to realise that "people don't and never did feel or think or dream for a second in that way; but all over the place, in your way." In other words she is claiming for herself the ability, or at least the intention, to see events out of time, to apprehend processes of thought and feeling as though they were pictorial shapes.

It is possible in *Mrs Dalloway* to find an attempt of this nature, a desire to make literature 'radial' rather than 'linear', to describe at once the "splashes in the outer air" and "the waves that follow one another into dark and forgotten corners." It may be that she acknowledges the extreme difficulty of such an undertaking when, in her next novel, she places a painter and a painting so near to the heart of her literary design and ends it with: "a line there, in the centre."

But most of Virginia's letters to Jacques Raverat are frivolous and uninhibited gossip. He—a Frenchman educated in England—had been one of the 'Neo-Pagans' and had married another—Gwen Darwin—in 1911. A letter from Jacques to Virginia praising *Monday or Tuesday* began a correspondence which lasted until his death in March 1925. He was now unable to walk or to write (his letters were dictated to his wife); in fact he was slowly and painfully dying. Virginia's instinctive response to suffering was always to write; and her way of showing practical sympathy in illness or distress was to write letters. She wrote long and fairly frequent letters to Jacques, and he wrote some extremely good letters in reply. "I like to please Jacques," she confided to her diary, and clearly Jacques was pleased. "Your letters," he wrote in December 1924, "particularly the last 3 or 4, have given me something, which very few people have been able to give me in these last years." They planned to meet again, but they never did; perhaps Virginia did not really want it. The pleasure of their friendship lay in its epistolatory character. In February 1925, a month before he died, Virginia did something that, so far as I know, she never did for anyone else. She sent him proofs of her unpublished novel. Gwen read *Mrs Dalloway* to him on his death-bed, omitting, for she found them too unbearably poignant, the passages describing the suicide of Septimus Warren-Smith.

On 8 April Virginia wrote in her diary:

> Since I wrote, which is these last months, Jacques Raverat has died; after longing to die; and he sent me a letter about *Mrs Dalloway* which gave me one of the happiest days of my life.

With Jacques' death, nothing seemed to remain of the Neo-Pagans. As Gwen wrote, it was "all over long ago." It died in 1914, though it was sick before. Rupert Brooke was gone; Frances Cornford had found another faith. The Olivier girls were married or had drifted away into very different worlds. Ka Cox too was married, to Will Arnold-Forster; "I feel you'll probably not like Will," she had written to Virginia; and she was right.

The Common Reader appeared on 23 April, *Mrs Dalloway* on 14 May. Virginia suffered the usual vicissitudes of feeling, winced at bad notices and rejoiced at good ones. By the end of May the worst was over: Morgan Forster liked *Mrs Dalloway*; Thomas Hardy had read *The Common Reader* with great pleasure. "Never," she was able to write in her diary, "have I felt so much admired."

Chapter Five

June 1925–December 1928

BETWEEN June 1925 and December 1928 Virginia wrote *To the Lighthouse* and conceived *The Waves*, the books which, in the opinion of many critics, are her greatest achievements. This may therefore be a suitable point at which to attempt an examination of her mind at work, even though, in such a scrutiny, we must abandon all pretence at chronological method and must adventure into an area which, manifestly, is not easily negotiated.

She herself has pointed out the dangers of such an undertaking.

Many scenes have come and gone unwritten, since it is today 4th September. A cold grey blowy day, made memorable by the sight of a kingfisher and by my sense, waking early, of being again visited by 'the spirit of delight'. "Rarely, rarely, comest thou, spirit of delight." That was I singing this time last year; and sang so poignantly that I have never forgotten it, or my vision of a fin rising on a wide blank sea. No biographer could possibly guess this important fact about my life in the late summer of 1926. Yet biographers pretend they know people.

They don't, or at least they ought not to. All that they can claim is that they know a little more than does the public at large and that, by catching at a few indications given here and there in recollections or writings, they can correct some misconceptions and trace, if they are very skilful or very lucky, an outline that is consistent and convincing, but which, like all outlines, is but tenuously connected with the actual form of the sitter in all lights, poses, moods and disguises.

To know the psyche of Virginia Woolf, and this is what she is in effect asking of a biographer, one would have to be either God or Virginia, preferably God. Looking from outside, one can go no further than what I have called the outline and for the rest one may guess, one may even build upon one's divinations, but never for a moment allowing oneself to forget that this is guesswork and guesswork of a most hazardous kind.

When, in September 1927, Virginia recalled Shelley's lines, we may fairly deduce that she was looking back at a period of unhappiness. The "fin rising on a wide blank sea"–one of her recurrent images–was a signal of disaster and she had seen it on that night in September 1923 when Leonard was so late coming home. Possibly these recollections are associated with another diary entry headed "A State of Mind" which she made on 15 September 1926:

> Woke up perhaps at 3. Oh it's beginning, it's coming–the horror–physically like a painful wave swelling about the heart–tossing me up. I'm unhappy, unhappy! Down–God, I wish I were dead. Pause. But why am I feeling this? Let me watch the wave rise. I watch. Vanessa. Children. Failure. Yes; I detect that. Failure, failure. (The wave rises).

This may be interpreted as: "Vanessa has three children; I have none."

> Oh they laughed at my taste in green paint!

So, we may be fairly sure, did she; this being–in broad daylight–some tease at Charleston, laughingly uttered, laughingly rebutted, and barely felt at the time. But now, in the small hours:

> Wave crashes. I wish I were dead! I've only a few years to live, I hope. I can't face this horror any more. (This is the wave spreading out over me.) This goes on; several times, with varieties of horror. Then, at the crisis, instead of the pain remaining intense, it becomes rather vague. I doze. I wake with a start. The wave again! The irrational pain; the sense of failure; generally some specific incident, as for example my taste in green paint, or buying a new dress . . . tacked on.

She was still desperately shy in dress shops, and although at about this time she congratulated herself on having at last learnt to face a shop assistant with nonchalant authority, it was but a temporary victory; she still hated buying clothes, particularly underclothes, and, when her purchases were criticised, she was mortified.

> At last I say, watching as dispassionately as I can, Now take a pull of yourself. No more of this. I reason. I take a census of happy people and unhappy. I brace myself to shove, to throw, to batter down. I begin to march blindly forward. I feel obstacles go down. I say it doesn't matter. Nothing matters. I become rigid and straight and sleep again and half wake and feel the wave beginning and watch the light whitening and wonder how, this time, breakfast and daylight will overcome it; and then hear L. in the passage and simulate, for myself as well as for him, great cheerfulness; and generally am cheerful by the time breakfast is over. Does everyone go through this state? Why have I so little control? It is not creditable, nor lovable. It is the cause of much waste and pain in my life.

During the 1920s Virginia's friends often remarked upon her exuberant high spirits.* She was a great social success but, reading her diary, one would hardly suspect that this was the case. In 1926 Roger Fry records a dinner at the Commercio Restaurant when "Virginia was in her grandest vein"; Virginia herself noted, on the previous day, "I tremble and shiver all over at the appalling magnitude of the task I have undertaken – to go to a dressmaker recommended by Todd [Miss Todd was then editor of *Vogue*], even, she suggested, but here my blood ran cold, with Todd." Or again, in 1928 Clive wrote: "The Woolves are in great glory" (19 February) and "Virginia is still on the crest of the wave" (2 March). She herself writes, on 18 March: "Since February I have been a little clouded with headache."

I suppose that most people, if their morale could be measured throughout the day, would show a fluctuation of psychic temperature which would astonish their friends. In Virginia's case the curves of the graph were, one suspects, unusually abrupt and the impression unusually deep and lasting, so that the despair of 1926 was vividly recalled in 1927.

But was it simply despair? The fin that rises above the water may indeed belong to an evil monster armed with razor teeth, but the monster is unseen, it lies in the depths, its character is uncertain.

Here, plunging recklessly, let us suppose that the wave, the fin, the creature from the abyss, was a signal that something was again quickening within her. To return to the autumn of 1926:

> ... it is not oneself but something in the universe that one's left with. It is this that is frightening and exciting in the midst of my profound gloom, depression, boredom, whatever it is. One sees a fin passing far out. ... All I mean to make is a note of a curious state of mind. I hazard the guess that it may be the impulse behind another book. At present my mind is totally blank and virgin of books.

And a month later:

> Monday, Ozzie Dickinson; Wednesday, Lady Colefax; Thursday, Morgan to meet Abel Chevalley, dine Wells to meet Arnold Bennett; Friday to Monday, Long Barn. So the week slips or sticks through my pages; rage, misery, joy, dulness, elation mix. I am the usual battlefield of emotions; alternately think of buying chairs and clothes; plod with some method revising To the Lighthouse; quarrel with Nelly (who was

* This was particularly true when she was with her immediate circle of friends; but she did not depend upon their presence. Professor William Empson recalls that "the only time I had the luck to meet her, which was when I was an undergraduate, I was quite ill with laughing at her jokes." BBC, 24 November 1953.

to catch the afternoon train today because I told a lie about a telephone) and so we go on. Maurice Baring and the Sitwells send me their books; Leonard forges ahead, now doing what he calls "correspondence"; the Press creaks a little at its hinges; Mrs. C[artwright]. has absconded with my spectacles; I find buggers bores, like the normal male; and should now be developing my book for the Press. All these things shoulder each other out across the screen of my brain. At intervals I begin to think (I note this, as I am going to watch for the advent of a book) of a solitary woman shaping a book of ideas about life. This has intruded only once or twice, and very vaguely; it is a dramatisation of my mood at Rodmell. It is to be an endeavour at something mystic, spiritual; the thing that exists when we aren't there.

The Waves, if it was *The Waves*, which Virginia had now begun vaguely to envisage, had not yet assumed a form sufficiently precise for her purpose and five years were to elapse before she could make her notions into a novel. When, in September 1927, she found herself echoing Shelley's despair the sequel, if one may call it a sequel, was to be something different. A month later a whole galaxy of ideas suddenly took shape in the most light-hearted and easily written of her novels.

The evidence suggests (it does no more) that moments of depression were followed by moments of creativity. Virginia, as will be seen in a later chapter, could profit by her illnesses. She needed to "float with the sticks on the stream; helter-skelter with the dead leaves on the lawn, irresponsible and disinterested and able, perhaps for the first time for years, to look around, to look up—to look, for example, at the sky." But she also needed, if she were to cope with the exacting task of describing that which she had seen in the heavens, to be well. In 1913 she had not been strong enough to cope with her vision, but in the years between 1925 and 1932 she was just healthy enough to cope with her own maladies. Nevertheless the effort was considerable and the balance between her illnesses and her constitution was a fine one, as she was to discover in the summer of 1925.

Although she was eager to begin work upon her novel, Virginia decided to postpone writing it until the beginning of August when she would be at Monk's House. The reception of *Mrs Dalloway* and *The Common Reader* had been of a kind to make society and the flatteries of society agreeable. She resolved to give her working time to journalism.*

* She had an additional motive: "I'm out to make £300 this summer by writing and build a bath and hot water range at Rodmell." *AWD*, p. 74, 19 April 1925.

. . . my mornings have all been spent writing–Swift or letters. So a whole tribe of people and parties has gone down the sink to oblivion –

Thus she wrote in her diary in July 1925. With the aid of Leonard's pocket book it is possible however to restore a fairly detailed calendar of these forgotten engagements. The record for the month of July will suffice.

On 1 July the Woolfs had Philip and Irene Noel-Baker to tea and dined out. On the 2nd Lytton's sister Dorothy Bussy came to tea; that evening was George Rylands' party, the party at which Berta Ruck performed. On 3 July Raymond Mortimer and Hope Mirrlees dined at Tavistock Square, Leo Myers and Daphne Sanger came in afterwards. On 5 July (Sunday) they went to a performance of *The Rehearsal*; on 6 July Virginia dined with Clive; on the 9th Lady Colefax and George Rylands came to tea, T. S. Eliot after dinner; on the following day, Friday 10th, they went to Rodmell, returning on Sunday to see Lytton's play, *The Son of Heaven*, at the Scala Theatre; on the 14th Julian Morrell, Ottoline's daughter, and Edward Sackville-West came to dinner, and the Thomas Marshalls (she had been Marjorie Joad when she worked in the Hogarth Press), John Hayward and Philip Morrell came after. On 15 July Virginia dined with the Morrells; on 16th July Angus came upstairs to tea; on the 17th Virginia, accompanied by Edward Sackville-West, joined a river party and dined at Formosa Place, Cookham, their host being George Young, the brother of Hilton Young; on the following day she saw Gwen Raverat and on the day after that, the 19th, she and Leonard lunched out with Morgan Forster and had Clive to dinner; after dinner Adrian came in to see them and he was followed by Ottoline, Julian and Philip Morrell. On the 21st Jack St John Hutchinson and Frances Marshall came to dinner; Francis Birrell and C. H. B. Kitchin, the novelist, joined them afterwards. On the 22nd Ann Wilkins from New York came on business; Edith Sitwell also came; on the 23rd Stella Benson and Angus Davidson came to tea; on the 24th the Harcourts–I do not know which Harcourts–came to tea and the Woolfs and Harold Nicolson dined with Raymond Mortimer. During the last week in July Leonard was suffering from sciatica and this put an end to their social engagements. Nevertheless this did not save them from some uninvited visitors, viz.: Roger Fry, Mary Hutchinson, Gwen Raverat, Geoffrey Keynes, Julian and Quentin Bell.

The work of the Press continued. Business, Virginia noted, had been brisk. She still worked as a compositor and a packer, and for her Maynard Keynes's pamphlet *The Economic Consequences of Mr Churchill*★ meant long hours in the basement with Leonard and the other workers in the Press,† answering the telephone, doing up parcels and attempting to meet the demand for the 10,000 copies printed. (Maynard Keynes, it may be noted, was married at St Pancras Registry Office on the 4th July that summer.) It is hardly surprising that, as she later observed, she was "riding on a flat tyre."

There was bound to be a reckoning. It came at Charleston on 19 August, when in those years there was always a birthday party. This anniversary fell so fortunately–all the family being there, the grouse being just high enough for eating, the weather usually propitious–that it was for some years celebrated with considerable brio. Brio, or at least noise–noise induced by good food and drink, by Clive's social volubility, by Virginia's sallies–describes the tone of the evening, until the clamour in that hot candle-lit room was suddenly stilled by Virginia, who rose, staggered, turned exactly the colour of a duck's egg and tried blindly and inefficiently to make her way out of the room. At that juncture, when most of the company sat in stupid amazement, two persons acted promptly: Leonard and Vanessa moved swiftly and decisively, with the efficiency of long training, to do what was necessary–to take Virginia away from the room to fresh air, to a bed, and to administer whatever medicines experience had shown to be useful.

This sudden collapse marked the beginning of a long bout of ill-health, with headaches and exhaustion, partial recoveries and new relapses, which lasted on and off through the rest of the year and was not finally overcome until the spring of 1926. Virginia realised that she had been overdoing it, that her life in London brought with it dangers which she could ignore only at her peril, and she resolved that she would in future see rather less of society and, when she did see it, take less trouble over it. This resolve was not altogether kept, but neither was it altogether broken. In subsequent years she was rather more careful about her social commitments.

The process of recovery was enlivened, but no doubt in some ways made more difficult, by the realisation that she had no lack of material for *To the Lighthouse*. The idea of it had come suddenly two

---

★ *The Economic Consequences of Mr Churchill*, a pamphlet dealing with the return by Britain to the Gold Standard and its probable consequences.

† These were: Angus Davidson, who came to the Press in December 1924 and stayed until the end of 1927; Bernadette Murphy, who arrived about the same time as Angus and was replaced the following July by Mrs Cartwright, who was to remain until 1930.

years earlier at Tavistock Square and it was now in a manner of speaking only waiting to be written. All that she needed was to be well enough to commit it to paper.

But that autumn, despite a promising start, she could do very little work; she remained idle and frustrated, first at Monk's House and then at Tavistock Square, leading what she called an "amphibious" life, half in, half out of bed; and when she could write something it was an essay *On Being Ill*. In addition she suffered from various vexations; one of these was connected with T. S. Eliot, another with Mrs Harold Nicolson.

In the autumn of 1925 T. S. Eliot, as Virginia put it, deserted the Hogarth Press. It was a rather unfair description of his conduct. What Eliot had done was to accept an editorship from the publisher who was reviving *The Criterion*. This gave him the financial security which Virginia had always wished him to have (and indeed the disposition of the Eliot Fellowship Fund became a matter of some difficulty), but, as a natural consequence, he was published by his new employer; and as a further consequence, he competed with *The Nation* for contributors. This, to Virginia, seemed conduct becoming only to the Underworld and it was some months before he was completely forgiven.

Mrs Harold Nicolson, who wrote under and indeed preferred to use the name of V. Sackville-West, was, in Virginia's words, "doomed to go to Persia." This, in more prosaic terms, meant that she was going, for a time, to join her husband in Teheran where he was Counsellor at the British Embassy. Of her, who must for convenience' sake be referred to as Vita, something has to be said, for at this time and for some years to come she was the most important person–apart from Leonard and Vanessa–in Virginia's life.

Vita would seem to have been invented for Virginia's pleasure. In her Virginia found a person of high lineage, but also one in whom there was something better–or at least more romantic than the blood of plain territorial magnates–a certain literary heritage; the child of an historic house, but also a house where the art of letters had been worthily cultivated–a Kentish *Academe*–and to crown it all, an exotic strain, the blood of disreputable Spanish gypsies, showing itself in the finest dark eyes imaginable, or perhaps in a certain grace of bearing, which might be called aristocratic but might equally well come from the streets of some Andalusian town.

Vita was certainly a very beautiful woman, in a lazy, majestic, rather melancholy way, charming with a charm which was largely unconscious—and the more lovable for that, intelligent and yet at the same time in an odd way stupid, blundering through life rather, with excellent intentions but without the acuteness, the humour, the malice, of Virginia. Add to these qualities the fact that she had a great admiration for the novels of Virginia Woolf and that she was herself a writer and she appears irresistible.

And yet for a time Virginia did resist her. Their first encounter, as we have seen, was at Clive's table, for Clive, despite the fact that she had no eyes for him, could not but admire Vita's rank, her beauty and her amiability of temper. He was quick to see her merits and to report to Virginia that Mrs Nicolson admired her, despite which, when she met "the lovely gifted aristocratic Sackville-West" she found her "Not much to my severer taste—florid, moustached, parakeet coloured, with all the supple ease of the aristocracy, but not the wit of the artist. She writes 15 pages a day—has finished another book—publishes with Heinemann's—knows everyone. But could I ever know her?"

I fancy that Virginia was a little frightened. No doubt she knew that Vita was a frank and unequivocal Sapphist. She probably became aware of Vita's feelings and perhaps acquired an inkling of her own at that first encounter; she felt shy, almost virginal, in Vita's company, and she was, I suspect, roused to a sense of danger. Since her marriage, no-one save Katherine Mansfield had touched her heart at all, and Katherine but slightly. She was still in love with Leonard. But suppose now, in middle age, someone else were to claim a place in her affections, might it not lead to something terrifying, something disastrous? Under the circumstances it was necessary that she should be indifferent, cold, hostile even, to Vita's charms.

Nevertheless, she was ready to see her again and although the friendship did not develop very fast, the Woolfs met the Nicolsons (mark those plurals) four times in the early months of 1923 and more frequently during 1924. In September 1925 Virginia writes to Vanessa of "our (Clive and my) Vita." By this time the friendship was well-established and Virginia, turning back to her diary entry for 15 December 1922, would, I think, have been slightly shocked and very much astonished.

The word 'friendship' has a coy look on this page and I would use the word 'affair' if I were perfectly certain of not being misunderstood. But, in fact, I myself know too little. What should or does one imply if one quite baldly says: "Virginia Woolf and Vita Sackville-West had a love affair between, shall we say, 1925 and

1929"? Vita was very much in love with Virginia* and being, I suspect, of an ardent temperament, loved her much as a man might have loved her, with a masculine impatience for some kind of physical satisfaction–even though Virginia was now in her forties and, although extremely beautiful, without the charm of her youth, and even though Vita herself was a little in awe of her. But the little evidence that we have suggests that Vita found Virginia unkind. Speaking of the seals of the General Post Office, Vita remarked in a letter to Virginia that they "are inviolable (like Virginia)." Again she accused her–this was in 1924, early in their relationship–of regarding their affections as literary material. "Look on it, if you like, as copy–as I believe you do on everything, human relationships included. Oh yes, you like people better through the brain than through the heart." The accusation was indignantly rejected but was not I think without truth. But not the whole truth–things are never so simple. Virginia felt as a lover feels–she desponded when she fancied herself neglected, despaired when Vita was away, waited anxiously for letters, needed Vita's company and lived in that strange mixture of elation and despair which lovers–and one would have supposed only lovers–can experience. All this she had done and felt for Katherine, but she never refers to Katherine, never writes of her as she does of Vita.

Vita for three days at Long Barn, from which L. and I returned yesterday. These Sapphists *love* women; friendship is never untinged with amorosity. In short, my fears and refrainings, my 'impertinence', my usual self-consciousness in intercourse with people who mayn't want me and so on–were all, as L. said, sheer fudge; and partly thanks to him (he made me write) I wound up this wounded and stricken year in great style. I like her and being with her and the splendour–she shines in the grocer's shop in Sevenoaks with a candle lit radiance, stalking on legs like beech trees, pink glowing, grape clustered, pearl

* Two undated letters from V. Sackville-West to Clive Bell give a notion of her sentiments:

"Virginia is just gone. She came back here with me–more entrancing than ever. Isn't it odd, dear Clive, how often our tastes (yours & mine) seem to coincide? But that is because we both have very good taste, or so I like to think."

And again:

"I saw Virginia today; incredibly lovely and fragile on two chairs under a gold cloak; with a weak voice and tapering hands; saying that she "felt stupid" and then giving vent to earthquaking remarks; but recovering, I think,–only *such* a liar about her own health that one doesn't know what to believe; but Leonard (a saner & more truthful barometer) seemed optimistic. My devotion increased; Virginia brilliant, one is inured to; but Virginia defeated is newly & surprisingly endearing. Dear Clive, I would go to the ends of the earth for your sister-in-law."

hung. That is the secret of the glamour, I suppose. Anyhow she found me incredibly dowdy. No woman cared less for personal appearance. No one put on things in the way I did. Yet so beautiful, etc. What is the effect of all this on me? Very mixed. There is her maturity and full breastedness; her being so much in full sail on the high tides, where I am coasting down backwaters; her capacity I mean to take the floor in any company, to represent her country, to visit Chatsworth, to control silver, servants, chow dogs; her motherhood (but she is a little cold and off-hand with her boys) her being in short (what I have never been) a real woman. Then there is some voluptuousness about her; the grapes are ripe; and not reflective. No. In brain and insight she is not as highly organised as I am. But then she is aware of this and so lavishes on me the maternal protection which, for some reason, is what I have always most wished from everyone. What L. gives me, and Nessa gives me and Vita, in her more clumsy external way, tries to give me. For of course, mingled with all this glamour, grape clusters and pearl necklaces, there is something loose fitting. How much, for example, shall I really miss her when she is motoring across the desert? I will make a note on that next year. Anyhow, I am very glad that she is coming to tea today and I shall ask her whether she minds my dressing so badly? I think she does. I read her poem; which is more compact, better seen and felt than anything yet of hers.

And to Vanessa, who wouldn't see Vita's perfections, she wrote:

Vita is now arriving to spend 2 nights alone with me & L. is going back. I say no more; as you are bored by Vita, bored by love, bored by me, & everything to do with me, except Quentin and Angelica; but such has long been my fate, & it is better to meet it open-eyed. Still, the June nights are long and warm; the roses flowering; and the garden full of lust and bees, mingling on the asparagus beds.

All of which might be a form of bravado and sisterly one-upman-ship. Finally, considering the case for – what is it, the prosecution? – take the evidence of Vita's monument, *Orlando*, of all Virginia's novels the one that comes nearest to sexual, or rather to homosexual, feeling; for, while the hero/heroine undergoes a bodily transforma-tion, being at first a splendid youth and then a beautiful lady, the psychological metamorphosis is far less complete. From the first the youth is a little uncertain of his sex; when he puts on petticoats he becomes, not simply a woman, but a man who enjoys being a woman. Orlando is also Virginia's most idealised creation; he/she is modelled near to the heart's desire (and not only to the heart) – near, in fact, to the glamorous creations of the novelette. Compare Virginia's treatment of him/her to the cool ironies of *Mrs Dalloway* or to the floral metamorphosis of Jinny in *The Waves*–a bouquet on a gilded chair–or the discreet glimpses of Jacob's loves.

There may have been–on balance I think that there probably was –some caressing, some bedding together. But whatever may have occurred between them of this nature, I doubt very much whether it was of a kind to excite Virginia or to satisfy Vita. As far as Virginia's life is concerned the point is of no great importance; what was, to her, important was the extent to which she was emotionally involved, the degree to which she was in love. One cannot give a straight answer to such questions but, if the test of passion be blindness, then her affections were not very deeply engaged.

Virginia certainly had her illusions about Vita; she could credit her with an almost impossible degree of charm and distinction, she could believe in her as a Kentish nymph, a blue-blooded dryad, an aristocratic goddess–but not as an author. She writes, says Virginia, "with complete competency, and a pen of brass." Usually Virginia was not unkind about Vita's writing, she found what she could to admire in the novels and the poetry, but she never extends her indulgence to the limits of what her conscience would allow, as she was always ready to do for Leonard. The reason, I think, is clear. She admired Leonard in a way that she could never admire Vita; she was not insensible to physical perfections and moral qualities but she could not really love without feeling that she was in the presence of a superior intellect.

And Vita comes to lunch tomorrow, which will be a great amusement and pleasure. I am amused at my relations with her: left so ardent in January–and now what? Also I like her presence and her beauty. Am I in love with her? But what is love? Her being 'in love' (it must be comma'd thus) with me, excites and flatters and interests. What is this 'love'? Oh and then she gratifies my eternal curiosity; who's she seen, what's she done–for I have no enormous opinion of her poetry.

It was, she felt, all rather a bore for Leonard–but not enough to worry him. Harold wrote to her to say how glad he was that Vita should have such a friend. The husbands took it all with admirable calm. It is perhaps significant that whereas neither Vanessa nor any other of Virginia's friends, except Clive, was really devoted to Vita, the closest, the nearest to devotion, was in fact Leonard.

How then, when all is said and done, shall we describe their relationship? I think we may call it an affair of the heart, but so far as Virginia was concerned that was where it began and that was where it ended. Nevertheless, when she returned from Sussex to London in the autumn of 1925, cured as she imagined but at once to be sent to bed by her doctor and not allowed to make her first sortie (to the Ballet) until 27 November, and learned that her friend was "doomed to go to Persia," she concluded that she was genuinely fond of Vita and minded her going very much indeed.

The Woolfs spent Christmas that year with the Bells at Charleston. Vita drove over from Long Barn to lunch on Boxing Day. "How beautiful she is," said Clive to Virginia after the guest had gone. "An aristocrat of ancient race," said Virginia to Clive. Leonard turned to Julian. "What snobs they are," he said.

This remark unleashed, as it was intended to unleash, furious expostulations and an argument which lasted the rest of the evening.

The early months of 1926 brought an improvement in Virginia's health. "Never," she reports, "never have I written so easily, imagined so profusely." *To the Lighthouse* seemed to be composed without effort; by 16 March she had written 40,000 words.

She was able to become more sociable and even to explore new territory, for, despite her excursions into Mayfair, Virginia believed that she was too much in Bloomsbury and that it would be good for her to measure herself against the standards of another milieu. These, in the Spring of 1926, were provided by Miss Rose Macaulay, a novelist and a person sufficiently close to and yet sufficiently distant from Virginia to be at once a welcome—in some lights a superior—friend and an effective assessor. It was therefore in a spirit, as one may suppose, not only of friendship but of enquiry that Virginia accepted an invitation to dine with Rose Macaulay at a restaurant on the evening of Wednesday 24 March.

It was a disastrous evening.

The Woolfs were very late. They had been machining and they hurried from Tavistock Square without changing the clothes or removing all the printer's ink that they had on. Virginia had assumed that they would dine at what she called a 'pothouse'; but this was no Bloomsbury dinner. Miss Macaulay received her guests in a very superior establishment. There were a dozen guests, all ladies and gentlemen of letters, all in pearls and white waistcoats; there was a platoon of waiters to serve them.

Leonard and Virginia were utterly unprepared for such a party; it was not the kind of party that they themselves would ever have given; they were conscious of being late, of having kept everyone waiting, of making a very bad impression. When Leonard was unnerved, the habitual trembling of his hands became wild and ungovernable. He now made conversation impossible by beating violently upon his soup plate, his spoon behaving as though it were a drum stick. It was not until he had drunk, or to speak more accurately, had distributed his soup (for but little can have reached his mouth) that the talk became audible. In Virginia's opinion it was none the better for that; it was what she called the "pitterpatter" of "baldnecked chickens." Who was to get what literary prize? Was Gerhardi as good as Tchekhov? Might *Shining Domes* by Mildred Peake be voted the best novel of 1926? To her it all seemed a whirl of meaningless jargon; presently her neighbour, Mr O'Riordan, made a remark about the Holy Ghost.

"Where is the Holy Ghost?" asked Virginia with sudden interest. The table fell silent.

"Wherever the sea is," replied Mr O'Riordan.

Am I mad? she wondered, or is this wit? and could only repeat: "The Holy Ghost?"

"THE WHOLE COAST!!" shouted Mr O'Riordan.

It was all very awkward and everyone felt that Virginia had disgraced herself. But Leonard was to have his turn too. Observing his neighbour's napkin upon the floor, he bent gallantly and picked it up only to discover that he was lifting her petticoat. The gesture, it seems, was misunderstood and the Woolfs crept home as soon as they decently could.

Virginia had said after a previous meeting with Rose Macaulay that it showed her own position "a good deal lowered and diminished," and this, she continued "is a part of the value of seeing new people." On this occasion she certainly got full measure; but I do not think that she was anxious to repeat the experience.

That same day had brought a more comfortable event and one more likely to have lasting consequences. For some time Virginia and her friends had felt that Leonard was wasting his talents as Literary Editor of *The Nation*. He ought, they felt, to be writing his own books instead of being tied down to this game of pursuing or putting off contributors—a dreary life with few rewards and few holidays. Then, on the morning of the Rose Macaulay party, Leonard, to whom Virginia had as yet said nothing, remarked as he made the coffee for breakfast: "I am going to hand in my resignation this morning."

"To what?"

"*The Nation*."

So that was that.

In April, Virginia finished the first part of *To the Lighthouse* and attacked Part II (Time Passes); she found it difficult but she was in good spirits and progressed. Nelly had given notice for, shall we say, the fiftieth time. This time it was to be final: it was no good going on, the work was too much for her, too many people came to the house. Virginia was desolate, but she was firm; she accepted it, and began seriously looking for someone else. Then on 27 April Nelly stopped her on the landing with a request: "Please, Ma'am, may I apologise. I am too fond of you ever to be happy with anyone else," which Virginia thought the greatest compliment she could receive. But, of course, it meant a return to the old emotional switchback, with this difference, that she would not, she swore, ever believe poor Nelly again when she threatened to leave. Nelly for her part had also probably come to the conclusion that she would never believe Virginia again when she threatened dismissal.

I saw this morning 5 or 6 armoured cars slowly going along Oxford Street; on each two soldiers sat in tin helmets, and one stood with his hand at the gun which was pointed straight ahead ready to fire. But I also noticed on one a policeman smoking a cigarette. Such sights I daresay I shall never see again; and don't in the least wish to.

But I think that, in a way, she was glad to have seen them. It was curious, strange, and perhaps historic, perhaps it was the beginning of the British Revolution; in fact it was the end of the General Strike. But in the anxious weeks that preceded the strike there were some of her friends who thought there would be civil war. 52 Tavistock Square became a centre of unusual activity, petitions were drawn up and cyclostyled, people came and went on bicycles carrying messages; Mr Pritchard, their tenant, genially declared that he was being trained to shoot Leonard. Friends came to listen to the Woolfs' wireless set, the only source of news apart from rumours.

Virginia discovered that she differed from Leonard; she thought him a tub-thumper, he thought her an irrational christian; she wanted peace, he wanted victory. She was glad when the strike collapsed but saddened by the fate of the miners who were left to struggle alone, and by what she considered the vindictive spirit of the employers.

Time Passes, the second part of *To the Lighthouse*, was finished on 25 May. She hoped to have the whole book done by the end of July. But once again she over-estimated her strength. Vita returned from Persia as the strike ended and with her, other social claims. There was a week-end at Garsington, when Virginia met Robert Bridges, and a meeting with H. G. Wells. She must have met him before this—Leonard knew him well—but this was a prolonged and clearly an interesting encounter. They did not like each other's books and Virginia had made her views clear in public, but they got on well enough. She thought him an odd mixture of bubble and solidity. He gossiped about Hardy and Henry James and outlined his plans for a ten-day week, unaware perhaps that Max Beerbohm had already put this notion into his mouth. From these encounters Virginia went to one which meant much more to her, with Thomas Hardy. I think she respected Hardy more than she respected any other living writer, and clearly she was delighted when she heard that he approved of *The Common Reader*. The meeting was a success, although, as so often happens when one meets the great, she was unable to frame the kind of question or elicit the kind of reply that she would have liked.

London in the summer of 1926 offered its usual attractions but Virginia, remembering her experience of the previous year did manage to exercise some self-restraint, and was at all events less exhausted by this summer than she had been by its predecessor. Even so she had "a whole nervous breakdown in miniature" at Monk's House at the end of July. The delights of the summer (it was a beautiful August), and even of new possessions, were in some degree spoilt by nervous irritability. It was, to be sure, very pleasing that *Mrs Dalloway* and *The Common Reader* had earned them lavatories and running hot water;* hitherto they had had an earth-closet and when Leonard and Virginia bathed they did so in a tin hip-bath on the kitchen floor. But Leonard planned to spend a part of their new wealth on his own kingdom, the garden, while Virginia wanted it to be devoted to more domestic comforts; and there was friction. Altogether it was a rather anxious and difficult time. She was trying to finish *To the Lighthouse*, and the end of a novel always gave her great trouble. In September she had moments of deep depression in which she described herself in her diary as an "elderly dowdy fussy ugly incompetent woman; vain, chattering and futile" and then she had her vision of a fin rising on a wide blank sea, and she woke in the early mornings with feelings of complete and utter despair.

Despite these vexations, *To the Lighthouse* made good progress. She wrote with heat and ease every morning. She did her two pages,

---

* "We are having two water closets made, one paid for by Mrs. Dalloway the other by the Common Reader: both dedicated to you." VW/VSW, 17 February 1926.

It has frequently been said that the MSS of Virginia's novels were put to a base use in the lavatories of Monk's House. My own recollection is that galley proofs were provided and these would, for a variety of reasons, have been more suitable.

and although her hope of finishing by the end of September was over-sanguine, she had reached the stage of rewriting in November and was planning another critical work on literature–a successor to *The Common Reader*. Finally, early in 1927, *To the Lighthouse* was ready for Leonard's approval and the proofs were read by March of that year.

1927 saw an evolution in the lives of people who were close to Virginia, which should be mentioned. Early in the year Duncan had gone to Cassis, where his mother and his aunt were staying, and there had fallen ill. His temperature soared alarmingly; Vanessa was told that he almost certainly had typhoid. It seemed a repetition of old horrors. She turned naturally to Virginia and Leonard; with their assistance she packed, settled outstanding affairs in London and transported Angelica, her servant and herself to Cassis within forty-eight hours of receiving the news. She arrived to find that Duncan had made a substantial recovery; it was not typhoid, but he was very weak. Vanessa established herself at Cassis, discovering what madness it was to remain in England during the winter months and how admirable a place Cassis was for a painter. Presently Clive announced his intention of joining them. On 28 January 1927 he had written to Vanessa to say that he was at last going to write that book about civilisation which had for so long been planned as a part of his magnum opus *The New Renaissance* and, furthermore, that he was very unhappy. He felt that he could not be comfortable unless he joined Vanessa and Duncan at Cassis. The reason for his unhappiness was that his long affair with Mary Hutchinson was coming to an end. The circumstances of that schism do not concern us apart from the fact that the break was not easily made (it caused great unhappiness to both parties), and that in the month of February there were still doubts and reservations on both sides.

Clive had always maintained that there was no-one more untrustworthy than Virginia and no more perfect model of indiscretion. It is therefore interesting that at this juncture, in many ways the most serious crisis of his life, he turned to Virginia for sympathy and advice. Almost at the same time Mary Hutchinson, divining perhaps that this would be the case and knowing that, in a way, Virginia was still one of the most important persons in Clive's life, telephoned her to ask her to soothe Clive–who was by now in a great state, talking wildly at parties and saying that he was miserable. Thus Virginia became, in some sort, the confidante of both.

"You'll get into trouble with the principals, one always does," wrote Vanessa. She was perfectly right. Virginia was already in trouble. What happened is not perfectly clear. It seems that she had a long interview with Clive. He came to tea; he described the situation and he asked her for her advice. Should he leave Mary and leave London, should he go to Cassis and write his book? Virginia thought he should. She did not like what she supposed to be Mary's influence upon Clive; she did not think the social whirl, the smart suppers and smart week-ends which she imagined to be Mary's natural milieu, were at all good for him.

Virginia I think had invented a character for Mary Hutchinson–a worldly glittering character which was far removed from the truth. As Mary herself put it, Virginia saw her as "a mere popinjay of fashion," a judgement which she found heart-breaking in its injustice. From her diaries and her letters it is clear that, at times, Virginia saw that this was unjust and was struck by the high moral qualities and serious character of Clive's friend; but the imaginary picture that she had drawn was equally real to her and it was on this that she relied at the present juncture. To Mary it must have appeared that, having applied to Virginia for help, she now found her maliciously and consciously plotting against her. There were some acrimonious exchanges culminating in an interview. The full dramatic impact of this encounter was muffled by the unexpected arrival of Vita's cousin Edward Sackville-West, a new friend of Virginia's, and so, while the two ladies glared at each other, for they were both angry, there was tea and a polite conversation about books until at length Mr Sackville-West departed. The discussion which then ensued began on a high note; but it ended in a renewal of friendship and confidences. Mary Hutchinson rebutted the charge that it was her mundanity which had lead Clive astray; Virginia was touched and convinced by her evident sincerity and they parted friends.

The rest of the affair does not concern us save that Clive, after a period of indecision, did go to Cassis, where Virginia was to meet him later in the year. In February the Woolfs had considered going to America to lecture and gave it up when they found that their expenses, which would not be covered, would leave practically nothing out of the lecture fees. They then thought of Greece and finally compromised on Sicily, stopping at Cassis on the way. The details of the tour may be omitted. We should however notice that the sea passage from Naples to Palermo was made memorable by the company, in Virginia's cabin, of a Swedish lady who complained that there was no lock to the door. "Madam," observed Virginia, "we have neither of us any cause for fear," which, happily, she took in good part. It was on this holiday that Virginia began to smoke cheroots. Rumour says that she smoked a pipe. I have found no evidence of this.

"I don't think I've ever enjoyed one month so much," she told her diary, and she said as much to Vanessa in a series of enthusiastic letters describing her travels. Vanessa read the letters aloud, which indeed she usually did with Virginia's letters, and Clive, then staying at Cassis and not making much headway with *Civilisation*, carried certain details with him back to Paris where, so Virginia believed, her enthusiasm was made fun of. She was cross enough to say that she would write no more letters to her sister. Luckily she did not persist in this resolve, and presently there was an epistolary exchange which was to be of some importance.

On 3 May Vanessa wrote from Cassis:

It is a work of absolute heroism to write to you. All my writing paper has been taken by Angelica to write a poem beginning The Robin hops on the window sill. Then having rescued one sheet I sit with moths flying madly in circles round me & the lamp. You cannot imagine what its like. One night some creature tapped so loudly on the pane that Duncan said "Who is that?" "Only a bat" said Roger "or a bird", but it wasn't man or bird, but a huge moth—half a foot, literally, across. We had a terrible time with it. My maternal instinct which you deplore so much, wouldn't let me leave it. [Vanessa's children were as enthusiastic in collecting butterflies and moths as their parents and relations had been before them.] We let it in, kept it, gave it a whole bottle of ether bought from the chemist, all in vain, took it to the chemist who dosed it with chloroform for a day—also in vain. Finally it did die rather the worse for wear, & I set it, & now, here is another! a better specimen. But though incredibly beautiful I suspect they're common—perhaps Emperor moths. Still I know how one would have blamed one's elders for not capturing such things at all costs so I suppose I must go through it all again. Then I remembered—didn't Fabre try experiments with this same creature & attract all the males in the neighbourhood by shutting up one female in a room?—just what we have now done. So probably soon the house will be full of them.

However, you'll only tell me its what comes of allowing instinct to play a part in personal relationships. What a lot I could say about the maternal instinct, but then also what a lot about Michael Angelo & Raphael. I wish you would write a book about the maternal instinct.

Virginia's reply ended thus:

By the way, your story of the Moth so fascinates me that I am going to write a story about it. I could think of nothing else but you & the moths for hours after reading your letter. Isn't it odd?—perhaps you stimulate the literary sense in me as you say I do your painting sense. God! how you'll laugh at the painting bits in the Lighthouse!

To the Lighthouse had, in fact, been published on 5 May. Vita, returning from Persia, found a copy awaiting her. Virginia had promised she would have a new book ready for her. It was inscribed: *Vita from Virginia* (*In my opinion the best novel I have ever written*). Vita was a little surprised at such shameless immodesty, but that night when she opened the book to read it in bed, she found that the inscribed copy was a dummy. Two copies had gone to Cassis – one for Vanessa and one for Duncan. And now, so far from wishing to break off the correspondence with her sister, Virginia became more and more anxious for a letter. By 15 May, unable to bear the suspense any longer, she wrote:

Dearest, no letter from you – But I see how it is – scene: after dinner: Nessa sewing: Duncan doing absolutely nothing.

Nessa (throwing down her work) Christ! There's the Lighthouse! I've only got to page 26 & I see there are 320. Now I cant write to Virginia because she'll expect me to tell her what I think of it.

Duncan Well, I should just tell her that you think it a masterpiece.

Nessa But she's sure to find out. They always do. She'll want to know why I think its a masterpiece.

Duncan Well Nessa, I'm afraid I cant help you, because I've only read 5 pages so far, & really I dont see much prospect of doing much reading this month, or next month, or indeed before Christmas.

Nessa Oh its all very well for you. But I shall have to say something: And I dont know who in the name of Jupiter all these people are (turns over some pages desperately). I think I shall make a timetable: its the only way: ten pages a day for 20 days is . . .

Duncan But you'll never be able to keep up ten pages a day.

Nessa (rather dashed) No. I suppose I shant. Well then, we may as well be hung for a sheep as for a goat – though whats the sense of saying that I never could see: a sheep is almost identical with a goat in some countries; except that one can milk a goat of course. Lord! I shall never forget Violet Dickinson at Athens & the Goat's milk But what was I saying when you interrupted me? Oh yes: I shall take the bull by the horns. I shall write to Virginia & say "I think its a masterpiece –"(she takes the inkpot & prepares to write, but finds it full of dead & dying insects). Oh Duncan, what have you done with the inkpot? Used it to catch flies in? But thats a beetle! Yes it is. Beetles have 12 legs: flies only 8. D'you mean to say you didnt know that? Well, I suppose you're one of those people who think a spider's an insect: Now if you'd been brought up in Cornwall you'd know that a spider's not an insect; its – No I dont think its a reptile: its something queer I know. Anyhow, I cant write to Virginia, because the ink is nothing but a mass of beetle or spider legs–I really dont know what they are: but one man's meat is another man's poison; & if you will use the inkpot to catch flies in, then I dont see how even Virginia herself could possibly expect, or even wish me to write to her–(they settle down again to discuss spiders etc.) etc. etc. etc.

Vanessa had in fact already written:

I think I am more incapable than anyone else in the world of making an aesthetic judgement on it–only I know that I have somewhere a feeling about it as a work of art which will perhaps gradually take shape & which must be enormously strong to make any impression on me at all beside the other feelings which you roused in me–I suppose I'm the only person in the world who can have those feelings, at any rate to such an extent–So though probably they don't matter to you at all you may be interested to know how much you did make me feel. Besides I daresay they do show something about aesthetic merits in your curious art of writing. Anyhow it seemed to me in the first part of the book you have given a portrait of mother which is more like her to me than anything I could ever have conceived of as possible. It is almost painful to have her so raised from the dead. You have made one feel the extraordinary beauty of her character, which must be the most difficult thing in the world to do. It was like meeting her again with oneself grown up & on equal terms & it seems to me the most astonishing feat of creation to have been able to see her in such a way–You have given father too I think as clearly, but perhaps, I may be wrong, that isnt quite so difficult. There is more to catch hold of. Still it seems to me to be the only thing about him which ever gave a true idea. So you see as far as portrait painting goes you seem to me to be a supreme artist & it is so shattering to find oneself face to face with those two again that I can hardly consider anything else. In fact for the last two days I have hardly been able to attend to daily life. Duncan & I have talked about them, as each had a copy, whenever we could get alone together, Roger too furious at being out of it for us to be able to do so when he was there.

Roger, however, was able to write six days later:

You won't want or expect criticisms from me–I'm not du métier. How little, I realized when I tried to imagine how I should describe the problems of a writer à la Lily Briscoe (in which by the by Vanessa and I both think you come through unscathed and triumphant though a little breathless and anxious perhaps). I know I should make a great mess of that.

So you won't get a criticism–only you can't help my thinking it the best thing you've done, actually better than Mrs. Dalloway. You're no longer bothered by the simultaneity of things and go backwards and forwards in time with an extraordinary enrichment of each moment of consciousness.

I'm sure that there's lots I haven't understood and that when I talk it over with Morgan he'll have discovered a lot of hidden meanings. I suspect for instance that arriving at the Lighthouse has a symbolic meaning which escapes me. But I wonder if it matters.

And to this Virginia replied regretting that she had not dedicated *To the Lighthouse* to Roger and acknowledging a debt of gratitude for his aesthetic guidance; he had kept her, she felt, on the right path. She continues:

I meant *nothing* by *The Lighthouse*. One has to have a central line down the middle of the book to hold the design together. I saw that all sorts of feelings would accrue to this, but I refused to think them out, & trusted that people would make it the deposit for their own emotions—which they have done, one thinking it means one thing another another. I can't manage Symbolism except in this vague, generalised way. Whether its right or wrong I don't know; but directly I'm told what a thing means, it becomes hateful to me.

Clive, back in London, wrote to Vanessa in May that the town seemed particularly dull and sad. "Only Virginia is sublimely happy, as well she may be—her book is a masterpiece." The view was pretty generally held by the critics, and a great many people wrote enthusiastically, although one complained that her descriptions of the fauna and flora of the Hebrides were totally inaccurate. The book sold better than its predecessors—3,873 copies (two of which were purchased by the Seafarers' Educational Society) in the first year.

That summer Virginia acquired a motor-car and a lover. The motor-car was an important addition to her life. The lover was Philip Morrell. Amiable and amorous, still handsome and with an honourable career behind him, he was nevertheless somehow ridiculous (or at least Virginia found him so). He pursued her briefly and cumbrously with unexpected visits and tentative love-letters; she eluded him without much difficulty. Neither Vita nor Leonard can have felt a moment's uneasiness on account of Philip.

The motor-car was considered a great luxury. Leonard at once became a skilful and knowledgeable driver; Virginia also took driving lessons and, as she considered, made good progress. But after taking their Singer through a hedge she decided (although no substantial damage was done) to let herself be driven. This indeed she found most enjoyable. The whole Sussex countryside, with its castles, seashores and great houses, suddenly became accessible; so too of course was Charleston and the Keynes's new home at Tilton. The social possibilities of the automobile were such that Vanessa, much to Virginia's amusement, placed a large notice on the gate leading to Charleston drive, bearing the word OUT.

Another important addition to Virginia's life was the gramophone. I do not think that the Woolfs had one until Leonard, who reviewed records for *The Nation*, purchased an expensive model. Virginia, who had a fairly catholic taste, developed a particular interest in Beethoven's late quartets, and they assisted those meditations which resulted finally in *The Waves*.

The pleasures of driving were country pleasures, the gramophone belonged also to the town and must have formed an ingredient of what was on the whole to be one of Virginia's happiest autumns. Not that, when the Woolfs returned to Tavistock Square at the end of September, they were particularly happy. They were troubled by that perennial problem, the young man in the Hogarth Press. Since the end of 1924 the young man had been Angus Davidson. He was one of the most amiable characters whom you could hope to meet. Unfortunately it was not amiability that Leonard was looking for. Already in 1926 Virginia was writing to Vanessa to say that the Press was going to make a loss that year and could not she, Vanessa, talk to Angus: he really ought to be more energetic. Vanessa did no doubt carry Virginia's message to Angus, who was taking his holiday with her and Duncan in Venice. But no amount of talking was going to remedy a situation in which Leonard and Angus continually got on each other's nerves.

One morning early in October 1927, Virginia left her studio at the back of No. 52 Tavistock Square, walked through into the offices of the Press, found Leonard and Angus together there and asked them the time.

She saw at once that she had made an unfortunate, or perhaps too apposite, a remark. Mrs Cartwright, the secretary, lowered her head over her typing and laughed. Virginia realised that she had come at the tail end of some terrific quarrel. She had in fact interrupted an argument which Leonard had begun by telling Angus that he was late for work. Angus denied the charge. Leonard persisted and produced his watch. Angus replied that his own watch was the better time-keeper. Leonard denied this; Angus refused to be outfaced. Leonard was sure of his facts; Angus doubted them. And so, the thing going on in this fashion – ding-dong, hammer and tongs, no one able to prove his point and time passing all the while unnoticed – they had got to the point at which there was nothing for it but to sally out and consult I know not what public monument–Euston Station, it may be–when Virginia, as though cued by a comic dramatist, put her head through the door and asked the time of day. They were both too vexed for laughter but it ended the dispute.

A few months later Angus and Leonard agreed, very wisely, that it would be best to part and, in November, the Woolfs wondered whether it might not be best to make an end of the Hogarth Press itself.

It was also at the beginning of October that Virginia's mind, which had for some time been simmering, suddenly boiled over. She had been contemplating two books: on the one hand that work of literary criticism which was to make a second volume to *The Common Reader*, which she had thought she would begin at Monk's House in August and with luck have finished by January, and on the other hand an imaginative work–the book she had vaguely seen dealing with a solitary woman shaping a book of ideas about life, or a semi-mystical, very profound life of a woman–a kind of play, it might be, she thought in February 1927. Then in May Vanessa had given this conception a slightly more definite form when she wrote about the moths. Connected with this was an idea for "Lives of the Obscure", or possibly of her friends–it was a favourite theme. This in turn had hardened into something much more definite in March–*The Jessamy Brides*–a comic version of the serious novel which still lay inchoate at the back of her mind. There were to be two poor solitary women at the top of a house with a view of Constantinople. The idea was still secondary–a pastime–when suddenly it presented itself in its final form. She wrote to Vita:

> Yesterday morning I was in despair. You know that bloody book which Dadie [Rylands] and Leonard extort, drop by drop, from my breast? Fiction, or some title to that effect. I couldn't screw a word from me; and at last dropped my head in my hands; dipped my pen in the ink, and wrote these words, as if automatically on a clean sheet: Orlando: A Biography. No sooner had I done this than my body was flooded with rapture and my brain with ideas. I wrote rapidly till 12. But listen; suppose Orlando turns out to be Vita. . . .

It was Vita–as she knew very well, for she had already told her diary that it was to be

> a biography beginning in the year 1500 and continuing to the present day called *Orlando*: Vita; only with a change about from one sex to another. I think, for a treat, I shall let myself dash this in for a week. . . .

The treat became an orgy. The work on fiction was abandoned

and in a state of high exhilaration she rushed into the writing of *Orlando*.

The book is interesting biographically, partly because it commemorates Virginia's love for Vita, and partly because we can trace so many of its elements to the incidents of Virginia's daily life in those years; for whereas *To the Lighthouse* was made from the passions and tragedies of her youth, *Orlando* was composed of materials which she noted hurriedly in her diary: Vita at Knole, showing her over the building–4 acres of it–stalking through it in a Turkish dress surrounded by dogs and children; a cart bringing in wood as carts had done for centuries to feed the great fires of the house; Vita hunting through her writing desk to find a letter from Dryden; Vita sailing through the Mediterranean in January 1926, with gold-laced captains off Trieste; Vita standing gorgeous in emeralds; a description of Vita and Violet Trefusis meeting for the first time upon the ice; Vita dressing her son as a Russian boy and his objection –"Don't," he said, "it makes me look like a girl"; Vita courted and caressed by the literary world; the homage of Sir Edmund Gosse, and indeed of Virginia herself.*

Then, early in September, Maynard and Lydia Keynes gave a party at Tilton. Jack (later Sir John) Sheppard enacted the part of an Italian *prima donna*, words and music being supplied by a gramophone. Someone had brought a newspaper cutting with them; it reproduced the photograph of a pretty young woman who had become a man, and this for the rest of the evening became Virginia's main topic of conversation.

Never had she worked so fast. She threw in everything that so beautifully, as it seemed so inevitably, lay to hand. In that autumn, "that singularly happy autumn," *Orlando* shoved everything aside.

Nevertheless she did have time to write an article for the *Atlantic Monthly* on E. M. Forster. Forster was the English contemporary for

---

* Sir Nicholas Greene is certainly a Gosse-like figure. Virginia had noticed how, at a gathering in Cambridge, Vita was "fawned upon by the little dapper grocer Gosse, who kept spinning round on his heel to address her compliments and to scarify Bolshevists; in an ironical voice which seems to ward off what might be said of him; and to be drawing round the lot of them thicker and thicker the red plush curtains of respectability." (*AWD (Berg)*, 30 October 1926). Obviously Nick Greene in his earlier avatar is less closely drawn from life and, if I am right in supposing that Virginia made use of a mirror in drawing him, it was for his pose rather than for his features, and the pose might have been provided by another model. Nevertheless something of Virginia's attitude in Vita's company is recorded in *Orlando*. She did then show a slight tendency to talk about the de l'Etang family. Vita, on the other hand, was rather inclined to dwell upon the humble origins of her Spanish forbears. (Cf. *Orlando*, p. 80.)

Virginia Woolf

Above Vanessa Bell in 1914

Right Ka Cox at Asham, 1914

Opposite above Margaret Llewelyn Davies and Leonard Woolf, 1916

Opposite below Virginia walking in Cornwall, 1916

Above Duncan Grant, Maynard Keynes and
Clive Bell at Charleston, 1919

Opposite above Barbara Bagenal, 1921
Opposite below Katherine Mansfield, 1920

Left Virginia Woolf, *c.* 1925

Left V. Sackville-West, 1926

Left Lydia Lopokova, *c.* 1920

Below Lady Ottoline Morrell by
Simon Bussy

Above Carrington and Ralph Partridge with Lytton Strachey at Ham Spray, 1930

Below Roger Fry, Desmond MacCarthy and Clive Bell at Charleston, 1933

Above Angus Davidson

Right George Rylands

Above T. S. Eliot

Below E. M. Forster

Above Julian Bell, 1932

Below Leonard and Virginia at Cassis, 1928

Above   Hugh Walpole

Opposite above   Leonard Woolf at Monk's House, *c.* 1933
Opposite below   Virginia with John Lehmann, *c.* 1931

Above   Virginia with Angelica Bell, 1932

Head of Virginia Woolf by Stephen Tomlin, 1931

whom she had most respect. His view of the world was not unlike hers. They loved and detested many of the same things. And yet there was between them a considerable barrier. Morgan was established as a novelist before she had published anything, but his career in fiction had ended, though she did not realise this, just when she was really beginning to find her voice. In a sense he belonged to an older generation. He was not deeply interested in–could not entirely sympathise with–her experiments in the handling of time, her probings into the mind. *Kew Gardens* and *The Mark on the Wall* had seemed to him "lovely little things," he had seen that *Night and Day* was a blind alley, but he was astonished to find the method used in these exquisite trifles also used, and, as it seemed to him, successfully used, in *Jacob's Room*, *Mrs Dalloway* and, his favourite to date, *To the Lighthouse*. And yet she had sacrificed a great deal–she had gone away from narrative, away from life.

They were a little afraid of each other. Morgan Forster was, I think, happier with his own sex. He found Virginia's feminism disturbing and felt that there was something a little too sharp, a little too critical, about her. "I don't think," he said, "that she cared for most people. She was always very sweet to me, but I don't think she was particularly fond of me, if that is the word." He was more at ease with Leonard; it was Leonard who urged him on when he despaired of finishing *A Passage to India* and believed it to be a failure. In a way I think that Forster was almost jealous of Leonard's affection for Virginia. He felt that Leonard was under-valued by Virginia's friends and resented, as Leonard did not, her growing eminence, the growing tendency to think of him as "her husband." And yet there was affection between them. Virginia was grateful for his praise, was touched when he informed her, before anyone else, that he had at last finished *A Passage to India*, and had, when all was said and done, a great admiration for his writings.

Still, a good deal had to be said and done. In *Mr Bennett and Mrs Brown* she had hailed Forster as one of the younger Georgians who were in revolt against Wells, Galsworthy and Bennett, but felt that somehow he had compromised. He had contrived to combine his own direct sense of the oddity and significance of character with Galsworthy's knowledge of the Factory Acts and Mr Bennett's knowledge of the Five Towns.

In 1927 Virginia wrote two rather severe articles about E. M. Forster. He saw one of them–at least–before publication and raised objections which led Virginia to feel, or at least to express, astonishment that this aloof, self-possessed man could be as sensitive, more sensitive indeed than she who had such a reputation for being thin-skinned.

In the first of her articles* she discussed E. M. Forster's critical work *Aspects of the Novel*. He seemed to her to be too ready to dismiss the claims of art as opposed to those of what he called "life"; it was an attitude which permitted him to do less than justice to Henry James.

But at this point the pertinacious pupil may demand: 'What is this "Life" that keeps on cropping up so mysteriously and so complacently in books about fiction? Why is it absent in a pattern and present in a tea party? Why is the pleasure that we get from the pattern in *The Golden Bowl* less valuable than the emotion which Trollope gives us when he describes a lady drinking tea in a parsonage? Surely the definition of life is too arbitrary, and requires to be expanded.'

To this E. M. Forster replied in a letter:

Your article inspires me to the happiest repartee. This vague truth about life. Exactly. But what of the talk about art? Each section leads to an exquisitely fashioned casket of which the key has unfortunately been mislaid and until you can find your bunch I shall cease to hunt very anxiously for my own.

I find the Continentals greater than the English not because Flaubert got hung up but because Tolstoy etc. could vitalise guillotines etc. as well as tea tables, could command certain moods or deeds which our domesticity leads us to shun as false. And why do you complain that no critic in England will judge a novel as a work of art? Percy Lubbock does nothing else. Yet he does not altogether satisfy you. Why?

Virginia replied:

Dear Morgan, I'm not particularly inspired to repartee by your letter. But I reply:—You say "Each sentence leads to a . . . casket of which the key has unfortunately been mislaid, and until you can find your bunch I shall cease to hunt very anxiously for my own."

Very well–but then I'm not writing a book about fiction. If I were, I think I *should* hunt a little. As a reviewer, which is all I am, it seems to me within my province to point out that both bunches are lost.

I agree that Tolstoi "vitalises the guillotine" &c. But by means of art I think; admitting that I can't define the word.

No; Percy Lubbock doesn't "altogether satisfy" me. But then I don't agree with you that he's a critic of genius. An able and painstaking pedant I should call him; who doesn't know what art is; so,

* *Is Fiction an Art?* first published in the *New York Herald Tribune*, 16 October 1927. Reprinted (revised) as *The Art of Fiction* in *Nation and Athenaeum*, 12 November 1927; VW, *Collected Essays*, II, p. 51. *The Novels of E. M. Forster*, published in *Atlantic Monthly*, Boston, November 1927; VW, *Collected Essays*, I, p. 342.

though his method of judging novels as works of art interests me, his judgments don't.   V.

The above is official & impersonal. Unofficially & personally I'm afraid I've hurt or annoyed you (perhaps I imagine it). I didn't mean to. The article was cut down to fit the Nation, and the weight all fell in the same place. But I'm awfully sorry if I was annoying.

Forster, it seems, was able to reassure her: she was not annoying, merely wrong. Right or wrong, her next article, *The Novels of E. M. Forster*, must surely have been annoying, for, while finding much to admire in his work she also finds much to blame and indeed finds fault with his entire method.

After Virginia's death, in his Rede Lecture, Morgan Forster returns to his side of the argument. She has all the aesthete's characteristics, selects and manipulates her impressions and is not a great creator of character, enforces pattern on her books, has no great cause at heart. She stands, therefore, at the very entrance of that bottomless cavern of dullness, the Palace of Art. She keeps out, says Forster, but I would surmise that he thought her too close for comfort—for his comfort anyhow. In much the same way she, I think, took the view that although Morgan comes very close to the pulpit, where he would be a bore, and terribly close to the Groves of Eleusis, where he would have been an embarrassment, he is saved from both these fates by a hair's breadth. In other words, each admired and each found a good deal to deplore in the work of the other.

About this time Virginia found herself engaged in a controversy—but it was a controversy of a very different kind—with T. S. Eliot. In February 1928 we find that she has been talking to him for two hours about God. Unfortunately the details of this conversation are not recorded. By all rights this should have been a far more momentous discussion than that slight difference concerning the character of the novel which preceded it. For Eliot had become an Anglo-Catholic, for him the whole universe was changed—his life was but an instant's preparation for eternity, he was (potentially at all events) saved for Heaven—while Virginia and Leonard were quite certainly damned. But in fact it seemed to her that his religious views need not be treated very seriously. She used to tease him about his beliefs and, with some ribaldry, beg him to explain them; but from such assaults he would retire, smiling, unruffled but unwilling to engage. Her own views never changed; after a momentary conversion in childhood she lost all faith in revealed religion and, while never committing herself to any positive declaration, she maintained an attitude sometimes of mild, sometimes of aggressive agnosticism. Using the word in a very wide sense we may find a "religious" element in her novels; she tended to be, as she herself put it, "mystical"; but she entertained no comfortable beliefs. That the Universe is a very mysterious place she would certainly have allowed, but not that this mysteriousness allows us to suppose the existence of a moral deity or of a future life.

Orlando went through the usual vicissitudes of her novels, but within a shorter space of time than most. Virginia began with an impetuous rush. Then there had been a loss of momentum. By December she had come to the conclusion that *Orlando* was bad. It would not be out, if it came out at all, until the autumn. In February she believed that she was finishing it and she had in fact finished writing it by 18 March 1928. Then the Woolfs set out again for Cassis by motor, reaching the Mediterranean on 2 April. It was on the whole a delightful holiday, although the return journey across the *Massif central* was almost too adventurous. "Often," she declared, "we were suspended on a precipice with the crows ogling us. Often only a hairsbreadth was between the left side wheel & a drop of some 80,000 feet." In fact it was a pretty agitating and tiresome journey, with many punctures, but at Cassis there had been agitations of a kind to worry her more. There was "Clive (who smacked me in public – curse him for an uneasy little up-start)."* This incident, the exact character of which is dubious, for it would have been unlike Clive to have resorted to actual physical demonstrations in public, and no-one seems to remember it, brought a contrite letter of apology in which he pointed out that he was very unhappy; to which Virginia replied that she for her part had been not only unhappy but insane. After all these years Virginia could still be driven to desperation by Clive. Twenty-four hours could be ruined – were ruined – and made utterly miserable simply because Clive made fun of her hat. It seems astonishing that he should have teased her so, or that she should so deeply have resented being teased by him. But on his part there was a kind of irritability and jealousy – a sense that she had no right not to be elegant, a sense that she was (as indeed she was) highly critical of him, so that in this way he could take his revenge; but also a more disinterested feeling that it was a part of everyone's duty to look as beautiful – and by beautiful he meant attractive, *soigné*, desirable – as possible. He resented and

---

* Cf. *Orlando*, p. 194. "Mr Pope left her with a bow. Orlando, to cool her cheeks, for really she felt as if the little man had struck her, strolled in the nut grove at the bottom of the garden."

always had resented the Stephen sisters' proud indifference to ornament–rather a kind of indifference which was in part modesty and in part sartorial incompetence–so that although they were sometimes beautifully dressed they were never well dressed. George, I suppose, had felt something the same about his half-sisters.

Virginia for her part really more than half wanted to be invisible. The whole business of clothes was a nightmare to her; and she was happiest when she could forget that anyone looked at her. It was when she was more or less in this happy condition that Clive could tumble her back into a state of self-conscious insecurity in what seemed to her an utterly merciless fashion, but to him was no more than a passing pleasantry.

This particular quarrel was in a way a continuation of the tensions which began in January of the previous year, when Clive, it may be remembered, had sought refuge from the miseries of love by applying himself to the composition of his book on civilisation. He had sent the first part of his manuscript to Virginia in November 1927, and she had called the opening chapters "brilliant, witty and suggestive." During the first months of 1928 they had seen a good deal of each other. But then at some point–perhaps when they were both at Cassis in April–Virginia had seen the rest of *Civilisation* and came to the conclusion, which she voiced privately after its publication, "that he has great fun in the opening chapters but in the end it turns out that Civilisation is a lunch party at no. 50 Gordon Square"–a just criticism, but one which, if given to the author in that form–and it was given in some form–must have been exceedingly mortifying. The quarrel was ended, or at least mended, when Clive wrote, and Virginia accepted, an elegant dedicatory chapter which prefaced the book when it appeared at the end of May.

In that month of May Virginia, rather shamefacedly, received the *Femina Vie Heureuse* prize (£40). Interest in her work was growing and has always persisted amongst the French. The ceremony itself was portentously dull; there was an eulogy by Hugh Walpole, which he himself described as "a rotten speech." To her it seemed that he was explaining at some length just why he disliked her novels so much. Nevertheless, she wrote a fulsome letter of thanks and invited him to dinner. Such formal insincerities are pardonable. But there was about her whole relationship with Walpole a certain lack of candour; that is to say, she praised his novels to his face rather more than she would have praised them to anyone else, and she made fun of him behind his back, though not unkindly. She was wrong in thinking that he did not like her work. He had in fact enormous admiration for her writing – for everything that she had written so far – and dreamed wistfully of producing novels which, like hers, would appeal to the intellectuals of Bloomsbury, to the happy few, instead of to the enormously lucrative public which he managed somehow always to capture. He admired her, was genuinely fond of her, any meeting with her was a delight – a special treat – for him. But also she terrified him. She for her part found him, as did everyone, a simple, lovable, faintly absurd and very teasable character. For all his terrors he found her approachable, he confided in her, described his life, his character, and the most intimate details of his sexual history, so that when she died he was almost relieved that certain of his secrets could now never be divulged.

In May 1928 Leonard saw the final version of *Orlando*; he liked it and Virginia was surprised to find that he took it more seriously than she expected; she of course found plenty of fault with it and, reading Proust, everything else appeared insipid and worthless. I think that she saw well enough that *Orlando* was not "important" among her works, but also she was content, feeling that, of its kind, it was good. That summer and autumn were not unhappy. With *Orlando* out of the way she began to prepare some lectures on Women and Fiction, to be delivered at Cambridge in October.

> Morgan was here for the weekend; timid, touchy, infinitely charming. One night we got drunk and talked of sodomy and sapphism, with emotion – so much so that next day he said he had been drunk. This was started by Radclyffe Hall and her meritorious dull book. They wrote articles for Hubert [Henderson, editor of *The Nation*] all day and got up petitions; and then Morgan saw her and she screamed like a herring gull, mad with egotism and vanity. Unless they say her book is good, she won't let them complain of the laws. Morgan said that Dr Head can convert the sodomites. "Would you like to be converted?" Leonard asked. "No" said Morgan, quite definitely. He said he thought Sapphism disgusting: partly from convention, partly because he disliked that women should be independent of men.

Radclyffe Hall's "meritorious dull book" was called *The Well of Loneliness*, and it created a good deal of excitement when it first appeared. It was a story of Sapphist love which today would hardly cause a moment's surprise; but in 1928 it was seized by the police. Those were the days when the Home Secretary, Joynson Hicks, was trying to cudgel the British public into purity and the question arose whether evidence of the book's literary merits was admissible. Hugh Walpole, Desmond MacCarthy and Virginia were all ready to go into the witness-box and testify in its favour. The difficulty, as will be seen, was that Miss Hall wanted her witnesses to declare that *The Well of Loneliness* was not only a serious, but a great work of art. This seemed too large a sacrifice in the cause of liberty.

However, the matter was compromised. Virginia went to testify at Bow Street but the magistrate, Sir Chartres Biron, ruled literary evidence out of court and the novel, a sincere though feeble effort, was condemned as though it had been any other piece of cheap pornography.

The case came on six days before the publication of *Orlando* and five days after Virginia had, in another manner, identified herself with the cause of homosexuality by spending a week in France alone with Vita. They set out from Monk's House on 24 September and the complexity of Virginia's affections is well illustrated by the fact that when the tour, which was to take them to Saulieu for a week, was imminent, she wrote to Vita, "I am melancholy, and excited in turn. You see, I would not have married Leonard had I not preferred living with him to saying goodbye to him." And yet on the morning of their departure the journey caused a small and sudden row between husband and wife. And yet again, when after three days' absence Virginia had no news from Leonard, she sent a telegram to make sure that all was well with him. And to Harold Nicolson she wrote:

... I was going to thank you for having married Vita; & so producing this charming & indeed inimitable mixture. ... Anyhow we had a perfect week, & I never laughed so much in my life, or talked so much. It went like a flash – Vita was an angel to me – looked out trains, paid tips, spoke perfect French, indulged me in every humour, was perpetually sweet tempered, endlessly entertaining, looked lovely; showed at every turn the most generous & magnanimous nature, even when there was only an old jug in the W.C. & she had lost her keys – in short it was the greatest fun.

It was a pleasant, and it may have been a perfectly innocent, excursion. Virginia returned refreshed, able to face the magistrate and, what was even more alarming, the critics.

"The great excitement," wrote Vanessa from London, "is Virginia's new book," and London was indeed well prepared, for the success of *To the Lighthouse* was recent in the public mind. *The Well of Loneliness* had given the sexual theme of the book topicality. The book itself was, from a publisher's point of view, perfect. By this time a great many people had discovered that Virginia Woolf was a novelist who must be tackled if one were to lay any claims to intellectual alertness. On the other hand, her manner of writing was still unfamiliar. For these *Orlando* came like an answer to prayer. Here was a work by a highbrow–a 'difficult' novelist–which nevertheless was easy, amusing, and straightforward in its narrative.

Vanessa had her doubts, so had Morgan; but the volume of praise, the enthusiastic letters, were impressive; so were the sales. It was, as Leonard said, the turning point in Virginia's career as a successful novelist. *To the Lighthouse* had sold 3,873 copies in the first year. *Orlando* sold 8,104 copies in the first six months. Financial anxieties were at an end. When in late October Virginia went to Cambridge and gave her lectures at Newnham and Girton there was, as Vanessa remembered, an atmosphere of triumph–a kind of ovation; Maynard Keynes came up with what seemed to her unnecessary *empressement*, saying, "Well there can be no doubt who is the famous sister now." Virginia's sales were still lower than those of Lytton, who published his *Elizabeth and Essex* in November of that year, but to her friends it was now clear that her genius burnt brighter. That autumn she was tempted by the idea of repeating her performance, of writing another *Orlando*. People felt that it was spontaneous and natural and this was a quality which she wanted to cultivate, but in fact she was waiting for something else. She was still haunted by the moths.

Chapter Six

1929–1931

IN January 1929 Leonard and Virginia travelled to Berlin. Harold Nicolson was now *en poste* there and Vita was with him; this, no doubt, supplied the chief motive for their journey. Vanessa and Duncan, who wanted to see the Berlin picture galleries, decided that they would go too.

> The Woolves [Vanessa observed] are enjoying themselves very much–Leonard is I think far more at home here than in Provence & Virginia finds all change fascinating. They don't of course quite know what to do. They walk miles rather than take a cab & go to the hotel restaurant where one pays about 10 marks for lunch rather than to some far better place where one could feed for a third as much. But it doesn't matter. I think Leonard has already got involved with socialists & Virginia with Vita who has a car & will whisk her about.

Vanessa disliked Germany, and Berlin did nothing to make her change her opinion; she found the Berliners kind but utterly unattractive (a view with which Virginia concurred) and was in a state of profound irritability most of the time. Something of her irritation finds its way into the letters which she addressed to Roger Fry. What she says in those letters of the disasters of the Berlin holiday is true enough, but her reflections on people are unusually severe and cannot be considered objective.

> The human situation here keeps us amused at odd moments. Virginia is of course a good deal involved with the Nicholsons [sic]. Vita is miserable here it seems. She hates Berlin & the Germans & I suspect will soon have to face a terrific crisis with Harold. He seems to me to be cut out for the diplomatic world to which he belongs. He reminds me of all the old official world I used to hate so & is really much like them, only perhaps he is nicer & I suppose must have more wits somewhere. Vita hardly ever comes to Berlin & when she does objects to the social duties, so that I suspect in the end he will have to give it up & then he'll be done for–Meanwhile the situation seems to be extremely edgy & is not improved by the Woolves' behaviour. Leonard swore he would go to no parties here & told Virginia to make this clear. She *says* she did so, but as soon as they arrived Harold announced that he had arranged two lunch parties for them, one to

meet a politician who specially wished to see Leonard. They shuffled and agreed to go to one & left the other vague till last night, when Leonard announced at supper after a concert (we were all there) that he did not mean to go. Harold was very cross – it was all most painful – & the Ws put it all on to our wishing to go to Potsdam that day. I think it was so transparent that we didn't get much blame, but it was very uncomfortable. However the Nicholsons seem to me such an unnecessary importation into our society that I can only leave Virginia to deal with them. We spent one of the most edgy & badly arranged evenings I can remember with them. We were to meet for dinner, all of us, & their two boys, so that we were 9. They hadn't ordered a table & of course none was to be had. It was horrid thawing weather, the streets covered with thick slush, & we hurried about from one restaurant to another trying to find room. At last we found it and had dinner. Then we went to see a Russian film called Storm over Asia. As we went in the younger boy was stopped by the man at the door who said he was too young to be allowed in – he's 11 or 12. Vita was furious & only made matters worse & enraged Leonard by pretending the people at the box office had told her it would be all right. We were all held up on the stairs & finally the wretched child had to be taken home by Vita. The film seemed to me extraordinary – there were the most lovely pictures of odd Chinese types, very well done. I enjoyed it immensely & was under the impression that everyone else did too until we got out into the street when it appeared that feeling was running very high on the question whether it was anti-British propaganda! No doubt it was – at least the feeblest part of it consisted of the flight of soldiers in British uniforms flying from Asiatics. Vita again enraged Leonard by asking him 6 times whether he thought they were meant for Englishmen – she and Harold both thought they weren't but managed to quarrel with each other all the same.* This discussion went on & on, all standing in the melting snow, & the general rage & uneasiness was increased by Eddy [Sackville-West] who was also of the party, who got into one of his regular old maidish pets, unwilling to stay or go home, flitting about from group to group like a mosquito. He always irritates the Nicholsons which I quite understand, but at the same time he's so far more intelligent than they are that I can't help sympathising with him. He had offered to take Duncan to see a little of Berlin night life & his one object was to avoid having to take Harold with them. But when at last the cold became too intense & Leonard and I between us managed to get a move on Eddy found

---

* I think that Vanessa was mistaken on this point; I do not think that Harold Nicolson doubted that the film was an attack upon British Imperialism in Asia. Vita may have had her doubts. Harold's position was made painful by the fact that he was his country's representative and that at the end of the film there was a small demonstration in the audience which could have been considered anti-British.

himself landed with Harold as well! Never have I spent such a thundery evening. As I was quite uninvolved however I got a good deal of amusement out of it. . . .

Virginia also was rather amused by the recollection of that disastrous but interesting entertainment, but, as Vanessa remarked, "Virginia lives in a world of her own."

As things turned out, Leonard's fears that the Berlin excursion might be too much for Virginia were fully justified. On 24 January they recrossed the North Sea. For the purpose of the voyage Vanessa gave Virginia a drug called *Somnifène* which she, Vanessa, had found an excellent preventive for seasickness. It was a fairly strong sedative and Vanessa warned Virginia on no account to exceed the stated dose. Virginia, according to her own account, took less than Vanessa had prescribed. Unfortunately the medicine clearly affected her with peculiar force. At Harwich she could hardly be roused. Leonard had to haul her like a sack into the train. There she relapsed at once into an unconscious condition, and upon reaching London was put to bed.

As in 1925, we find that what for someone else might have been a temporary set-back was for her the beginning of a long bout of ill-health. She was in bed for three weeks; she had one of her "first rate headaches," with all the usual symptoms—"pain, and heart jumps and my back aches, and so on." For six weeks she couldn't work. Vita wrote anxious half-apologetic letters, Virginia replied reassuringly; Vanessa felt some guilt about the *Somnifène*, and Leonard had to set her mind at rest. Altogether the *post mortem* on the Berlin visit was a good deal longer than the visit itself.

But this illness was another of those long fallow periods—fallow in the true sense—a period when her mind was ploughed and harrowed and made ready for its next sowing and harvesting. In January she was already beginning to compose *The Moths* in her head, and later she wrote to the author: "I am writing an entirely new kind of book. But it will never be so good as it is now in my mind—unwritten."

Perhaps I ought not to go on repeating what I have always said about the spring. One ought perhaps to be forever finding new things to say, since life draws on. One ought to invent a fine narrative style. Certainly there are many new ideas always forming in my head. For one, that I am going to enter a nunnery these next months; and let myself down into my mind; Bloomsbury being done with. I am going to face certain things. It is going to be a time of adventure and attack, rather lonely and painful I think. But solitude will be good for a new book.

Of course, I shall make friends. I shall be external outwardly. I shall buy some good clothes and go out into new houses. All the time I shall attack this angular shape in my mind. I think *The Moths* (if that is what I shall call it) will be very sharply cornered. I am not satisfied though with the frame. There is this sudden fertility which may be mere fluency. In old days books were so many sentences absolutely struck with an axe out of crystal: and now my mind is so impatient, so quick, in some ways so desperate.

There were other unwritten books to which she had committed herself, and of these the one that interested her most was the one concerned with women and fiction; it was based upon the two lectures which she had given in Cambridge in October 1928. She addressed herself to the task of turning them into a book with some enthusiasm. It was finished by the middle of May and in October the book was published under the title *A Room of One's Own*. It is, I think, the easiest of Virginia's books, by which I mean that it puts no great burden on the sensibilities. The whole work is held together, not as in her other works by a thread of feeling, but by a thread of argument—a simple well-stated argument: the disabilities of women are social and economic; the woman writer can only survive despite great difficulties, and despite the prejudice and the economic selfishness of men; and the key to emancipation is to be found in the door of a room which a woman may call her own and which she can inhabit with the same freedom and independence as her brothers. The lack of this economic freedom breeds resentment, the noisy assertive resentment of the male, who insists on claiming his superiority, and the shrill nagging resentment of the female who clamours for her rights. Both produce bad literature, for literature—fiction, that is—demands a comprehensive sympathy which transcends and comprehends the feelings of both sexes. The great artist is Androgynous.

This argument is developed easily and conversationally, striking home in some memorable passages but always lightly and amusingly expressed. It is that rare thing—a lively but good-tempered polemic, and a book which, like *Orlando*, is of particular interest to the student of her life. For in *A Room of One's Own* one hears Virginia speaking. In her novels she is thinking. In her critical works one can sometimes hear her voice, but it is always a little formal, a little editorial. In *A Room of One's Own* she gets very close to her conversational style.

If truth is not to be found on the shelves of the British Museum, where, I asked myself, picking up a notebook and a pencil, is truth?

Thus provided, thus confident and enquiring, I set out in pursuit of truth. The day, though not actually wet, was dismal, and the streets in the neighbourhood of the Museum were full of open coal-holes, down which sacks were showering; four-wheeled cabs were drawing up and depositing on the pavement corded boxes containing, presumably, the entire wardrobe of some Swiss or Italian family seeking fortune or refuge or some other desirable commodity which is to be found in the boarding-houses of Bloomsbury in the winter. The usual hoarse-voiced men paraded the streets with plants on barrows. Some shouted; others sang. London was like a workshop. London was like a machine. We were all being shot backwards and forwards on this plain foundation to make some pattern. The British Museum was another department of the factory. The swing-doors swung open; and there one stood under the vast dome, as if one were a thought in the huge bald forehead which is so splendidly encircled by a band of famous names. One went to the counter; one took a slip of paper; one opened a volume of the catalogue, and . . . . .

It is tempting to continue, and indeed those who wish to know what kind of a person Virginia Woolf was in the autumn of 1928 should do so. But because it is, after all, a book, because she is leading us through London and into that perplexing labyrinth, the Reading Room of the British Museum, in order to say some very trenchant things about the relationship of men to women, she must make an argument, and resist the temptation of following her fancies. Swiss families entering Bloomsbury boarding-houses, men with plants on barrows, were to her infinitely seductive; she could fill them with romance. The Italians might be refugees flying from Fascism or perhaps from the Austrians (she was sometimes a little uncertain about dates). The men with barrows might collect lizards or play the harp. She is too good an advocate to wreck her arguments by pushing such enquiries further, as she might have done when talking. They are only tentatively suggested, but the conversational tone of voice is there. It is a serene voice, the voice of a happy woman who loves life, loves even the rattle of coal down the pavement coal-hole, and loves, how much more, that "subtle and subterranean glow which is the rich yellow flame of rational intercourse. No need to hurry, no need to sparkle," when you can light a cigar, blow that dense satisfying cloud of vapour into the air and talk nonsense about the underlying music of conversation, the absurdities of dogs, the peculiarities of Manx cats. . . .

A mongoose had just run into the bathroom at Monk's House—Nelly is terrified. Or, driving from Lewes to Sevenoaks: "We met an elephant on the road here only the other day—I fancy they are common in this part of Kent. Why, there is another. Well, perhaps it is only an old sow. But you wouldn't usually find a sow that looked so much like an elephant in any other part of England."

"She lives," said Clive, "half in a world of solid reality, half in a Victorian novel" (and she could make others do likewise); but she did so adventuring gaily, noting advancing age without too much distress, conscious always of the flight of time, "reckoning how many more times I shall see Nessa," but with great good humour, with always the comforting reflection – important, I think, for Leslie Stephen's daughter – that she was richer than she had ever been before. Now she could go into a shop and buy a pocket-knife if she wanted one without thinking about the cost. It might not be the noblest of pleasures, but to those who have had to stint and save and calculate it may be one of the most solid. "I like printing in my basement best, almost:" she wrote about this time; "no, I like drinking champagne and getting wildly excited. I like driving off to Rodmell on a hot Friday evening and having cold ham, and sitting on my terrace and smoking a cigar with an owl or two." And yet she could also write: "What a born melancholic I am"; and in a sense this also was true.

She had worries. She made the most of them. She invented others. There was Vita. Vita remained admirable and charming; it was a pleasure to see her and it was a pleasure too when that summer Harold finally decided to quit the diplomatic service. He had written to Leonard and Virginia to ask if they would think it disgraceful if he were to accept a post on Beaverbrook's *Evening Standard*. Presumably they did not. Indeed they congratulated him warmly when on 15 September they heard of his decision to leave the Service for good. But Vita had friends – a Sapphist circle – which Virginia found decidedly unsympathetic. Perhaps Vita found in them a relief from the too-chaste, the too-platonic atmosphere of 52 Tavistock Square and Monk's House, and perhaps Virginia was jealous. At all events Virginia found them second-rate; they engendered a school-girl atmosphere, and although she was conscious of being unkind to Vita she was unable to resist the temptation of telling her what she thought. Poor Vita discovered a certain acidity in her friend's communications – "adders' tails or viper's gall," as Virginia put it (with considerable zoological inexactitude). And so their friendship was for a time agitated.

It was perhaps also a vexation that the Hogarth Press now made its one bad blunder, rejecting *Brothers and Sisters* by Ivy Compton-Burnett, which Leonard, it is said, did not like. It is uncertain whether

Virginia ever saw the manuscript but she admitted later that they had made a mistake.

Then there was Vanessa. Between her and Virginia there was a kind of tacit competition; the one was brilliantly articulate and a successful artist, the other was silent, and as a painter somewhat overshadowed by Duncan Grant's growing fame. But she had three children; she had that ruthless artistic egotism which could say: "I need sunlight and peace at Cassis even more than I need my sister's company" (not that she probably said it out loud); she had, in a word, things that Virginia did not have and she led a life, even though it was devoted to what Virginia called "a low art," which seemed enviably enjoyable and romantic. When, early in June 1929, the Woolfs went to Cassis for a week and tasted the delights of intense heat, cheap wine and cigars and that peculiar languid serenity which is induced by the ease and abundance of Mediterranean life as the visitor knows it, Virginia entered into negotiations for a house, "La Boudarde," a few hundred yards from "La Bergère" where Vanessa lived. She wanted it, I think, in order to be even with her sister and at the same time to experience something which Vanessa had and which she, Virginia, had not. It was another example, too, of the way in which they were drawn together as though by some capillary attraction. Thus Vanessa had followed Virginia to Sussex, thus Virginia had made her way back from Richmond to Bloomsbury. But "La Boudarde" was not a realistic proposition, as Leonard, I imagine, saw from the beginning. Virginia could live in two establishments but not in three. Nor, without impossibly exhausting journeys, could she live so far from London and the Press. Leonard was not really as fond of Cassis as were the Bells, and neither, Virginia discovered later on, was she. The attempts to furnish the Cassis house became more and more half-hearted and in 1930 the enterprise was quietly dropped.

> Of course there are the Woolves too, whom I have seen twice since you were here, and in my opinion Virginia is in a bad way and ought to stay in the country. She will not of course; and so I daresay will go into a madhouse instead. And then what will all the ladies say? (*Clive Bell to Frances Marshall*, Charleston, 11th September 1929).

Clive was unduly pessimistic (if he really meant what he said), but it was true that Virginia's health had not been good. The return from Cassis had been followed by what she described as a "helter skelter random rackety summer," and at Monk's House there had been some unusually unpleasant scenes with Nelly. Also the page proofs of *A Room of One's Own* demanded particular attention. But, when these and other matters had been disposed of:

> . . . I must think of that book again and go down step by step into the well. These are the great events and revolutions in one's life–and then people talk of war and politics. I shall grind very hard; all my brakes will be stiff; my springs rusty. But I have now earned the right to some months of fiction and my melancholy is brushed away, so soon as I can get my mind forging ahead, not circling round.

And three days later:

> And so I might fill up the half hour before dinner writing. I thought on my walk that I would begin at the beginning: I get up at half past eight and walk across the garden. Today it was misty and I had been dreaming of Edith Sitwell. I wash and go into breakfast which is laid on the check tablecloth. With luck I may have an interesting letter; today there was none. And then bath and dress; and come out here and write or correct for three hours, broken at 11 by Leonard with milk and perhaps newspapers. At one, luncheon–rissoles today and chocolate custard. A brief reading and smoking after lunch; and at about two I change into thick shoes, take Pinker's lead and go out–up to Asheham hill this afternoon, where I sat a minute or two, and then home again along the river. Tea at four, about; and then I come out here and write several letters, interrupted by the post, with another invitation to lecture; and then I read one book of the Prelude. And soon the bell will ring and we shall dine and then we shall have some music and I shall smoke a cigar; and then we shall read–La Fontaine I think tonight and the papers–and so to bed. . . . Now my little tugging and distressing book and articles are off my mind my brain seems to fill and expand and grow physically light and peaceful. I begin to feel it filling quietly after all the wringing and squeezing it has had since we came here. And so the unconscious part now expands; and walking I notice the red corn and the blue of the plain and an infinite number of things without naming them; because I am not thinking of any special thing. Now and again I feel my mind take shape, like a cloud with the sun on it, as some idea, plan or image wells up, but they travel on, over the horizon, like clouds and I wait peacefully for another to form, or nothing–it matters not which.

These words, surely, were written in an interval of fruitful tranquillity. But even her illnesses could yield spiritual dividends. On 10 September she wrote: "Six weeks in bed now would make a masterpiece of *Moths*"; it was a thought to which she was to return some months later when the *Moths* had been rechristened *The Waves* and she was again ill.

If I could stay in bed another fortnight (but there is no chance of that) I believe I should see the whole of *The Waves*. . . . I believe these illnesses are in my case—how shall I express it?—partly mystical. Something happens in my mind. It refuses to go on registering impressions. It shuts itself up. It becomes chrysalis. I lie quite torpid, often with acute physical pain—as last year; only discomfort this. Then suddenly something springs.

But the process of gestation was slow and there was very little progress that autumn either at Rodmell or in London. The Woolfs had decided to see as few people as possible in Sussex, and in fact they did see rather less of their old friends that summer; but some younger ones were invited: Janet Vaughan, Madge's daughter, then beginning her career as a scientist; Lyn Irvine, a young Cambridge graduate who, with considerable competence and enterprise, was trying to make a living by her pen; and William Plomer. In 1925 Plomer had sent to the Hogarth press from Zululand a manuscript which both Leonard and Virginia had thought extraordinarily good, and which they published. In 1929 he reached England and they met and liked him; they asked him to Rodmell for a week-end in August and Virginia persuaded him to talk about himself. She was much interested by what he had to say and considered him a more solid and a more serious character than most of the young men of her acquaintance. Nevertheless, when she brought him over to Charleston her behaviour was abominable. "Mr. Plomer," she began, "has been telling me all about himself. He is descended from Shakespeare and also from William Blake." Needless to say he had said nothing of the kind and, indeed, he shyly attempted to explain what he *had* said, but it was no good. Virginia had imagined so fascinating and so astonishing a conversation that she could not keep it to herself. The result, of course, was to make it appear that he, who was the quietest and most modest of men, had been outrageously self-important and vainglorious.

"I am afraid," he said to her next day, "that I was very inadequate last night." Virginia apologised for the Bell family party. He replied that it had been delightful. I hope he was not too insincere. Certainly the family party attacked Virginia very severely when they next met, but she seemed perfectly unconscious of any cruelty to the guest whom she had brought, and to whom, judging from her diary entries, she certainly wished no ill.

The Woolfs returned to London on 3 October. Here they seemed to have lived pretty quietly, with few social engagements and no great excitement other than the publication of *A Room of One's*

Own on the 24th, which brought the usual crop of appreciative letters. Clive was one of the few who didn't like it; he thought that Virginia should stick to works of the imagination. It sold extremely well.

That autumn, which was devoted to *The Waves*, was distracted by Nelly; she again gave notice and did so as Virginia was attempting to dismiss her (which was provoking). She was to leave on 12 December; on 2 December she asked to be allowed to stay and a compromise was reached: they would try one more month. And then there was an excavator's pumping machine which made a spasmodic and exasperating noise; and to the thumping of the pump was added the far worse noise of dance music from the hotel which had arisen behind them in Woburn Place; every night No. 52 Tavistock Square shook with the din and this of course drove Virginia frantic. In the end they had to go to law to get it silenced.

More agreeable, but hardly less destructive of the peace that she needed for the composition of *The Waves*, were her social duties. As an aunt, as a sister, she felt obliged to go to a New Year party in Vanessa's studio at No. 8 Fitzroy Street; it was for her niece Angelica, who was twelve years old – a fancy-dress affair, everyone being disguised as a character from *Alice in Wonderland*. Roger had most appropriately disguised himself as the White Knight. He was dressed in white Jaeger pants, chain armour, cricket pads, his whiskers were green, he had fastened to his person an infinity of objects – candles, mousetraps, tweezers, frying-pans, scales jingling from a brass chain. The children crowded round him; he was the *pièce de résistance* of a highly successful evening. Returning from the party by way of Francis Street, the Woolfs witnessed a social injustice of the kind that made Leonard's blood boil. Two men passing on the other side of the road jeered at a rather tipsy middle-aged tart. She retorted fiercely, shrieking out something about bollocks, bulls and buggers. "Whore," they roared back, and then, perceiving a policeman, bolted. A bottle of beer crashed behind them on the pavement. The woman was not so agile and the policeman began to bully and goad her into saying something for which she might be arrested. Leonard found this intolerable. Flinging himself between the policeman and the woman he said, "Why don't you go for the men who began it? My name's Woolf and I can take my oath that the woman is not to blame." A small crowd accumulated, as such crowds do; moved by Leonard's eloquence it took the woman's side. Immediately she lost her head and nearly spoilt her case by abusing the policeman. The ex-District Officer of Hambantota Province told someone to take her away. The policeman was cowed. "We parted almost amicably," said Leonard in his account of the affair, "and as the crowd broke up I saw Lydia standing on the outskirts under a gas-lamp gazing with amazement at me and the policeman."

Mrs Keynes had good reason to be amazed, for not only was the scene unusual, but it was made more so by the fact that Leonard was still in his party dress. He was Lewis Carroll's Carpenter, complete with paper hat, green baize apron and chisels, while Virginia wore the paws and ears of the March Hare. It was typical of Leonard that this aspect of the matter never occurred to him. What the effect of so strange an apparition may have been on the policeman one cannot tell.

It is a wonder, when one considers the number of interruptions, pleasant and unpleasant, that Virginia made any progress at all with *The Waves*. Nevertheless, in January 1930, she found herself rather more fluent than she had been throughout the autumn. When, in February, she was again ill, her imagination was busy with the Hampton Court scene. But in February she encountered the most disastrous interruption of all–Ethel Smyth.

"An old woman of seventy-one has fallen in love with me," wrote Virginia. "It is at once hideous and horrid and melancholy-sad. It is like being caught by a giant crab."

And yet it was not all hideous and horrid and melancholy-sad. Ethel was, as Virginia said more than once, a game old cock. Her vitality was so terrific. She fumbled and blustered and bawled her way through life, without vacillations or hesitations or doubts of her own tremendous genius as a musician. Virginia admired the headlong impetuosity of her conversation and of her writing, her startling freedom of expression. She was absurd–grotesque even, brave as befitted a General's daughter, one who would ride straight to a bullfinch, tumble, remount, ride on regardless of either pain or ridicule–a gallant figure whom it was impossible not to admire, perhaps to love. And then, how could Virginia resist so much admiration? "I don't think," Ethel wrote, "I have ever cared for anyone more profoundly...", "for eighteen months I really thought of little else." Ethel admired Virginia for her beauty–"for her most wonderful speaking voice and the distinction and the fascination no words can describe"–and yet from a very early date she could see another side to Virginia.

I think she has very grave faults. Absolutely self-absorbed and (no wonder), jealous of literary excellence; (couldn't see the point of D. H.

Lawrence until he was dead). Ungenerous, indeed incapable of knowing what generosity means, I had almost said, but she recognizes it in others. In Vita, for instance, who I think is the only person except Vanessa Bell . . . and Leonard, . . . whom she really loves. . . . She is arrogant, intellectually, beyond words yet absolutely humble about her own great gift. Her integrity fascinates me. To save your life, or her own, she could not doctor what she thinks to be the truth. Of religion she has no conception. Her views, and the views of all that Bloomsbury group, about it are quite childish. Also their political views. They think all aristocrats are limited and stupid, and swallow all the humbugging shibboleths of the Labour Party. . . .

This entry in Ethel's diary–written about 1933–is in many ways interesting. It shows some of the misunderstandings and some of the perceptions that made the relationship between the two women difficult. The references to Virginia's socialism were written, I fancy, with Leonard in mind. I doubt whether Ethel herself was deeply religious or very deeply political, but she saw in the tenets of what she was pleased to call Bloomsbury an affront to her own notions of good form, and this difference, social rather than ideological, was one of the things that separated her from Virginia. Virginia did not refrain from mocking at and abusing Ethel's beliefs.

Virginia's arrogance, the kind of arrogance that made her contemptuously dismiss the novels of Maurice Baring which Ethel considered masterpieces of the highest order, or, worse still, some of Ethel's friends, was real enough. For rather the same reason she could appear ungenerous, although to me the charge seems the most unjust that Ethel makes. Nor were Virginia's affections so limited as her friend supposed, although here again we may see a personal application: undoubtedly Virginia never loved Ethel half so much as Ethel herself wished to be loved. And of course she *was* self-absorbed. But in this accusation there is something more than a little comic, for here indeed it was a case of Greek meeting Greek. Ethel was a fascinating person but also incredibly demanding. Vita Sackville-West tells us:

how angry she could get when her friends didn't answer her letters in detail. Poor Virginia Woolf, endlessly patient under this loving persecution, had to endure long questionnaires: "You haven't answered my questions one, two, three, four–right up to twenty. Please reply by return of post." Ethel seemed to command endless time, and to expect her friends to command equal leisure. Blinkered egoism could scarcely have driven at greater gallop along so determined a road. But although often a nuisance, Ethel was never a bore.

Ethel and Virginia appear to have met on 20 February 1930, and thereafter, as was usual in any matter which concerned Ethel, things went on at a thundering pace. She burst into the room at four in the afternoon, in a three-cornered hat and a tailor-made suit, and found Virginia resting on a sofa. "Let me look at you . . . I have brought a book and a pencil. I want to ask . . . First I want to make out the genealogy of your mother's family. Old Pattle–have you a picture? No, well now–the names of his daughters." Fifteen minutes later they were on Christian name terms. She had thought of nothing for ten days but of seeing Virginia; she was in rhapsodies about *A Room of One's Own*, and didn't much care for Vita's friends. She said writing music was like writing novels, that orchestration was colouring. She lived in the country because of her passion for games, for golf. She had been thrown off her horse two years ago while hunting. She rode a bicycle. She was very strong. And so it went on until half-past seven, when she had to leave for Woking.

Virginia was impressed. There was something fine and tried and experienced about Ethel besides the rant and the riot and the egoism; and perhaps after all she was not such an egotist as people made out. As for Ethel, she, I think, was in love with Virginia before she even met her.

The honeymoon period was short. Virginia could not keep up with Ethel's demands or conform to the reckless pace of her friendship. Towards the end of April Ethel declared that she was disillusioned. Virginia replied that she was glad of it; she hated illusions.

With this exchange the friendship might have come to an end, but there was a reconciliation on the 1st of May. Ethel came to tea, she met Vanessa, who became her confidante–she wrote innumerable letters to both sisters, often twice a day to Virginia–and later that month, after Leonard and Virginia had returned from a business holiday, travelling their books in Devon and Cornwall, there were more meetings, and so it continued throughout the summer. When in August the Woolfs were at Monk's House, Ethel wrote to Virginia and told her that in getting to know her, she had felt an emotion comparable only to that which she had experienced when first she heard the music of Brahms.

Then she came to spend a night at Rodmell and Virginia meditated on "this curious unnatural friendship. I say unnatural because she is so old, and everything is incongruous." There had been, as Virginia said, some interesting moments.

"D'you know, Virginia, I don't like other women being fond of you."

"Then you must be in love with me Ethel."

"I have never loved anyone so much. . . . Ever since I saw you I have thought of nothing else. . . . I had not meant to tell you. But I want affection. You may take advantage of this."

And some affection Virginia was ready to give her. She was such a splendid old thing–"an indomitable old crag"–so assured, sometimes so quick, so practical, and she had a certain smile, very wide and benignant.

Ethel, Vita, Vanessa and Duncan, and writing *The Waves* were what she called the "elements" of that summer of 1930, and it was surely Ethel who made her describe it as "a very violent summer." Being violent it was, of necessity, exhausting and one afternoon in late August when Maynard and Lydia Keynes had come to Monk's House, Virginia, having placed a sprig of white heather in a vase (it had been sent by an admirer), walked down the path with Lydia:

If this don't stop, I said, referring to the bitter taste in my mouth and the pressure like a wire cage round over my head, then I am ill: yes, very likely I am destroyed, diseased, dead. Damn it! Here I fell down–saying "How strange–flowers". In scraps I felt and knew myself carried into the sitting room by Maynard. Saw L. look very frightened; said I will go upstairs; the drumming of my heart, the pain, the effort got violent at the doorstep; overcame me; like gas; I was unconscious; then the wall and the picture returned to my eyes; I saw life again. Strange, I said, and so lay, gradually recovering, till 11, when I crept up to bed. Today, Tuesday, I am in the lodge and Ethel comes–valiant old woman! But this brush with death was instructive and odd. Had I woken in the divine presence it would have been with fists clenched and fury on my lips. "I don't want to come here at all!" so I should have exclaimed. I wonder if this is the general state of people who die violently. If so, figure the condition of Heaven after a battle.

It is possible that this "brush with death" gave Virginia an idea of how she would finish *The Waves*. She continues:

I will use these last pages to sum up our circumstances. A map of the world.

Leaving out the subject of Nelly, which bores me*, we are now much

* It may bore the reader too; but it seems only proper to note that Nelly had an operation in May 1930 and was convalescent throughout the summer. In her absence Virginia employed daily servants and was so well pleased by the arrangement that, while continuing to pay her wages, she refused on grounds of her health to let Nelly return to work. In November 1930 Virginia wrote dismissing her finally; but Nelly's dismay and her arguments, supported as they were by Leonard, overcame Virginia's resolution, and she returned for a further trial period from 1 January 1931. Nelly's fellow-servant, Lottie, had left the Woolfs and taken service with the Stephens in 1924.

freer and richer than we have ever been. For years I never had a pound extra; a comfortable bed, or a chair that did not want stuffing. This morning Hammond delivered 4 perfectly comfortable armchairs–and we think very little of it.

I seldom see Lytton; that is true. The reason is that we don't fit in, I imagine, to his parties, nor he to ours; but that if we can meet in solitude all goes as usual. Yet what do one's friends mean to one, if one only sees them 8 times a year? Morgan I keep up with in our chronically spasmodic way. We are all very much aware of life and seldom do anything we do not want to. My Bell family relations are young, fertile and intimate. . . . Julian is publishing with Chatto and Windus. As for Nessa and Duncan, I am persuaded that nothing can be now destructive of that easy relationship, because it is based on Bohemianism. My bent that way increases–in spite of the prodigious fame (it has faded out since July 15th; I am going through a phase of obscurity: I am not a writer; I am nothing; but I am quite content) I am more and more attracted by looseness, freedom and eating one's dinner off a table anywhere, having cooked it previously. This rhythm (I say I am writing the Waves to a rhythm, not to a plot) is in harmony with the painters'. Ease and shabbiness and content therefore are all ensured. Adrian I never see. I keep constant with Maynard. I never see Saxon. I am slightly repelled by his lack of generosity; yet would like to write to him. Perhaps I will. George Duckworth, feeling the grave gape, wishes to lunch with Nessa; wishes to feel again the old sentimental emotions. After all, Nessa and I are his only women relations. A queer cawing of homing rooks this is. I daresay the delights of snobbishness somewhat fail in later life–and we have done–"made good", that is his expression.

My map of the world lacks rotundity. There is Vita. Yes. She was here the other day, after her Italian tour with 2 boys; a dusty car, sandshoes and Florentine candlepieces, novels and so on tumbling about on the seats. I use my friends rather as giglamps: There's another field I see–by your light–over there's a hill. I widen my landscape.

George (now Sir George) came to lunch at Charleston, corpulent, complacent and gluttonous. Virginia used to describe his demeanour on that occasion with a kind of amused horror. It was not an enlivening reunion; neither was Mrs Woolf's annual visit to Monk's House which took place at the end of September and consumed a day that might have been given to *The Waves*. It was most unwillingly sacrificed, for she was a vain, querulous, utterly commonplace old person connected to Virginia only by the circumstance of marriage. She had to be fed on sweet cakes and conversational bromides; she demanded sympathy and admiration and, if denied these treats, might dissolve into reproachful tears.

These were only some of the time-consuming interruptions of what Virginia described nevertheless as the happiest, the most satis-factory summer since they came to Monk's House.

The Woolfs returned to London on 4 October and Virginia set to work to finish *The Waves*. On 15 October she records a bad start and felt that she must return to Rodmell, which she did, apparently with good results. "Alas, too numb brained to go on with Bernard's soliloquy this morning"–this she wrote on 8 November, and on 2 December: "No, I cannot write that very difficult passage in the Waves this morning." She took a week off before attempting to tackle the last lap–Bernard's final speech. The Woolfs spent Christ-mas at Rodmell and the end seemed in sight when Virginia was struck down by influenza; at the very end of the year she was able, cautiously, to resume work. But there were difficulties: the cold at Monk's House was intense and she found that her wits were frozen; all she could do was to write a few staggering sentences. A visit to Charleston brought little comfort. She found it depressing; the painters teased her, so did Clive; the young reminded her of her age–they seemed to sneer, to mock, and certainly they did not help her to write *The Waves*.

Again at Tavistock Square, Bernard's speech continued to present difficulties.

I could perhaps do B[ernard]'s soliloquy in such a way as to break up, dig deep, make prose move–yes I swear–as prose has never moved before; from the chuckle, the babble to the rhapsody. . . .

Now this is true: *The Waves* is written at such high pressure that I can't take it up and read it through between tea and dinner; I can only write it for about one hour, from 10 to 11.30. And the typing is almost the hardest part of the work.

Still *The Waves* had to be written. It ground on somehow until 20 January when, lying in her bath, Virginia was struck by an idea. It excited her so much that, for a time, *The Waves* became more impossible than ever. It was to be a sequel to *A Room of One's Own*. It would be called *Professions for Women* perhaps. For a week she could think of nothing else and Bernard remained tongue-tied. The idea was triggered off by a speech that she delivered on 21 January at a meeting organised by Philippa Strachey and the London National Society for Women's Service. Virginia spoke to an audi-ence of two hundred people; Ethel, in a blue kimono and a wig, spoke also. It was on the whole a successful occasion, although Leonard, so it appeared to Virginia, was somewhat exasperated by it all. Possibly he foresaw that she would have a temperature of 99 on the following morning and again be unable to work.

By 26 January she had shaken off the feminist pamphlet and hoped to finish *The Waves* within three weeks. By 2 February she believed she would have finished by the 8th. "Oh Lord the relief when this week is over." It had, she felt, been at least a brave attempt and oh, the delight to be free again. But on that very day she had to go and hear Ethel rehearse *The Prison*. This was a fascinating experience – an audience of fat, elderly, satin-swathed ladies in a vast Adam house in Portland Place and Ethel, shabby, vigorous, impetuously conducting with a pencil, convinced that she was as great as Beethoven. And who knows, reflected Virginia, perhaps she *was* a great composer? And then on the 4th, Leonard's day was ruined by jury service and Virginia's by the fact that her doctor, Ellie Rendel, who was to have come to enquire into her persistent high temperature at 9.30 sharp, thus leaving the morning free for writing, was an hour and a half late. It was a little thing, the reader may think – a morning's work lost – but the frustrations that such a delay can cause, the accumulated exasperation when one is interrupted again and again as one attempts to finish a task, is one of the major miseries of life. It is as though one were crushed beneath a multitude of counterpanes unable to breathe until at length they are cast off and with each attempt to throw them away something happens, they fall back again, stifling, oppressive, inevitable.

But now at last the end really was in sight, and indeed she was able to keep exactly to the timetable she had proposed for herself on 2 February. On the morning of the 7th she wrote:

Here in the few minutes that remain, I must record, heaven be praised, the end of *The Waves*. I wrote the words O Death fifteen minutes ago, having reeled across the last ten pages with some moments of such intensity and intoxication that I seemed only to stumble after my own voice, or almost, after some sort of speaker (as when I was mad). I was almost afraid, remembering the voices that used to fly ahead. Anyhow, it is done; and I have been sitting these 15 minutes in a state of glory, and calm, and some tears, thinking of Thoby, and if I could write Julian Thoby Stephen 1881–1906 on the first page. I suppose not. How physical the sense of triumph and relief is! Whether good or bad, it's done; and, as I certainly felt at the end, not merely finished, but rounded off, completed, the thing stated – how hastily, how fragmentarily I know; but I mean that I have netted that fin in the waste of water which appeared to me over the marshes out of my window at Rodmell when I was coming to an end of *To the Lighthouse*.

If, as many critics assert, *The Waves* was Virginia's masterpiece, then that morning of Saturday, 7 February 1931, may be accounted the culminating point in her career as an artist.

This chronicle of Virginia's final efforts to finish her novel has obliged me to pass over an event of some importance in her life.

On 27 October 1930 Leonard and Virginia decided to make an end of the Hogarth Press. They might perhaps continue to publish their own works and those of a few friends, together with those which they actually printed themselves; but the Press would cease to be a large business. The motives which governed this resolution were not new. The Press deprived the Woolfs of liberty and imposed altogether too much labour. If Virginia could have had her way the decision would not have been reversed; she found the work, and particularly her own employment as a reader, onerous and dispiriting. But Leonard could not easily destroy the remarkable edifice which he had built. I have little doubt that it was he who decided to try once more to enlist an intelligent adjutant. The young man whom he found this time was Julian's friend John Lehmann. He had recently left Cambridge; they had just accepted his poems for publication. He was to become manager, to run the press under Leonard's supervision and eventually to become a partner.

Virginia met him early in the New Year: "a tight aquiline boy, pink, with the adorable curls of youth; yes, but persistent, sharp."

The arrangement lasted less than two years, although it was not to be the end of the connection between John Lehmann and the Hogarth Press. It strengthened the first tenuous contacts between the Woolfs and those remarkable young writers of the Left—Stephen Spender, C. Day Lewis, W. H. Auden and Christopher Isherwood—whose work John Lehmann promoted through the Press. And of course it meant that the idea of bringing the whole business to an end was quietly dropped.

Virginia went out and had her hair curled. Vanessa didn't like the effect and Virginia was chagrined. Then she quarrelled with Ethel. They were both in a state to quarrel with anyone. Virginia, depressed and exhausted by so much effort, wrote on 11 April: "I have finished the worst novel in the language," which, of course, was partly fake modesty but also contained, I think, a germ of real despair, the knowledge that she had not after all achieved that perfect work of art which must always remain unachieved. Ethel's work, *The Prison*, after a successful performance in Edinburgh, was not well received in London. She displayed, as it seemed to Virginia, a tawdry, paltry vanity. Moreover, the things that Virginia and Ethel did not like about each other were becoming more and more obvious to each of them. Ethel's overwhelming egotism and incessant raucous demands for attention gave Virginia headaches. She felt she was being attacked, overwhelmed, submerged, and she reacted fiercely in defence of her own personality. Each saw the other as the aggressor, each felt some misgivings about the other's friends. Ethel disapproved of Bloomsbury, what she knew of it—although she did like Duncan and Vanessa and she was amiable with the younger generation, but there was little love lost between her and Leonard and I think that she saw a vague background of frivolous long-haired atheists and socialists who were not impressed by her music, who perhaps made fun of her—that potent hostile unnamed Bloomsbury of the imagination, which has enraged so many unsuccessful artists. Virginia was equally, if not even more, unappreciative of Ethel's friends and relations. Matters seem to have come to a head in June 1931. Again Virginia was unwell, despite the fact that in May the Woolfs had taken a memorable but wet holiday carrying them as far as Brantôme and Montaigne's house. Ethel irritated her by saying that there was nothing wrong with her save her liver. No doubt it was kindly meant, and the postcard decorated with a picture of a sick monkey which accompanied it was intended obviously as a joke, but Virginia was in no mood for such joking. With a headache which gnawed like a rat as she retyped *The Waves*, and then the correction of the retyping, no, it didn't seem to her a bit funny. Their relations deteriorated until on 29 June Ethel seems to have burst out in a letter which Virginia called sordid and ridiculous. She meditated a scathing reply, or so it seems, and finally contented herself with a laconic note. "I suppose from your tone that you don't want to come here on Monday." She didn't. There was an interval of hurt silence. At the end of it Ethel came, in a sense, to apologise—that is to say, to explain, to defend, to extenuate, while her tea grew cold and her parentheses grew endless. When she had gone Virginia wrote to her saying in effect: this must not happen again. Ethel, she explained, demanded too much sympathy. It was a fault into which Sir Leslie had fallen in his dealings with his children. The result would inevitably be estrangement. Virginia had, in fact, discovered that she was the stronger of the two. She could up to a point dictate the terms of their friendship. Ethel could loom and strut and talk her head off, but when Virginia was silent, Ethel was undone; she needed Virginia. Virginia liked, was entertained by and in a way sympathised with her, but she could do perfectly well without her. On these terms the friendship could, and indeed did, continue, but not without altercations.

All this must be imagined against the final miseries of correcting the typescript copy of *The Waves*.

On 17 July she wrote: "Yes, this morning I think I may say I have finished." The novel could be submitted to Leonard. Would he perhaps condemn it, no doubt in some qualified fashion, and find it too difficult, too incoherent? Two days later he came out to her in the garden house at Rodmell and said that the first hundred pages were indeed very difficult, but: "It is a masterpiece, the best of your books." She felt inexpressible relief, and walked off in the rain "as light as a trout." Now she could count her blessings—so hard to count when they really need counting: what with the Press and her work, she had a "hoard"* of £860, and material luxuries: a Heal's bed, a wireless, electric light, a Frigidaire; she could make a dress allowance to her niece Angelica, who would soon be old enough to value such things—and set herself to write something light and easy and untroubling—a biography of Mrs Browning's dog, Flush.

Moreover she had settled not only Ethel's hash but Stephen Tomlin's, for Tomlin, a charmer whose charm totally failed to work upon Virginia, had nevertheless persuaded her to sit to him for a sculptured head. Posterity may be glad that he did so. No-one else had any cause to be glad. For somehow Virginia managed to forget, in agreeing to the proposal, that the sculptor must inevitably wish to look at his sitter and Virginia should have recollected that one of the things she most disliked in life was being peered at. A very few friends had been allowed to make pictures; some were made by stealth. She didn't like being photographed, but if a painter or a photographer is unwelcome, how much more so a modeller? The man with the camera may be offensive but his offence is swiftly committed. The painter is worse in this respect, but he may, like Lily Briscoe, be supposed to regard you as no more than a part of the composition—an interesting but perhaps not an essential accent. But a sculptor has but one object: yourself—you from in front, you from behind, you from every conceivable angle—and his is a staring, measuring, twisting and turning business, an exhaustive and a remorseless enquiry. Virginia couldn't stand it. His face staring

* "At the end of the year I worked out what the actual expenditure had been and also the total actual combined income, and then the excess of income over expenditure was divided equally between us and became a personal 'hoard', as we called it, which we could spend in any way we liked." Leonard Woolf, *Downhill* . . . p. 142.

into hers appeared ugly, obscene and impertinent. It seemed an insult to her personality, pinning her down, wasting her precious time–insufferable.

In vain Vanessa tried to ease matters by coming with her and making a sketch of her own. Ethel came too. Nothing answered. Tomlin was intolerable. He insisted on making plans to suit his own convenience. Then he was not punctual and she, Virginia, had to plod along dusty streets–a proceeding which if the object had been different she would have found delightful–to reach his studio, and in short she was, as Vanessa said, in "a state of rage and despair," so that after four short sittings–how short time seems to those who paint and how long to those who sit–she struck. Two further sessions were by some prodigy of persuasion vouchsafed, and then she would have no more of it. She was free of the affliction. Poor Tomlin was miserable. The work had to be left unfinished without any hope that it would ever be brought to a satisfactory conclusion.

Now the final irony is this: Stephen Tomlin's best claim to immortality rests upon that bust. It is not flattering. It makes Virginia look older and fiercer than she was, but it has a force, a life, a truth, which his other works (those I have seen) do not possess. Virginia gave him no time to spoil his first brilliant conception. Irritated, despondent, reckless, he pushed his clay into position and was forced to give, while there was still time, the essential structure of her face. Her blank eyes stare as though in blind affronted dismay, but it is far more like than any of the photographs.

So far as Virginia herself was concerned, by August 1931 the business was over. And so she could face the proofs of *The Waves*, Mrs Woolf for lunch, Lady Colefax come to cadge an invitation to Monk's House, and Maynard, foretelling doom, destruction, crisis and war so eloquently that she wondered whether she was not fiddling while Rome burned.

On 19 August she writes, "My proofs did go–went yesterday; and I shall not see them again." And so *The Waves* was committed to the public and she took to her bed with a headache and slept and read *Ivanhoe*, with which she found fault. How could her father have taken the archery scene seriously? And all those unreal heroines? And yet she still liked it better than *Judith Paris* by Hugh Walpole.

It is worth looking for a moment at her reactions to this book, for they provide a test of her sincerity. On 1 September 1931 she noted:

. . . it's a London Museum book. Hugh bouncing with spurious enthusiasm–a collection of keepsakes–bright beads–unrelated. Why? No central feeling anywhere–only "I'm so vital–so big–so creative".

True, it's competent enough, spare in the wording–but words without roots. Yes that's it. All a trivial litter of bright objects to be swept up.

A fortnight later, when the first copies of *The Waves* had been sent out, the first reactions came from Hugh, not directly, and probably in a distorted form. They were unfavourable. Virginia's latest novel, he told his friends, was a disappointment–"all about nothing –exquisitely written, of course." The report gave Virginia a day of acute anguish, which was to turn to acute delight when on the following day John Lehmann wrote an enthusiastic letter. It was the first of many and thereafter she was once more floated on a tide of success. On 4 November Hugh wrote and congratulated her on the second edition. Her sales were almost half those of *Judith Paris*.

I was delighted to see that *The Waves* went into a second edition so quickly. Much of it beat me because I couldn't feel it to be real. Very odd this reality–so personal and unreasonable–but some of it is lovely and I feel that I am wrong about my "reality".

To which she replied:

My dear Hugh, And I'd been meaning to write to you, but unlike you, I never, never do what I mean to. How d'you get the time? . . . Well– I'm very much interested about unreality & *The Waves*–We must discuss it (I mean why do you think *The Waves* unreal, & why was that the very word I was using of *Judith Paris*). "These people aren't *real* to me"–though I do think; & you won't believe it, it had all kinds of qualities I admire & envy. But unreality does take the colour out of a book, of course; at the same time, I don't see that it's a final judgment on either of us–You're real to some–I to others. Who's to decide what reality is? Not dear old Harold, anyhow, whom I've not heard [Harold Nicolson had been broadcasting about both *Judith Paris* and *The Waves*], but if as you say, he sweeps us all into separate schools, one hostile to the other, then he's utterly–damnably wrong, & to teach the public that's the way to read us is a crime & a scandal, & accounts for the imbecility which makes all criticism worthless. Lord– how tired I am of being caged with Aldous, Joyce & Lawrence! Can't we exchange cages for a lark? How horrified all the professors would be!

This seems to me a temperate reply–no doubt it would have been less temperate if it had been written at the time when Hugh's reported chatter had cast her into a tumult of anguished feelings. By November she could write with a growing assurance of success. Presently Morgan Forster wrote to say that he felt he had encountered a classic, something which, I surmise, he would hardly have said about *Judith Paris*. Nevertheless, Hugh had given her deep pain and she found in his words a confirmation of the gossip which had reached her. Her retort omits that which would have been needlessly offensive—her sense of Hugh's posturing; it mentions and exaggerates the good qualities which she notes in her diary and it goes to the root of the matter as she saw it—the fundamental unreality of Hugh's imagined world.

"But Oh the happiness of this life." Thus she wrote on 16 November, and although she goes on to note some minor vexations—differences with Vita and with Leonard, whose own book *After the Deluge*, was not quite the success that they had hoped for, still, "my happiness is too substantial to be tarnished." Ethel was, for the time being, on her best behaviour, Vita was really very agreeable. The General Election had, it was true, been disastrous for Labour and the country was in a condition of economic crisis. In Sussex the Labour Party candidate had disgraced himself by building the ugliest imaginable house on the top of Rodmell Hill—a feat which brought from Leonard the memorable statement: "You have done the impossible—you have ruined the view for everyone else without getting a view for yourself" and led Virginia to declare that she would not vote for him. But none of this counted against Morgan's words, against the solid fact that her extraordinary venture into fiction had succeeded. Yes, that autumn she was happy, although exhausted, and there were more things to write. *Flush* was going well. She meditated a book to be called *The Tree*, and the feminist pamphlet and a second *Common Reader*. But her happiness was to be short.

On 6 December she had agreed, no doubt at Leonard's request, to lead an invalid's life until Christmas—no writing, no parties. On 10 December she did, however, amuse herself by writing a letter to Lytton. She had dreamed of him the night before and in her dream they were both young again and in fits of laughter. She had no news, nothing to say except "when you're in London with the tulips & Waley's white flannels, please come and see your old and attached friend Virginia." During the past few years they had met infrequently. She found him charming when they did meet—mellowed, his eyes twinkling behind his spectacles, altogether benign and at peace with her. *Elizabeth and Essex* she had not liked; she found it a disappointing book. Virginia, though she still felt some envy, could all the same regret this and welcome *Portraits in Miniature*, for in these essays she thought that Lytton dealt with congenial material in the form which exactly suited his pen. When she wrote to him in December 1931 he was ill. By the time that her letter reached Ham Spray his illness had become acute. By Christmas Eve all hope seemed gone. Virginia and Leonard sat over the fire at Monk's House and wept unashamedly. They talked about death, the coming of old age, the loss of friends. Then on Christmas Day a telephone message revived their hopes. Lytton was rather better, and this improvement was maintained; the relief was exquisite. And so, agitated but hopeful, Lytton's state seeming to go up and down, they waited for news, and on 14 January drove down to Ham Spray. The Bear at Hungerford was full of melancholy Stracheys reading detective novels or solving crossword puzzles. Pippa sobbed on Virginia's shoulder: "He is so ill, how can he get better?" The house was full of nurses, very efficient, very orderly; the routine of illness had been well established. Carrington moved about scarcely knowing people. They did not see Lytton, but were told he was pleased at their coming.

A fancy dress party in Vanessa's studio had been planned for 21 January. Should it go on? James Strachey telegraphed "Much better again" and the party took place. But already when the guests were arriving, the noise and laughter beginning, Virginia, Duncan and Vanessa were sobbing quietly in a corner, for they knew now that James's telegram had been wrongly transmitted: "much better" should have read "much weaker"—in fact Lytton had died that afternoon.

Chapter Seven

1932–1934

ON 25 January 1932, Virginia was fifty years old, she had written six novels, she was famous, and Lytton was dead. She felt physically and morally exhausted. She was distressed by the loss of an old friend, and Leonard, whose friendship went further back, was perhaps even more saddened. They both felt, I think, that the world had lost an artist who had never quite found himself, never quite justified the hopes of his Cambridge contemporaries, never written that "supreme" book of which they had believed him capable.

The idea of a biography of Lytton was discussed and, some time later, his sisters–some of them–suggested that Virginia might write "something." But to give any notion of what Lytton had really been like, it was, everyone agreed, necessary to deal frankly with his sexual adventures. At that time this seemed completely impossible. It was taken for granted that no true life could be written and Virginia did not want to write anything else.

Meanwhile the *sequelae* of Lytton's death were causing anxiety and sorrow. As we have seen, Carrington had married Ralph Partridge largely because she could in this way continue to be with Lytton; thereafter she had remained his devoted companion. Before his death she had talked of following him; when it was imminent she had tried to kill herself and now there could be no doubt that she would make a second attempt. Oliver Strachey, dining with the Woolfs, took a very commonsensical view of the matter. If she really wanted to kill herself why should anyone try to stop her? She had a right to dispose of her own life. It might be a good plan for her to wait until the shock of the thing had worn off but then . . . Suicide seemed to him a perfectly sensible act. Why could not the other inhabitants of Ham Spray leave her alone?

This is the kind of view that it is more easy to take when one is not actually in touch with the person who contemplates death. Ralph Partridge, at all events, was determined to save his wife if he could; he believed that it was important that she should see people and not mope alone at Ham Spray. He asked the Woolfs to visit her. And so, one fine cold morning in March, they motored out to Wiltshire and came to that pretty house with its long verandah facing the downs. Carrington opened the door in her little jacket and socks; she wore a twisted necklace; her great blue eyes were pale with anguish. She had not expected them to come, there had been a muddle; she had sent a telegram . . . "But I do everything wrong."

They entered. The house was cold, Lytton's room very neat. She had wanted to keep it just as Lytton had left it, but the Stracheys thought this morbid. She contrived a good lunch for them, brightened a little and even managed to find a laugh or two. After lunch Leonard suggested a walk. She took them to "her grove"; the trees there, she said, had a flower that smelled very sweet in summer. Then she left them; she had some letters to write. Leonard went to do something to the car; Virginia wandered for a time in the garden, and then returned to the sitting-room; presently Carrington found her there, and offered tea. Together she and Virginia went upstairs to Lytton's room and there she broke down and wept in Virginia's arms.

She sobbed and said she had always been a failure. "There is nothing left for me to do. I did everything for Lytton. But I've failed in everything else. People say he was very selfish to me. But he gave me everything. I was devoted to my father. I hated my mother. Lytton was like a father to me. He taught me everything I know. He read poetry and French to me."

Carrington's intention was clear. Virginia's was not. She, who had twice attempted to kill herself, could neither preach nor lie. She would not, she could not, pretend that there was no sense in what Carrington said.

I said life seemed to me sometimes hopeless, useless, when I woke in the night and thought of Lytton's death. I held her hands. Her wrists seemed very small. She seemed helpless, deserted, like some small animal left. She was very gentle; sometimes laughing; kissing me; saying Lytton had loved his old friends best. She said he had been silly with young men. But that was only on the top. She had been angry that they had not understood how great he was. I said I had always known that. And she said I made too much of his young friends. . . . And this last year Lytton made up his mind to be middle aged. He was a realist. He faced the fact that Roger [Senhouse] could not be his love. And we were going to Malaga and then he was going to write about Shakespeare. And he was going to write his memoirs, which would take him ten years. It was ironical, his dying, wasn't it. He thought he was getting better. He said things like Lear when he was ill. I wanted to take you to see him the day you came, but I was afraid to. James and

Pippa said one must not run any risk and it might have upset him. " No, of course not " I said. " Roger will take the books of course – he will have to." And what else did we say? There was not much time. We had tea and broken biscuits. She stood by the fireplace. Then we said we must go. She was very quiet and showed no desire for us to stay.

As they were going she produced a little French box.

"James says I mustn't give away Lytton's things. But this is alright. I gave it to him."

She seemed frightened of doing wrong, like a child that has been scolded. At the door she kissed Virginia repeatedly.

" Then you will come and see us next week – or not – just as you like? " " Yes, I will come, or not " she said. And kissed me again and said goodbye. Then she went in.

On the following evening Stephen Tomlin came round to break the news. Early that morning Carrington had shot herself. Even in this she had half failed and she died slowly, in great pain. It was impossible for Virginia not to feel in some measure responsible. It would have been wrong to lie to Carrington; but she might have argued more strongly in favour of life. One may doubt whether any arguments could have deflected Carrington from her purpose.

There had to be an inquest; but the Coroner was a sensible man, and he accepted Carrington's story of an accident. Neither Leonard nor Virginia was called as a witness. They went, as they had already planned, on a short excursion by car to East Anglia, spending nights at Cambridge and at Cromer and with Roger Fry near Ipswich. Virginia noted Carrington's married name, Partridge, on tombstones and over grocers' shops. On 15 April they set off with Roger and his sister Margery Fry for Greece.

Yes, but what can I say about the Parthenon – that my own ghost met me, the girl of 23, with all her life to come. . . .

A lot of things had changed, the country seemed more beautiful than before, the inhabitants seemed nicer, the inns cleaner and of course Greek art was quite different with Roger to talk about it, to draw their attention to Byzantine work, to prevent too whole-hearted an acceptance of classical sculpture, to praise the architecture, to see that nothing of importance was passed over.

"It's all likely to end in bugs, quarrels, playing chess, disputing about expeditions & so on," wrote Virginia to Vanessa and in fact, on the face of it, this did seem a danger, all the more so because

Margery was the kind of female philanthropist whom Virginia tended to admire rather than to like. But it was all right; Margery fell in love with Virginia and told her the entire story of her life which, though melancholy in the extreme, was of course fascinating. And the spectacle of the two Frys, who between them seemed to know everything that could be known about the art, architecture, folk-lore, fauna, flora, geography, geology and history of Greece, was amusing, as also was their energy which, despite Roger's usual ill-health, was prodigious. Roger's audacity in attempting impossible roads and dealing with unruly mules and muleteers, visiting in-accessible monasteries, climbing mountains and playing continual games of chess with Leonard who, to his vexation, continually won them, was diverting yet admirable. There was even, to Virginia's perception, some charm in the discovery that when Roger with one Demotic Grammar and Leonard with another and Virginia herself with tags from the classical tongue attempted to ask the way, they had purchased two black kids and a bowl of sour milk. It was above all Roger's character, "so humane, so sympathetic, so indomitable," that she appreciated and that made the pleasure of the holiday. For the rest, a postcard to Julian Bell may serve to suggest their activities.

> We have seen vultures, buzzard, eagles, bee eaters, blue thrushes, temples, ruins, statues, Athens, Sparta, Corinth—& are just off to a monastery. So goodbye.

The homecoming was not agreeable. In the Hogarth Press the differences between John Lehmann and Leonard were now such that, after an increasingly contentious summer, it seemed best to bring the arrangement to an end. Then there was a hostile review in *Scrutiny* which made Virginia think that, from now on, she would be under attack. But this does not quite account, nor could she herself account, for the fact that by the end of May she felt "nearer to one of those climaxes of despair that I used to have than at any time these ten years." I think that her health had been bad ever since she reached the concluding passages of *The Waves*; the tragedies of the winter must have been psychologically unhealthy and she needed, not a holiday, but a rest.

The trouble was that she hardly knew how to rest, to rest volun-tarily, that is; when a "headache" knocked her down and out and it became too painful to do anything but rest, she would lie on a sofa; she could even be persuaded to do so for a little time after the pain itself had ceased to issue commands; but in general she found it exceedingly hard to be doing nothing. There was always a book, usually a good deal of journalism, numerous letters to write, and a diary to keep. In addition to this, she was by nature physically energetic. The picture of continual illnesses, headaches, exasperation and despair is a true one, but it may suggest another picture of languid and lethargic debility; and this would be false. She was still, at this time, working in the Hogarth Press, often enough parcelling up books. And although this exercise was irregular, her walks— seven, eight or more miles every afternoon leaping over ditches, climbing up hills, negotiating barbed-wire or brambles if she were in the country—continued to be an habitual pleasure whenever she had health enough to undertake them.

During these years, however, her walks from Monk's House became less agreeable to her than her long rambles through London. The reason was simple. The country was being spoilt. All along the valley, it seemed, from Lewes to the sea, villas, bungalows, dog-racing tracks and other ugly incongruities were creeping in; what its ultimate fate might be was made very clear by the creation of Peacehaven. This had once been a very lovely and wild-looking stretch of downland between Rottingdean and Newhaven. Now the whole sea coast had been made into a kind of holiday slum, a hopelessly ugly agglomeration of mean squat bungalows. But, from Virginia's point of view, there was worse to come. Asham, which they might have regained for a thousand pounds soon after their establishment at Monk's House, was now sold to a cement-making Company and so, bang in the middle of their view from the grassy terrace of Monk's House, bang in the middle of the loveliest stretch of the South Downs and that to which Virginia was nostalgically attached, went tractors, lorries, excavators and scaffolding. Asham itself was blotted out of sight by vast corrugated iron sheds, the valley was coated with toxic white dust, the air was made nauseous, the grass became foul, trees died and the hill itself was hollowed out as though it had been a diseased tooth.

Virginia, coming across such evidence of 'progress' on her afternoon walks, was in despair. Writing to Ethel Smyth in January 1932 she uses coarser language than is usual in her letters when she describes the capitalists responsible for these works as "damnable buggers." Duncan and Vanessa, with the usual perversity of painters, found a certain beauty in the new buildings at Asham and Virginia tried, pathetically enough, to share their view; "I intend to see them," she said, "as Greek temples." But it was no good. Maynard's confident belief that the Cement Company was utterly unsound and would certainly go smash even before its buildings were complete (it prospers to this day) was much more comforting and, if it had not been for his assured optimism, the Woolfs, who had often talked of leaving Rodmell, might actually have done so.

"I don't like old ladies who guzzle," said Virginia; she referred to Ethel,* who certainly champed and chawed at her food with some ferocity. It is perhaps worth noting that Virginia was always critical of her friends' behaviour at table. Her sensitivity on this point was perhaps connected with her own phobias about eating, phobias which, when she was ill, could make her starve herself and, at ordinary times, made her always very reluctant to take a second helping of anything. George Duckworth, Julian Bell, Kingsley Martin were all, at various times, severely condemned for eating with too little grace and too much enthusiasm. From this we may perhaps conclude that Virginia's condemnation of Ethel was not wholly rational. Certainly, at this time, Ethel had a real grievance against her friend. For Ethel was still in love with Virginia, and so inevitably made scenes, scenes which Virginia found disgusting, repellent and tedious. In self-defence she chased Ethel away and declared that she would have nothing more to do with her. For a time she *did* break off relations altogether.

Ethel, her woes and her demands, form a *leitmotif* of these years, an important and an exasperating part of Virginia's life. There were crises in July 1932 and again in February 1933 and early in 1934, when Ethel celebrated her 75th year and there was a kind of Smyth Festival with special performances of her compositions and a lunch, at which Sir Thomas Beecham made facetious remarks which reduced Virginia to despair. Her *Mass* was performed before Royalty, and the nobility and gentry were subsequently entertained by Ethel at Lyons' Corner House. This brought on another quarrel. In June 1934 Ethel wrote to Vanessa, "I rather think she's through with me"; but she wasn't. In July Ethel discovered that she owed the Inland Revenue £1,600; she was ruined. Virginia's sympathies were aroused. And so it went on.

For a time Ethel seemed to transfer her affections from Virginia to Vanessa. Vanessa was to do the décor for Ethel's ballet *Fête Galante*.

* "The reason why Ethel Smyth is so repulsive, tell Nessa, is her table manners. She oozes; she chortles; and she half blew her rather red nose in her table napkin. Then she poured the cream—oh the blackberries were divine—into her beer; and I had rather dine with a dog. But you can tell people they are murderers; you cannot tell them that they eat like hogs. . . . She was however full—after dinner—of vigorous charm; she walked four miles; she sang Brahms; the sheep looked up and were not fed. And we packed her off before midnight." VW/QB, 19 September 1933.

The vicissitudes of that project, detailed in endlessly loquacious letters, were something appalling. And here too Ethel began to feel a sentimental attachment and to resent the fact that her passion was not returned. "You are a little like your sainted sister in some respects," wrote Ethel tartly. This was true; they both liked Ethel in small doses and neither wanted to swallow her whole; but Vanessa could manage her better and was more ready, if necessary, calmly and finally to shut the door in Ethel's face.

To return to 1932: at the beginning of the year Virginia had written her *Letter to a Young Poet*, which arose out of discussions with John Lehmann, and which was published as No. 8 in a series of shilling booklets, *The Hogarth Letters*, in July 1932. The second *Common Reader* made its appearance in October and was reprinted in November. The preparation, revision and correction of this "bunch of articles" was virtually the only writing, save for a little journalism and one or two experimental stories, that she undertook during the first nine months of 1932. She completed it with "no sense of glory; only of drudgery done." *Flush*, which she had started in August 1931, before *The Waves* was published, was taken up again after she had finished work on the *Common Reader*; on 16 September she was at work on the penultimate chapter.

In November 1931 she had written to George Rylands, thanking him for his kind remarks about *The Waves*.

> . . . I'm full of ideas for further books, but they all develop from *The Waves*. Now if *The Waves* had seemed to you a barren and frigid experiment—merely Virginia hanging to a trapeze by her toenails—then I should have felt, Why go on? and as I can't go back, even so far as *Mrs. Dalloway* and *The Lighthouse*, I should have come to an awkward pass, and have probably taken a vow of silence for ever. That's why your encouragement is a draught of champagne in the desert and the caravan bells ring and the dogs bark and I mount—or shall in a few months—my next camel. Not that I mean to begin another of these appalling adventures yet awhile.

A year later she had found her theme; but it does not appear to have developed from *The Waves*. Indeed *The Pargiters* was to be completely different from *The Waves*; it was to be what she called a novel of fact, a narrative, and almost as much of a conventional story as *Night and Day*. It was:

> . . . to take in everything, sex, education, life etc.: and come, with the most powerful and agile leaps, like a chamois, across precipices from 1880 to here and now. That's the notion anyhow, and I have been in

such a haze and dream and intoxication, declaiming phrases, seeing scenes, as I walk up Southampton Row that I can hardly say I have been alive at all, since 10th October.

Everything is running of its own accord into the stream, as with *Orlando*. What has happened of course is that after abstaining from the novel of fact all these years–since 1919–and N[ight] & D[ay] is dead–I find myself infinitely delighting in facts for a change, and in possession of quantities beyond counting: though I feel now and then the tug to vision, but resist it. This is the true line, I am sure, after *The Waves*–the Pargiters–this is what leads naturally on to the next stage– the essay novel.

Monday, December 19th

Yes, today I have written myself to the verge of total extinction. Praised be I can stop and wallow in coolness and downs and let the wheels of my mind–how I beg them to do this–cool and slow and stop altogether. I shall take up *Flush* again, to cool myself. By Heaven, I have written 60,320 words since October 11th. I think this must be far the quickest going of any of my books. . . .

It is impossible to read these words without pain and pity; it is as though one saw Virginia run gaily and swiftly out upon a quicksand. For, whatever we may think of the final result (*The Pargiters* became *The Years*), it was for her a pitfall, very nearly a death trap. She entered with delight into most of her novels, but never with such lighthearted confidence as now; and never was she to be so thwarted, baffled, anxious and miserable in her writing.

In January 1933 she had to deal with *Flush*. She prided herself on the care that she took in making this trifle fit for the Press, but she was anxious to be rid of it–she wanted to get back to *The Pargiters*. When she did so the book ran without a check until April.

In March 1933 Virginia was offered an Honorary Degree by the University of Manchester; she refused it as she had previously refused to give the Clark lectures at Cambridge.*

The Clark lectures had tempted her considerably and she half

---

* "It is an utterly corrupt society I have just remarked, speaking in the person of Elvira Pargiter, and I will take nothing that it can give me etc. etc.: Now, as Virginia Woolf, I have to write–oh dear me what a bore–to the Vice-Chancellor of Manchester University and say that I refuse to be made a Doctor of Letters. And to Lady Simon, who has been urgent in the matter and asks us to stay. Lord knows how I'm to put Elvira's language into polite journalese. What an odd coincidence!" *AWD*, p. 195, 25 March 1933.

The Clark lectures were offered and refused in February 1932. In March 1939 Virginia refused a Doctorate from the University of Liverpool. *AWD* (*Berg*), 3 March 1939.

regretted it when she had posted her letter to the Master of Trinity; how pleased, she reflected, her father would have been if he could have known that his daughter was to be asked to succeed him. Her friends also felt that she was rather absurd to refuse the Doctorate, but in both cases she felt that one of the dangers of becoming an established writer was that one would come to terms with the academic machine; and she had it in mind to attack that machine in her next book. She was a little caustic about Roger when he became Slade Professor at Cambridge.

Perhaps she still felt something of the old jealousy which had consumed her when she saw her brothers going to Cambridge and herself left behind. Young women were admitted to the campus but they were still unfairly treated and the Universities remained to a large extent a preserve of the other sex. But also she distrusted academic criticism altogether.* During the summer of 1933 she was able to discuss the point with T. S. Eliot. Eliot was at this time painfully disengaging himself from his first marriage and Virginia was the sympathetic auditor (perhaps not always sympathetic for there were moments when she thought that Vivien was being badly treated) of his domestic troubles. By September 1933, however, these were in a fair way to solution and the two authors were able to discuss other questions. Eliot interested her by saying that he was now no longer so sure that there was a science of criticism; the critics had exaggerated the intellectuality and the erudition of his poetry, he found that they got things very wrong. They agreed–or perhaps it might be more true to say that Virginia persuaded him to agree–that the teaching of English in Universities was idiotic. I believe also that she felt, in the case of certain teachers of English, that they showed in their writings so little understanding of the language that they could hardly discuss their betters, the genuine masters of English, without being guilty of arrogance.

If this was the case she was not wholly consistent, for, during that autumn of 1933, she attempted to criticise an art in which she herself had no skill. Sickert was having an exhibition in London and she went to it with Vanessa. She was delighted by what she saw. She had always liked his work–it seemed to her all that painting ought

---

* To her nephew Julian, when he took a chair of English at Wuhan University, she wrote: "But why teach English? . . . all one can do is to herd books into groups, and then these submissive young, who are far too frightened and callow to have a bone in their backs, swallow it down; and tie it up; and thus we get English Literature into A B C; one, two, three; and lose all sense of what its about." VW to Julian Bell, 1 December 1935.

to be. Vanessa, who was very fond of Sickert, said that Virginia ought to write to the artist and tell him what she thought. In his reply Sickert said: "I have always been a literary painter, thank goodness, like all the decent painters. Do be the first to say so."* Clive gave a dinner-party for them to meet again–a highly successful evening. Fortified by wine and turkey, cigars and brandy, Sickert kissed the ladies' hands, sang a French song, told the story of his life, made jokes about Roger, repeated that he was a literary painter–a romantic–and assured Virginia that she was the only person who understood him.

The result was *Walter Sickert: a Conversation*, a small pamphlet and no doubt a minor work, but interesting in that it shows Virginia adventuring into an unfamiliar field. She was very conscious of her own temerity, was careful to explain her own limitations, but determined nevertheless to advance her own view of painting. What she admired in Sickert was his "literature"–"Not in our time will anyone write a life as Sickert paints it," and she compares him as an artist with Dickens, Balzac, Gissing and the earlier Arnold Bennett. It would have been difficult to choose an approach to the art of painting more completely opposed to that of her sister, and I fancy that she was rather frightened of what Vanessa would say. From Sickert himself she had nothing to fear. When in the following year the pamphlet was published, he turned up at tea-time wearing a green peaked cap, sang a few bawdy songs over his cake, smoked a cigar and exclaimed against the criticism of Clive and Roger. They didn't know a picture from a triangle whereas she, Virginia (kissing her hand), was an angel: her criticism had been the only criticism that had ever been worth having in all his life.

Flush appeared in October 1933. It was, as she had foreseen, a success; but on this occasion she feared success almost as much as she usually feared blame. The critics would like it for reasons which did her no credit; she would be admired as an elegant lady prattler. Judging from the reviews she was not far wrong. Her problem now, she felt, would be how to cope with the kind of popularity that lady prattlers achieve. In spite of which, such is human perversity, I do not believe that she would have welcomed the comments of Ethel Smyth, who wrote to Vanessa saying that it was the kind of book that gave her "the kick screams." One may be fairly sure that this criticism never reached Virginia's ears.

* "I would suggest that you *saute pardessus* all paint-box technical twaddle about art which has bored and will always bore everybody stiff." Walter Sickert to VW, n.d.

Biographically *Flush* is interesting, for in a way it is a work of self-revelation. As it is, I imagine, one of the least read of her novels, it may be useful to tell the reader that Flush was Elizabeth Barrett Browning's spaniel, given her by Miss Mitford; he was stolen and Miss Barrett had to retrieve him from a thieves' den in the East End of London; she took Flush with her when she eloped with Browning, and he ended his days in Florence. The narrator is Virginia herself but an attempt is made to describe Wimpole Street, Whitechapel and Italy from a dog's point of view, to create a world of canine smells, fidelities and lusts.

Ottoline, writing to congratulate Virginia said: "Don't you sometimes *hug* your dog–I did my darling Socrates–hugged him & hugged him–and kissed him a thousand times on his soft cheeks." "No," would have been Virginia's truthful reply to this question. She was brought up with dogs in the home, she had always kept dogs and liked them; but she was not, in the fullest sense of the word, a dog lover.

The original of Flush was a golden cocker spaniel called Pinka which had been given to Virginia by Vita. It became, essentially, Leonard's dog. Neither Leonard nor Virginia ever "hugged it and hugged it." Leonard had a feeling for animals which was, on the surface at all events, extremely unsentimental. He was gruff, abrupt, a systematic disciplinarian, extremely good at seeing that his dogs were obedient, healthy, and happy. Whenever one met Leonard there would be a brief shouting match between him and whatever dog or dogs happened to be there, at the end of which the animals would subside into whining passivity and Leonard would be transformed from a brutal Sergeant-Major into the most civilised of human beings.

But Virginia's attitude was much less understandable. She nearly always had a dog, she took a dog with her when she went for a walk and did, up to a point, control the creature. Sometimes, when talking, she would slowly caress Pinka's nose, thoughtfully stroking it in the wrong direction. She was fascinated by all animals but her affection was odd and remote. She wanted to know what her dog was feeling–but then she wanted to know what everyone was feeling, and perhaps the dogs were no more inscrutable than most humans. *Flush* is not so much a book by a dog lover as a book by someone who would love to be a dog. In all her emotional relationships she pictured herself as an animal; to Vanessa she was a goat or sometimes a monkey, sometimes even a cartload of monkeys–*les singes*; to Violet Dickinson she was half monkey, half bird–Sparroy;

to Leonard she was–surprisingly enough–Mandrill (and he Mongoose); to Vita she was Potto (a cocker spaniel, I think). These animal *personae*, safely removed from human carnality and yet cherished, the recipients indeed of hugs and kisses, were most important to her, but important as the totem figure is to the savage. Her dog was the embodiment of her own spirit, not the pet of an owner. Flush in fact was one of the routes which Virginia used, or at least examined, in order to escape from her own human corporeal existence.

1934 began with the great Ethel festival and a burst of work in which Virginia wrote the air-raid scene in *The Pargiters*. This effort ended with ten days in bed and then, on 15 February, there was a tremendous row with Nelly, who flatly refused to cook dinner so that the Woolfs were driven out raging to a restaurant. Virginia swore that this should be the end. She would dismiss Nelly on 27 March before they went to Rodmell for Easter. Leonard, who was often Nelly's advocate, might protest; but neither should deflect her from her purpose. She had been weak too often; now at last, she told herself, she was absolutely determined. But, as the moment approached, she looked forward to the interview with growing dismay, counting the days before it was due, longing to have it over, unable to concentrate upon her novel. The day came. The interview took place; it was a miserable business but at last it was done and, when they returned to Tavistock Square on 10 April, Nelly was out of the house. Even so she made some efforts to return, until she found another job and the long unhappy association was over at last.

Despite some real affection and sympathy on both sides and despite some acts of true generosity, it had been an uneasy and an agitating relationship. Nelly could bring out the worst in Virginia and when, in her diary, she writes of Nelly in anger Virginia is at her least sympathetic. The relationship, as she knew, was a mischievous one and at times they both made the worst of it.

Henceforth, in London Nelly was replaced by a daily–steady, silent, unselfish Mabel–and in the country by another, and it says something for the personal relationship that they there established, and which lasted for the rest of Virginia's life, that Louie Everest, who came and 'did' for them at Rodmell, was able to risk a fairly exasperating joke on her employer and to be, and know that she would be, forgiven.* Here however tempers were not tried by the

* ". . . another year, I thought well you've had me two or three times, I'm going to have Mrs. Woolf April Fool. Whether she will like me after or not I don't know. But we had a certain lady lived in the village who ran the Women's

difficulty of having a resident. It was this I think that made it so hard to deal with Nelly; she was so much a part of the family. Life without indoor servants, which they had seen as the possible result of their poverty in 1918, was now a sign of their increasing wealth. They were beginning to be able to afford the kind of appliances which made indoor servants unnecessary.

At the end of April they took a fortnight's holiday in Ireland; it was pleasant, though wet and on the whole uneventful. But at Waterville Leonard opened *The Times* and saw George Duckworth's obituary. It was years since Virginia had escaped from George and so she could indulge in some slightly sentimental reminiscences; he had after all been extremely kind to them when they were little. The period of revolt, that time when he stood for the kind of life which they felt must be thrown aside or it would crush them, was long past.

To the younger generation, the generation of Virginia's nephews and nieces, George was no more than a name and the 'Georgian' view of life no more a menace than the megatherium. But were they perhaps lacking in something that had been granted to their elders? Were they altogether fortunate in not having had to struggle against Victorian morality? Maynard Keynes said that they lacked a religion. It was, he continued, addressing a dinner party in Clive's flat at 50 Gordon Square, it was a fine thing to fight against, but a still finer thing to be brought up in the Christian tradition. They, the young, would never get so much out of life as their elders. They were trivial and, in their lusts, like dogs. T. S. Eliot agreed from the other side of the table, whereupon Virginia asked him to define his belief in God; as usual he evaded her. And then, as dinner came to an end, Julian came blundering in, and Maynard, reminded of his theme, remarked that the young had no religion save Communism and this was worse than nothing. Moreover, it was founded upon nothing better than a misunderstanding of Ricardo. Given time he would deal thoroughly with the Marxists, and indeed all the other economists, and then there would be no more economic stress.

Institute. Who had a very loud domineering voice. Which frightened the life out of Mrs. Woolf, she couldn't bear the voice of this lady. So I went up to her study and said, this lady was here and could she speak to her about the Women's Institute. So she rushed out of her room, down into her bedroom, combed her hair, made herself look tidy and come and sat in the dining room, and then discovered there was no lady in the dining room. So I was able to get on back at her; she really laughed and laughed about it; but I didn't think she really would " Mrs Louie Mayer, BBC/TV, *Omnibus*, 18 January 1970.

"And then," asked Maynard, "how will you live, Julian, you who have no moral strictness?"

"We miss your morality," Julian admitted. "But I prefer *my* life in many ways."

"The young are too anxious to publish, you publish too soon."

"That's to make our names and make money; we want to chip in before the talk has changed."

"It's because you have no sense of tradition, of continuity. It was different in my day," said Maynard. "I could take 15 years over a book. I wanted to take longer and longer. You write and publish at 18."

Eliot agreed, and so, I imagine, did Virginia. Then the talk wandered to the morals and beliefs of the Jews, to Montagu Norman, Major Douglas and Social Credit. It was all very much Maynard's monologue that evening; he ended by describing the manner in which new Fellows were made at King's. He was, at this time, very much in love with tradition, with the idea of moral stability, with a conservatism which some of his younger friends found increasingly distasteful. For them tradition, conservatism, the respectability of ancient ceremonies, was at best an irrelevance, at worst the cloak for something much more sinister.

In January 1933 Hitler had become ruler of Germany and in April of that year Virginia met Bruno Walter, the conductor. "Our Germany," he exclaimed, "our Germany, which I loved, with our tradition, our culture. We are now a disgrace." But it was not until after the events of 30 June 1934 that Virginia became imaginatively aware of what was happening in Germany. It was then, when General von Schleicher, his wife and others, were dragged out of their beds and slaughtered without the pretence of a trial, without a thought of mercy, that Virginia, like a great many people in this country, felt that Germany was in the hands of thugs, of people without scruples, decency or pity, and she was horrified, all the more so when she read articles in the British press in which the Führer was extolled as a truly great man, a real leader.

For Virginia's juniors, those who were politically conscious, the massacres of 30 June were something completely different. To them it was a matter of hope, almost of rejoicing, that the Nazis should be at each others' throats. When these rogues started to kill each other it seemed as though, for the first time in their lives, they were usefully employed. For us the shock had come earlier, in the first weeks of Hitler's tyranny, or even before that, when the political murders of 1932 showed us, not only what stuff the Nazis were made of, but how the German people, by supporting the murderers, had abandoned the cause of human decency.

But as yet Virginia was not really worried about politics. In 1934 she was much more worried about her novel, which in January had been renamed *Here and Now*. The honeymoon period was coming to an end; there were still moments when, as she put it, she was in "full flood," but such moments were becoming more and more infrequent.

At Rodmell on 27 August she wrote: "I am trying to start the nameless book again; and of course find it grinding, to try to get back into those stiff boots"; on the 30th: "After three days' grind, getting back, I am I think floated again"; on 2 September:

I don't think I have ever been more excited over a book. . . . I wrote like a–forget the word–yesterday; my cheeks burn; my hands tremble. I am doing the scene where Peggy listens to their talking and bursts out. It was this outburst that excited me so. Too much perhaps. I can't make the transition to Elvira's speech easily this morning.

And then came a piece of news that swept everything aside.

Roger died on Sunday. I was walking with Clive on the terrace when Nessa came out. We sat on the seat there for a time. On Monday we went up with Nessa. Ha [Margery Fry] came. Nessa saw Helen [Anrep].* Tomorrow we go up, following some instinct, to the funeral. I feel dazed; very wooden. Women cry, L. says: but I don't know why I cry,–mostly with Nessa. And I'm too stupid to write anything. My head all stiff. I think the poverty of life now is what comes to me; and this blackish veil over everything. Hot weather; a wind blowing. The substance gone out of everything.

* Since 1926 Helen Anrep had been living with Roger Fry, as his wife. As Roger put it: "il n'y a que la formule qui manque." See VW, *Roger Fry*, p. 255.

Chapter Eight

1934-1936

They played Bach. Then the coffin moved slowly through the doors. They shut. They played again–Anon, I think; old music. Yes, I liked the wordlessness; Helen [Anrep] looking very young and blue eyed and quiet and happy. That is much to remember her for. I kissed her on the lips in the courtyard. Then Desmond came up: said "Wouldn't it be nice to walk in the garden? Oh we stand on a little island" he said. "But it has been very lovely" I said. For the first time I laid my hand on his shoulder and said "Don't die yet." "Nor you either" he said. "We have had wonderful friends" he said.

ROGER'S death was a more intimate and a more desolating event than the death of Lytton. Lytton was her past, Roger her present. It was, as she said, "a horrid time," and the worst of it was that she had to suffer, not only from her own sense of loss, but from Vanessa's grief.

It was more than twenty years now since the affair with Roger had come to an end; but Vanessa could make a friend of her lover and so, despite some very painful transitional periods, Roger had, bit by bit, come back into the family circle on a new, happier and less romantic footing. He brought his own contribution to the symposium of Bloomsbury, a vintage old and dry, but generous and heart-warming. In his presence people became at once more lively and more serious, livelier because there was something naturally cheerful and ebullient in his nature, more serious because, behind the gaiety, certain things were taken so very much for granted–the need for intellectual honesty, for aesthetic probity, a respect for certain values: tolerance, charity, good humour. Roger had always believed in them, as his friend Lowes Dickinson believed in them, but in a more robust way, and without that kind of weak and whimsical hopelessness which made Lowes Dickinson at once so charming and so exasperating. Roger was altogether more earthy, more sensual, more resilient, and yet, in his way, just as unworldly, just as "pure".

To these qualities of humour and integrity he joined, and it was this that made him so important to Virginia and to Bloomsbury, a gift for friendship. This was surprising in him, for certainly he was not tractable; he could, and did, impose his will upon others; he was capable of spending six hours on end in a picture gallery and of making his friends do likewise, and at the same time he was, in a way, a figure of fun. He was laughed at by his friends for his scientific open-mindedness which verged upon sheer credulity, for his panaceas, for his prophecies of cosmic doom, for his White-Knightly inventions. But neither his tyrannies nor his absurdities put any real strain upon his friends or his friendships. He knew well enough that he was mocked at; he could laugh at his own gullibility—though usually *after* he had been disillusioned—and he could smilingly allow that he might be a dictator, although it made him no less dictatorial. But Roger's genius for friendship could stand a much more severe strain than this. All his life he had wanted to be a painter. The critic, the art historian, the lecturer, were roles forced upon him, disguises which he cast away as soon as he could get back to his easel. He wanted to paint great pictures and—love apart—I should say that the happiest moments of his life were spent in front of a canvas while the unhappiest were those when the picture hung unsold, damned with the faint praise of the critics and the unspoken condemnation of his friends. Virginia, however, dealt neither in unspoken condemnation nor in faint praise; seizing a trowel (an instrument which she would not have employed in literary criticism) she laid on her praise in thick creamy slabs.

So my dear Roger, don't go palming yourself off on me as a broken down failure, because such shifts are utterly unworthy; & I now can't, for very shame, tell you how much I liked—but I know I liked all the wrong things, the colour, the charm, the sentiment, the literary power —your little landscape at Heals.

Or again:

I could trace so many adventures & discoveries in your pictures, apart from their beauty as pictures—& some seemed to me surprising in their beauty—but then as you know I'm a partial & imperfect judge of that. What intrigued me & moved me to deep admiration was the perpetual adventure of your mind from one end of the room to the other. How you have managed to carry on this warfare, always striding ahead, never giving up or lying down & becoming inert & torpid & commonplace like other people, I can't imagine.

Roger was grateful and perhaps it was her praise which led him, half seriously, to express the hope that she might one day be his biographer.

When on 18 November Margery Fry came to tea to discuss the matter with Virginia, this suggestion had already been canvassed, but they were both half inclined to think that a collection of essays written by different hands might be better. Margery should describe his youth, Nathaniel Wedd should write about Roger at Cambridge, Clive and Sickert should describe his later life in London, Desmond, and Virginia herself, his place in Bloomsbury and Julian, Anthony Blunt and Gerald Heard might write about his later years.

This scheme never came to anything, but the idea of a 'Life' persisted. In July 1935 there was a Memorial Exhibition of Roger's paintings at Bristol. Virginia was asked to speak at the opening; she found it a heavy and an unrewarding task, for the Fry family— Roger's daughter and five sisters—did not seem to like what she said. She realised also that, if there were to be a 'Life,' the relations would want to manage everything. And then she asked herself, "Have I the indomitable courage" to start another book? For by now *The Years* had become a nightmare.

The manner in which Virginia finally got committed to this task is not perfectly clear. Helen Anrep was strongly in favour of her writing Roger's biography and took credit for the result. Margery Fry, who was literary executor, seems to have been undecided. Vanessa I think favoured the idea; Ottoline on the other hand was against it and so was Julian Bell. What Leonard advised, or whether at this stage he offered any advice, I do not know. At a later date he expressed the view that Virginia had undertaken a task for which she was not well equipped. ". . . she could deal with facts and arguments on the scale of a full-length book only by writing against the grain, by continually repressing something which was natural and neces- sary to her peculiar genius." I imagine that most critics would agree. But in addition to the difficulties inherent in the form that she had chosen, Virginia had to tackle problems which were peculiar to this particular subject.

There was a side of Roger's life which needed to be described by an artist or by an art historian and this was a task which might be, perhaps will be, accomplished by some author who can stand away from the passions, prejudices and fashions of our time. This was a study for which Virginia had not, and did not pretend to have, the equipment. The other story that might have been told was the tragic—but at times comic—story of Roger's love affairs. A great part of this story was well known to Virginia. But this she could not make public. "How," she wrote to Vanessa, "how to deal with love so that we're not all blushing?" "I hope you won't mind making us all blush, it won't do any harm," Vanessa bravely replied. But Virginia was born in 1882 and I do not think that she, or anyone else that I can think of born before 1900, could in cold print have set down the tale of a sister's adulterous passion.* But even if she could have brought herself to be perfectly unreserved, the Fry sisters would have been deeply distressed. It was only when Helen Anrep insisted that the truth about her should be told that Virginia was able to deal frankly if briefly with Roger's last love affair.

The effect of these inhibitions was bad for the book. A crucial period of Roger's life was made tremendous by Cézanne and by Vanessa. I doubt whether Virginia could have given the whole of Roger's feelings and of his adversaries' feelings about Cézanne. Vanessa she did understand, and she might have described her love affair with Roger beautifully; but she was prevented from doing so. Thus in the end she was thwarted both by what she knew and by what she did not know; and the life of Roger, which should have been a rest after *The Years*, became a further torment. This, however, is an anticipation.

The last months of 1934 and the beginning of 1935 were made unhappy and constituted a period of what Virginia called "human emptiness," not only because Roger was dead, but also for another reason. On 10 March the Woolfs drove in a snowstorm from Rodmell to Sissinghurst to see Vita. As they took their leave Virginia realised that their passionate friendship was over. There had been no quarrel, no outward sign of coldness, no bitterness, but the love affair–or whatever we are to call it–had for some time been quietly evaporating, and that particular excitement had gone out of her life, leaving a blankness, a dullness.

At about this time Virginia began, as she had anticipated, to suffer from a good deal of hostile criticism. Prince Mirsky and Frank Swinnerton attacked her, the one as a peddler of capitalist narcotics, the other as a clever intellectual snob. They caused pain; but a deeper and a more lasting wound was inflicted by Wyndham Lewis.

Men Without Art was advertised on 11 October 1934 in *The Times Literary Supplement*. Virginia knew at once that she would be attacked, nor was she mistaken. A chapter was devoted to her and she was dismissed as a nonentity–she is "extremely insignificant . . .," she is "taken seriously by no-one any longer today." These criti-

* "If I could have shirked all the relations, I might have said more–but as it is, No, I don't think one can so disregard human feelings:–a reason not to write biographies,–yet if one waits the impression fades." VW to Shena Simon (Lady Simon of Wythenshaw), 25 January 1941.

cisms concern us only in so far as they were a psychological event in her life. She read the chapter on 14 October and for the next two days was completely miserable. She certainly took Wyndham Lewis very seriously; she acknowledged that he made "tremendous and delightful fun" of *Mr Bennett and Mrs Brown*, she considered whether she ought to attend to and to act upon his strictures, then, having faced her critic, she assured herself that the pain was over But it was not and, on the next day, 15 October, she opened her heart to Leonard, walking with him in Kensington Gardens, and then again to Ethel Smyth. They were both, in their different ways, kind and comforting and she was grateful to them. On the 16th she again told herself that she was cured. On 2 November a letter by Wyndham Lewis to *The Spectator*, where he had been accused of malice by Stephen Spender, brought all the pain back again.

The disquieting thing about Wyndham Lewis's criticism was not simply that it was clever, ably written and severe, but that it was in a quite special way belligerent. This belligerence showed itself–paradoxically–in passages which can only be described as apprehensive. Lewis was a man with a grievance, he believed that he had been driven to lead "the life of the outlaw." Virginia, so far as I can discover, never referred to him in print; but she might easily be regarded as a representative of that ill-defined and largely imaginary body which, so Lewis imagined, had as its chief object the destruction of Wyndham Lewis. Of this sinister gang he was, it would seem, terrified. Therefore, although willing enough to wound, he was half afraid to strike and, when he did strike, he tried to shirk the responsibility for his words–"I don't say it–others do."

This timorous quality in the criticism of Wyndham Lewis should not have disturbed Virginia but I suspect that, in her more anxious moments, it did. Criticism by stealth is more contemptible, but it is not for that reason less injurious than outright, straightforward condemnation. The idea that she had an enemy who was waiting for his opportunity, a critic who wanted to hurt rather than to argue, to impugn rather than to judge, was I believe a contributory factor in Virginia's almost hysterical attitude to criticism, or, more exactly, to the potentialities of criticism, during the next three years.

Hostile criticism was now to become more and more frequent. She tried to be indifferent to it, she tried to profit by it, and sometimes she tried to answer it with her pen. She failed in all three endeavours. She could never really be indifferent either to praise or to blame (and this I suspect is true of nearly all artists, although it was particularly true in her case); the critics had not very much to offer her that she would or could use, and she was not a good controversialist. Leonard had often to persuade her not to rush impetuously into the correspondence columns of the papers. Criticism was a thing that had to be endured, like headaches and insomnia.

She had a sense at this time that her reputation must decline, nor was it an unreasonable supposition, apart from the fact that she felt deeply apprehensive about the reception of *The Years*. There was the equally important fact that she had reached a position the eminence of which made her an obvious target for those critics who like to take a shy at the Establishment. In writing *Mr Bennett and Mrs Brown* Virginia had seen as her natural antagonists Wells, Bennett and Galsworthy, while her natural allies were (not without some reservations) E. M. Forster, D. H. Lawrence, T. S. Eliot, James Joyce and Lytton Strachey. It was possible, in 1924, to see the party warfare of literature in those terms. Ten years later it was no longer possible. Wells was now the only survivor of the old guard and, of what had been the younger generation, Lawrence was dead, Lytton was dead, E. M. Forster had ceased to write novels and there had been no major work from Joyce since 1922. The English novelists of roughly her own generation were Compton Mackenzie, Aldous Huxley, J. B. Priestley, Hugh Walpole, David Garnett and Rose Macaulay; they none of them seemed to be carrying forward the revolution which, in 1924, she had believed to be imminent. Having lost both her adversaries and her collaborators she stood very much alone. I don't think that this, in itself, worried her. But, as the survivor of a movement that had spent its impetus, she might fairly be regarded as being, in her turn, a reactionary and the natural adversary of the young. To me the wonderful thing is not that she was the object of criticism, but that those criticisms were for the most part so mild and so limited. For her manner of writing was not one to arouse the enthusiasm of young people in the 'thirties. To many she must have appeared as an angular, remote, odd, perhaps rather intimidating figure, a fragile middle-aged poetess, a sexless Sappho and, as the crisis of the decade drew to its terrible conclusion, oddly irrelevant—a distressed gentlewoman caught in a tempest and making little effort either to fight against it or to sail before it. She made far less of an attempt than did Forster to contribute something to the debates of the time, or rather, when she did, it was so idiosyncratic a contribution that it could serve no useful purpose.

This is a picture which requires some qualification, as the following pages will show. But it is true that during these years the temper of literature was changing, or at all events that a large and important contingent of young poets and novelists were calling for a literature that would lead to effective political action.

Here it is perhaps necessary to remind the reader that in 1933–the year of the publication of *Flush*–Hitler came to power and the Japanese were overrunning Manchuria; in the following year there was what looked like the first stage of a Fascist revolution in France; in 1935 the Italians invaded Abyssinia, in 1936 the Spanish Civil War began, in 1937 the Japanese took Shanghai and Pekin and in 1938 the Nazis annexed first Austria and then the Sudetenland. As the reactionaries went from strength to strength those who opposed them had to consider whether force should be countered by force. Virginia hated violence–she associated it with masculine assertiveness. But were we then to scuttle like frightened spinsters before the Fascist thugs? She belonged, inescapably, to the Victorian world of Empire, Class and Privilege. Her gift was for the pursuit of shadows, for the ghostly whispers of the mind and for Pythian incomprehensibility, when what was needed was the swift and lucid phrase that could reach the ears of unemployed working men or Trades Union officials.

And yet her critics were on the Right rather than on the Left. There were many of the younger writers who knew her personally; through Julian and through John Lehmann she knew Isherwood, Stephen Spender and Day Lewis and her relationship with the anti-Fascist poets was, on the whole, easy, friendly and cordially appreciative. They, knowing her, must also have known that although her prose could never be an effective vehicle for conveying political ideas, her attitude to politics was of a kind that they found sympathetic.

Of course, in a sense, she had been in Left-Wing politics for much longer than they had. But then her attempts to deal with political reality were bewildering, and at times exasperating, both to her and to those who had to collaborate with her. I recall her during these years at the meetings of the Rodmell Labour Party, a small group of which she was, for a time, the Secretary, and I remember my despair, when I was trying to get the party to pass resolutions urging the formation of a United Front–or something equally urgent, vital and important–and Virginia managed to turn the debate in such a way that it developed into an exchange of Rodmell gossip. In this of course she was much nearer to the feelings of the masses, if one may thus describe the six or seven members of the Rodmell Labour Party, than I was. I wanted to talk politics, the masses wanted to talk about the vicar's wife.

After one such meeting Virginia did ask me why, in my opinion, things had gone so very wrong with the world during the past few years. I replied with what I suppose was the stock answer of any young socialist: the world economic crisis, of which the American stock-market crash was the grand symptom, was the prime cause; it had bred unemployment, revolution, counter-revolution, economic and political nationalism, hence Communism, Fascism and war ... all these things were but the effects of an economic cause. She was frankly amazed, neither agreed nor disagreed, but thought it a very strange explanation. To her, I think, it appeared that the horrible side of the universe, the forces of madness, which were never far from her consciousness, had got the upper hand again. This to her was something largely independent of the political mechanics of the world. The true answer to all this horror and violence lay in an improvement of one's own moral state; somehow one had to banish anger and the unreason that is bred of anger. Thus she tended, unlike Leonard, to be an out-and-out pacifist; she never made this clear in terms of policy, but it was her instinctive reaction, the feminine as opposed to the masculine–"the beastly masculine"– reaction.

When in October 1935 she and Leonard went to the annual Conference of the Labour Party in Brighton, they witnessed the celebrated debate between Ernest Bevin, representing Collective Security, and George Lansbury, the Pacifist leader. Bevin demolished Lansbury. They were both horrified by his methods–"like an enormous frog crushing a smaller frog," said Virginia; but whereas Leonard distinguished carefully between Bevin and his policy (of which on the whole he approved), Virginia thought only of the drama and horror of the occasion.*

In December of that year she attended a gathering of antiFascist intellectuals. Such gatherings provided one of the many disheartening political spectacles of the time–the supposed demonstration of unity and solidarity invariably ending in a vicious dispute between Communists and Pacifists. Virginia felt amazed admiration at the competence and loquacity of the politicians, but her chief reaction was dismay that Leonard would have to serve on yet another committee. She had already got into trouble with her more conservative friends by lending her name to a Communistinspired anti-Fascist exhibition, and with the Left by her unwilling-

* She also noted Leonard's political shrewdness. When the meeting rose to its feet and sang "For he's a jolly good fellow" (referring to George Lansbury), Leonard turned to Virginia and said, "Now they can get rid of him." (p. i., QB)

ness to advocate the use of violence. She was persuaded by the charming secretary of the Artists' International Association in 1936 to write an article for the *Daily Worker*, and was then attacked by the Editor of that paper for her lack of Marxism. She could not quite keep out of politics–how could she when she detested Fascism and Fascism was becoming every day more menacing?

But the machinery of politics exasperated and bewildered her. As a celebrity and one whose sympathies were with the Left she was continually approached by politicians who wanted to use her name. She might be, and indeed was, expected to give an immediate reply to a journalist who rang up to know what she thought of the Supreme Court's verdict in the Scottsboro Case;* she was asked, very frequently, to lend her name to organisations which might or might not be controlled by the Communist Party. In such cases she could usually turn to Leonard for advice. But sometimes she herself was persuaded to serve on committees or to be present at conferences. In 1935 we find E. M. Forster trying to induce both her and Leonard to attend a meeting of anti-Fascist intellectuals in Paris.

Oh my dear Virginia, fancy if you and Leonard came after all! What a delight, and what a fortification against communists who will probably try to do the silly! Yes, I am going, so is Aldous, we are trying to persuade Gerald Heard, and there is even a hope of Desmond. Charles Mauron will be there. I do beg you both to come, if only for a day or two. I don't suppose the conference is of any use–things have gone too far. But I have no doubt as to the importance of people like ourselves *inside* the conference. We do represent the last utterances of the civilised.

On this occasion Forster failed. But she could not always resist his appeals, witness a letter to Ethel Smyth written in August 1936.

I was pressed by E. M. Forster to be on a committee–they bothered me to take part–endless correspondence: I refused to budge, finally resigned. But it was harrowing. A woman called Ellis Williams ran amok. Gide and other famous French abused me.

She had to have a problem presented in personal terms before it could capture her imagination. When a fainting girl came down the area steps of 52 Tavistock Square and begged for a glass of water– she had not eaten all day and had been tramping from place to place looking for work–the horrors of unemployment became real to

---

* I.e.: the finding of the Supreme Court in 1935, when the verdict of an all-white Alabama jury upon two Negroes accused of rape was reversed.

her. Dynastic dramas were of course immediately acceptable; she enjoyed the Abdication crisis of 1936 immensely.

Critics and politicians played a growing part in Virginia's existence; they were both unwelcome interruptions in a life which was principally devoted to the increasingly miserable business of trying to write *The Years*. But there were, of course, other interruptions, pleasant and unpleasant, which should be noted.

In January 1935 *Freshwater*,* a play which she had begun twelve years before and had then entirely rewritten, was acted in Vanessa's studio. The performance was somewhat marred by Clive and his brother Cory, spectators who laughed so loud and so long that the dialogue was practically inaudible.

In the spring of 1935 the Woolfs, taking what had become their annual excursion abroad, decided to drive to Rome, there to meet Vanessa and some of her family. I was astonished then (I am astonished still) that Leonard chose to travel by way of Germany.

It is true that the Woolfs had the privileges of foreigners and that they were armed with a letter from Prince Bismarck at the German Embassy in London; it is also true that, in the event, Mitz, Leonard's marmoset (which bore a striking likeness to the late Dr Goebbels), created so strong and so favourable an impression that the Woolfs never had to use their letter of recommendation. Nevertheless, only a slight misfortune was needed in order to create a frighteningly unpleasant incident. In fact they came very near to such a misfortune when they blundered into a Nazi demonstration near Bonn. Not, I think, that they had to fear arrest or physical brutality; but for Virginia a mere show of hostility, of truculence, or of Aryan arrogance, would have been sufficiently shattering. It was the only time, so far as I know, when Leonard took an unjustifiable risk with Virginia's nerves.

Leaving Germany they drove through the Alps to Verona, and thence by way of Bologna, Florence, Perugia and Spoleto to Rome, where Vanessa awaited them. From Rome they made excursions to

* *Freshwater, a Comedy in Three Acts*, deals with the home life of Virginia's great-aunt Mrs Cameron (the photographer) and her friends on the Isle of Wight. There are two versions: the first was written about 1923 (MH/A 25a); the second (MH/A 25b) is the one performed in 1935. A copy in Vanessa Bell's hand (MH/A 25c) has, in addition, a list of props and the cast which acted at the first and only performance at No. 8 Fitzroy Street. Vanessa Bell took the part of Mrs Cameron, Mr Cameron was played by Leonard Woolf, Lord Tennyson by Julian Bell, Ellen Terry by Angelica Bell, G. F. Watts by Duncan Grant, John Craig by Ann Stephen and Eve Younger doubled the parts of Mary (the maid) and Queen Victoria.

the Villa d'Este and to Monte Cassino and in Rome itself there was
not only the Vatican and the Borghese but the rag market to be
visited; here Vanessa was in her element, purchasing cheap crockery
with splendid avidity and reminding Virginia of other journeys in
the days when they were young.

At the *Poste Restante* there was a letter from No. 10 Downing
Street; the Prime Minister would be glad to recommend to His
Majesty . . . In fact it was the offer of a C.H.* Virginia's comment in
her diary was a simple No.

Soon after their return to Tavistock Square Julian Bell arrived in
a state of high excitement; he had been offered and had accepted a
Chair of English at the University of Wuhan. He would be in China
for three years. Virginia regretted his going, yet approved of it; he
had been too long in Cambridge and London, now he would grow
up and it would be good for him. Her nephews, unlike her nieces,
were a cause of exasperation, and exasperation brought a sense of
guilt. She never failed to be irritated by Vanessa's silliness, as she
thought it, on the subject of her children. Even at a dinner which she
and Leonard had purposely arranged to cheer Vanessa up at a time
when she was very much saddened by the loss of Roger, the unlucky
subject of Julian's poems could produce a wrangle in which the
sisters hurt each other when each only wanted to be comforting and
comfortable. In the same way, when I had an exhibition of pictures,
Virginia was grieved by her inability to find anything to say to
Vanessa in praise of them. It was a constant cause of sadness, this
friction between the childless and the maternal sister.

On 5 November 1935 Virginia again recorded what she called
"a specimen day."† By this she meant not a normal day but rather,
I think, a specimen of the distractions, worries, absurdities, that make
up one's life. In other passages she complains that she has had no
time in which to write her diary because there had been too many
"specimen days."

> A specimen day, yesterday: a specimen of the year 1935, when we are
> on the eve of the Duke of Gloucester's wedding: of a general election:
> of the Fascist revolution in France; and in the thick of the Abyssinian
> War: it being mild warm November weather: at 2.30 we went to the
> B.B.C. and listened to some incomparable twaddle soliloquy which
> the B.B.C. requests me to imitate (a good idea, all the same, if one
> were free), with all the resources of the B.B.C. behind one: real railway

* Companion of Honour. This order consists of the Sovereign and not more
than 65 members.
† Possibly a reference to Walt Whitman.

trains; real orchestras; noises; waves, lions and tigers etc. At 3. we reach Dorland Hall*; a loudspeaker proclaiming the virtues of literature, the Princess Louise having just declared the show open and said that books are our best friends. There we meet old stringy Rose Macaulay, beating about like a cat a-hawking odds and ends; Gerald Duckworth, covered with small prickly red squares, as if he had fallen on his face in a bramble bush; Unwin; and so out: home: at 5.15, telephone: the Baroness Nostitz has arrived early: will we see her now: up she comes; a monolithic broad faced Hindenburg, bulky; can't get in and out of my chair; says Germany is the better for Hitler–so they say: but of course I'm not a politician: I want to get some young man to lecture on English poetry: has a rather hard, dominating impassive eye: slow; stately; must have been a beauty; statuesque; aristocratic; then a card: in comes the Indian: stays till 7.30; was turned out of a carriage in Bengal. "That's an Indian!" the lady cried. "If you don't go, I shall kick you". He jumped out, happily into bushes, as the train was going 15 miles an hour. Liberty, justice. A girl who shot at the Governor. Hatred of the British rule: still, it's better than the Italian. Mussolini is paying their fare and hotel bills in order to get them to side with him. "You are our allies. The British will be turned out." And now Morgan rings up–what about Jules Romains? Will you meet him? [This was politics.] May 1 lunch to discuss the French question. And so we go on. Another specimen day.

But the "specimen day" began at 2.30; by that time the real day, the working day, was done. Usually it was devoted to *The Years*; but there were distractions. In 1935 Virginia was reading and making some preliminary notes for the Roger Fry biography, also she was anxious to write *Three Guineas*–at times very anxious. In April 1935 she had met E. M. Forster on the steps of the London Library, the Committee of which had, he told her, been discussing whether to admit ladies as Committee members. Virginia supposed that she was about to be invited to serve; but she was not. Having raised her expectations Forster proceeded to disappoint them. Ladies were troublesome, ladies were impossible, the Committee wouldn't hear of it. Virginia was furious and her projected book, which at this point was called *On Being Despised*, received a new impetus.

Nevertheless, although she could be distracted, she could not for long be diverted from the task of finishing her novel.

The history of the writing of *The Years* was something like this: it began very joyously in the autumn of 1932 and proceeded without a check until June of the following year (1933). Then Virginia's efforts became more spasmodic. She was "in flood" in June, and

* I.e. the Sunday Times Book Exhibition.

again in July; there were difficulties in August and a rearrangement of all the first part. "I have stopped inventing the Pargiters," she writes on 20 August; then she began to rewrite but there was not a word done in October, and on 29 October she declares, "No, my head is too tired." But Part 4 was finished in December and 1934 began with another burst of creative energy; she was at work on the air-raid scene in February, in March she was checked again: Nelly's dismissal hung over her and there were decorators in the house; and then in May, despite influenza on her return from Ireland, she started Part 7 and things went fairly well; in June she lost momentum and regained it; in July "that particular vein" was worked out, and she rested, priming herself for a further effort, getting "a little fresh water" in her well. By August she believed that she could at last see the end of it and, at the time of Roger's death, she was working on the last chapter with some excitement and enthusiasm; the last words of the first draft were written on 30 September 1934.

This was the end of the beginning; so far the progress of *The Years* had been not unlike that of her other novels, apart from the fact that the draft was so very long. Too long, she felt, and decided that drastic cuts must be made. In October, as we have seen, she was very much unnerved by Wyndham Lewis's criticisms; they rein-forced doubts that she already felt about the "nameless book"; for a moment she thought of recasting it in the light of the criticisms that had been made of her other work. She rejected the notion, but still felt thrown out of gear so that she could not work again until November, when she started the rewriting. By 2 December she was so far recovered as to think it rather good. But 1935 brought a set-back. "I am taking a fortnight off fiction. My mind became knotted" (23 January). "Sara is the real difficulty" (20 February), and then, a week later, "writing and writing and rewriting the scene by the Round Pond. . . . It won't be done before August." It was all revision and like many authors she found this the hardest and the saddest part of writing. "Since October 16 I have not written one new sentence but only copied and typed" (6 March). And then later in that month came more hostile criticism and she makes a rather grim observation: "The only thing worth doing in this book is to stick it out." Accordingly she rewrote the entire chapter, and not without some satisfaction. "I think I have actually done the Raid this morning" (28 March).

The difficulty of the work was bad for her nerves and her temper. What Leonard suffered from Ethel Smyth she began to suffer from Kingsley Martin, who was perpetually telephoning or calling to lay his problems before Leonard. He, like Ethel, was a gross feeder, he shovelled the grub into his mouth; he was a bore, a time-waster, and how Leonard could endure so much of his company she could not conceive. In April, when he appeared at Monk's House, his visit was followed by a violent headache and *The Years* had to be given up until after their tour of Holland, Germany and Italy. But that excursion did not cure her. On their return they found their dog Pinka had just died; this depressed Leonard. Virginia complained of "the fidgets"–her name, since childhood, for bouts of intense nervous irritability; she found it very hard to get back into the mood for working at her novel: "I wish for death," she exclaims on 5 June. Mrs Woolf had to be entertained, and then Leonard, as though his family were not affliction enough, complained of Mabel's cooking and her carelessness (she had broken the gramophone) and found Mabel herself a poor substitute for Nelly. There was a domestic explosion and Virginia, with the insouciance of a well-blackened kettle, accused Leonard of not knowing how to deal with servants. The dispute did not last long–their disputes never did–but it produced headaches, despite which she finished what she called a "wild retyping" on 15 July, and in August at Rodmell was making a further typed version at the rate of 100 pages a week and clearly felt a resurgence of energy. Eleanor's day was concluded "with the usual pangs and ecstasies" on the 29th. But this effort had to be paid for: on 5 September she had to stop work; "I can't pump up a word"; on the 6th she declares that she will wrap her brain in green dock leaves, just as she had wrapped her legs in them as a child when they were stung by nettles. She had never had such a "hot balloon" in her head as rewriting *The Years*: it was so long, and the pressure so terrific. Towards the end of September she was dealing with Sally and Maggie in the bedroom; it was, she thought, the most difficult writing she had ever undertaken; but still she hoped to finish by Christmas.

Almost every day of their two months at Monk's House had brought some distraction or interruption in terms of visitors or excursions. On 30 September Virginia went with Leonard to the first day of the Labour Party Conference at Brighton and as a result of this she was so preoccupied with ideas for the book which was finally to emerge as *Three Guineas* that she could hardly think of her novel. But in London again she settled down to regular work on it and set herself a target; she would deliver the completed manuscript by February. It had been decided that *The Years* should be put into galley before Leonard was asked to read it. This was something new and the reasons for it are not clear; perhaps she was afraid of what he might say and wanted to defer the evil moment for as long as possible. Certainly she was terribly anxious about the book and it was making her unwell. On 18 December she writes: "I've had a bad morning at *The Years*," and ten days later: ". . . almost extinct, like a charwoman's duster; that is my brain; what with the last revision of the last pages of *The Years*." Two days later: ". . . it's no go. I can't write a word: too much headache" (30 December). For three days she lay still and tried to vegetate. "My head," she observed on 4 January "is still all nerves; and one false move means racing despair."

The *Life* of Roger Fry was now beginning to become a counter-attraction; she longed to be at it and to abandon this wearing and wearying work of fiction. Already she had read a great many of Roger's letters. In December she had tackled his aesthetic theories. She determined that she would make herself work at *The Years* until midday each day and then relax with the biography. One morning she caught herself cheating: she had contrived to read 11 as 12 on her watch and had stolen an hour from the novel. A few days later she re-read what she had written and was appalled: "Seldom have I been more completely miserable," she wrote; it was feeble twaddle. But there seemed nothing for it: she went on working and she went on getting headaches and on 10 March, 132 pages went to the printer.

Then, for a few days, things seemed to go rather better. But March was a bad month. Hitler was on the Rhine and, suddenly, Virginia recognised that the nightmare of war had returned. The growing international crisis aggravated her own private worries and they were now acute. Her diary records violent alternations of feeling concerning the value of her novel. On 18 March she believed that *The Years* might be very good, on the 19th it seemed hopelessly bad, on the 20th she regained courage, on the 21st she lost it, and so on. Never had she worked so hard at a book and never, since the days when she was finishing *The Voyage Out* and slipping fast towards madness, had she experienced such acute despair on re-reading what she had written. On 24 March she realised, as she was walking in the Strand, that she had begun to talk to herself aloud. She became increasingly alarmed by her own state but managed never-theless to totter on; she rewrote the passage dealing with Eleanor in Oxford Street for the twentieth time on 29 March and on 8 April posted the last batch of typescript to the printer from Rodmell.

Now will come the season of depression, after congestion, suffocation. . . . The horror is that tomorrow, after this one windy day of respite—

oh the cold north wind that has blown ravaging daily since we came, but I've had no ears, eyes, or nose: only making my quick transits from house to room, often in despair—after this one day's respite, I say, I must begin at the beginning and go through 600 pages of cold proof. Why, oh why? Never again, never again . . .

Although Leonard was not to read the novel in manuscript, he read some of the galley proofs as they came from the printer, and, without at all committing himself, he gave Virginia the impression that he was disappointed. Nor was this an entirely false impression: Leonard read enough to have his doubts; he was seriously alarmed by Virginia's condition. "It's terrible about Virginia," wrote Duncan to Vanessa. "It's much better to put the book away. But I wonder why Leonard thinks it may not be so good." Virginia's own doubts and the doubts that she divined in Leonard were enough to bring her to the verge of collapse. All her novels were a cause of anxiety and depression, but this one was by its very nature particularly shattering to her nerves. She had been content, and the critics had been content, with *Jacob's Room*; *Mrs Dalloway* had been the logical outcome of that achievement and, having written *Mrs Dalloway*, she could adventure in the same direction: *To the Lighthouse* and *The Waves* followed naturally, each novel consolidating the ground for its successor. She had known where she was going and she became increasingly certain, as did her public, that she had taken the right path.

But *The Years* was something different, a step back, or at least a step in another direction. It could easily be a wrong direction—a *cul-de-sac*—and if it were, then her friends would be saddened and her enemies—she had recently become well aware that she had enemies—would rejoice. The old nightmare that had visited her when she finished *The Voyage Out*, the nightmare of the jeering crowd, returned. And so, faced by six hundred pages of cold proof, fearful of Leonard's judgement, tortured by repeated and incapacitating headaches, she felt madness coming upon her.

Leonard took her to Cornwall, and as usual Cornwall did her some good. But when she returned to London she was ordered by her doctor to rest at Monk's House. For two months her diary was left untouched. She lost half a stone in weight. A letter to Ethel Smyth written at the end of this time gives a notion of what she was suffering:

. . . never trust a letter of mine not to exaggerate that's written after a night lying awake looking at a bottle of chloral & saying No, no no, you shall not take it. It's odd how sleeplessness, even of a modified kind, has the power to frighten me. It's connected I think with those awful times when I couldn't control myself.

This was written on 4 June 1936; a week later she wrote in her diary:

. . . at last after two months dismal and worse, almost catastrophic illness—never been so near the precipice to my own feeling since 1913—I'm again on top.

But it was scarcely true. Very slowly, very painfully, she set about the task of correcting her proofs. She had to take a great deal of rest, and was continually obliged to stop—the pain in her head, her feelings of complete despair and failure—were too intense. Writing again to Ethel she said: "I have to consider the appalling nuisance that I am to Leonard—angel that he is." Leonard's angelic qualities were soon to be tested. For at length, on the 2nd of November, after pains and difficulties which it would be otiose to record, the proofs were all corrected and handed to him for inspection. Virginia herself had made up her mind, or at least she thought she had. She had re-read *The Years* and concluded that it was impossibly bad. The proofs would have to be destroyed; it was throwing away two or three hundred pounds, and four years of her life had been wasted. But it was better, in a way it was a relief, to face the situation frankly. All this she said to Leonard, who answered that she might perhaps be wrong; he would read it and tell her what he thought.

Leonard was not able to start his reading until late in the day. After a round of weary trivialities and excursions they came home in the evening and Leonard began to read. He read in silence. Leonard's silences could be pretty frightening and certainly Virginia was frightened; as he read on she fell into a kind of feverish doze, a sort of miserable half-sleep. Meanwhile Leonard was feeling both disappointed and relieved. The book was a failure—but it was not so disastrous a failure as Virginia supposed. It would therefore be possible to tell a lie; if he told her the truth he had very little doubt that she would kill herself.

Suddenly he put down the proof and said, "I think it's extraordinarily good."

Chapter Nine

November 1936–September 1939

ON 24 November 1936 Virginia noted in her diary:

> . . . I've been on the whole vigorous and cheerful since the wonderful revelation of L[eonard]'s that night. Now I woke from death–or non being–to life! What an incredible night–what a weight rolled off!

But although Leonard's duplicity had succeeded in its main purpose, Virginia needed more reassurance than he could give; she had been severely shaken; nor were her ills to be ascribed simply to her novel and the state of mind that her novel engendered. She suffered from swollen veins, a sense of falling, a feeling that the blood was not reaching her head, and a tendency, when she was alone, to fall into a sort of trance or coma, symptoms which she attributed, no doubt correctly, to the change of life.

She welcomed distractions now; was glad that she had Lord Robert Cecil to tea, glad to be lunching with Mme de Polignac and Nadia Boulanger, glad of the company of Ethel Smyth, of Dorothy Wellesley and of older friends, glad of the Abdication crisis with all its picture-book absurdities, glad in fact of anything which could make her forget that she had, with her own hands, lit a fuse which would burn steadily for the next few months and explode a charge beneath her feet when *The Years* was thrown upon the world. Under the circumstances, work and society might both be used as opiates, and so she saw a great many people and returned to *Three Guineas*. Whatever else may be said for or against that work it was certainly therapeutic; she had always to be writing something; but *this* writing induced none of those aesthetic miseries which always accompanied her novels. It enabled her to let off steam, to hit back at what seemed to her the tyrannous hypocrisy of men.

The New Year opened with misfortunes. Stephen Tomlin died early in January, and two weeks later Miss West, one of the employees of the Hogarth Press. Both these deaths left Virginia with a feeling of guilt–she felt now that she had been unreasonable in the matter of Tomlin's sculpture, and recalled his good qualities; she felt also that she should have been more sociable, more accessible, to the workers in the Press. But a far more serious disaster threatened when Leonard was taken ill at the beginning of February 1937. It seemed to be a serious liver complaint, or diabetes, or perhaps prostate–the doctors didn't know what. Leonard himself remained calm, took to his bed, lived upon rice pudding and continued, as always, to work very hard at politics, journalism and the business of the Press. But it was not so easy for Virginia to remain calm; if Leonard were in hospital, or worse, she would be left alone to face the crisis which now lay hardly more than a month ahead. So that when, on 12 February, they drove off together to Rodmell with a complete medical pardon, it was with a sense of relief, of sheer overflowing joy, such as she does not often record during these years. And three days later she noticed with complacency that 38 pages of *Three Guineas* were now written.

Saturday, February 20th

I turn my eyes away from the Press as I go upstairs, because there are all the review copies of *The Years* packed and packing. They go out next week: this is my last week-end of comparative peace. What do I anticipate with such clammy coldness? I think chiefly that my friends won't mention it; will turn the conversation rather awkwardly. I think I anticipate considerable lukewarmness among the friendly re-viewers–respectful tepidity; and a whoop of Red Indian delight from the Grigs who will joyfully and loudly announce that this is the long-drawn twaddle of a prim prudish bourgeois mind, and say that now no one can take Mrs. W. seriously again. But violence I shan't so much mind. What I think I shall mind most is the awkwardness when I go, say to Tilton or Charleston, and they don't know what to say. And since we shan't get away till June I must expect a very full exposure to this damp firework atmosphere. They will say it's a tired book; a last effort. . . . Well, now that I've written that down I feel that even so I can exist in that shadow. That is if I keep hard at work. . . .

Monday, March 1st

I wish I could write out my sensations at this moment. They are so peculiar and so unpleasant. Partly T[ime]. of L[ife]. I wonder? A physical feeling as if I were drumming slightly in the veins: very cold: impotent: and terrified. As if I were exposed on a high ledge in full light. Very lonely. L. out to lunch. Nessa has Quentin, don't want me. Very useless. No atmosphere round me. No words. Very apprehensive. As if something cold and horrible–a roar of laughter at my expense were about to happen. And I am powerless to ward it off; I have no protection. And this anxiety and nothingness surround me with a vacuum. It affects the thighs chiefly. And I want to burst into tears, but have nothing to cry for. Then a great restlessness seizes me. I think I could walk it off–walk and walk till I am asleep. But I begin to dislike that sudden drugged sleep. And I cannot unfurl my mind and apply it calmly and unconsciously to a book. And my own little scraps look dried up and derelict. And I know that I must go on doing this dance on hot bricks till I die. This is a little superficial I admit. For I can burrow under and look at myself displayed in this ridiculous way and feel complete submarine calm: a kind of calm moreover which is strong enough to lift the entire load: I can get that at moments; but the exposed moments are terrifying. I looked at my eyes in the glass once and saw them positively terrified. It's the 15th March approaching I suppose–the dazzle of that head lamp on my poor little rabbit's body which keeps it dazed in the middle of the road. (I like that phrase. That gives me confidence.)

Tuesday, March 2nd

I'm going to be beaten, I'm going to be laughed at, I'm going to be held up to scorn and ridicule–I found myself saying those words just now. Yet I've been absorbed all the morning in the autobiography part of *Three Guineas*. And the absorption is genuine: and my great defence against the cold madness that overcame me last night. Why did it suddenly point itself like a rain cloud and discharge all its cold water? Because I was switched off doing Pictures in the morning: and then at the play*; I suddenly thought the Book Society has not even recommended *The Years*. That's true; but the B.S. is not an infallible guide. Anyhow these days of waiting must be a dull cold torture. I shall be happy enough this time next month I've no doubt. Meanwhile, suffer me now and again to write out my horror, this sudden cold madness, here. It is partly T. of L. I think still. And it won't be anything like so bad in action as in prospect. The worst will be that the book will be treated with tepid politeness, as an effusive diluted tired book. All my other books have stirred up strife; this one will sink slowly and heavily. But when that's said, need I fear more? I may get praise from some people. Indeed I think there must be some 'seriousness' in it. And I can feel a little proud that I have faced the music; that we have sold 5,000 before publication: that we shall get some money; that I'm doing my share, and not merely subsiding into terrified silence. Also my own psychology interests me. I intend to keep full notes of my ups and downs for my private information. And thus objectified, the pain and shame become at once much less. And I have proved to my own conviction that I can write with fury, with rapture, with absorption still.

On the morning of Friday, 12 March, Leonard brought *The Times Literary Supplement* to Virginia as she lay in bed. It carried a

* *Le Misanthrope.*

favourable review; and so, later in the day, did *Time and Tide*; on Sunday the *Observer* added two columns of praise; it became obvious that *The Years* was a success, so far as the newspapers were concerned at all events. Virginia's old friends were less enthusiastic; Maynard, so far as I know, was the only one of them to give his unqualified approval. But Virginia's fears had been so intense, the public acclaim was so great, the triumph of the book, in terms of copies sold, was so emphatic that she could feel little save relief. There were some unfavourable notices to be sure; but they were nothing to what she had expected.

The success of *The Years* became news to such an extent that the *New York Times* sent a journalist to get personal details; he rang up and was told that he could look at the outside of 52 Tavistock Square if he chose. But he was not to be denied. He appeared at Monk's House in a Daimler and Virginia found that he had walked into her sitting-room and was coolly taking notes. She fled unobserved, and presently Leonard managed to get rid of him. Virginia was incensed by such behaviour, as I suppose anyone might be. But her reaction was odd. She burst into an almost hysterical outburst of half-rhymed prose, rather like a parody of Joyce.*

The Woolfs had arranged to take a holiday early in May; but before leaving for France Virginia had the satisfaction of accomplishing two pieces of business. On 29 April she broadcast. It was not her only broadcast but it is of interest as it was the only one to be recorded; and it seems worth noting, for the benefit of posterity, that this record is a very poor one. Her voice is deprived of depth and resonance; it seems altogether too fast and too flat; it is barely recognisable. Her speaking voice was in fact beautiful – though not so beautiful as Vanessa's – and it is sad that it should not have been immortalised in a more satisfactory manner.

On the day of her broadcast, while Leonard was checking the stock in Virginia's studio, the Woolfs once again discussed the question of the Hogarth Press and resolved that they must either give it up altogether or radically change its organisation. It was by no means the first time that they had decided this; but now, they were in earnest. The little hobby, involving a hand press and a few pounds of type, had become a considerable business. But for Virginia it was inconvenient and worse than inconvenient. It kept her in London when she should have been in the country; it obliged her to read manuscripts when she should have been writing them. It was a worry, a distraction, it had been a source of endless disputes

* See Appendix B.

between Leonard and the young men whom he had brought in as apprentice managers, and, because it was emotionally important to him, it was a source of agitation to her.

In October 1937 a solution presented itself:

> ... suddenly L. developed the idea of making the young Brainies take the Press as a co-operative company (John [Lehmann]: Isherwood: Auden: Stephen [Spender]). All are bubbling with discontent and ideas. All want a focus: a manager: a mouthpiece: a common voice. Would like L[ehmann] to manage it. Couldn't we sell and creep out?

Only John Lehmann was sufficiently interested in the possibilities of the Hogarth Press to consider buying them out altogether. But by this time it was so large a concern that he could afford only fifty per cent of the business. He bought out Virginia. It was not a very good arrangement—indeed it had all the disadvantages of the old one, with the added drawback that Leonard and his new partner were bound by a commercial marriage from which neither could easily escape. "There were," writes John Lehmann, "checks and clashes ... though Virginia's presence helped to cool our fevers and bring us back to the understanding that really underlay our differences." But in April 1937 these plans and these mistakes were still in the future, and Virginia could take her holiday with the comforting assurance that the burden of the Press was to be lifted off her back and that *The Years* had, after all, not been a total disaster.

On the other hand there were still abundant causes for unhappiness. Janet Case was ill; she had taught Virginia Greek and was one of the few people who had known her intimately during the opening years of the century; she had remained a steadfast friend. Now it was clear that she was dying. "No one," wrote Virginia to Margaret Llewelyn Davies, "not Leonard even, knows how much I have to thank Janet for." And now Virginia sent her letters, visited her, and at last, when she died in June 1937, wrote her obituary for *The Times*. When the Woolfs were in France in May, news came that Maynard Keynes was desperately ill, and they drove through the Dordogne expecting, in every newspaper, to read that he was dead. He recovered, thanks largely to Lydia's care, but there was another calamity in preparation, one which was, in a way, more dreadful.

Julian Bell had written from China late in 1936 to say that he was coming home in the Spring. His main object was to take an active part in politics, and soon it appeared that he intended to go to Spain to fight for the Republic. Virginia, as soon as she became aware of this, wrote begging him to remain where he was; but in vain.

From this time Vanessa's happiness was at an end. The spectacle of her dumb despair added to the horror of those weeks in the Spring of 1937 when Virginia was preparing herself as best she might for the publication of *The Years*. She certainly felt some anger against her nephew; she felt that he must know what torture he was inflicting, and it was very hard for her to sympathise with the emotions of a young man who felt that he could not leave other people to do his fighting for him; still less could she sympathise with the excited interest of one who saw in warfare itself an art form to be enjoyed for its own sake. To her, therefore, Julian's attitude seemed quite incomprehensible.

Things were made worse by the fact that Julian allowed himself to be deflected a little from his purpose. His first idea, that he would leave the boat at Marseilles and go straight to Spain, was abandoned. He returned to England in March and other political occupations, suggested by Leonard, were proposed as substitutes and not altogether rejected. Nevertheless, when he came home, it was at once clear to Virginia that something had happened to him. He had grown up. There was a new authority, a new tension in his manner. Presently he declared that he must go to Spain, if not as a soldier, then as an ambulance driver. For Vanessa it was as though a small window of hope were shuttered and bolted; she continued, in a sense, to enjoy Julian's company—now he was her dearest child—though with an intolerably aching heart. Virginia saw and understood everything and could do nothing about it; like Vanessa, she was convinced that if he did go to Spain he would not return.

They were right: he left for Spain on 7 June; he was killed on 18 July. The matter concerns us only in as much as it concerned Virginia. She was appalled by her own loss; but it was Vanessa's affliction that hurt her most. Virginia, being in London, was of necessity a witness of her sister's first shocking paroxysms of grief. Thereafter she was a daily visitor at Vanessa's bedside, giving what consolation she could, trying with every device of her imagination to make Vanessa's existence bearable.

Discussing Julian's action with Leonard's friend W. A. Robson, Virginia could allow that "there is a kind of grandeur . . . which somehow now & then consoles one. Only to see what she has to suffer makes one doubt if anything in the world is worth it." The spectacle of this daily renewed torture was something that might shake the reason and the nerves of anyone, especially of Virginia. But like Thoby's death thirty years earlier it was a challenge to which she rose. She was hardly aware of how well she did and it was a surprise to her when she discovered–at a later date–that while Vanessa lay in bed in what she herself called "an unreal state," it seemed to her that Virginia's voice was the only thing that kept life from coming to an end.

Throughout August and September Vanessa was an invalid. Only very slowly was she able to return to something like normal life and to paint a little. "I shall be cheerful, but I shall never be happy again," she told Virginia. The Woolfs drove her down to Charleston late in July and themselves moved to Monk's House so that Virginia might see her daily: "the only point in the day," as Vanessa said, "that one could want to come." Thus Virginia continued to be the witness of a misery that she could not cure. She had to prevent herself from thinking about it too much. Any day when she could not get to Charleston she wrote, and Vanessa, receiving these notes, would sometimes remark with a wintry little smile, "Another love letter from Virginia," and went on to say sadly that she found it difficult to respond to Virginia's affection: "When she is demonstrative I always shrink away." Not that Virginia's affection was unimportant–far from it. Virginia had helped her more than she could say; but she was unable to express her gratitude to Virginia herself. She had to write to Vita who, as Vanessa knew, would see that her message reached its destination.

Seven months later Vanessa did manage to be rather more explicit: Virginia, remembering that Julian's birthday fell on 4 February, wrote a line of affection. Vanessa replied: "I couldn't get on at all if it weren't for you," and went on to regret that she was such an emotional wet blanket.

Virginia, at the time of Julian's death, had been getting on very well with *Three Guineas*; now for some time she found this work impossible and instead wrote an account of her nephew and of their last meetings.* Later on, when she returned to her book during the autumn, she found that it became in a large measure a kind of argument with Julian, or rather with what she supposed to be Julian's point of view.

That autumn *The Years*, having sold very well in England, became a best-seller in the United States and for the first time she found herself really wealthy. As she observed, in October, "We have the materials for happiness, but no happiness." She had but two consolations: the continued easy progress of *Three Guineas*, and Leonard. In October she felt a sudden impulse to take a holiday in Paris. She looked up trains, she asked Vanessa about hotels. Then Leonard

* See Appendix C.

said that he didn't want to go and she discovered, to her enormous satisfaction, that if he didn't come with her it wasn't worth going. It was like falling in love again and the pleasure was exquisite. But even the joy which derived from a solid and happy marriage had its Janus head. Early in 1938 Leonard had a return of the malady which had so alarmed Virginia a year before. The scare on this occasion was greater than before, and lasted longer, although it brought the same happy conclusion. Virginia was impatient with the doctors, and Helen Anrep, who was seeing a good deal of her (for now the *Life* of Roger was beginning in earnest), was touched by this concern and by her evident pride in doing things for Leonard.

This evil brought another in its train. Vanessa, who had been genuinely and unaffectedly distressed when Leonard seemed dangerously ill, grew bored and impatient with the description of his symptoms when once he was out of danger; nor, I think, did she altogether conceal her impatience. She was in fact profoundly irritated by Leonard at this time and throughout 1938, for in the preparation of a memorial volume* devoted to Julian she was continually encountering Leonard's not unreasonable caution concerning the work that he was to publish, and his dislike of what he rather impatiently called "Vanessa's necrophily." In fact her anxiety that Julian's genius should be recognised, and the Woolfs' scepticism concerning that genius, were even more likely to breed quarrels after his death than they had been during his lifetime. To make matters more difficult, the inevitable administrative disputes with John Lehmann over the Press were now beginning. Some of these disputes were concerned with the memorial volume and Vanessa tended to take John's side.

Three Guineas was published in June 1938. It is the product of a very odd mind and, I think, of a very odd state of mind.† It was intended as a continuation of *A Room of One's Own*, but it was written in a far less persuasive, a far less playful mood. It was a protest against oppression, a genuine protest denouncing real evils and, to the converted, Virginia did not preach in vain. A great many women wrote to express their enthusiastic approval; but her close

---

* *Julian Bell. Essays, Poems and Letters.* Edited by Quentin Bell, with contributions by J. M. Keynes, David Garnett, Charles Mauron, C. Day Lewis and E. M. Forster. The Hogarth Press, 1938.

† ". . . the book which was like a spine to me all last summer; upheld me in the horror of last August: and whirled me like a top miles upon miles over the downs. How can it all have petered out into diluted drivel? But it remains, morally, a spine: the thing I wished to say, though futile." *AWD (Berg)*, 12 March 1938.

friends were silent, or if not silent, critical. Vita did not like it, and Maynard Keynes was both angry and contemptuous; it was, he declared, a silly argument and not very well written. What really seemed wrong with the book–and I am speaking here of my own reactions at the time–was the attempt to involve a discussion of women's rights with the far more agonising and immediate question of what we were to do in order to meet the ever-growing menace of Fascism and war. The connection between the two questions seemed tenuous and the positive suggestions wholly inadequate.

The book was pretty severely attacked; but on the whole Virginia does not seem to have minded very much. There was, however, one critic of whom she was obliged to take notice, for she was a woman and a very eloquent woman. Her name was Agnes Smith and she lived near Huddersfield. At the time of the publication of *Three Guineas* she was unemployed. In a long, fluent and forceful letter she objected that Virginia had said nothing about working women. Of what use was it to suggest that women should refuse to manufacture arms when they were only too glad to have the opportunity to manufacture anything? She herself was living on a dole of 15s. a week, and she described how when her nephew, a small child, cried for an extra piece of cake, and got it, it had meant that she herself had nothing more to eat for the rest of the day. From Agnes Smith's next letter it is clear Virginia replied that *Three Guineas* had been explicitly addressed to women in a more fortunate social position; but the tone of that letter must also have encouraged her correspondent to write again and, although I think that they never met, they continued to write to each other, at intervals, until the end of Virginia's life.

But the true criticism of *Three Guineas* came from events; for the events of 1938 did not turn upon the Rights of Women but upon the Rights of Nations. In March, when Hitler invaded Austria, Virginia had written in her diary: "When the tiger . . . has digested his dinner he will pounce again." It was indeed becoming difficult to think of anything save the growing menace of war. *Roger Fry* was not a very potent diversion.

In April, however, she was struck by the idea of a book about England and English literature to be called, perhaps, *Poyntzet Hall*. In June, after the publication of *Three Guineas*, the Woolfs took a holiday in Scotland. Virginia wrote to Vanessa:

> Well, here we are in Skye, & it feels like the South Seas–completely remote, surrounded by sea, people speaking Gaelic, no railways, no London papers, hardly any inhabitants. Believe it or not, it is (in its

way, as people say) so far as I can judge on a level with Italy, Greece or Provence. No one in Fitzroy Street will believe this; & descriptions are your abhorrence–further the room is pullulating & popping with Edinburgh tourists, one of whom owns spaniels, like Sally [her dog], but "all mine are gun trained, the only thing they won't carry being hares"–so I can't run on, did you wish it. Only–well, in Duncan's highlands, the colours in a perfectly still deep blue lake of green & purple trees reflected in the middle of the water which was enclosed with green reeds & yellow flags, & the whole sky & a purple hill– well, enough. One should be a painter. As a writer, I feel the beauty, which is almost entirely colour, very subtle, very changeable, running over my pen, as if you poured a large jug of champagne over a hair- pin. I must here tender my congratulations to Duncan upon being a Grant. We've driven round the island today, seen Dungevan [*sic*], encountered the children of the 27th Chieftain, nice red headed brats: the Castle door being open I walked in; they very politely told me the Castle was shut to visitors, but I could see the gardens. Here I found a gamekeepers larder with the tails of two wild cats. Eagles are said to abound & often carry off sheep: sheep & Skye Terriers are the only industries; the old women live in round huts exactly the shape of skye terriers; & you can count all the natives on 20 feet: but they are very rapacious in the towns, & its no use trying to buy anything, as the price, even of Sally's meat, is at least 6 times higher than in our honest land. All the same, the Scotch are great charmers, & sing through their noses like musical tea kettles. The only local gossip I've collected for you is about your Mr Hambro's wife–the one who was drowned in Loch Ness. We met a charming Irish couple in an Inn, who were in touch, through friends, with the Monster. They had seen him. He is like several broken telegraph posts & swims at immense speed. He has no head. He is constantly seen. Well, after Mrs Hambro was drowned, the Insurance Company sent divers after her, as she was wearing 30,000 pounds of pearls on her head. They dived & came to the mouth of a vast cavern, from which hot water poured; & the current was so strong, & the horror they felt so great, they refused to go further, being convinced the Monster lived there, in a hollow under the hill. In short, Mrs Hambro was swallowed. No drowned body is ever recovered & now the natives refuse to boat or to bathe. That is all the local gossip. And I will NOT describe the colour.

They returned at the beginning of July to find that *Three Guineas* was selling very well, to the "fearful niggling drudgery" of the biography, and to a different kind of monster.

They were at Rodmell in September when war began to seem inevitable. Kingsley Martin, who, so it appeared to Virginia, sought Leonard in every crisis, much as a timid bothering child might come running to its Nanny, telephoned on the 26th in a state of panic and implored Leonard to return to London. The Woolfs drove up together. It was raining; men were digging trenches. Kingsley was melodramatic and tedious; it never became clear why he wanted Leonard; the telephone rang continually.

Virginia escaped to the London Library to look up *The Times* of 1910 on the first Post-Impressionist exhibition. There, in the basement, an old man came gently dusting.

"They're telling us to try on our masks, Madam.'
"Have you got yours?"
"No, not yet."
"And shall we have war?"
"I fear so, but I still hope not. I live out at Putney. Oh they've laid in sandbags; the books will be moved; but if a bomb strikes the house ... May I dust under your chair?"

She went to the National Gallery; someone was lecturing to quite a large audience on Watteau. Then she returned to Tavistock Square; plans had to be made to evacuate the Press. They drove back through torrential rain to Monk's House. It seemed curiously sane and beautiful after London. At 10.30 that night the local Air Raid Warden brought their gas masks.

On 28 September they expected a declaration of war; instead they heard that Mr Chamberlain was on his way to Munich; the 'Settlement' was made on the following day. "We have peace without honour for six months," said Leonard, and the postman expressed the same opinion at much greater length on the doorstep. Virginia felt that it was probably true; still, the sense of reprieve was tremendous and she could work again.

But the work on which she was engaged could not please her. The discipline of facts, facts pure and simple, without a novelist's licence or the opportunity for polemics, bored her. *Pointz Hall* was now her relaxation; it was beginning to become *Between the Acts* and it could on occasion give her a day's pleasure. But *Roger Fry* had somehow to be written. Difficulties accumulated; there was the unspoken censorship of the Fry sisters, that of her own feelings, and there was Helen Anrep. She was sorry for Helen Anrep; she liked her (most of the time), but Helen could be trying. Encouraged by Vanessa, she had persuaded Virginia to become one of the guarantors of a new School of Drawing and Painting (which later became known as "The Euston Road School"). This didn't worry Virginia–she was rich now–neither should it have worried her that she lent Helen £150; but it did.

The lamentable story of that loan, which amused Vanessa a good deal, began in October 1938 when Helen Anrep dined with the Woolfs at Tavistock Square. After dinner, she and Virginia discussed the progress of Roger's biography; they talked about his ruthlessness–yes, he was ruthless, although his motives were pure and good; they discussed the breach between Roger and Sir William Rothenstein (whom Virginia was later to interview and to find very agreeable). Then, most unluckily, the talk turned to the subject of *Three Guineas*. Helen Anrep, who prided herself on speaking her mind and was always ready, with a kind of mock imperiousness, to tax her friends with their faults, told Virginia what she thought of her book. Helen's overbearing way amused some people; it annoyed others. Virginia was one of the others. With apparent humility she told Helen that probably she was right; she, Virginia, was not gifted for any writing save fiction or criticism; ought she not then to abandon the *Life* of Roger? Helen, I surmise, was appalled by this application of her criticisms; but worse was to come. Virginia now became solicitous about Helen's financial situation. It appeared that she could not meet her commitments. Virginia offered to pay off her overdraft. Helen, after some hesitation, accepted.

Virginia had attempted to redress the balance of her ruffled feelings by a large gesture; she regretted it almost at once, particularly when she discovered that the overdraft was not, as she had supposed, a matter of some fifty pounds but one hundred and fifty. All the old Stephen money terrors awoke within her; she was shooting Niagara; she had been reckless; she would be ruined. It gave her sleepless nights and, even though she must have known that her alarms were absurd and that the sales of *The Years* made such generosities perfectly safe, she could not be easy in her financial conscience until she had rewritten and sold an old story, *Lappin and Lapinova*, to America.

Meanwhile Helen herself was far from easy. Somehow, she felt, she must repay Virginia. In 1939 she was trying to economise for this purpose. In the Spring of 1940 she wrote to Vanessa, "if only I could ever get enough money ahead to pay Virginia even a small instalment I should breathe more happily"; and at length, in February 1941, she managed to save £25 and sent it to Virginia. To crown the sad absurdity of the transaction it appears that Helen's insolvency, like Virginia's terrors, was purely imaginary. The muddle of her accounts was so great that she had imagined a deficit which never existed.

"We have reached a time of life," said Duncan, "when we must expect our friends to die." In the year 1938 it must have seemed to

Virginia that this was indeed the case. Ottoline died in April, Ka Cox in May. The death of Ka affected her chiefly because she felt it so little; for many years now they had met to remember rather than to renew their friendship. The loss of Ottoline was much more felt. Virginia wrote an obituary of her for *The Times*. The world seemed greatly impoverished by the disappearance of that fantastic being; there had been something grand about her and, in later years, something rather touching and lovable.

At the end of the year Jack Hills died–but he indeed was "a figure from the past"; and in June 1939 Mark Gertler committed suicide. Public events were not of a kind to dissipate the general gloom. Franco was in Barcelona in January 1939; he was in Madrid (and Hitler in Prague) by March. Julian's life seemed, more than ever, to have been thrown away. "Maynard, even Maynard," wrote Virginia, "can't find much that's hopeful now." England was full of refugees. Freud was in Hampstead and the Woolfs went to see him. He gave Virginia a narcissus and talked, as everyone then talked, about Hitler. It would take a generation, he said, to work out the poison. And what were they, the English, going to do? He struck Virginia as an alert, "screwed up shrunk very old man," an "old fire now flickering" and, as they all knew, near to extinction.

And all the time she was working on Roger; she brought what she called the "first sketch" to an end on 11 March 1939, and hoped to have it all finished by July; but it was not. On 12 July, "For the first time for weeks, after being so damnably down in the mouth . . . I've worked with some pleasure at R[oger]." In that month there was yet another death, that of old Mrs Woolf, Leonard's mother. It did not touch Virginia deeply, and yet she was saddened. The poor old creature had been very silly and very boring, she had wasted a lot of Virginia's time and yet, in a way, Virginia was fascinated by her and deeply sorry for her, for she was a lonely self-pitying person who tried to keep up a fiction of intense family affection to which Leonard, despite a strong sense of filial duty, could not respond. With Virginia, she played an odd, unreal game, in which each tried to act out the not very suitable part allotted to them by fate.

But there was still plenty of fun. That is a fact which must be stated but which it is difficult to convey. Virginia's diaries, it is true, become increasingly despondent; private miseries and public events struck with overwhelming force, but still, she was not overwhelmed. Neither Vanessa nor Virginia ever courted sorrow, or wallowed in grief as their father had done when *he* was bereaved.

It was their instinct to remain as cheerful as they could, and the new friends whom Virginia made in the 'thirties—as for instance Elizabeth Bowen, Shena Simon, Stephen Spender—did not carry away with them the impression of an old and gloomy authoress, frustrated in her work, bereaved and menaced. At Monk's House and at 52 Tavistock Square the prevailing sound was still one of laughter; it might take some courage to go on laughing at that time, but an appearance—and indeed a reality—of gaiety was maintained.*

In June 1939 the Woolfs took a holiday in Brittany. Virginia had always wanted to visit Les Rochers and pay her respects to a great predecessor.† They returned to face the business of moving house. No. 52 Tavistock Square was to be pulled down and the area redeveloped. Together with their friendly tenants the solicitors Messrs Dolman and Pritchard, they looked for and found a suitable house in Mecklenburgh Square. They left their old home on 25 July. At the same time various new additions to Monk's House were completed. The Bells simultaneously were making further additions to Charleston. There was a general atmosphere of retreat and fortification in the country, of making all secure and shipshape before the coming of the storm.

Virginia spent much time walking about the City of London; it was almost as though she were saying goodbye to it. There was not much time in which to do so, for in August "last year's mad voice" was heard again; and this time a defiant answer had become inevitable.

* Virginia wrote one of the gayest and one of the most hilarious of her letters to Vanessa at the height of the Munich crisis. Unfortunately it is not a letter which can, at present, be published.

† *Madame de Sevigné*, which was published, together with other essays, in *The Death of the Moth* (1942), was almost certainly written at this period.

Chapter Ten

1939–1941

ON the morning of 3 September 1939, Virginia and Leonard sat arguing in their new sitting-room at the top of Monk's House while they waited for Mr Chamberlain to speak to the nation. Virginia said it was 'they' who made wars; 'we' as usual remained outside and had no voice in our fate. And supposing the Allies were to win—then what?

"Better to win the war than to lose it," replied Leonard. This in fact had become the only choice. Virginia more than half agreed and yet, to face those harsh alternatives was difficult for her—difficult also for the nation at large, and for nine months we most of us refused to do so.

At Monk's House the first effect of the war was to produce a kind of peace. Yards of blackout material were bought and made into curtains (Virginia's blackout was not very efficient and she was in trouble with the police at least once). Pregnant mothers, hurriedly evacuated from the capital, were decanted from buses and presently drifted disconsolately back to London; the first sirens sounded the first false alarm. Virginia and Leonard returned to their usual tasks and diversions; throughout that wonderfully fine autumn they played bowls up and down their undulating green. But Virginia was under no illusions, or at least she had fewer illusions than most of us. The war, it seemed to her, was beginning in cold blood, the killing machine was starting silently, but it was not the less deadly for that. It was working very efficiently in Poland and, when the Poles had been conquered, "we shall be attended to." And, while the newspapers indulged in the kind of jolly hubristic patriotism which Virginia particularly disliked, Kingsley Martin brought dark rumours of chaos, inefficiency and despair.

The biography still had to be finished; that ungrateful task plagued her all through the autumn and winter, and from time to time she took refuge in *Pointz Hall*, which she had been writing intermittently all through 1939. She also began to write her memoirs, which, unfortunately, are incomplete.

When war broke out she decided to return to journalism and to write for *The New Statesman*. She did this partly because she took it for granted that she and Leonard would be impoverished by the war, partly for reasons which are not easy to understand. Journalism represented, in some way, a kind of patriotic gesture, or at least a way of meeting the emergency, though in what way the war effort, or indeed her private income, would benefit by the fact that she now gave time to articles on Sir Walter Scott or Horace Walpole, it would be hard to say. I think also that she simply felt that she wanted to be doing something different. Everyone else, it seemed, had found or was looking for a new employment; so would she. T. S. Eliot wrote to say that he half expected to meet her in Russell Square directing the traffic and wearing an Air Raid Warden's tin hat.

In that 'phoney' period of the war there were no air raids, but raids were expected and when, in October, the Woolfs drove to London and were confronted by large posters at Wimbledon declaring "THE WAR BEGINS. HITLER SAYS: NOW IT'S ON," Virginia remarked to Leonard that it seemed foolish to have chosen that particular day for their visit. They appeared to be driving into a trap and she was frightened; but not for very long; later she felt that there was sufficient community of sentiment in the capital to allow her to merge her private emotions with those of others. London seemed sober and businesslike. At night it was dark and so unsocial that she wondered whether she might not be seeing the end of urban life and the beginning of a time when badgers and foxes, owls and nightingales would populate the darkened city. But by day there were more familiar manifestations. Mrs Sidney Webb–"like the veins of a leaf when the pulp has been eaten away"–presiding over lunch in a spacious Victorian room with sideboards and maids; the ordered conversation: ten minutes for Virginia and ten for Leonard; sharp remarks about Wells and Shaw. Mrs Webb said she was thankful for her Victorian training in morality; "I said we were moral in fighting that morality. Now there's a morality to make again." The old Fabian marched on and Virginia, as usual, found her uncommonly depressing and was glad to leave her.

She tried to bring some order into their new home in Mecklenburgh Square, which was still in a state of confusion and most uncomfortable. The kitchen seemed too small, everywhere else too large, the stairs were bad, there were no carpets. The staff of the Press were uneasy, Sally the spaniel was unwell. Virginia felt useless, fretful and *désœuvrée*. After a week of London they returned to the peace of Monk's House.

In the ensuing months–until their house became uninhabitable in

September 1940–Leonard and Virginia would drive up to London every other week and spend a few days there.

Nevertheless it was many years since Virginia had spent so much of her winter in the country–not in fact since 1913. It was an experience which interested, depressed and exalted her. In a way it was the fulfilment of a dream, the dream of escaping from London, of getting away from Colefax and her like and from the Press, of having abundant leisure in which to read and to write and very little company save their own. Better still, she need no longer feel, as she usually did in the country, that she was "out of things." "Things" seemed to have vanished, or at all events to have left town. Moreover at this time Virginia seems to have wanted, or half wanted, to be "out of things." She had, she decided, come to a stage in her career in which fame would leave her. She would become "an outsider"– it might be just as well. Living in the country she might claim to be living the part. However, living alone in the country, particularly if you have a book on your hands that won't come right and won't get finished, can be boring. Monk's House at that time was a decidedly cold house and the winter of 1939/40 was quite dramatically cold.* Snow made roads impassable, the brooks froze solid, and there was ice even on the tidal Ouse. Then there was a sudden thaw, followed by an even more sudden frost, so that all the country seemed glazed with diamond-clear ice which at sunset and sunrise gave it a prismatic splendour of unbelievable beauty.

After Christmas there was one last Bloomsbury celebration, Angelica's twenty-first birthday party which, since wartime shortages had not yet made themselves felt, could be celebrated with some *éclat*. Lydia danced for the last time and Duncan danced with her, Marjorie Strachey sang *The Lost Chord*, a young German refugee gave a parody of the Führer, and Virginia obliged with *The Last Rose of Summer*, of which she knew, or invented, a great many verses. Everyone was gay, everyone knew that there would be no more such gaieties.

---

* The cold at Monk's House was so intense that Morgan Forster, vainly seeking to warm himself by the "Cosy Stove" in his bedroom, burnt his trousers. At Charleston he was warmer; but here the house caught fire. He celebrated these events on the back of a National Gallery Concert programme:

> "*To a cosy stove, installed in a hospitable homestead*
>
> "O hearth benign! O decent glow!
> My trousers, blackened down below,
> Accuse not thee, but praise the zest
> Which burns the host before the guest."

"Oh, it's a queer sense of suspense, being led up to the spring of 1940." Virginia wrote this in her diary on 8 February; she felt that we were all being led to an altar, a sacrificial altar garlanded with blossoms of flame. Towards the end of February she had influenza and for a long time was unable to shake it off; nevertheless Leonard clearly thought her well enough–morally and mentally–to endure a very severe criticism of *Roger Fry*. It was, he said, merely analysis, not history; she had chosen the wrong method, seen it from a dull angle made even more dull by so many dead quotations. No doubt he added that, like everything of hers, it had things in it which could only have been hers, and very good they were; but this, characteristically, she does not record. It was a painful conversation; she felt as though she were being pecked with a very strong, hard beak. Although Leonard had not been enthusiastic about *Three Guineas*, this was the first time that he had given her an entirely adverse criticism. He was rational, impressive, definite and emphatic; and he convinced her that she had failed–almost. She was not certain however that his motives were quite pure; unconsciously he might be moved by a lack of sympathy for Roger, a lack of interest in his personality. She had sent her manuscript, or parts of it, to two other judges, Margery Fry and Vanessa. She would await their verdict.

"It's *him* . . . unbounded admiration," wrote Margery, with more enthusiasm than grammar. And Vanessa wrote:

> Since Julian died I haven't been able to think of Roger. Now you have given him back to me–Although I cannot help crying I can't thank you enough.

These judgements prevailed. Vanessa's commendation was, in its way, sufficient. To bring back Roger to those who knew him was a great part of Virginia's intention. Whether Leonard's verdict may not have been nearer to that of those who did not know Roger is another matter. Virginia was certainly made happy again by these assurances. She could go ahead with the dreary task of correcting proofs without too much despair, and on 13 May they were posted back to the printer.

On 10 May the Germans had invaded Belgium and Holland, on the 14th the Dutch army surrendered, on the 28th the Belgians followed suit and on 14 June, Paris fell.

Virginia, as we have seen, had not been living in a fool's paradise; she had suspected that things would go badly and she saw in these events, I think, no more than the continuance and intensification of a nightmare that had been going on for five or six years. She was still instinctively opposed to the idea of armed resistance; she was not uncritical when Leonard announced his intention of joining the Local Defence Volunteers. That he should wear an arm-band, a bandolier or a uniform seemed ridiculous. But her qualms about fighting the enemy did not make the enemy himself appear any less terrifying. It was disturbing to find that the bestial stupidity of the Fascist, his belief in the most puerile nonsense, was allied to immense military science and valour. Our own leaders seemed elderly, dull-witted and timorous. Nor could she take comfort from the oratory of our leaders, or from the new sense of desperation and resolution in the British people. Old Ethel Smyth stoutly declaring "of course we shall fight *and* win," two days after the fall of Paris, could excite her admiration, but she brought no comfort and no conviction. Neither did Winston Churchill, and still less the newspaper myths of laughing heroic tommies, the cheery brittle optimism of the BBC and of the politicians. There might be something in it not wholly false; but it was tainted with falsehood and there was an uglier side to our conduct in the national emergency. Refugees, as she knew from personal experience, were being incarcerated for no fault save their nationality, and a soldier came limping home from Dunkirk to Rodmell with stories of panic, demoralisation, looting, and utter military incompetence.

As the battle approached, and it became more and more likely that we should be defeated, Virginia's existence seemed to become unreal or at least incongruous; the activities and sentiments of her daily life were completely at variance with the appalling struggle on which her fate depended. Thus, when she sent off the proofs of the *Life* of Roger, she could speak of "peace and content" well knowing how grotesquely such a statement must read on the third day of the Battle of France; "So my little moment of peace comes in a yawning hollow." A week later, when the drama in the Low Countries was reaching its climax, Desmond MacCarthy and G. E. Moore came to stay at Monk's House–Desmond battered and dishevelled, but charming and talkative as ever; Moore, at sixty-five a shade less impressive than he had seemed in the days when Virginia Stephen had listened to him in mute reverence at the Sangers, but still noble in his disinterestedness. Desmond read him *The Hound of the Basker-villes* in the garden before lunch and in the afternoon they all went over to Charleston. There they discussed Moore's famous taciturnity: he was accused of silencing a generation. "I didn't want to be silent," he replied. "I couldn't think of anything to say." And at any rate he had never silenced Desmond, who presumably started talking to the cat and the towel-horse in his nursery. And over the hills came the reverberation of the cannon-fire.

Still more unreal was the Woolfs' jaunt to Penshurst with Vita. They visited the house, with its banqueting hall, its disappointing furniture, its memories of Elizabeth and Essex, the shell of Lady Pembroke's lute and Sidney's shaving glass, its tidy lawns, goldfish ponds and the old lord, garrulous, excruciatingly bored by his life, living for his game of cards in Tonbridge. On that day Paris fell.

July brought the publication of *Roger Fry* and something of the usual anxieties which Virginia always felt on such occasions. With it also came the fear of invasion. For Virginia and Leonard this meant something worse, in a way, than the universal annihilation which awaits us today if our rulers decide to destroy us. Leonard, in the last of his autobiographical volumes, gives an account of what the Fascist menace must have meant for him. I quote it, because it supplies the image that stared Leonard and Virginia in the face in July 1940.

> Jews were hunted down, beaten up, and humiliated everywhere publicly in the streets of towns. I saw a photograph of a Jew being dragged by storm troopers out of a shop in one of the main streets in Berlin; the fly-buttons of the man's trousers had been torn open to show that he was circumcised and therefore a Jew. On the man's face was the horrible look of blank suffering and despair which from the beginning of human history men have seen under the crown of thorns on the faces of their persecuted and humiliated victims. In this photograph what was even more horrible was the look on the faces of respectable men and women, standing on the pavement, laughing at the victim.

This then was the quality of the enemy who now had victory almost within his grasp and who, having achieved it, would be released from all restraints. Even if one were optimistic enough to believe that there might be a grain of pity or magnanimity in the heart of such an enemy, it was quite certain that there would be none for a Jewish socialist and his wife; for them the gas chamber would be an unlooked-for mercy. Leonard and Virginia had the advantage, if it was an advantage, of knowing enough about their adversary to be free from illusions. On 13 May, when the battle was at its height, they had discussed the question of suicide. They decided to poison themselves with the fumes of their car and Leonard kept enough petrol for this purpose in his garage; later they managed to get sufficient morphia from Adrian for a lethal dose. Throughout May and June Virginia refers frequently to the question of how and when they should make an end of themselves. Believing the war to be lost, she hardly doubts the necessity will arise, and looking into the future she sees nothing: "I can't conceive," she wrote, "that there will be a 27th June 1941."

And so, for three months, she lived on the brink of a precipice, always tensed to throw herself over. But towards the end of this period, fate provided a sort of cure, or so it seems, in the form of actual rather than imagined dangers. Throughout August and September she witnessed those odd scraps of air fighting which were all that people on the ground were usually able to perceive of the Battle of Britain. These contests in the sky were, as often as not, incomprehensible to the onlooker. Tiny sharp accents of light wheeled and vanished high in the air and then a great plume of smoke, with perhaps, an elegant botanical parachute above it, signified that someone, English or German, one could not tell which, had been shot down. But at times the events were more understandable and more dramatic; one might see a low-flying plane with enemy markings, hear the pop-pop-pop of cannon-fire, the disconcerting noise of bullets ripping the air, the whistle and crash of bombs.

They came very close. We lay down under the tree. The sound was like someone sawing in the air just above us. We lay flat on our faces, hands behind head. Don't close your teeth, said L. They seemed to be sawing at something stationary. Bombs shook the windows of my lodge. Will it drop I asked? If so, we shall be broken together. I thought, I think, of nothingness—flatness, my mood being flat. Some fear I suppose. Should we take Mabel to garage. Too risky to cross the garden L. said. Then another came from Newhaven. Hum and saw and buzz all round us. A horse neighed in the marsh. Very sultry. Is it thunder? I said. No, guns, said L., from Ringmer, from Charleston way. Then slowly the sound lessened. Mabel in kitchen said the windows shook. Air raid still on: distant planes . . . The all clear 5 to 7. 144 down last night.

Shattering, nerve-racking though such experiences must have been, unfit though Virginia was to be at the periphery, let alone the centre of a battle, I think that the effect may have been therapeutic. From the time when she came literally under fire, the talk of suicide ceased.

I remember her at this time reading aloud to the Memoir Club the account which she had written for the Rodmell Women's Institute of the Dreadnought Hoax; there was much laughter and applause, she seemed cheerful and certainly not at all suicidal. No doubt it was different when she rang up Sissinghurst and heard Vita's voice with the bombs falling all around her and did not know, when she rang off, whether she would ever hear Vita again.

The war moved inland; Rodmell was by no means out of danger but London was now the chief target. Both Virginia and Vanessa suffered material damage in the bombardment. And now the old competition between them was, in the strangest way, renewed. When Mecklenburgh Square was blasted Virginia was in despair for two reasons: it was exasperating to have moved into what was now an uninhabitable house while still paying rent for No. 52 Tavistock Square which remained untouched; it was also annoying when Vanessa's studio (and Duncan's next door) was entirely destroyed so that her own broken windows and fallen ceilings seemed but a paltry disaster. She was positively relieved when No. 52 Tavistock Square shared the fate of No. 8 Fitzroy Street and she felt, as Vanessa did when her studio went up in flames, an odd, unaccountable sense of exhilaration. But when they went to London to see what could be done about the damage and to arrange for the removal of the Hogarth Press, she experienced different emotions: amazement at the stouthearted stoicism of old Mr Pritchard and his sister, and, to quote a letter to Ethel Smyth:

> . . . what touched and indeed raked what I call my heart in London was the grimy old women at the lodging house at the back, all dirty after the raid, & preparing to sit out another . . . And then the passion of my life, that is the city of London–to see London all blasted, that too raked my heart.*

On top of all this came a private trouble, perfectly silly and petty and unnecessary, but worth mentioning if only to show how Virginia was torn between the cosmic disasters of war and the little *ennuies* of private life. There was a furnished cottage to let at Rodmell. Helen Anrep wanted to be near her friends and Vanessa told her about it. In a telephone conversation between Vanessa and Virginia, Virginia understood that Helen was coming to live in Rodmell permanently. For a moment the dangers of invasion were forgotten, or rather the threat of invasion now came from the Anrep family, a prospect equally grim. There was a sisterly quarrel as heated as any for years. It was soon over; Helen only intended a short stay anyway; but while the altercation lasted it was violent and painful.

In May 1940, speaking to the Workers' Educational Association

---

* "When the Germans bombed London, she [Virginia] calculated the serious damage in terms of decreased book-sales." (Michael Holroyd, *Lytton Strachey*, Vol. I, p. 404.) I have found no record of these singular calculations.

in Brighton, Virginia gave expression to her irritation with some of the poetry of the Left Wing intellectuals. Her lecture was published later under the title of *The Leaning Tower*. *The Leaning Tower* got her into a great deal of trouble with Left Wing writers, and this is natural enough, for she was rude, and for all I know mistaken, about their poetry. But it is in many ways a thoughtful essay, the final statement of a socially conscious writer, and it expresses much that is true. Virginia saw how intimately the history of English literature is conditioned by the English class structure, and how even the Left Wing movement of the 'thirties derived its nature from an essentially bourgeois society. She believed that the young socialist writers of her time did not, despite their ideological stance, transcend the boundaries of class and were indeed condemned to a certain obliquity of vision by reason of their class origins, and always would be so condemned unless they could create a classless society.

Where Virginia differed from most of the younger socialists was in her frank and unequivocal acceptance of the importance of the class structure in literature. Where others attempted to cross the barriers of class, or even to deny their existence, she frankly recognised them and, in so doing, recognised that she herself was in an isolated position within a divided society. As she makes clear in *The Leaning Tower*, she did not consider that this was a desirable state of affairs; but neither did she think that it was a state of affairs which could be altered by pretending that it did not exist. It was here that she parted company, not only with the Left, but with the Right.

The point is well brought out by an earlier essay. In *The Niece of an Earl* she wrote:

... our ignorance of the aristocracy is nothing compared with our ignorance of the working classes. At all times the great families of England and France have delighted to have famous men at their tables, and thus the Thackerays and the Disraelis and the Prousts have been familiar enough with the cut and fashion of aristocratic life to write about it with authority. Unfortunately, however, life is so framed that literary success invariably means a rise, never a fall, and seldom, what is far more desirable, a spread in the social scale. The rising novelist is never pestered to come to gin and winkles with the plumber and his wife. His books never bring him into touch with the cat's-meat man, or start a correspondence with the old lady who sells matches and bootlaces by the gate of the British Museum.

As a sympathetic critic puts it:

The subject of her writing was the little world of people like herself, a small class, a dying class, ... a class with inherited privileges, private incomes, sheltered lives, protected sensibilities, sensitive tastes. Outside of this class she knows very little.

This, for a novelist, is certainly a limitation, but there is some advantage in being aware of one's own limits.

Commenting on *The Niece of an Earl*, Jacques Emile Blanche wrote:

> ... je me permets de vous avouer que m'étonne une autre phrase de cet essai où vous exprimez comme une certitude, que les gens de notre classe ne connaissent pas l'ésprit du peuple, "of the old woman who sells matches and bootlaces at the gates of the British Museum." J'ai beaucoup causé avec "the plumber and his wife"–avec toutes sortes d'ouvriers, à la ville et à la campagne–et il est facile de sé mettre a leur niveau; ou mieux; c'était facile. La guerre de classes, qui fait rage ici, sous le souffle de Moscou, transforme les plus gentils en des brutes effrayantes.

This may serve as a classic instance of the writer who believes that he knows the lower classes, knows how he can bring himself "to their level," loves them quite genuinely so long as they play the role that he expects of them but whose affection, when that role changes, turns to hatred.

Virginia's attitude is the exact opposite. She did not demand love from her social inferiors or feel hatred when love was refused. She felt so little love for the proletariat that she wanted to abolish it and in abolishing it to abolish the class society. Her attitude, in that it resulted from a correct assessment of the character of the society in which she lived, enabled her in *The Leaning Tower* to make a very penetrating analysis. At the same time it was politically sterile in that it ignored those social affections on which political action usually depends. This, for those who suffered from the political blunders of her generation, was profoundly irritating. Benedict Nicolson, Vita's son, who was at that time on active service, read her biography of Roger while he was living in conditions of great stress and danger. He wrote to Virginia to express his exasperation. Bloomsbury, it seemed to him, had been living in a fool's paradise, enjoying cultivated pleasures while it neglected the first duty of the intellectual, which is to save the world from its follies. That disagreeable task had been left to him and his generation.

Virginia was clearly both irritated and impressed by his arguments. She wrote her reply with some care and, when it was finished, her letter was quite as fierce as his. In a subsequent exchange they both regained their tempers and the correspondence ended in a spirit of charity, if not of agreement. Apart from its acerbities and

some points which related simply to Roger Fry's achievements as a critic, the argument turned on the social responsibility or irresponsibility of Bloomsbury in the years between the wars Virginia did not defend Bloomsbury, as she might have done, by questioning the validity of the term in such a connection and pointing out that, if Leonard and Maynard Keynes belonged to Bloomsbury, it would be hard to accuse that body of total indifference to public affairs.*
She rested her case on the view that artists are unable, substantially, to influence society and that this was true even of the greatest writers: Keats, Shelley, Wordsworth or Coleridge. And this was the defence most applicable to her. As we have seen, she had attempted to be politically active; it was the ability, not the inclination, that was lacking. Only in *A Room of One's Own* does she exhibit any great persuasive power and, politically, she was a much less influential writer than Harriet Beecher Stowe.

This exchange took place in August 1940; by that time the Battle of Britain was approaching its climax and Virginia was passing from a mood of apprehension to one of quiet imperturbability.

Her serenity was perhaps a necessary prelude to the storm–by which I mean that the workings of Virginia's mind may have been such that she had to pass from the terror of June 1940 to the final agony of March 1941 by way of an euphoric interval, and that this may have been just as much a part of her mental illness as all the rest. At the same time we may note that the happier phase of that autumn–though not the subsequent relapse–could be directly related to public events. In August and September the threat of invasion continued; but at least it was clear that this island was capable of resistance, the enemy was not going to win command of the air without a tremendous struggle; and presently it began to look as though he were not winning it at all. Invasion was postponed from week to week until, clearly, it would be delayed until the Spring. London might be bombed and blazing but Leonard was not yet compelled to wear a yellow star. And, at the end of the year, a pale star of Victory shone over Africa.

It was satisfactory that Mabel went off to live with her sister. Mabel was the London maid; she had never played as important a role in Virginia's life as had Nelly; she was an easier, more placid, less disastrously interesting character. Nevertheless the Woolfs were

---

* In a draft for her letter of 24 August 1940 she does make this point, and, defending herself, alludes to her own work for Morley College, the Suffrage movement, and the Women's Co-operative Guild. This is omitted in the letter that she sent to Benedict Nicolson.

glad when she left; she was only at Rodmell because it was impossible to ask anyone to stop in London at that time. All the work that the Woolfs needed doing at Monk's House could be done by Louie, who lived in the village and with whom they both got on very well (Louie indeed was to remain with Leonard for the rest of his life). Thus the great servant problem was solved at last.

Bombs went on falling, and on 29 September one fell very close to Monk's House. Virginia swore at Leonard for slamming the window so noisily and then, realising what it was, went out on the lawn to see the raider chased back over Newhaven; but such things no longer worried her. She reflected that she was leading a lazy life. Leonard brought her breakfast in bed, as he had done for so many years, and there she read a book; she took a bath, then she saw Louie and made her household dispositions; then she went out to her lodge in the garden to work at *Pointz Hall*. Never had a novel of hers flowed so rapidly, so effortlessly from her pen; there were no checks, doubts, despairs, struggles or revisions. There was another book. Several drafts for a first chapter remain and two chapters are complete. It was called *Anon*, and was to be a kind of history of literature; it was to be written for Duncan in order to explain to him what English Literature was about. The difficulty was, she said, that she had reached a point at which she had to explain Shakespeare; his genius was universal and her book might therefore be rather long. In the intervals of writing she took pleasure in observing the landscape; she altered the position of her table in order to get a new aspect of the very beautiful flat country that lay between her and Mount Caburn. In November it became more beautiful than ever before; a bomb had burst the river bank and the waters of the Ouse, pouring out over the water-meadows, swept right up to her garden and formed a lovely inland sea visited by multitudes of water fowl. This was a source of great delight. Having surveyed the view and lighted a cigarette – "to tune up" as she put it – she would write until midday. Then came a pause to look at the newspapers, then she typed until one o'clock. Their lunch was frugal, the food shortage was now becoming acute; but with an appetite so sharply set, she ate whatever there was to eat more heartily than ever before; she even confesses at this period to an occasional guzzle, when guzzling was possible. Vita, having a farm, could make handsome presents and in November 1940 was thanked in the following terms:

> I wish I were Queen Victoria. Then I could thank you. From the *depths* of my *Broken* WIDOWED heart. *Never* NEVER NEVER have we had such a *rapturous* ASTOUNDING GLORIOUS–no, I can't get the hang

of the style. All I can say is that when we discovered the butter in the envelope box we had in the household—Louie that is—to look. That's a whole pound of butter I said. Saying which, I broke off a lump & ate it pure. Then in the glory of my heart I gave all our week's ration—which is about the size of my thumb nail—to Louie—earned undying gratitude: then sat down & ate bread and butter. It would have been desecration to add jam. You've forgotten what butter tastes like. So I'll tell you—its something between dew & honey. Lord, Vita!—your broken po, your wool; & then on top your butter!!! Please congratulate the cows from me, & the dairymaid, & I would like to suggest that the calf should be known in future (if its a man) as Leonard if a woman as Virginia.

Think of our lunch tomorrow! Bunny Garnett and Angelica are coming: in the middle of the table I shall put the whole pat. And I shall say: Eat as much as you like. I can't break off this rhapsody, for its a year since I saw a pound, to tell you anything else. I don't think anything else seems important. Its true all our books are coming from the ruined house tomorrow: all battered & mildewed. Its true I've been made Treasurer of the Women's Institute. Also I want to ask you about lantern slides of Persia; & will you come and talk; but this is mere trifling. Bombs fall near me—trifles; a 'plane shot down on the marsh—trifles; floods damned—no, nothing seems to make a wreath on the pedestal fitting your butter.

They've never sent me your book from the Press, damn them.

Here L[eonard] breaks in: If I'm writing to you, will I add his deepest thanks

for the

Butter.   V.

After lunch Virginia read the newspapers more seriously, went for a walk and perhaps did a little manual work, gathering and storing apples, or bread-making. Tea followed, and after tea there might be letters to write, followed by some more typing and reading or writing in her diary. Then it was time to cook the dinner and to eat it, to listen to some music on the gramophone, to read, doze, or embroider until it was time for bed.

She compared this life to the scramble, the frustrations, the interviews, telephonings, social engagements and social prevarications of her life in London. Here she was happy, very free, disengaged—"a life that rings from one simple melody to another. Yes: why not enjoy this after all those years of the other?"

Such an existence provided few incidents worthy of record. Their continued residence and the necessities of war brought the Woolfs much more into village life, and on the whole Virginia enjoyed this, although there were some village bores whom she grew to dread.

But in this period of no headaches, no exasperations, and smoothly running work, she seemed almost imperturbable. She enjoyed it when Morgan wrote asking her to join the Committee of the London Library, as she had said that he would one day, and she was able to take a little revenge for herself and her sex by refusing to be "a sop" to public opinion. She enjoyed it when Lady Oxford sent her a statuette of Voltaire and letters of some absurdity written from the Savoy Hotel during the Blitz. In the New Year she enjoyed going to Charleston and to Cambridge and, clearly, she enjoyed a visit from Elizabeth Bowen.

Miss Bowen was at Rodmell on 13 and 14 February 1941 and has recorded her memories of that visit. She describes Virginia kneeling on the floor—they were mending a torn curtain—

> and she sat back on her heels and put her head back in a patch of sun, early spring sun, and laughed in this consuming, choking, delightful, hooting way . . . and it has remained with me. So that I get a curious shock when I see people regarding her entirely as a martyred, or a definitely tragic sort of person claimed by the darkness.

When did the laughter end and the darkness begin? It is hard to say. She finished *Between the Acts* on 23 November, and the ending of a novel was always a period of danger for her; but throughout December she seems to have been happy enough. There are passages in her diary for January, February and March which, with hindsight, may be considered ominous. From the middle of January Leonard was very anxious about her; but there is no entry in his diary relating to her health until 18 March, when he writes: "V.n.w." [Virginia not well]. Six days later, on 24 March, she wrote to John Lehmann to say that she did not want *Between the Acts* to be published. By that time it was clear to Leonard that her situation had become critical.

It was a symptom of Virginia's madness that she could not admit that she was mentally ill; to force this knowledge upon her was, in itself, dangerous. But by 26 March Leonard had become convinced that the risk must be taken and that she must be persuaded to see a doctor. For this purpose it was far better that she should see someone whom she knew and liked. As it happened the Woolfs had a friend who was also a physician with a practice in Brighton. Octavia Wilberforce lived with Elizabeth Robins, the actress, who had been a friend of Virginia's mother. Both ladies were clearly fascinated by Virginia. Miss Robins returned to America in 1940, but Octavia, who owned a farm and had seen that Virginia was growing thin and pallid, would send presents of butter and cream to Monk's House. Virginia declared that she would like to write Octavia's portrait and appears to have begun something of the sort, Octavia coming now and then to sit—that is to say, to talk with her.

On March 21 she came to tea and Leonard told her what the situation was.

For the next five days Octavia herself was ill in bed. On the 27th Leonard rang her up. He had persuaded Virginia to see Octavia as a friend and as a doctor. He sounded desperate. Octavia also was desperate. She could only just crawl out of bed, but, heroically, she concealed this fact from Leonard, and it was arranged that he should bring Virginia over to Brighton that afternoon.

The interview was difficult. Virginia at once declared that there was nothing the matter with her. It was quite unnecessary that she should have a consultation; she certainly would not answer any questions.

"All you have to do," said Octavia, "is to reassure Leonard." Then she added that she knew what kind of symptoms Virginia felt, and asked to examine her. In a kind of sleep-walking way Virginia began to undress and then stopped.

"Will you promise, if I do this, not to order me a rest cure?"

"What I promise is that I won't order you to do anything that you won't think it reasonable to do. Is that fair?"

Virginia agreed and the examination continued, but not without many protests. She was like a child being sent up to bed. In the end she did confess some part of her fears, fears that the past would come back, that she would be unable to write again. Octavia replied that the mere fact that she had had this trouble before and that it had been cured should be a reason for confidence. If you have your appendix removed, she said, nothing will remain but the scar; a mental illness can be removed in the same way if you don't inflame the wound by dwelling upon it.

At the end she took Virginia's hand, a cold thin hand she found it, saying: "If you'll collaborate I know I can help you and there's nobody in England I'd like more to help." At this Virginia looked a little happier—"detachedly pleased," as Octavia put it.

Then there was a private consultation between Octavia and Leonard. What were they to do; should Virginia be under the surveillance of a trained nurse? It might easily be a disastrous measure. It seemed, both to Leonard and to Octavia, that the consultation had done some good. The Woolfs went back to Rodmell and Octavia returned to bed. She wrote Virginia a note, as gentle and as reassuring as she could make it, and on the following evening rang up, but by that time it was too late.

On the morning of Friday 28 March, a bright, clear, cold day, Virginia went as usual to her studio room in the garden. There she wrote two letters, one for Leonard, one for Vanessa—the two people she loved best. In both letters she explained that she was hearing voices, believed that she could never recover; she could not go on and spoil Leonard's life for him. Then she went back into the house and wrote again to Leonard:

Dearest,

I feel certain I am going mad again. I feel we can't go through another of those terrible times. And I shan't recover this time. I begin to hear voices, and I can't concentrate. So I am doing what seems the best thing to do. You have given me the greatest possible happiness. You have been in every way all that anyone could be. I don't think two people could have been happier till this terrible disease came. I can't fight any longer. I know that I am spoiling your life, that without me you could work. And you will I know. You see I can't even write this properly. I can't read. What I want to say is I owe all the happiness of my life to you. You have been entirely patient with me and incredibly good. I want to say that—everybody knows it. If anybody could have saved me it would have been you. Everything has gone from me but the certainty of your goodness. I can't go on spoiling your life any longer.

I don't think two people could have been happier than we have been.

V.

She put this on the sitting-room mantelpiece and, at about 11.30, slipped out, taking her walking-stick with her and making her way across the water-meadows to the river. Leonard believed that she might already have made one attempt to drown herself; if so she had learnt by her failure and was determined to make sure of it now. Leaving her stick on the bank she forced a large stone into the pocket of her coat. Then she went to her death, "the one experience," as she had said to Vita, "I shall never describe."

APPENDIX A
Chronology

1912

4–6 June   Virginia unwell and in bed; for the rest of June and July she is much occupied, introducing Leonard to her friends and relations, meeting his family, spending week-ends at Asham and one at Walberswick

10 August   Marriage of Virginia Stephen and Leonard Woolf at St Pancras Registry Office. They go to Asham for two days, return to London, and then stay at the Plough Inn, Holford, Somerset

18 August   Leonard and Virginia leave *via* Dieppe for their honeymoon, spent travelling in Provence, Spain and thence by sea to Italy; on 28 September they are in Venice

3 October   The Woolfs return to 38 Brunswick Square. On 8th Leonard starts work as Secretary to the 2nd Post-Impressionist Exhibition at the Grafton Galleries (until 2 January)

Late October   The Woolfs move to rooms at 13 Clifford's Inn; they divide their time between these and Asham

December   Virginia unwell with headaches, Leonard with malaria. They are at Asham for Christmas and again early in the new year

1913

January   Leonard consults medical advisers as to the wisdom of Virginia having a child. She is suffering from headaches and sleeping badly. On 13th he begins to keep a daily record of her state of health

25 January–1 February   The Woolfs stay at Harbour View, Studland, for Virginia's health, returning to London for two weeks and then spending a long week-end at Asham

22–23 March   The Woolfs stay at Ditchling with the Gills

9 March   The manuscript of *The Voyage Out* is delivered to Gerald Duckworth. Virginia goes to Liverpool, Manchester, Leeds, York, Carlisle and Leicester with Leonard, who is studying the Co-operative movement; they return to London on 19 March, and then go to Asham for Easter with Adrian Stephen and Saxon Sydney-Turner

1–11 April	At Asham with Marjorie Strachey and Sydney-Turner
12 April	*The Voyage Out* accepted for publication by Duckworth
19 April	The Woolfs go to Asham for a fortnight. Back in London, they attend *The Ring* at Covent Garden
16 May–2 June	At Asham; Desmond MacCarthy and Lytton Strachey stay one week-end and Janet Case another
6–8 June	The Woolfs are at Cambridge, staying at Newnham with Virginia's cousin the Principal
9–12 June	The Woolfs go to Newcastle-upon-Tyne to attend Women's Co-operative Congress, returning to London with Margaret Llewelyn Davies. Virginia not well
19 June–7 July	The Woolfs are at Asham. Guests are Oliver and Ray Strachey, H. T. J. Norton, E. M. Forster, Lytton Strachey and Molly MacCarthy
12 July	The Woolfs lunch with Beatrice and Sidney Webb during a week's stay in London
16–21 July	At Asham; Lytton Strachey to stay. Virginia increasingly depressed and unwell
22 July	The Woolfs go to Keswick for Fabian Society Conference; Virginia ill. They return to London on 24th and next day consult Sir George Savage. Virginia enters nursing home at Twickenham
11 August	Virginia leaves nursing home for Asham
22 August	Leonard takes Virginia to London to see Drs Savage and Head; they go next day to the Plough Inn, Holford. Virginia's depression, delusions and resistance to food increase
2 September	Katherine Cox joins the Woolfs at Holford; on 8th they all return to London, to 38 Brunswick Square
9 September	Virginia sees Drs Wright and Head; in the evening she attempts suicide
20 September	Virginia is taken by Leonard to Dalingridge Place, Sussex, where she remains until November under the care of Leonard and nurses
18 November	Virginia is moved with two nurses to Asham; her condition slowly improves
3–5 December	Leonard is in London arranging to vacate Clifford's Inn rooms
1914	
January	Virginia is now able to read and write letters; she undertakes typewriting for Lytton Strachey, whom Leonard visits in Wiltshire
16 February	Virginia's last nurse leaves

APPENDIX A

7–18 March	Ka Cox, Janet Case and Vanessa Bell each come to stay with Virginia at Asham while Leonard is away
6 April	The Woolfs go to London to consult Dr Craig; they stay with Janet Case in Hampstead
8–30 April	In Cornwall–St Ives, Carbis Bay and Godrevy
1 May	Return *via* London to Asham, where they remain all summer save for a visit to London in June (dentist) and Leonard's visits to Birmingham and Keswick for conferences
7 July	Leonard buys Virginia a bicycle
4 August	Declaration of war
6 August	The Woolfs spend a night in London and then go to Northumberland, staying at Wooler and Coldstream until 15 September, when they return to London. House-hunting
30 September	To Asham for a week
9 October	The Woolfs go into lodgings at 65 St Margaret's Road, Twickenham; and on 16th they move to 17 The Green, Richmond
November–December	Virginia is apparently recovered, seeing friends, attending cookery classes. The Woolfs spend a week end at Lytton Strachey's cottage in Wiltshire, and Christmas near him at Marlborough

1915

1 January	Virginia starts to write a diary
25 January	Virginia's 33rd birthday; she and Leonard resolve to buy a printing press and to take Hogarth House, Richmond
18 February	Virginia has headache and sleeps badly; early stage of recurrence of mental breakdown. By 4 March she is excited and violent, and nurses are called in
25 March	Virginia is taken to nursing home, while Leonard undertakes the move to Hogarth House
26 March	Publication of Virginia's first book, *The Voyage Out*
1 April	Virginia is brought to Hogarth House; four nurses in attendance. April and May are the most violent and raving months of her madness
June	Beginning of gradual improvement in Virginia's condition. By August Leonard is able to take her out for drives or in a wheel-chair
11 September–4 November	The Woolfs live at Asham with one nurse, a cook and a housemaid
4 November	Return to Hogarth House. Virginia is gradually returning to normal life; the nurse leaves 11 November

22–30 December	Christmas at Asham; James Strachey and Noel Olivier are guests
1916	
January	Virginia leads a comparatively normal life at Hogarth House
1 February	Nelly Boxall and Lottie Hope come as cook and housemaid. The Woolfs are at Asham for a week-end in February
6–15 April	Virginia has influenza, after which she goes to Asham for three weeks. Lytton Strachey and C. P. Sanger are guests for Easter
5 May	The Woolfs return to Hogarth House
20–22 May	The Woolfs stay with Roger Fry at Durbins near Guildford
30 May	Leonard is examined and rejected by Army Medical Board
17–19 June	The Woolfs spend week-end in Sussex with Mr and Mrs Sidney Webb; George Bernard Shaw is a fellow guest
7 July	The Woolfs go to Asham until mid-September, interrupted by a visit to Vanessa at Wissett in Suffolk (21–24 July) and the succeeding week at Hogarth House
15–19 August	G. E. Moore and Pernel Strachey at Asham. Subsequent guests include Adrian and Karin Stephen, Alix Sargant-Florence, James Strachey, R. C. Trevelyan, the Waterlows and Roger Fry
16 September	The Woolfs return to Richmond and go on 18th to Carbis Bay
2 October	Return to Hogarth House
c. 4 October	David Garnett, Carrington and Barbara Hiles spend a night at Asham (uninvited)
17 October	Virginia lectures to Richmond Branch of Women's Co-operative Guild
20–24 October	The Woolfs are at Asham. Vanessa has recently moved to Charleston, four miles away, but they are unable to meet
21 December	The Woolfs go to Asham; Ka Cox comes for Christmas
1917	
2 January	The Woolfs visit Charleston; Virginia stays the night. On 4th they return to Hogarth House. Virginia is again writing for *The Times Literary Supplement*

23 March	The Woolfs order a printing press in Farringdon Road
3–17 April	Easter holiday at Asham. C. P. Sanger and Marjorie Strachey to stay
24 April	Printing press delivered to Hogarth House. The Woolfs remain at Richmond until August, with short visits to Asham and to R. C. Trevelyan
July	Publication No. 1 of The Hogarth Press: *The Mark on the Wall* and *Three Jews*
3 August– 5 October	The Woolfs are at Asham. Virginia enters brief notes in a diary (*Berg*). Guests include G. Lowes Dickinson, Lytton Strachey, Katherine Mansfield, Philip Morrell, Sydney Waterlow, Desmond MacCarthy
8 October	Virginia starts regularly writing a diary (*AWD* (*Berg*)). Emma Vaughan gives her bookbinding equipment to Virginia
10 October	Foundation of the 1917 Club; Leonard on committee
29 October	Virginia goes to Asham with Saxon Sydney-Turner, then on to Charleston, while Leonard goes to Bolton, Manchester and Liverpool
2 November	Return to Hogarth House
17–19 November	The Woolfs first visit to Garsington Manor, home of Philip and Lady Ottoline Morrell; Lytton Strachey and Aldous Huxley are fellow guests
15 November	The Woolfs buy a larger second-hand press; on 21st Barbara Hiles starts work as part-time assistant in the Hogarth Press
19 December	First General Meeting and Dinner of the 1917 Club
20 December	The Woolfs go to Asham for Christmas holiday; visits to Charleston and *vice versa*; Ka Cox to stay
1918	
3 January	Return to Hogarth House. Virginia is setting type, writing for *TLS*, and making frequent visits to London, to libraries, 1917 Club, etc.
8 February	Virginia is in bed for a week with influenza; she goes with Leonard to Asham on 19th, thence to Charleston on 1 March, returning to Hogarth House on 2nd
12 March	Over 100,000 words of *Night and Day* written
21 March–5 April	The Woolfs are at Asham for Easter; Lytton Strachey to stay
14 April	Harriet Weaver comes to tea at Hogarth House with the manuscript of *Ulysses*
May	Publication of Lytton Strachey's *Eminent Victorians*
16–28 May	The Woolfs are at Asham; Roger Fry to stay
15–17 June	The Woolfs stay with the Waterlows at Oare, Wiltshire

10 July	First copies of Katherine Mansfield's *Prelude*, printed at the Hogarth Press, are sent out
20–22 July	The Woolfs stay at Tidmarsh with Lytton Strachey and Carrington
27–29 July	The Woolfs stay at Garsington with the Morrells
31 July	The Woolfs go to Asham for summer. Guests include Adrian and Karin Stephen, Sidney and Beatrice Webb, Mark Gertler
7 October	Return to Hogarth House; on 13th H. A. L. Fisher calls with news of the war ending
11 November	Armistice Day; guns announce peace
15 November	T. S. Eliot comes to Hogarth House; first meeting with Virginia
21 November	Virginia finishes *Night and Day*. Printing *Kew Gardens*; frequent visits to Katherine Mansfield at Hampstead
14–16 December	Virginia stays week-end at Durbins, near Guildford, with Roger Fry
20 December	Virginia goes to Asham; Leonard comes next day
25 December	Birth of Angelica Bell at Charleston; on 28th Julian and Quentin Bell are brought to Asham

1919

1 January	The Woolfs return to Hogarth House with Julian and Quentin Bell
2 January	Virginia has a tooth extracted and is subsequently in bed for a fortnight; on 9th the Bell children are sent home to Gordon Square
January–March	Domestic crises at Charleston; Virginia sends Nelly to help
26 February	Death of Lady Ritchie (Aunt Anny)
28 February	The Woolfs go to Asham; are given notice to leave the house
4 March	Virginia spends a night at Charleston and returns next day to Hogarth House. Printing T. S. Eliot's *Poems*
1 April	*Night and Day* submitted to Gerald Duckworth
25 April	The Woolfs go to Asham for ten days; house-hunting in district
7 May	Virginia takes three cottages in Cornwall. Duckworth accepts *Night and Day*
12 May	*Kew Gardens* by Virginia, *The Critic in Judgement* by J. M. Murry and *Poems* by T. S. Eliot published by the Hogarth Press
27 May	The Woolfs go to Asham; house-hunting
2 June	Leonard returns to town; Virginia goes to Charleston for the night; next day she buys the Round House in Lewes and returns to Hogarth House

21–23 June	Virginia stays at Garsington for the week-end; G. L. Dickinson, Aldous Huxley and Mark Gertler are also there
26 June	The Woolfs go to Lewes to look at the Round House and on to Asham; on 27th and 28th they look at Monk's House
1 July	Auction sale of Monk's House, Rodmell; bought by the Woolfs for £700
19 July	Peace Treaty signed
29 July	The Woolfs go to Asham for the whole of August; guests include Hope Mirrlees and E. M. Forster
1 September	The Woolfs move to Monk's House, Rodmell
6 October	The Woolfs return to Hogarth House
20 October	*Night and Day* is published by Duckworth
8–10 November	The Woolfs stay at Tidmarsh with Lytton Strachey and Carrington; Saxon Sydney-Turner is also there
1–19 December	Leonard ill with malaria
20–27 December	Virginia in bed with influenza
29 December	The Woolfs go to Monk's House

1920

8 January	Return to Hogarth House
18 January	Virginia goes to Guildford to stay overnight with Roger Fry
7–9 February	The Woolfs go to Aldbourne for week-end with Ka (*née* Cox) and Will Arnold-Forster
21 February– 1 March	The Woolfs are at Monk's House
4 March	First meeting of the Memoir Club
25 March–7 April	The Woolfs are at Monk's House for Easter; from 30 April–4 May; and for a week-end at end of May
11 May	Leonard is offered nomination as Labour candidate for the Combined English University Constituency
7 June	Virginia goes to London; has tea with Clive Bell, dinner with Vanessa; story of "Mad Mary" and vivid bus ride to Waterloo
24–28 June	The Woolfs are at Monk's House
22 July	The Woolfs go to Monk's House for two months. On 2 and 23 August Virginia goes to London to see Katherine Mansfield (their last meeting)
28 August	Carrington and Ralph Partridge stay the week-end; the latter is invited to join the Hogarth Press
September	Lytton Strachey stays several days and T. S. Eliot one night at Monk's House. Virginia is writing *Jacob's Room*

1 October	The Woolfs return to Hogarth House. Ralph Partridge starts part-time work in the Press on 6th
22 December	The Woolfs go to Monk's House for Christmas holiday

1921

2 January	Return to Hogarth House, whence they make two excursions: to Woodcote (Philip Woolf) and on to Tidmarsh (Lytton Strachey) on 28–29 January; and to Monk's House on 22–28 February
7 or 8 March	Publication of *Monday or Tuesday*
16–18 March	Virginia accompanies Leonard to an adoption meeting in Manchester
23–31 March	The Woolfs stay at Zennor, near the Arnold-Forsters
April	Publication of Lytton Strachey's *Queen Victoria*
22–25 April	The Woolfs are at Monk's House
18 May	Desmond and Molly MacCarthy and Roger Fry dine at Hogarth House; Desmond's conversation written down
21 May	Marriage of Ralph Partridge and Dora Carrington
June–July	Virginia unwell; no diary entries between 7 June and 8 August. The Woolfs are at Monk's House from 18 June to 1 July; and return there on 28 July
August–September	Virginia is convalescent; she is unable to work or see visitors until mid-September. T. S. Eliot stays 24–25 September
6 October	Return to Hogarth House
4 November	Last words of *Jacob's Room* written
November	Excursions to Monk's House on 5th, and to see Philip Woolf and then Lytton Strachey on 19th
1–3 December	Leonard goes on political business to Manchester and Durham
20 December	The Woolfs go to Monk's House for Christmas holiday

1922

2 January	Return to Hogarth House
January–February	Virginia has influenza on 7 January, a relapse on 22 January and is an invalid throughout February; she is visited frequently by Clive Bell
25 February	Richmond G.P. Dr Fergusson recommends that Virginia see a heart specialist; she has a persistent high temperature throughout March
7–27 April	The Woolfs are at Monk's House
May	Virginia's temperature and heart still causing anxiety. She has three teeth extracted

27–29 May	The Woolfs go to Tidmarsh to visit Lytton Strachey, Carrington and Ralph Partridge; E. M. Forster and Gerald Brenan are also there
c. 2–10 June	The Woolfs are at Monk's House, whence they attend the 'Co-operative Conference at Brighton presided over by Margaret Llewelyn Davies
July	Virginia is finishing *Jacob's Room*; anxiety about her lungs
15–17 July	Virginia stays at Garsington, where she meets Augustine Birrell and J. T. Sheppard
1 August–5 October	The Woolfs are at Monk's House. On 9 August Virginia sees a specialist in London, who finds no tuberculosis, but identifies pneumonia germs in her throat. House guests are Sydney Waterlow, Lytton Strachey, E. M. Forster and T. S. Eliot; question of the Eliot Fellowship Fund is discussed
27 October	*Jacob's Room* is published by the Hogarth Press
4–5 November	The Woolfs stay at Tidmarsh with Lytton Strachey; the future of Ralph Partridge and the Hogarth Press under consideration until the end of the year
17 November	General Election; Leonard fails to win a University seat
14 December	The Woolfs dine with Clive Bell; first meeting with Vita Sackville-West (Mrs Harold Nicolson)
21 December	The Woolfs go to Monk's House for Christmas holiday

1923

1 January	Return to Hogarth House
9 January	Death of Katherine Mansfield
15 January	Virginia is ill in bed with a temperature; unwell for rest of the month. On 29th Marjorie Joad comes to work full-time at the Hogarth Press; Ralph Partridge leaves on 14 March
3–5 February	The Woolfs go to Cambridge for the week-end; they dine at King's, see *Oedipus Rex*, visit Newnham, and dine with Maynard Keynes
February–March	*The Nation* remodelled; Virginia attempts to get the literary editorship for T. S. Eliot; it is offered to and accepted by Leonard on 23 March
27 March	The Woolfs go to Spain *via* Paris, reaching Granada on 31st. They stay with Gerald Brenan at Yegen from 4–13 April, then travel by stages back to Paris. Leonard returns home on 24th; Virginia follows on 27th April. Leonard starts work on *The Nation*
25–27 May	The Woolfs are at Monk's House

2–3 June	The Woolfs stay at Garsington; Lytton Strachey is also there; "37 people to tea," including Lord David Cecil, E. Sackville-West, L. P. Hartley, Mrs Asquith
Late June	Virginia retires from her task of providing speakers for the Richmond Branch of the Women's Co-operative Guild
1 August– *30 September*	The Woolfs are at Monk's House; house guests include Francis Birrell and Raymond Mortimer, Mrs Mary Hamilton, E. M. Forster, Lytton Strachey and the Partridges; from 7–10 September they stay at Lulworth with Maynard Keynes; Lydia Lopokova, George Rylands and Raymond Mortimer are also there. Virginia is writing first version of *Freshwater*, and *The Hours* (*Mrs Dalloway*)
October–November	Virginia looks for a London house
December	The Woolfs are at Monk's House from 1–3 December and again from 21st

1924

1 January	Return to Hogarth House
January–March	Virginia finds 52 Tavistock Square, Bloomsbury on 8 January, buys the lease on 9 January, and moves there on 13–15 March
17–28 April	The Woolfs are at Monk's House for Easter
9–10 May	The Woolfs stay at Tidmarsh with Lytton Strachey and the Partridges
17–19 May	The Woolfs stay at Cambridge; they lunch with George Rylands at King's; plan of his joining Hogarth Press considered. Virginia lectures to The Heretics on Modern Fiction (*Mr Bennett and Mrs Brown*)
5–9 June	Whitsun holiday at Monk's House
28–29 June	The Woolfs stay at Garsington; fellow guests include Lord Berners and T. S. Eliot
2 July	George Rylands starts work at the Hogarth Press
4 July	Virginia taken by V. Sackville-West to Knole; she meets Lord Sackville, Lady Dorothy Wellesley and Geoffrey Scott
30 July–2 October	The Woolfs are at Monk's House; Virginia is working on *Mrs Dalloway*. Guests include George Rylands, Norman Leys, V. Sackville-West and Karin and Ann Stephen
8 October	*Mrs Dalloway* finished. The Woolfs visit Lytton Strachey in his new home, Ham Spray House, near Hungerford
30 October	*Mr Bennett and Mrs Brown* is published

25 November	George Rylands decides to leave the Hogarth Press at the end of the year; his successor, Angus Davidson, starts work on 10 December
24 December	The Woolfs go to Monk's House; Angus Davidson stays for Christmas

1925

3 January	Return to Tavistock Square; the Woolfs remain there until 26 March with one week-end at Monk's House, 6–8 February. Angus Davidson is working in the Hogarth Press
22 January	Virginia is ill and in bed for about two weeks
February	Marjorie Joad leaves the Hogarth Press; Bernadette Murphy comes
6 February	Virginia sends proofs of *Mrs Dalloway* to Jacques Raverat; he dies on 7 March
26 March–7 April	The Woolfs go to Cassis, and stay at Hotel Cendrillon
9–13 April	Easter at Monk's House
23 April	*The Common Reader* is published
2–3 May	The Woolfs stay at Cambridge; they meet John Hayward and Richard Braithwaite and many old friends
14 May	*Mrs Dalloway* published. Virginia thinking of *To the Lighthouse*
May–July	Virginia leads a very social life in London, with two week-ends at Monk's House and one at Thorpe-le-Soken with Adrian and Karin Stephen
July	Bernadette Murphy leaves the Hogarth Press; Mrs Cartwright comes
4 August	Marriage of John Maynard Keynes and Lydia Lopokova
5 August–2 October	The Woolfs are at Monk's House. On 19 August Virginia collapses at Charleston, and is unwell, seeing few visitors, throughout the holiday
October–November	Virginia is unwell and inactive at Tavistock Square
7 November	Death of Madge Vaughan
2 December	Virginia goes to the ballet; her first night out for two months
17–20 December	Virginia stays with V. Sackville-West at Long Barn, near Sevenoaks; Leonard joins them on 19th
22–28 December	The Woolfs stay with the Bells at Charleston (builders at Monk's House); V. Sackville-West to lunch there on 26th

1926

8 January	Virginia starts German measles at Tavistock Square and is unwell for the rest of the month; she begins

	again on *To the Lighthouse*. V. Sackville-West goes to Persia
6–8 February	The Woolfs are at Monk's House
16 March	40,000 words of *To the Lighthouse* written
24 March	Leonard gives in his resignation as Literary Editor of *The Nation*. Disastrous "literary" dinner with Rose Macaulay
13–18 April	The Woolfs go to Iwerne Minster; and travel books in Dorset
29 April	Virginia finishes first part of *To the Lighthouse* and begins Part 2, which she finishes on 25 May
3–12 May	General Strike.
27–30 May	The Woolfs go to Monk's House, to which improvements have been made
11–15 June	Virginia is at Monk's House; Leonard stays two days and V. Sackville-West the next two
26–27 June	The Woolfs stay at Garsington; fellow guests include Aldous Huxley, Siegfried Sassoon, E. Sackville-West. They visit Robert Bridges at Boar's Hill
23 July	The Woolfs go to Dorchester to visit Thomas Hardy
27 July	The Woolfs go to Monk's House; Virginia exhausted and resting. Very few visitors; among them Rose Macaulay, Angus Davidson and Stephen Tomlin. Virginia depressed
14 October	Return to Tavistock Square
23–25 October	The Woolfs stay at Cambridge; they see Edmund Gosse, Pernel Strachey, F. L. Lucas and V. Sackville-West
4 November	The Woolfs dine with H. G. Wells to meet Arnold Bennett; the following day they go to Long Barn to spend the week-end with V. Sackville-West
22–28 December	The Woolfs spend Christmas with the Arnold-Forsters in Cornwall
1927	
January	Virginia finishing *To the Lighthouse*. She and Leonard at Monk's House from 5–9 January; 15th–17th she is at Long Barn and visits Knole; on 29 January V. Sackville-West returns to Persia. The Woolfs consider and reject the idea of going to America
9 February	Virginia has her hair shingled
25–27 February	The Woolfs are at Monk's House
Mid-March	Virginia conceives the idea of *The Jessamy Brides*
30 March–28 April	The Woolfs spend a week with the Bells at Cassis and then travel to Palermo, Syracuse, Naples and Rome, where they stay for a week

APPENDIX A

30 April	Vanessa writes to Virginia describing the moths at Cassis
5 May	*To the Lighthouse* is published
18–19 May	Virginia visits Oxford with V. Sackville-West and then goes to Monk's House for the week-end
Early June	Virginia is in bed for a week with headache; she goes to Monk's House for a week on 8th; on 16th she sees V. Sackville-West presented with the Hawthornden Prize
28–29 June	The Woolfs with the Nicolsons and others travel to Yorkshire to see the total eclipse of the sun
July	Virginia spends two week-ends with V. Sackville-West at Long Barn. The Woolfs buy a Singer car. Virginia broadcasts
27 July–1 August	Virginia stays with Ethel Sands and Nan Hudson at the Château d'Auppegard, near Dieppe; she meets J. E. Blanche
August–September	The Woolfs are at Monk's House. House guests include V. Sackville-West, Raymond Mortimer, E. M. Forster. Numerous excursions by motor car
5 October	Virginia starts to write *Orlando* "as a joke." The Woolfs return to Tavistock Square on 6th
8 November	Clive Bell sends Virginia first part of *Civilisation*. Correspondence with E. M. Forster about art and life
9 December	Angus Davidson is to leave the Hogarth Press
24 December	The Woolfs go to Charleston for Christmas; and on to Monk's House on 27th
1928	
2 January	Return to Tavistock Square. Virginia is working on *Orlando*. On 14–15 January she stays at Long Barn. Towards the end of the month she is in bed with headache, and again, with influenza, in mid-February
9–12 March	The Woolfs are at Monk's House. *Orlando* is finished on 17 March
26 March	The Woolfs cross to Dieppe and drive to Cassis, arriving on 2 April. They stay at Colonel Teed's house, Fontcreuse, near the Bells and Duncan Grant. They start home on 9 April, reaching London on 16th
April–June	Virginia is awarded the *Femina Vie Heureuse* prize. The Woolfs spend the last week-ends in April, May and June at Monk's House
9–11 June	The Woolfs visit Janet Case at Lyndhurst

24 July	The Woolfs go to Monk's House. V. Sackville-West stays on 29th and 30th; other guests this summer are E. Sackville-West, E. M. Forster, Richard Kennedy and Mrs Woolf. They buy the field adjoining Monk's House
24 September	Virginia and V. Sackville-West travel to Paris, Saulieu, Vézelay and Auxerre, returning to Monk's House on 1 October
2 October	The Woolfs return to Tavistock Square
11 October	*Orlando* is published
20 October	The Woolfs with V. Sackville-West, Vanessa and Angelica Bell, go to Cambridge. In this and the following week Virginia reads to the women's colleges two papers which are revised to become *A Room of One's Own*
9 November	*The Well of Loneliness* case is heard at Bow Street
November– December	Virginia and Vanessa organise a series of parties. On 10 November the Woolfs go to Cambridge to see Lydia Lopokova act; on 24–25 November they are at Rodmell, where they buy a cottage; and again on 15–16 December. Third edition of *Orlando* ordered
27 December	The Woolfs go to Monk's House; Richard Kennedy comes for one night

1929
3 January	Return to Tavistock Square
16 January	The Woolfs travel to the Prinz Albrecht Hotel in Berlin, where they are joined on the 18th by Vanessa and Quentin Bell and Duncan Grant. Harold Nicolson is *en poste* at the Embassy; Vita and E. Sackville-West are also in Berlin
24–25 January	Return journey *via* Harwich; Virginia suffers from the effects of *Somnifène* and is ill for several weeks; she is further affected by the noise of a pumping machine near Tavistock Square
March	Virginia is writing the final version of *A Room of One's Own* and thinking about *The Moths*
3–7 April	The Woolfs go to Monk's House; and again later in the month, making arrangements to have two new rooms built on
3–6 May	To Monk's House, and again at Whitsun, 17–23 May
30 May	General Election. The Woolfs drive to Rodmell to vote; return next day *via* Long Barn to Tavistock Square
4–14 June	The Woolfs go to Cassis for a week, by train; they

	stay at Fontcreuse. Vanessa Bell and Duncan Grant are there
19–23 June	The Woolfs are at Monk's House. Virginia has a bad throat and headache
July	At Monk's House 5th–8th, 12th–14th and 20th–23rd
27 July–6 October	At Monk's House; guests include Ka Arnold-Forster, William Plomer, Janet Vaughan, Lyn Irvine, F. L. Lucas. Virginia suffers from intermittent headaches and melancholy. Visits to Long Barn to see V. Sackville-West and to Worthing to see Mrs Woolf
September	Harold Nicolson resigns from the Diplomatic Service
30 September	The Woolfs attend the Labour Party Conference in Brighton
24 October	*A Room of One's Own* is published
20 November	Virginia broadcasts. The Woolfs are disturbed by dance music from an hotel in Woburn Place and take legal action
21 December	To Monk's House; Virginia's new bedroom ready. They see the Keyneses and V. Sackville-West

1930

5 January	The Woolfs return to Tavistock Square. On 15th Virginia dines with Henry Harris in Bedford Square to meet the Prime Minister, &c; on 18th to Angelica Bell's party at 8 Fitzroy Street. On 31st the case against the Imperial Hotel Company is decided in the Woolfs' favour
9 February	Death of C. P. Sanger. On returning from two days at Monk's House, Leonard is ill, succeeded by Virginia, who has an intermittent temperature for the rest of the month
February	Plans for a new periodical are discussed between Woolfs, Bells, Roger Fry and Raymond Mortimer (unrealised)
20 February	Virginia's first meeting with Ethel Smyth, who henceforth is a constant visitor
1–8 March	The Woolfs are at Monk's House; and again from 21st–24th. Virginia is writing *The Waves*
31 March	Mrs Cartwright leaves the Hogarth Press
April	The Woolfs are at Monk's House 4th–6th; and again at Easter, 16th–27th
29 May	Virginia finishes first version of *The Waves*
4–11 May	The Woolfs make a tour of Somerset, Devon and Cornwall travelling books, returning through Hampshire to Monk's House. Nelly Boxall is ill all the month and on 29th goes into hospital

5–10 June	The Woolfs are at Monk's House; and again 20th–21st. Virginia is rewriting *The Waves*; and seeing a good deal of V. Sackville-West and Ethel Smyth, both of whom she visits
July	The Woolfs are at Monk's House 4th–6th, 12th–14th and from 29th. They make short visits to Cambridge, to Woking to see Ethel Smyth, and to Long Barn
August–September	At Monk's House. Leonard drives to London about once a week, Virginia sometimes accompanies him. Guests are Ethel Smyth, V. Sackville-West, Alice Ritchie, E. M. Forster. On 29 August Virginia faints in the garden and is ill for ten days. Her new bedroom becomes the sitting-room. On 10 September the Woolfs go to Sissinghurst Castle, V. Sackville-West's new home, for the day
1 October	The Woolfs lunch with the Bells at Charleston to meet George and Margaret Duckworth
4 October– December	Return to Tavistock Square. Four week-ends are spent at Monk's House. Virginia is leading a sociable life in London, dining out with Lady Rhondda, Lady Colefax, etc., as well as seeing old friends and family
23 December	The Woolfs go to Monk's House for Christmas; Virginia is ill in bed from 24th–30th
1931 *7 January*	Return to Tavistock Square. Nelly Boxall returns to work as cook-housekeeper
12 January	Virginia meets John Lehmann, the prospective partner in the Hogarth Press; he starts work on 21st, when Virginia addresses the Society for Women's Service
23–25 January	The Woolfs are at Monk's House. Henceforth their general intention is to spend every other week-end (from Friday to Sunday), usually rather longer at Easter, Whitsun and Christmas, and the whole or August and September, at Rodmell
7 February	Virginia records the end of *The Waves*
14–15 February	The Woolfs drive with Vanessa to Cambridge to see Purcell's *Faery Queen*; they see E. M. Forster, George Rylands and others
27 February	Virginia goes to Sissinghurst to stay overnight with V. Sackville-West
28–29 March	The Woolfs drive to Liphook to stay with Sidney and Beatrice Webb

2–9 April	Easter at Monk's House
16–30 April	The Woolfs tour western France by car, from Dieppe to La Rochelle, Brantôme, Poitiers, Le Mans, Dreux, Caudebec and back
3 May	Return to Tavistock Square after Virginia has spent two days at Monk's House
21–28 May	Whitsun holiday at Monk's House after Virginia has spent two days in bed with a headache blamed on Ethel Smyth
July	Virginia sits to Stephen Tomlin for a sculptured head
17–19 July	The Woolfs are at Monk's House. Virginia finishes correcting and retyping *The Waves*, which Leonard reads and declares a masterpiece
25–26 July	The Woolfs stay at Oare with Sydney and Margery Waterlow
30 July	The Woolfs go to Monk's House for the summer. Virginia begins writing *Flush* and corrects proofs of *The Waves*; some days of headache. Visitors include V. Sackville-West, Lady Colefax, Ethel Smyth, John Lehmann, Sir George and Lady Margaret Duckworth, Kingsley Martin and Lyn Irvine
1 October	Return to Tavistock Square. Leonard gives six broadcasts at weekly intervals
8 October	*The Waves* is published
24 November	Virginia has headaches and has to remain inactive for a month
22 December	The Woolfs go to Monk's House for Christmas. Lytton Strachey is dangerously ill
1932	
10 January	Return to Tavistock Square
14 January	The Woolfs drive to Ham Spray to visit Lytton Strachey, who is too ill to see them; lunch with Pippa Strachey
21 January	Death of Lytton Strachey
31 January	Virginia finishes writing *A Letter to a Young Poet*; she works on *The Common Reader: Second Series*
February	Virginia is invited to deliver the Clark Lectures at Cambridge, but declines
10 March	The Woolfs drive to Ham Spray to see Carrington, who the following day kills herself
12–15 March	The Woolfs drive to Cambridge to see *Hamlet* with George Rylands; then to King's Lynn, Cromer, Norwich, and to spend a night with Roger Fry near Ipswich

23 March–3 April	Easter at Monk's House; the Woolfs visit V. Sackville-West at Sissinghurst Castle and Ethel Smyth and Maurice Baring at Rottingdean. Cement works being erected at Asham
15 April	The Woolfs, with Roger and Margery Fry, set out for Greece, *via* Paris and Venice, reaching Athens on 20th; they return by Orient Express *via* Belgrade and reach Monk's House on 12 May
15 May	Return to Tavistock Square. Discussions concerning organisation of the Hogarth Press; John Lehmann is to stay as adviser, Miss Scott Johnson as manager, with three clerks
June–July	Virginia leads a very sociable life, going to Monk's House every other week-end
1 July	*A Letter to a Young Poet* is published; on 11th *The Common Reader: Second Series* is finished
26 July	The Woolfs go to Monk's House. Very hot August weather: on 11th Virginia faints from heat and is unwell for some days. Visitors include Stella Benson, Mrs Woolf, Mr and Mrs T. S. Eliot, V. Sackville-West, Ethel Smyth and William Plomer
25–26 August	The Woolfs go to Thorpe-le-Soken to visit Adrian and Karin Stephen, returning to Monk's House *via* Tavistock Square
31 August	John Lehmann leaves the Hogarth Press
October	The Woolfs return to Tavistock Square; on 3–5 October they attend the Labour Party Conference at Leicester
13 October	*The Common Reader: Second Series* is published. Virginia begins "making up" *The Pargiters* (*The Years*)
1 November	Virginia's heart "galloping", which restricts her activity
20 December	The Woolfs go to Monk's House for Christmas; the Keyneses come to lunch and tea on Christmas Day
1933	
2 January	The Woolfs go to London for one night, to Vanessa's party
15 January	Return to Tavistock Square. Virginia is correcting *Flush*
February	Virginia begins twice weekly Italian lessons
March	Virginia is offered, and refuses, an Honorary Doctorate of Manchester University
13–23 April	The Woolfs are at Monk's House for Easter
5–27 May	The Woolfs drive through France and *via* the Grande

	Corniche and Pisa to Siena, returning by Lucca, Lerici, Avignon and Chartres to Monk's House
28 May	Return to Tavistock Square. Virginia is working on *The Years*
1–7 June	Whitsun at Monk's House
June–July	The Woolfs are very active and sociable; there is a revival of intimacy with Lady Ottoline Morrell, whom Virginia encourages in writing her memoirs
27 July	To Monk's House for the summer. Virginia is completely exhausted and in bed early August. Visitors include Elizabeth Read, Ethel Smyth, Kingsley Martin, V. Sackville-West, Leopold Campbell-Douglas, W. A. Robson, T. S. Eliot, E. M. Forster. Virginia begins again on *The Years*
Early September	Virginia is offered the Leslie Stephen lectureship at Cambridge, which she declines
23 September	The Memoir Club meets at Tilton (the Keyneses); E. M. Forster stays with the Woolfs; on 24th there are eleven people for tea at Monk's House
3–4 October	The Labour Party Conference at Hastings; Leonard attends both days, Virginia the first
5 October	*Flush* is published; the Woolfs go to Sissinghurst for the day
7 October	Return to Tavistock Square. Fortnightly visits to Monk's House continue (Friday to Sunday). On 11–12 November the Woolfs go to Ipsden to stay with Rosamond (Lehmann) and Wogan Philipps; on 30 November Virginia goes to Oxford to visit H. A. L. Fisher
15 December	Virginia dines with Clive Bell to meet Walter Sickert
21 December	The Woolfs go to Monk's House for three weeks. The Keyneses and V. Sackville-West and her sons come on Christmas Day
1934 7 January	The Woolfs go to London for the day, Leonard to the funeral of his sister Clara
14 January– end March	Return to Tavistock Square. Fortnightly visits to Monk's House continue. Virginia is suffering from recurrent headaches. In February she finishes revising *Sickert* and returns to work on her novel. Vanessa is painting her portrait
28 March	Nelly Boxall finally leaves the Woolfs' service. They go to Monk's House for a fortnight over Easter. E. M. Forster comes to stay for the Memoir Club meeting at Tilton on 8 April

22 April	The Woolfs drive to Monk's House and thence, by Salisbury and Fishguard, to Ireland; they visit Elizabeth Bowen at Bowen's Court; at Waterville on 1 May they read of George Duckworth's death; they go to Galway and Dublin and return by Holyhead and Stratford-on-Avon
9 May	Return to Tavistock Square. Virginia has influenza and is in bed for a week, after which they go to Monk's House for Whitsun (17–22 May). She is again ill in London, so they return to Monk's House for another week. They go to *Figaro* at Glyndebourne
11 June	Return to Tavistock Square. Virginia has French lessons with Janie Bussy twice a week; she returns to work on *The Years*
25 July	Leonard acquires a marmoset
26 July	The Woolfs go to Monk's House for the summer; Mabel comes as their new cook, Louie Everest as daily help. Visitors include Enid Bagnold, Saxon Sydney-Turner, William Plomer, Lyn Irvine, Karin, Ann and Judith Stephen, George Rylands
9 September	Death of Roger Fry; the Woolfs go to his funeral at Golders Green on 13 September
30 September	Virginia finishes first draft of *The Years* and is unwell for several days
7 October	Return to Tavistock Square. Virginia is depressed over her novel and Wyndham Lewis's detractions
20–21 October	The Woolfs go to a New Fabian Research Bureau conference at Maidstone. On 25th *Walter Sickert: a Conversation* is published. Virginia meets W. B. Yeats at Lady Ottoline Morrell's house
15 November	Virginia starts rewriting *The Years*
21 December	The Woolfs go to Monk's House for Christmas; very wet
1935	
2 January	Death of Francis Birrell
13 January	The Woolfs return to Tavistock Square
18 January	Virginia's play *Freshwater* performed before friends in Vanessa's studio at 8 Fitzroy Street
February–April	Alternate week-ends at Monk's House. Virginia is revising *The Years* and seeing a great many people
18–24 April	Easter at Rodmell
1 May	The Woolfs set out *via* Harwich for a tour of Europe by car. They spend a week in Holland, three days in Germany and cross the Brenner Pass into Italy

	on 13 May; they reach Rome on 16 May and find Vanessa, Angelica and Quentin Bell there; they start home on 24th and drive through France, reaching Monk's House on 31 May
2 June	Return to Tavistock Square until 6th, when they go back to Monk's House for Whitsun. Two visits to Glyndebourne
2 July	Virginia goes to spend a night with the Tweedsmuirs (Susan Buchan) in the Cotswolds
12 July	The Woolfs drive to Bristol, where Virginia opens an exhibition of Roger Fry's paintings; they return by Avebury, Lechlade and Kelmscott
24 July	"Reconciliation dinner" for John Lehmann
25 July	The Woolfs go to Monk's House for the summer. Visitors include Stephen Tennant, Leonard's relations, W. A. Robson, Margery Fry and T. S. Eliot. They make day visits to London, to Worthing, to Sissinghurst, to Dorking (to see Margaret Llewelyn Davies).
29 August	Julian Bell leaves Newhaven for China. Exceptionally stormy weather
September	Virginia decides to call her book *The Years*; she is rewriting it
30 September–2 October	The Woolfs attend the Labour Party Conference in Brighton; they hear Bevin's attack on Lansbury
5 October	Return to Tavistock Square. Virginia is reading Roger Fry's letters and making notes for a possible biography
14 November	General Election. The Woolfs vote at Rodmell and drive voters to the poll at Patcham
20 December	To Monk's House for Christmas holiday. Very wet
1936	
1 January	Virginia is in bed with headache; three bad days
8 January	Return to Tavistock Square. Virginia is revising *The Years* and reading for *Roger Fry*
20 January	Death of King George V; accession of Edward VIII
24–26 January	The Woolfs go to Monk's House and on to Canterbury, where Leonard lectures to the Workers' Educational Association
9 February	The Woolfs attend a meeting of Vigilance, an organisation of anti-Fascist intellectuals, at Adrian Stephen's home
February	Virginia is working very hard, is not very well, and limits her social engagements
March	The Woolfs go to see Lydia Lopokova playing in

	Ibsen. There is a general preoccupation with the worsening political situation. Part of *The Years* is sent to the printer, but the greater part is still being revised and retyped
3 April	The Woolfs go to Monk's House for Easter. Virginia sends last batch of manuscript of *The Years* to the printer on 8th, collapses into bed and remains at Rodmell for a month, able to do nothing
3 May	Return to Tavistock Square; Virginia sees Dr Rendel. They then set out by car for a tour of the south-west, to Weymouth, Lyme Regis and to Cornwall, where they stay three nights with the Arnold-Forsters at Zennor; they return *via* Coverack and Shaftesbury to Monk's House and Tavistock Square, which they reach on 22 May
23 May	Virginia begins work again–not more than 45 minutes a day permitted by her doctor
29 May–10 June	The Woolfs return to Monk's House, following the doctor's recommendation
10–25 June	Return to Tavistock Square for a fortnight's trial. Virginia is correcting proofs of *The Years* with great suffering
25–30 June	The Woolfs are at Monk's House. After a further week in London they return there and remain until October. Virginia is very unwell; no entry in her diary from 23 June to 30 October; few visitors–mostly family to play bowls with Leonard
11 October	Return to Tavistock Square. Virginia seems much better; on 19th she goes to stay a night with Ethel Smyth at Woking, and begins to entertain and to go out again
2 November	Virginia is in despair; Leonard reads proofs of *The Years* and reassures her; she finishes work on it on 30 November
November	Roger Fry's friend Charles Mauron is in London and meets the Woolfs. Virginia begins writing *Three Guineas*
December	The Abdication crisis; King Edward abdicates on 10th
17 December	The Woolfs go to Monk's House for Christmas; Christmas lunch with the Keyneses
1937	
1–4 January	Ann and Judith Stephen stay at Monk's House. On 8th the Woolfs have tea with Elizabeth Robins and Octavia Wilberforce in Brighton
9 January	Funeral of Stephen Tomlin

16 January	Return to Tavistock Square. On 21st Miss West, the manager of the Hogarth Press, dies
February	Virginia is working on *Three Guineas*; Leonard is not well and sees specialists; by 22nd he is given a clean bill of health
12–15 March	The Woolfs are at Monk's House. Julian Bell returns from China with the intention of enlisting in the International Brigade in Spain
15 March	Publication of *The Years*
25 March–4 April	The Woolfs are at Monk's House for Easter. On 1 April they drive to Minstead in the New Forest to see Janet Case, who is dying
29 April	Virginia broadcasts
7–25 May	The Woolfs tour south-western France by car, staying some days at Souillac and visiting Les Eyzies, Albi, George Sand's house at Nohant, and Maintenon. Maynard Keynes is seriously ill
29 May–6 June	The Woolfs are at Monk's House
6 June	Farewell dinner for Julian Bell at 50 Gordon Square; he leaves next day to drive an ambulance in Spain
June–July	Virginia is again active and sociable; some week-ends are spent at Monk's House
15 July	Death of Janet Case
20 July	The news is received of Julian Bell's death on 18 July
29 July	The Woolfs drive Vanessa to Charleston, and then go to Monk's House until October. Virginia is a constant support to her sister and family. Dorothy and Janie Bussy, Judith Stephen and T. S. Eliot stay at Monk's House. Day visits to London, to Dorking to see Margaret Llewelyn Davies, and to Sissinghurst. Virginia is working on *Three Guineas*
10 October	Return to Tavistock Square. On 12th Virginia finishes *Three Guineas*
October–December	The Woolfs go once a fortnight to Monk's House; 12–13 November they are at Cambridge, Leonard speaking at the Union. Virginia is unwell at the beginning of December, and anxious about Leonard's health
22–29 December	The Woolfs are at Monk's House for Christmas; Leonard is ill, so returns to London and is examined at the Royal Northern Hospital on 31 December
1938	
1–11 January	Leonard stays in bed; specimens found "normal"
14–23 January	To Monk's House for Leonard's convalescence

24 January	Virginia is ill at Tavistock Square with a temperature
1 March	John Lehmann takes over Virginia's share of the Hogarth Press
12 March	Hitler invades Austria
14–24 April	The Woolfs are at Monk's House for Easter. Lady Ottoline Morrell dies on 21 April. Virginia is working at *Roger Fry* and thinking about *Poyntz Hall* (*Between the Acts*)
14–15 May	The Woolfs go to Haslemere to stay with Ray and Oliver Strachey
22 May	Death of Mrs Arnold-Forster (Ka Cox)
1–11 June	The Woolfs are at Monk's House. *Three Guineas* is published on 2 June
16 June–2 July	The Woolfs go by car *via* the Roman Wall to Scotland and the Western Isles
28 July	The Woolfs go to Monk's House for the summer; guests include V. Sackville-West, Lady Colefax, E. M. Forster and Molly MacCarthy (for Memoir Club meeting, 11 September), Noel Olivier Richards and Richard and Ann (Stephen) Llewelyn Davies. Weekly visits to London, and for one night (26–27 September) during the Munich crisis
16 October	Return to Tavistock Square; the Woolfs make fortnightly visits to Monk's House
20 December	To Monk's House for Christmas. Snow. On 24th Jack Hills dies; also Leonard's marmoset, Mitz. To Tilton and Charleston on Christmas Day.
1939	
15 January	Return to Tavistock Square. The Woolfs go twice a month to Rodmell for week-ends
28 January	The Woolfs visit Sigmund Freud at Hampstead
2 March	Virginia speaks at an exhibition of book jacket designs at the Central School of Arts and Crafts
3 March	Virginia is offered and refuses an Honorary Doctorate of Liverpool University
6–24 April	The Woolfs are at Monk's House for Easter. Virginia is not very well
25 May	At Monk's House for Whitsun
5–20 June	The Woolfs go from Rodmell to France, to make a tour by car in Brittany and Normandy
22 June	Return to Tavistock Square
2 July	Death of Mrs Woolf, Leonard's mother
25 July	The Woolfs go to Monk's House for the summer
17 August	To London to move the Hogarth Press to 37 Mecklenburgh Square, W.C.1; on 24th they move their

	personal possessions there, and return to Rodmell. Crisis atmosphere in London
1 September	Germany invades Poland; on 3rd England declares war
September	Hogarth Press clerks each stay two or three days at Monk's House; other guests are Kingsley Martin, Stephen Spender, John Lehmann and Judith Stephen
13–20 October	The Woolfs stay at Mecklenburgh Square. Henceforward they live at Monk's House, going to London usually once a week, sometimes for the day, sometimes staying a few days
October–December	At Monk's House. Regular meetings of the Rodmell Labour Party are held there. Guests are T. S. Eliot, E. Sackville-West, W. A. Robson, John Lehmann

1940

6 January	Party for Angelica Bell at Charleston; guests include the Woolfs, the Keyneses, Marjorie Strachey and Duncan Grant
12–13 January	E. M. Forster stays at Monk's House
February	6th–7th, John Lehmann to stay; 12th–16th, in London; 17th–19th, Sally Graves (Mrs Chilver) stays at Monk's House; 24th, Virginia is ill with influenza, but on 26th goes to Mecklenburgh Square, where she stays in bed
2 March	Return to Monk's House. The manuscript of *Roger Fry* is sent to Margery Fry and to Vanessa. Virginia is mostly ill and in bed until 21 March. 27th–28th, Margery Fry stays at Monk's House
9 April	German invasion of Norway and Denmark
23–24 April	V. Sackville-West stays at Monk's House
27 April	Virginia lectures to the Workers' Educational Association in Brighton (*The Leaning Tower*)
10 May	Germany invades Holland and Belgium
18–21 May	Desmond MacCarthy and G. E. Moore stay at Monk's House
10 June	Italy enters the war
14 June	The Woolfs visit Penshurst with V. Sackville-West; Paris falls to the Germans
17–20 June	The Woolfs stay at Mecklenburgh Square; Adrian Stephen provides them with a lethal dose of morphia
25–27 June	Elizabeth Bowen stays at Monk's House
15–16 July	St John and Jeremy Hutchinson stay at Monk's House
23 July	Virginia reads her account of the Dreadnought Hoax to the Women's Institute in Rodmell

25 July	Publication of *Roger Fry: A Biography*
August–September	Battle of Britain; daily air raids. John Lehmann, Ann and Judith Stephen, Benedict Nicolson stay at Monk's House. The Memoir Club meets at Charleston on 1 September. Helen Anrep stays in Rodmell
10 September	The Woolfs drive to London; Mecklenburgh Square has been bombed, their house severely damaged, and they cannot reach it
23 September	The Hogarth Press is moved from Mecklenburgh Square to Letchworth, Hertfordshire
18 October	The Woolfs drive to London for the day; see 52 Tavistock Square in ruins
7 November	Virginia refuses E. M. Forster's request to propose her for the Committee of the London Library
4 December	Furniture and books arrive from Mecklenburgh Square for storage at Monk's House and in the village
14 December	The Hogarth Press printing machine is delivered to Monk's House

1941

1 January	Dr Octavia Wilberforce has tea at Monk's House; she now comes fairly often from Brighton, bringing cream, etc.
11–13 February	The Woolfs drive to London and go by train to Cambridge, where they see Pernel Strachey and George Rylands; they also visit the Hogarth Press at Letchworth
13–15 February	Elizabeth Bowen stays at Monk's House
17–18 February	V. Sackville-West stays at Monk's House
26 February	Virginia finishes *Pointz Hall* (*Between the Acts*)
8 March	To Brighton; Leonard lecturing to the Workers' Educational Association, Virginia fighting despondency
18 March	Leonard becomes seriously alarmed by Virginia's deteriorating state
27 March	The Woolfs go to Brighton to consult Dr Wilberforce about Virginia's condition
28 March	Virginia Woolf drowns herself in the River Ouse

APPENDIX B

The Years was published on 15 March 1937; on Easter Sunday, 28 March, Virginia Woolf made the following entry in her diary (AWD (Berg)) at Monk's House, Rodmell

... Yesterday a reporter for the New York Times rang up: was told he could look at the outside of 52 [Tavistock Square] if he chose. At 4.30 as I was boiling the kettle a huge black Daimler drew up. Then a dapper little man in a tweed coat appeared in the garden. I reached the sitting room: saw him standing there looking round. L. ignored him. L. in the orchard with Percy. Then I guessed. He had a green notebook and stood looking about jotting things down. I ducked my head—he almost caught me. At last L. turned and fronted him. No, Mrs W. didn't want that kind of publicity. I raged: a bug walking over one's skin—couldn't crush him. The bug taking notes. L. politely led him back to his Daimler and his wife. But they'd had a nice run from London—bugs, to come and steal in and take notes.

The typescript original (MH/A 19) of the following contains a certain number of typing errors which have been corrected in accordance with Virginia's obvious intentions.

FANTASY UPON A GENTLEMAN WHO CONVERTED HIS IMPRESSIONS OF A PRIVATE HOUSE INTO CASH

He wished to see, J.B., the lady of the house, did he?
There he sat, in the morning, the precious morning,
in the spring of the year, on a chair; J.B.
Yes, I see; I see, the unbaked crumpet face;
with a hole for a mouth; and a blob at the lips;
the voluble half closed lips; gooseberry eyes;
his lack of attraction; his self satisfaction;
sitting there, in the chair in the spring of the year;
taking time, air, light, space; stopping the
race of every thought; blocking out with his tweeds
the branches; the pigeons; and half the sky.
Monarch of the drab world; of the shifting shuffling
uneasy, queasy, egotist's journalist's pobbing and
boobling, like a stew a-simmer, asking for sympathy
dousing the clean the clear the bright the sharp in
the stew of his greasy complacency; his self satisfaction
his profound unhappy sense of his lack of attraction;
his desire to be scratched cleansed, rubbed clean of
the moss and the slime; demanding as a right,

other people's time; sitting there on the chair;
blocking out the light with his rubbed grease stained tweeds.
Why did he want to be 'seen'. What corkscrew
urge from the surge of his stew, his gobbets and
gibbets forced him out of the here, to this chair,
to be seen? when the spring was there?
to be seen sitting there, sprawling, self conscious,
conscious only of nothing, blear eyed, blubber
lipped, thick thumbed, squirming, to be seen,
Brown like a bug that slips out on a lodging house
wall; J.B. John Bug; James Bug Bug bug bug, as he
talked he slipped like a bug malodorous glistening
but only semi transparent; as if while he talked he
sipped blood. my blood; anybodies blood to make a
bugs body blue black. There he sat on the chair,
with his hair unbrushed; his mouth dribbling; his eyes
streaming with the steam of some lodging house stew.
A bug; Always on the wall. The bug of the house
that comes. But if you kill bugs they leave marks
on the wall. Just as the bug's body bleeds in pale
ink recording his impressions of a private house
in the newspapers for cash.

Virginia Woolf and Julian Bell

Julian Bell was killed in Spain on 18 July 1937. Virginia's memoir of him is dated 30 July 1937. The manuscript (MH/A 8) runs to some 7,000 words, and was made use of by Peter Stansky and William Abrahams in their dual biography of Julian Bell and John Cornford, Journey to the Frontier *(1966). It is printed here in the belief that it illuminates Virginia's own character and personality: some less relevant passages have therefore been omitted.*

I am going to set down very quickly what I remember about Julian,—partly because I am too dazed to write what I was writing: & then I am so composed that nothing is real unless I write it. And again, I know by this time what an odd effect Time has: it does not destroy people—for instance, I still think perhaps more truly than I did, of Roger, of Thoby: but it brushes away the actual personal presence.

The last time I saw Julian was at Clive's, two days before he went to Spain. It was a Sunday night, the beginning of June—a hot night. He was in his shirtsleeves. Lottie* was out, & we cooked dinner. He had a peculiar way of standing: his gestures were, as they say, characteristic. [They reminded one of a sharp winged bird—one of the snipe here in the marsh] He made sharp quick movements, very sudden, considering how large & big he was, & oddly graceful. I remember his intent expression; seriously looking, I suppose at toast or eggs, through his spectacles. He had a very serious look: indeed he had grown much sterner, since he came back from China. But of the talk I remember very little; except that by degrees it turned to politics. L. & Clive & Julian began to talk about Fascism, I daresay: & I remember thinking, now Clive is reining himself in with L.: being self restrained: which means there's trouble brewing. (I was wrong, as L. told me afterwards.) Julian was now a grown man: I mean, he held his own with Clive & L.: & was cool & independent. I felt he had met many different kinds of people in China. Anyhow, as it was hot, & they talked politics, V[anessa]. & A[ngelica]. & I went out into the Square, & then the others came, & we sat & talked. I remember saying something about Roger's papers, & telling Julian I should leave them to him in my will. He said in his quick way, Better leave them to the British Museum. & I thought, That's because he thinks he may be killed. Of course we all knew that this was our last meeting—all together—before he went. But I had made up my mind to plunge into work, & seeing people, that summer.

* Lottie Hope, who had once been the Woolfs' servant, now worked for Clive Bell at 50 Gordon Square.

I had determined not to think about the risks, because, subconsciously I was sure he would be killed; that is I had a couchant unexpressed certainty, from Thoby's death I think; a legacy of pessimism, which I have decided never to analyse. Then, as we walked towards the gate together, I went with Julian, & said, Won't you have time to write something in Spain? Won't you send it us? (This referred of course to my feeling, a very painful one, that I had treated his essay on Roger too lightly.) And he said, very quickly—he spoke quickly with a suddenness like his movements—"Yes, I'll write something about Spain. And send it you if you like." Do I said, & touched his hand. Then we went up to Clive's room: & then they went: we stood at the door to watch them. Julian was driving Nessa's car. At first it wouldn't start. He sat there at the wheel frowning, looking very magnificent, in his shirt sleeves; with an expression as if he had made up his mind & were determined, though there was this obstacle—the car wouldn't start. Then suddenly it jerked off—& he had his head thrown slightly back, as he drove up the Square with Nessa beside him. Of course I noted it, as it might be our last meeting. What he said was 'Goodbye until this time next year.'

We went in with Clive & drank. And talked about Julian. Clive & L. said that there was no more risk in going to Spain than in driving up & down to Charleston. Clive said that only one man had been hurt by a bomb. And he added, But Julian is very cool, like Cory [Clive's brother] & myself. It's spirited of him to go, he added. I think I said, But it's a worry for Nessa. Then we discussed professions: Clive told us how Picasso had said, As a father, I'm so glad my son does not have one. And he said, he was glad Julian should be a 'character'; he would always have enough money to get bread and butter: it was a good thing he had no profession. He was a person who had no one gift in particular. He did not think he was born to be a writer—No he was a character, like Thoby. For some reason I did not answer, that he was like Thoby. I have always been foolish about that. I did not like any Bell to be like Thoby, partly through snobbishness I suppose; nor do I think that Julian was like Thoby, except in the obvious way that he was young & very fine to look at. I said that Thoby had a natural style, & Julian had not.

There was also the damned literary question. I was always critical of his writing, partly I suspect from the usual generation jealousy; partly from my own enviousness of anyone who can do in writing what I can't do: & again (for I can't analyse out the other strains in a very complex feeling, roused partly by L.; for we envied Nessa I suspect for such a son; and there was L.'s family complex which made him eager, no, on the alert, to criticise her children because he thought I admired them more than his family) I thought him very careless, not 'an artist', too personal in what he wrote, & "all over the place". This is the one thing I regret in our relationship: that I might have encouraged him more as a writer. But again, that's my character: & I'm always forced, in spite of jealousy, to be honest in the end. Still this is my one regret; & I shall always have it; seeing how immensely generous he was to me about what I did—touchingly proud sometimes of my writings. But then I came to the stage 2 years ago of hating 'personality'; desiring anonymity; a complex state which I would one day have discussed with him. Then, I could not sympathise with wishing to be published. I thought it wrong from my new standpoint—a piece of the egomaniac, egocentric mania of the time. (For that reason I would not sign my Janet article). But how could he know why I was so cool about publishing his things? Happily I made L. reconsider his poems, & we published them.

I could be hurt sometimes by his rather caustic teasing, something like Clive's, & I felt it more because I have suffered from Clive's caustic & rather cruel teasing in the past.—Julian had something of the same way of "seeing through one"; but it was less personal, & stronger. That last supper party at Clive's I remember beginning a story about Desmond. It was about the L.S. lecture.* I said "Desmond took it very seriously as a compliment." And I could not remember who had had the L.S. lectureship and said "Didn't David [Cecil] do it?" & then Julian gave his flash of mockery & severity & said Ah, how like you. That's what you said—looking at Clive as though they both joined in suspecting my malice: in which he was that time wrong. But not always. I mean he had claws & could use them. He had feelings about the Bells. He thought I wanted to give pain. He thought me cruel, as Clive thinks me; but he told me, the night I talked to him before he went to China, that he never doubted the warmth of my feelings: that I suffered a great deal: that I had very strong affections.

But our relationship was perfectly secure because it was founded on our passion—not too strong a word for either of us—for Nessa. And it was this passion that made us both reserved when we met this summer.

I was so anxious to do everything to stop him from going that I got him to meet Kingsley Martin once at dinner, & then Stephen Spender, & so never saw him alone—except once, & then only for a short time. I had just come in with the Evening Standard in which The Years was extravagantly praised, much to my surprise. I felt very happy. It was a great relief. And I stood with the paper, hoping L. would come & I could tell him when the bell rang. I went to the top of the stairs, looked down, & saw Julian's great sun hat (he was amazingly careless of dress always—would come here with a tear in his trousers) & I called out in a sepulchral voice "Who is that?" Whereupon he started, & laughed & I let him in. And he said What a voice to hear, or something light: then he came up; it was to ask for Dalton's telephone number. He stood there; I asked him to stay and see Leonard. He hesitated, but seemed to

* The Leslie Stephen Lecture at the University of Cambridge.

make up his mind that he must get on with the business of seeing Dalton. So I went & looked for the number. When I came back he was reading the Standard. I had left it with the review open. But he had turned, I think to the politics. I had half a mind to say, Look how I'm praised. And then thought No, I'm on the top of the wave: & it's not kind to thrust that sort of thing upon people who aren't yet recognised. So I said nothing about it. But I wanted him to stay. And then again I felt, he's afraid I shall try to persuade him not to go. So all I said was, Look here Julian, if you ever want a meal, you've only to ring us up. Yes he said rather doubtingly, as if we might be too busy. So I insisted. We can't see too much of you. And followed him into the hall, & put my arm round him & said You can't think how nice it is having you back. & we half kissed; & he looked pleased & said Do you feel that? And I said yes, & it was as if he asked me to forgive him for all the worry; and then off he stumped, in his great hat and thick coat.

When I was in that horrid state of misery last summer with the proofs of The Years, in such misery that I could only work for 10 minutes & then go & lie down, I wrote him my casual letter about his Roger paper, & he only answered many weeks later to say he had been hurt;* so hadn't written: & then another letter of mine brought back the old family feeling. I was shocked at this, & wrote at once, in time to catch him before he started home, to say don't let us ever quarrel about writing, & I explained & apologised. All the same, for this reason, & because of his summer journey, & also because one always stops writing letters unless one has a regular day, we had one of those lapses in communication which are bound to happen. I thought, when he comes back there'll be time to begin again. I thought he would get some political job & we should see a lot of him.

This lapse perhaps explains why I go on asking myself, without finding an answer, what did he feel about Spain? What made him feel it necessary, knowing as he did how it must torture Nessa, to go? He knew her feeling. We discussed it before he went to China in the most intimate talk I ever had with him. I remember then he said how hard it was for her, now that Roger was dead; & that he was sorry that Quentin was so much at Charleston. He knew that: & yet deliberately inflicted this fearful anxiety on her. What made him do it? I suppose its a fever in the blood of the younger generation which we can't possibly understand. I have never known anyone of my generation have that feeling about a war. We were all C.O.'s in the Great war. And though I understand that this is a 'cause', can be called the cause of liberty & so on, still my natural reaction is to

* Virginia's letter is lost. Julian, in his reply from Wuhan (5 December 1936), says: "I was rather hurt at your not liking my Roger better—which was most unreasonable of me, but I think your letter caught me at the moment when one feels most sensitive about one's work, when its finished past altering and at the same time is still a part of oneself."

fight intellectually: if I were any use, I should write against it: I should evolve some plan for fighting English tyranny. The moment force is used, it becomes meaningless & unreal to me. And I daresay he would soon have lived through the active stage, & have found some other, administrative, work. But that does not explain his determination. . . .

A Note on Sources and References

The notes which follow are intended to direct those who may wish to pursue such matters to the sources I have used. To avoid spattering the main text with distracting numerals, a page number and salient phrase are used to identify the quotation or statement whose origin is here documented.

The principal *published* sources are listed in the Bibliography on p. 282, where abbreviated titles used in the notes are given in full. Page references are given to English editions, and to the first edition of Virginia Woolf's books.

The *unpublished* material to which reference is made is for the greater part contained in three collections (more fully described in the Foreword to Volume I), namely: the Henry W. and Albert A. Berg Collection of English and American Literature in the New York Public Library (Berg); the Charleston Papers in the Library of King's College, Cambridge (CH); and what I have called the Monk's House Papers (MH). These, which formed a part of the estate of the late Leonard Woolf, now belong, thanks to the generosity of Mrs Ian Parsons, to the University of Sussex. In the notes I have identified material from these three repositories by the abbreviations given here in brackets.

In 1955 Leonard Woolf began to assemble copies of Virginia Woolf's letters with the intention of publishing them. The intention was abandoned, but the copies were retained. It is thus that I am familiar with letters whose whereabouts I do not always know. Many remain in private hands; others may have reached the Academic Center of the University of Texas, whose important collection of writers' letters I have unfortunately been unable to visit.

I have also drawn upon various family documents which remain in the possession of the heirs and descendents of Sir Leslie Stephen. The following are referred to by abbreviations: *The Mausoleum Book*, written by Leslie Stephen after the death of his wife Julia in 1895 (MBk); copies of the Stephen children's family newspaper, the *Hyde Park Gate News*, for 1891, 1892 and 1895 (HPGN); and six manuscript memoirs by Vanessa Bell (VB/MS I–VI).

In referring to Virginia Woolf's *Diaries, 1915–1941*, I cite wherever possible the selection published by the Hogarth Press in 1953 under the title *A Writer's Diary* (abbreviated to *AWD*); references to the unpublished portions of the original now in the Berg Collection are prefixed *AWD (Berg)*.

A NOTE ON SOURCES AND REFERENCES

Original documents are transcribed as faithfully as possible, so that errors in spelling and punctuation may be ascribed to the writer, not to the printer.

The following initials are used in place of full names:

CB	Clive Bell	QB	Quentin Bell
DG	Duncan Grant	RF	Roger Fry
EMF	Edward Morgan Forster	SST	Saxon Sydney-Turner
ES	Ethel Smyth	VB	Vanessa (Stephen) Bell
GLS	Giles Lytton Strachey	VD	Violet Dickinson
JMK	John Maynard Keynes	VSW	V. Sackville-West
LW	Leonard Woolf	VW	Virginia (Stephen) Woolf

Hearsay evidence is indicated by the abbreviation *p.i.* followed by the name of my informant.

REFERENCES

VOLUME 1

CHAPTER ONE

Page
1 Imprisonment for debt . . . James Stephen, *Considerations on Imprisonment for Debt* . . ., 1770, passim
2 "want of birth . . ." Leslie Stephen, *Life of Sir James Fitzjames Stephen*, p. 7
2 "What then was to be done?" James Stephen, *Memoirs*, p. 188
3 *War in Disguise* . . . James Stephen, *War in Disguise; or the Fraud of the Neutral Flags*, 1805
5 "Mr Over-Secretary Stephen." Leslie Stephen, *op. cit.*, p. 46
5 "Did you ever know your father . . ." *ibid.*, p. 63
7 "to be weak is to be wretched . . ." *ibid.*, p. 80
8 "He has lost all hope . . ." *p.i.* (*VW*)
8 "Oh Almighty Lord . . ." *Book of Common Prayer*: for Fair Weather
11 "She and I had our little contentions." *MBk*, p. 17
12 "I got up and found . . ." *MBk*, p. 16
12 "Now Milly has loved me . . ." *MBk*, p. 43
13 "All life seemed a shipwreck . . ." *MBk*, p. 30
13 . . . a permanent loss of faith. *MH/A 6*
13 "I am in love with Julia!" *MBk*, p. 36
14 According to Virginia's cousin . . . H. A. L. Fisher, *An Unfinished Autobiography*, Oxford, 1940, pp. 10–12. See also: E. F. Benson, *As We Were*, 1930, p. 87, and Paul Savile, *Val Prinsep and Royal Academy Painting*, a Mastership Dissertation (Magdalen College, Oxford), 1970
14 The sequel is interesting . . . See E. F. Benson, *As We Were*, 1930, pp. 92–95
16 "she doubled the generosity . . ." VW (quoting Mrs G. F. Watts), introduction to *Victorian Photographs of Famous Men & Fair Women by Julia Margaret Cameron*, Hogarth Press, 1926, p. 3
16 "where only beautiful things . . ." Quoted by Helmut Gernsheim, *Julia Margaret Cameron*, 1948, p. 15
17 her "dear heart, her lamb." *Mrs Jackson to Mrs Leslie Stephen*, passim
18 Mrs Ramsay's relationship with her husband . . . See Mitchell A. Leaska, *Virginia Woolf's Lighthouse*, 1970, chapter 5
18 . . . little tails . . . *p.i.* (*VB*)

CHAPTER TWO

Page
23 The arrival of Adrian . . . See footnote, p. 116
23 "She reminded me always . . ." *VB/MS I*
24 . . . scratching a distempered wall . . . *p.i.* (*VB*)

REFERENCES

Page

24 "The Saint" *VB/MS I*; also *MH/A 6*

24 "purple with rage" *VB/MS I*

25 some indifferent verses . . . Reprinted in F. W. Maitland, *Sir Leslie Stephen*, 1906, p. 318

25 "MY DEAR GODPAPA . . ." *VW to J. R. Lowell*, on a letter from Leslie Stephen, 20 August 1888. (The Houghton Library, Harvard University)

25 "Clementé, dear child . . ." *VB/MS I*

27 Singing was better . . . *VW/VD*, [c. 27 December 1902] (Berg); also *VB/MS I*.

28 "How sweet it was . . ." *HPGN*, 21 March 1892

28 "So the boy turned him lose . . ." *HPGN*, 7 March 1892

29 "Rather clever, I think," *VB/MS I*

29 "Young children should be nipped . . ." *HPGN*, 18 January 1892

29 "Miss Millicent Vaughan . . ." *HPGN*, 14 March 1892

29 ". . . the prince of talkers . . ." *HPGN*, 21 March, 9 May, 7 November 1892

29 "I cannot make up plots . . ." *AWD*, p. 116, 5 October 1927

29 *The Midnight Ride. HPGN*, 25 January, 1 February, 1892

30 ". . . you have jilted me . . ." *HPGN*, 6 June 1892

30 *A Cockney's Farming Experiences. HPGN*, 22 August 1892 *et seq*

30 "That day . . . is stamped . . ." *HPGN*, 16 May 1892

32 "On Saturday morning . . ." *HPGN*, 12 September 1892

32 Family life at St Ives . . . *VB/RF*, 29 September 1930 (CH)

32 Mr Wolstenholme . . . *MBk*, p. 61

33 Rupert Brooke . . . From Stella Duckworth's *1893 Diary* it is clear that it was in August and September that the Brookes met the Stephens at St Ives, rather than in April 1899 as Christopher Hassall (*Rupert Brooke*, 1964, p. 30) states. The Stephens had in any case left St Ives by 1895. See also: *Mrs Mary Ruth Brooke to VW*, 18 August 1918 (MH)

34 William Fisher . . . *William Wordsworth Fisher* (later Admiral Sir W. W. Fisher) *to Mrs Leslie Stephen*, 5 August [1891]

35 "The felicious family . . ." *HPGN*, 22 August 1892

35 . . . the scene in *The Years* . . . p.i. (*VB*). See VW, *The Years*, p. 29

37 . . . a novel of manners . . . "Extracts from the Diary of Miss Sarah Morgan" in *HPGN*, 14 and 21 January 1895; article beginning "I dreamt one night that I was God . . ." *ibid.*, 11 February 1895

37 a report of the wedding . . . *HPGN*, 21 January 1895

37 "from the tooth of time" *HPGN*, 25 February 1895

37 "For the last fortnight . . ." *HPGN*, 4 March 1895

38 Mrs Jackson had written . . . *Mrs Jackson to VB*, 11 July 1890

38 "Ah, thank Heaven, there is no post . . ." *MH/A 5*

38 . . . crushed and cramped in the womb . . . *AWD (Berg)*, 3 December 1923

39 "fits of the horrors" *MBk*, p. 68

CHAPTER THREE

Page

40 "Her death . . . was the greatest disaster . . ." *MH/A 6*

40 . . . a panegyric on 'My Julia' *MBk*

40 "Oriental gloom" *MH/A 6*

41 . . . "trifles," but also . . . *MBk*, p. 69

Page

45 in 1896 she did keep a diary . . . It is referred to in the *1897 Diary* (Berg) on 18 January, but has not been preserved

47 "My Julia . . ." *MBk* (addendum), p. 82

47 "he has picked my pocket . . ." *Florence Burke to VW*, 30 April 1928, enclosed with *VW/VB*, 9 May 1928 (Berg)

48 "like the smack of a whip" *MH/A 5*

50 "DENIZENS OF THE KITCHEN . . ." *p.i.* (*VB*)

50 "O Leslie, what a noble boy . . ." *1897 Diary*, 6 January (Berg)

50 "I hope, though I still hope . . ." *Leslie Stephen to Mrs Herbert Fisher*, 14 November 1897

50 "I did some Greek." *1897 Diary*, 3 March (Berg)

51 "Gracious, child, how you gobble" *VW/VSW*, 19 February 1929 (Berg)

51 "Ginia is devouring books . . ." *MBk* (addendum), p. 84

51 Hakluyt's *Voyages* . . . *AWD*, p. 150, 8 December 1929

52 "rather nasty . . ." *Leslie Stephen to Thoby Stephen*, 6 February 1897

53 the "dreadful idea" . . . *1897 Diary*, 7 March (Berg)

53 "Do you think that I may be allowed . . ." *Leslie Stephen to Thoby Stephen*, 27 March 1897; "arrived at father's tailor in Bond St where father ordered himself a whole new suit for the wedding." *1897 Diary*, 29 March (Berg)

53 "about as amusing to me" *Leslie Stephen to Thoby Stephen*, 27 March 1897

54 "third rate actresses . . ." *1897 Diary*, 18 April (Berg)

54 "a good many selfish pangs . . ." *MBk* (addendum), p. 84

55 "Stella was worse . . ." *1897 Diary*, 29 April (Berg)

56 "She . . . irritated me extremely" *1897 Diary*, 12 June (Berg)

56 "unreasonable enough" *1897 Diary*, 4 May (Berg)

56 "This Sunday a most distinct . . ." *1897 Diary*, 9 May (Berg)

57 "I growl at everything . . ." *1897 Diary*, 13 June (Berg)

57 "relentless, thundery sunless heat" *1897 Diary*, 24 June (Berg)

57 "three months of . . . horrible suspense" *VB/MS II*

57 "goodbye" *1897 Diary*, 17 July (Berg)

CHAPTER FOUR

Page

58 "the ghastly mourners" *MH/A 6*

59 "My mother was a saint" H. A. L. Fisher, *An Unfinished Autobiography*, Oxford 1940, p. 15

59 "My dear Virginia . . ." *p.i.* (*VW*)

59 "The Fishers would have made Eden . . ." *VW to Emma Vaughan*, 30 August [1903] (MH)

60 "She talks . . . every minute of the day" *VW to Thoby Stephen*, 5 December 1897 (CH)

60 "the most ungainly creatures . . ." *VB/MS II*

60 . . . ugly and sweated . . . *VW/ES*, 18 May 1931 (Berg)

61 "Madge is here . . ." *p.i.* (*VW*). Also: *AWD* (Berg), 2 June 1921

61 "Terrible long dinner . . ." *1897 Diary*, 25/26 September (Berg)

62 "poor boy, . . ." *MH/A 5*

62 "when he was sad, she should be sad; . . ." *MH/A 6*

Page
62 "Did you hear me call" *MH/A 6*
63 "And you stand there like a block . . ." *MH/A 5*
63 "What an aggravating young woman . . ." *VB/MS II*
65 ". . . the edge of this . . . [cloud]" *Warboys Diary*, 1 September 1899 (Berg)
66 *VW to Emma Vaughan* (MH)
68 "very white and shrivelled" *VW to Emma Vaughan*, 23 October 1900 (MH)
70 "I don't get anybody to argue . . ." *VW to Thoby Stephen*, n.d. [early May 1903] (CH)
72 "So you take their side too" *MH/A 5*
73 (Everyone has forgotten me) *MH/A 5*
74 "Hyde Park Gaters" *Adrian Stephen to VB*, n.d. [April/May 1941] (CH)
74 "Why won't my whiskers grow?" *p.i.* (*VB*)
74 "Why won't that young man go?" *p.i.* (*VB*); alternatively: "Why can't he go? Why can't he go?" *VW*, *Collected Essays*, 1967, "Leslie Stephen", vol. IV, p. 78
74 "Oh Gibbs, what a bore you are" *MH/A 15*
77 ". . . the truth of it is, . . ." *VW to Emma Vaughan*, 8 August 1901 (MH)
77 "they're not used to young women . . ." *MH/A 14*
78 "One day when William Rufus . . ." *p.i.* (*VW*)
79 her drawers fell down . . . *VW/VD*, 2 October 1902 (Berg)
79 In an essay written at this time . . . "Thoughts upon Social Success" in *HPG Diary*, 15 July 1903 (Berg)
79 "I went to *Two Dances* . . ." *VW/VD*, n.d. [?27 December 1902] (Berg)
80 . . . a difficult husband . . . *VD/VB*, 20 July 1942 (CH)
81 "SHE IS AN AGED GOAT" *p.i.* (*VB*)
82 "I consider this to be equivalent . . ." *MBk* (addendum, 23 April 1902), p. 90
82 "They have, I suppose, explained . . ." *Leslie Stephen to Thoby Stephen*, 9 November 1902
82 "her only fault . . ." *Leslie Stephen to Mrs Herbert Fisher*, 14 September 1902
82 "We . . . showed her to her room . . ." *MH/A 26*; see also: *Friendship's Gallery* (Berg)
83 "You remind me . . . of Mrs Carlyle." *VW/VD*, 4 May 1903 (Berg)
84 "Ginia . . . continues to be good . . ." *Leslie Stephen to Mrs Herbert Fisher*, 8 July 1900; also 11 August 1901; also *VW/VD*, [28 January] 1904 (Berg)
85 "The aimiable ladies . . ." *Leslie Stephen to Thoby Stephen*, 22 November 1902
85 "Rather too fashionable" *VW/VD*, 4 May 1903 (Berg)
85 to at least one observer . . . *p.i.* (*Desmond MacCarthy*)
85 "I am Henry James." *VD/VB*, 14 May 1942 (CH)
85 "Three mornings I have spent" *VW/VD*, n.d. [?December 1903] (Berg)
85 "This illness" *VW/VD*, 28 November 1903 (Berg)

CHAPTER FIVE

Page
88 "I wonder how we go on . . ." *VW/VD*, [c. 23] March 1904 (Berg)
88 "to prove to myself . . ." *VW/VD*, 10 November 1904 (Berg)
88 "a strange race . . ." *VW to Emma Vaughan*, 25 April 1904 (MH)
89 Clive Bell and *his* friend . . . *VW/VD*, 7 May 1904 (Berg); also *VB to Margery Snowden*, 3 May 1904 (CH)

REFERENCES

CHAPTER SIX

Page

112 ... her own continuing life ... *AWD* (*Berg*), 26 December 1929

112 She addressed herself to Lytton ... *SST/LW*, 4 September and 22 November 1908 (MH); also *GLS/CB*, 18 November 1907 (CH)

112 In a manuscript written at the end of her life ... *MH/A 5*

114 He was pompous, polished ... *VW/VD*, 28 and 30 December, 1 and 3 January, 1907 (Berg)

114 "However I suppose she knows ..." *Henry James to Mrs W. K. Clifford*, 17 February 1907 (Harvard University, Houghton Library). I am indebted to Professor Leon Edel who called my attention to this letter.

115 "I hate her going away" *VW/VD*, n.d. [6 February 1907] (Berg)

115 "numb and dumb" *VW/VD*, n.d. [?8 February 1907] (Berg)

115 "Beatrice [Thynne] comes round, ..." *VW/VD*, 15 February 1907 (Berg)

116 "fifteen years younger ..." *VW/VD*, April 1903 (Berg)

116 the editors of the *News* ... *HPGN*, 27 June and 1 November 1892

116 unfairly but inevitably ... *p.i.* (*LW*)

116 The Dwarf ... *p.i.* (*VB*)

116 he did not believe in G. E. Moore. *p.i.* (*Adrian Stephen*)

117 one witness ... *p.i.* (*Duncan Grant*)

117 "Virginia ... must marry." *VW/VD*, n.d. [?29 December] 1906 and 3 January 1907 (Berg)

118 he had a certain eccentric absurdity ... See E. F. Benson, *As We Were*, 1930, pp. 134–139

119 all her "unpublished works" *VW/VD*, [10 December] 1906 (Berg)

119 she hated "pouring out tea ..." *VW/VD*, 15 February 1907 (Berg)

119 "a serious interview" *VW/VD*, n.d. [16 March 1907] (Berg)

121 "Country going to the dogs ..." *VW/VD*, n.d. [?7 July 1907] (Berg)

121 tried to hide from Mrs Humphry Ward *p.i.* (*VW*); but see: DG, "Virginia Woolf" in *Horizon*, 1941, vol. III, no. 18, p. 406

121 "Nessa & Clive live ..." *VW to Madge Vaughan*, 6 November 1907 (MH)

121 the dog Hans ... DG, *op. cit.*

122 "Miss Stephen, do you *ever* think?" *p.i.* (*DG*)

122 ... an account of her father and mother. *MH/A 6*

122 She was also writing ... *1906–1908 Diary* (Berg)

122 hoping "that old Henry James" ... *VB/VW*, 14 August 1907 (MH)

122 "... we went and had tea ..." *VW/VD*, [25 August 1907] (Berg)

123 On 27 December, 1907 ... Minute Book of *The Play Reading Society*

124 "It was a spring evening ..." *MH/A 16*

125 "I'm going to have a man and a woman ..." *VW/VD*, n.d. [?November 1903] (Berg)

125 "My only defence ..." *VW to Madge Vaughan*, n.d. [?June 1906] (MH)

CHAPTER SEVEN

Page

128 she might end by marrying Saxon. *LW/GLS*, n.d. [1 February 1909] (MH)

128 "amazingly beautiful" *DG/GLS*, 7 April 1907 (CH)

Page
128 found him charming . . . *VB to Margery Snowden*, n.d. [April 1907] (CH)
128 hitching up his trousers . . . *MH/A 16*
128 "That Mr Grant" DG, "Virginia Woolf" in *Horizon*, 1941, vol. III, no. 18, p. 402
129 "I should like Lytton as a brother . . ." *VB/VW*, n.d. [11 August 1908] (MH)
129 Clive . . . suggested that Lytton . . . *CB/VW*, n.d. [12 January 1911] (MH)
130 he lacked . . . magnanimity, *AWD* (*Berg*), 24 January 1919
130 "Yes they are exquisite . . ." *VW/CB*, n.d. [?9 August 1908]
131 they were tolerant as well as charming . . . Hilton Young (Lord Kennet of the Dene), an unpublished memoir. I am grateful to the present Lord Kennet for allowing me to look at this ms.
132 like an ill-omened cat. *VW/VD*, 13 May 1908 (Berg); see also *VW/GLS, Letters*, p. 13, [28 April 1908]
132 With a sense of desertion . . . *VW/VD*, 13 May 1908 (Berg)
133 "My dear Virginia . . ." *p.i.* (*CB*)
133 "it will be some time before I can separate . . ." *VW/VD*, [15 October 1907] (Berg)
134 She could, she said, have forgiven . . . *p.i.* (*VB*)
135 "about the honourable wounds . . ." *CB/VW*, 3 May 1908 (MH)
135 "You brought a tear to my eye . . ." *VW/CB*, n.d. [6 May 1908]
135 "Do you remember" *CB/VW*, 3 May 1908 (MH)
135 "On the top of Rosewall, . . ." *CB/VW*, 7 May 1908 (MH)
136 "Why . . . do you torment me . . ." *VW/CB*, n.d. [6 May 1908]
136 "I wonder what *you* have said . . ." *VB/VW*, 4 May 1908 (MH)
137 "Couldn't you . . . call her Apricot?" *VB/VW*, n.d. [8 August 1908] (MH)
137 "Or Barcelona" *CB/VW*, 23 August 1908 (MH)
137 "write rather well . . ." *VW/VD*, 30 August 1908 (Berg)
137 "I think a great deal . . ." *VW/CB*, n.d. [19 August 1908]
137 a letter to Emma Vaughan . . . *VW to Emma Vaughan*, n.d. [August 1908] (MH)
138 a note book . . . I have been unable to trace the original of this; Leonard Woolf had a copy made from it. It was used during the expedition to Greece in 1906, and brought to Italy in 1908 and 1909
139 . . . screaming at each other, *p.i.* (*VW*)
139 "Vanessa and Virginia are both . . ." *CB/SST*, 17 September 1908 (CH)
139 "Does it savour of paradox . . ." *SST/CB*, 21 September 1908 (CH)
139 "an admirable man" *VW/VD*, n.d. [4 October 1908] (Berg)

CHAPTER EIGHT

Page
141 "paradise of married peace . . ." *GLS/LW*, 19 February 1909
141 a sexual coward . . . *VW/ES*, 26 June 1930 (Berg)
142 she preserved his letter . . . *Anon to VW*, 30 March [1909] (MH); also *VW/VD*, n.d. [27 March 1909] (Berg)
142 "Life . . . is certainly very exciting" *VW to Madge Vaughan*, 21 March 1909 (MH)
143 landing "as the first cock . . ." *VW/VD*, n.d. [27 March 1909] (Berg)
143 "that unnatural Florentine society" *AWD* (*Berg*), 21 August 1929

REFERENCES

Page

143 "like a transfixed hare" *Greece/Italy 1906–1909 Notebook* (see note to p. 138)

143 The slightest, the most natural ... *AWD (Berg)*, 7 December 1917

143 "I was ... unhappy that summer" *AWD (Berg)*, 21 August 1929

143 "tiresome" in the Bargello *VB/VW*, n.d. [10 May 1909] (MH)

144 "It was rather melancholy ..." *VB to Margery Snowden*, 10 May 1909 (CH)

144 "We have just got to know ..." *VW to Madge Vaughan*, n.d. [Early Summer 1909] (MH)

145 "wonderful friends ..." *et. seq.*, *MH/A 16*

148 "What's the pudding?" *p.i. (VB)*

148 shopping with Adrian ... *Adrian Stephen to VB*, 9 August 1909 (CH)

150 "We must be a curious sight" *Adrian Stephen to VB*, 18 August 1909 (CH)

150 "There is a great crowd ..." *VW/VB*, 16 August 1909 (Berg)

150 "It is of no use ..." *Adrian Stephen to VB*, 18 August 1909 (CH)

150 "The grossness of the [Germans] ..." *VW/VB*, n.d. [8 August 1909] (Berg)

150 "Saxon is dormant ..." *VW/VB*, n.d. [10 August 1909] (Berg)

151 "Saxon is ... almost sprightly." *VW/VB*, n.d. [19 August 1909] (Berg)

151 "... it begins to dawn on me ..." *SST/CB*, 9 August 1909 (CH)

152 "a bi-sexual bathing dress" *VW/VD*, 21 September 1909 (Berg)

152 "I was most agreeably entertained" *Walter Lamb to CB*, 21 March 1909 (CH)

153 "Now we are back again ..." *VW/GLS, Letters*, p. 34, [6 October 1909]

153 "a book which one may still buy ..." *MH/B 21*

154 "expected to be the chef d'oeuvre" *CB/VW*, n.d. [8 November 1909] (MH)

154 "My feeling is that you have impaled ..." *Reginald Smith to VW*, 10 November 1909 (MH)

155 "Suppose I stayed here ..." *VW/CB*, 26 December 1909

CHAPTER NINE

Page

157 "like a seedy commercial traveller" Adrian Stephen, *The "Dreadnought" Hoax*, p. 18

157 ... the author of many practical jokes. See Joseph Hone, "Henry Cole, King of Jokers" in *The Listener*, 4 April 1940

158 she had two days' notice. *Daily Mirror*, 15 February 1910

158 Vanessa was dismayed ... *VB to Margery Snowden*, 13 February 1910 (CH)

159 "*Entaqui, mahai, kustufani*" Adrian Stephen, *op. cit.*, p. 26

159 "A rum lingo they speak" *p.i. (DG)*; also Adrian Stephen, *op. cit.*, p. 28

159 "Oh Miss Genia, Miss Genia!" *p.i. (VW)*

160 "very good looking ..." *Daily Mirror*, 14 February 1910

160 a letter from Dorothea ... *Dorothea Stephen to VW*, 3 March 1910 (Berg)

161 Ever since January 1906 ... *p.i. (VB)*

161 she could neither do sums ... *VW to Janet Case*, 1 January 1910 (MH)

161 Miss Rosalind Nash ... *Rosalind Nash to VW*, 19 January 1910 (MH)

161 "... names like Cowgill ..." *VW/VD*, n.d. [27 February 1910] (Berg)

161 a bloodless, inhuman ... *VW to Janet Case*, n.d. [?December 1909] (MH)

161 a novel by H. G. Wells ... *VW/VD*, n.d. [27 February 1910] (Berg)

162 Clive reported ... *CB/SST*, 2 and 13 April 1910 (CH)

162 "... more to mitigate my own lot ..." *VW/SST*, n.d. [13 June 1910]

Page

163 "Virginia since early youth . . ." *VB/CB*, 25 June 1910 (CH)

163 "I shall say . . ." *VW/VB*, 24 June 1910 (Berg)

164 "They reverence my gifts, . . ." *VW/VB*, 28 July 1910 (Berg)

164 She "was transformed . . ." CB, *Old Friends*, p. 117

165 "a dark devil" *VW/VB*, 28 July 1910 (Berg)

165 "one cannot help . . ." *VB/VW*, 29 July 1910 (MH)

165 "Oh dear . . ." *VB/VW*, 5 August 1910 (MH)

167 Early in that year . . . *MH/A 16*; *VB/MS VI*

168 imagined a dreadful repetition . . . *VW/VD*, 25 May 1911 (Berg)

168 Roger in command. VW, *Roger Fry*, p. 170

170 human nature changed . . . VW, *Mr Bennett and Mrs Brown*, p. 5

170 Vanessa and Virginia . . . *p.i.* (*VB and DG*); also *VB/MS VI*

170 it was whispered that . . . *MH/A 16*

170 "*en France ça aurait . . .*" *p.i.* (*CB*); also *Adrian Stephen to VB*, n.d. [April/May 1941] (CH)

170 "Beloved, It is great devotion . . ." *VW/VB*, n.d. [21 July 1911] (Berg)

172 long and slightly absurd letters. *Walter Lamb to VW*, 23 and 25 July 1911 (MH)

172 Clive, Walter Lamb and Sydney Waterlow . . . *Sydney Waterlow to CB*, 1 August 1911 (CH); *Walter Lamb to VW*, n.d. [August 1911] (MH); *Walter Lamb to CB*, n.d. [end July 1911] (CH)

172 Clive never spoke to him again. *p.i.* (*CB*)

173 in "the heart of young womanhood" *VW/CB*, n.d. [23 January 1911]

173 "Miss Cox is one of the younger . . ." *VW/CB*, n.d. [23 January 1911]

174 she supplied a word . . . Christopher Hassall, *Rupert Brooke*, p. 280; but see the review by VW of "The Collected Poems of Rupert Brooke" in the *Times Literary Supplement*, 8 August 1918

174 If Adrian is to be trusted . . . *Adrian Stephen to CB*, n.d. [c. 25 August 1911] (CH)

174 The visit began badly . . . Hassall, *op. cit.*, p. 281

175 "Oh, its quite alright, . . ." *MH/A 16*; and Marjorie Strachey on *Woman's Hour*, BBC Home Service, 26 April 1967

175 "Julia would not have liked it." *MH/A 16*

176 "Yesterday I finished . . ." *VW/CB*, 18 April 1911

176 "I could not write . . ." *VW/VB*, n.d. [1 June 1911] (Berg)

176 She seems to have had . . . *VW to Sydney Waterlow*, 9 December 1911

177 "Woolf came to tea" *VB/CB*, n.d. [?31 December 1911] (CH)

177 "He is of course very clever . . ." *VB/CB*, 11 October 1911 (CH)

178 "stupid degraded circle . . ." *LW/GLS*, 2 July 1905 (MH)

178 It was on this point . . . *LW/GLS*, 2 July 1905 (MH)

179 even took up painting . . . *LW/VW*, 28 February 1912 (MH); LW's *Diaries*, 1911, 1912 (MH)

179 "Dear Mr Wolf . . ." *VW/LW*, 8 July 1911 (MH)

179 "it was not a cottage . . ." *VW/LW*, 31 August 1911 (MH)

180 "I must see you . . ." *LW/VW* (telegram), 10 January 1912 (MH)

180 "My dear Virginia . . ." *LW/VW*, 11 January 1912 (MH)

181 ". . . I can try & write . . ." *LW/VW*, 12 January 1912 (MH)

181 "There isn't really . . ." *VW/LW*, n.d. [13 January 1912] (MH)

182 ". . . how glad I shall be . . ." *VB/LW*, 13 January 1912 (MH)

182 "coldest day for 40 years;" *VW to Katherine Cox*, 7 February 1912

REFERENCES

Page

182 "a touch of my usual disease . . ." *VW to Katherine Cox*, 7 February 1912
182 "I shall tell you wonderful stories . . ." *VW/LW*, n.d. [5 March 1912] (MH)
184 ". . . I want to see you . . ." *LW/VW*, 29 April 1912 (MH)
185 "What a career . . ." *VW/LW*, 1 May 1912 (MH)
186 "No, I shan't float . . ." *VW to Molly MacCarthy*, n.d. [?March 1912]
187 "I hope you aren't getting too much worried . . ." *VB/VW*, 28 May 1912 (MH)

VOLUME II

CHAPTER ONE

Page

1 Virginia and Leonard are engaged . . . *VB/RF*, 2 June 1919 (CH)
1 "Ha! Ha!" *VW/GLS, Letters*, p. 40, 6 June 1912
1 He wrote to her to say . . . *CB/VW*, n.d. [June 1912] (MH)
1 Everyone seemed to be cross . . . *VB/RF*, 2 June 1912 (CH)
2 "An engagement seems . . ." *VB/GLS*, 5 June 1912
2 "My Violet . . ." *VW/VD*, 4 June 1912 (Berg)
2 The case of Madge . . . *p.i.* (*LW*)
3 "A sandwich . . ." *VW to Janet Case*, n.d. [June 1912] (MH)
4 "Work and love . . ." *VW/VD*, n.d. [13 June 1912] (Berg)
4 Saturday, 10 August . . . *VW/VD*, 5 August 1912 (Berg)
4 the official business . . . *VB to Margery Snowden*, 20 August 1912 (CH)
4 a very good way . . . *VW to Janet Case*, n.d. [17 August 1912] (MH)
5 In Barcelona . . . *VB/VW*, 2 September 1912; accounts of the honeymoon journey also in *VW to Katherine Cox*, 4 September 1912 and *VW/SST*, 17 September 1912
5 "chronically nomadic . . ." *VW to Molly MacCarthy*, 28 September 1912
5 "Why do you think . . ." *VW to Katherine Cox*, 4 September 1912; see also *DG/VW*, 23 September 1912 (MH)
6 "They seemed very happy . . ." *VB/CB*, 27 December 1912 (CH); see also *CB to Molly MacCarthy*, 31 December 1912 (CH)
6 "She dislikes the possessiveness . . ." *VSW, Journal of Travel*, 25 September 1928
6 "My Violet, Yesterday . . ." *VW/VD*, 11 October 1912 (Berg)
7 "an abominable race . . ." *VW/VD*, 24 December 1912
7 "a kind of tortured intensity" LW, *Beginning Again*, p. 143
8 buying horses and a cow . . . *VW/VD*, 24 December 1912
8 "Virginia has been very nice . . ." *VB/RF*, 24 December 1912 (CH)
8 sisterly bickerings . . . *VB/CB*, n.d. (CH); see also *CB to Molly MacCarthy*, n.d. [March 1913] (CH)
9 "I wish Woolf didnt irritate . . ." *VB/RF*, 7 January 1913 (CH)
9 "The whole moral significance . . ." Draft of a letter from *LW to Edward Arnold* in reply to his of 17 February 1914 (MH)
10 economic problems . . . *VW/VD*, 11 April 1913 (Berg)
10 "I expect to have it rejected," *VW/VD*, 11 April 1913 (Berg)
12 "My eyes are bruised," *VW to Katherine Cox*, 16 May 1913

Page

12 "He seems to have thought . . ." *VB/RF*, 26 July 1913 (CH)

13 A few miserable shaky . . . *VW/LW*, 7 letters, n.d., but postmarks for 26 July and 1, 3, 4, 5 August 1913 (MH)

14 "Virginia" she reported . . . *VB/CB*, 23 August 1913 (CH)

16 Dr Head, nurses, Vanessa . . . I am indebted to Sir Geoffrey Keynes for a description of these events; see also *VB/JMK*, 9 September 1913 (CH); *LW to R. C. Trevelyan*, 13 September 1913 (MH); *Sir George Savage to LW*, 9 September 1913 (MH); also footnote p. 17

17 "Woolfe bicycled over . . ." *CB to Molly MacCarthy*, n.d. [25 September 1913] (CH)

18 "Oh you know very well . . ." *p.i.(LW)*

19 a kind of treaty . . . *LW/VW*, 19 June 1914 (MH)

20 This idea filled Leonard . . . *VB/RF*, 2 August 1914 (CH)

20 "It is thought . . ." *VW to Katherine Cox*, 12 August 1914

21 "At one end of the room . . ." *VW to Janet Case*, 10 December 1914 (MH)

22 "Saturday, January 2nd [1915]" *AWD (Berg)*

23 "The Sidney Webbs ask us . . ." *VW to Margaret Llewelyn Davies*, [9 December 1914] (MH)

23 "which everyone . . ." *AWD (Berg)*, 27 January 1915

24 "My dear Margaret . . ." *VW to Margaret Llewelyn Davies*, [25 February 1915] (MH)

26 "I saw Woolf yesterday . . ." *VB/RF*, 27 May 1915 (CH)

26 "played out" *Jean Thomas to VD*, 9 April 1915 (Berg)

26 "Ka had been to see Virginia . . ." *VB/RF*, 25 June 1915 (CH)

CHAPTER TWO

Page

28 "Here at last . . ." "Some Press Opinions" printed at the back of *Night and Day*, 1919

28 "That is not a word . . ." *ibid.*

28 One sentence "more or less . . ." *VW to Molly MacCarthy*, 15 December 1914

29 "Your letter still delights me." *VW to Margaret Llewelyn Davies*, n.d. [c. 1 August 1915] (MH)

29 "I think it is about time . . ." *VW/GLS, Letters*, p. 53, 22 October 1915

30 "It has vanished . . ." *VW to Katherine Cox*, 19 March [1916]

31 Lady Robert *did* . . . *VW/VB*, 7 June 1916, with enclosure *Lady Robert Cecil to VW*, n.d. (Berg)

32 "My industry . . ." *VW/GLS, Letters*, p. 62, 25 July [1916]

32 "I am very much interested . . ." *VW/VB*, 30 July 1916 (Berg)

32 "I wish you'd leave Wissett . . ." *VW/VB*, 4 May 1916 (Berg)

33 "I think the Woolves . . ." *VB/GLS*, 24 October 1916

33 "some pollution theory . . ." *GLS/VB*, 25 October 1916 (CH)

34 "We are not at all anxious . . ." *VW/VB*, 11 September 1916 (Berg)

35 "we have had nothing but brilliancy . . ." *VW to Margaret Llewelyn Davies*, 25 June 1920 (MH)

36 "for we mothers . . ." *VW to Margaret Llewelyn Davies*, 24 January 1917 (MH)

37 "decidedly an interesting creature . . ." *GLS/VW, Letters*, p. 61, 17 July 1916

37 "If," said Virginia . . . *VW/GLS, Letters*, p. 62, 25 July 1916

CHAPTER THREE

Page
69 "We had thought . . ." *Athenaeum*, 26 November 1919
69 ". . . I should need . . ." *AWD (Berg)*, 18 February 1919
70 "The inscrutable woman . . ." *AWD (Berg)*, 22 March 1919
70 "a steady discomposing . . ." *AWD (Berg)*, 31 May 1920
71 "We think we now deserve . . ." *AWD (Berg)*, 28 December 1919
71 "This is our last . . ." *AWD (Berg)*, 7 January 1920
72 "It is true I have . . ." *AWD (Berg)*, 15 November 1919
72 "The day after my birthday . . ." *AWD*, p. 23, 26 January 1920
74 "This made my drive . . ." *AWD (Berg)*, 8 June 1920
74 "Lay by my side . . ." *Jacob's Room*, p. 107; *Mrs Dalloway*, p. 124
74 "a clubman's view . . ." *AWD (Berg)*, 2 April 1919
76 "putting his ox's shoulder . . ." *AWD (Berg)*, 18 October 1920
76 Friday, February 18th [1921] *AWD (Berg)*
77 "a mass of corruption . . ." *AWD (Berg)*, 8 April 1921
77 "and its that . . ." *AWD*, p. 32, 9 April 1921
78 he thought it marvellous. *AWD*, p. 33, 12 April 1921
78 "very complex" *AWD (Berg)*, 12 December 1921
78 "Carrington grows older . . ." *AWD (Berg)*, 31 January 1921
79 "Well," Virginia observed . . . *AWD (Berg)*, 12 December 1920
79 "Oh dear no," *AWD (Berg)*, 31 January 1921
79 "He was very shrewd . . ." *AWD (Berg)*, 15 May 1921
79 "put a pistol . . ." LW, *Downhill . . .*, p. 72
80 "You mustn't think . . ." *Carrington, Letters &c*, p. 178
80 "You must not believe . . ." *ibid.*, p. 183
80 "with her love of stirring . . ." Holroyd, *Lytton Strachey*, vol. II, p. 398
80 "He told her that Virginia . . ." *ibid.*, p. 401
80 "So Carrington did . . ." *AWD (Berg)*, 23 May 1921
81 "I'm not sure . . ." *AWD (Berg)*, 18 February 1919
83 a chest of drawers . . . *RF/VB*, n.d. [18 May 1921] (CH)
83 "These, this morning . . ." *AWD (Berg)*, 8 August 1921
84 "had passed the limits . . ." *AWD (Berg)*, 4 February 1922
85 ". . . I am seeing Clive . . ." *AWD (Berg)*, 12 March 1922
85 ". . . We talked from 4.30 to 10.15 . . ." *AWD (Berg)*, 24 March 1922
85 "I hope I shan't . . ." *CB/VB*, 1 March 1922 (CH)
86 "He sang it and chanted it . . ." *AWD (Berg)*, 23 June 1922
86 prepared a circular . . . Holroyd, *Lytton Strachey*, vol. II, p. 366
86 "After Joyce . . ." *AWD (Berg)*, 27 September 1922
87 "amazingly well written . . ." *AWD*, p. 47, 26 July 1922
88 "this nervous man . . ." *AWD (Berg)*, 29 October 1922
88 "You have freed yourself . . ." *T. S. Eliot to VW*, 4 December 1922

CHAPTER FOUR

Page
89 ". . . forging ahead . . ." *AWD (Berg)*, 3 January 1923
90 "I can foresee . . ." *VW/VB*, 22 December 1922 (Berg)
91 "Mrs Murry's dead!" *AWD (Berg)*, 16 January 1923
91 "Yet even in this light . . ." *Jacob's Room*, p. 217
91 and it was he . . . *Berta Ruck to QB*, 11 September 1971

REFERENCES

Page

92 "Never allow a Sailor ..." G. H. W. Rylands, *BBC/TV Omnibus*, 18 January 1970

92 "Leonard thinks himself ..." *AWD* (*Berg*), 7 February 1923

92 "poor dear Tom ..." *AWD* (*Berg*), 19 February 1923

92 "Perhaps because Virginia lacked ..." Gerald Brenan, *South from Granada*, 1957, chapter 13; see also *VW/VSW*, 15 April 1923 (Berg) and *VW/RF*, 16 April 1923

93 *To Spain.* Reprinted in *The Moment*, 1947

94 "I lie & think ..." *VW/LW*, 17 April 1922 (MH)

95 "glowing and gleaming ..." *VW to Jacques Raverat*, 29 November 1924

95 "My boast ..." *VW/CB*, 9 April 1922

95 "Lady Londonderry ..." *VW/CB*, 9 April 1930

96 "Leonard thinks less well of me ..." *AWD* (*Berg*), 26 May 1924

96 Virginia was more like ... *VB to Margery Snowden*, 15 April 1923 (CH)

97 "... her social approach ..." Ralph Partridge, *Portrait of Virginia Woolf*, BBC Home Service, 29 August 1956

99 "I am a great deal interested ..." *AWD*, p. 55, 4 June 1923

99 "I took up this book ..." *AWD*, p. 57, 19 June 1923

100 "sheer weak dribble". *AWD* (*Berg*), 6 August 1923

100 "And I meant to record ..." *AWD* (*Berg*), 15 October 1923

101 "back again tomorrow ..." *AWD* (*Berg*), 23 January 1924

102 No. 52 ... Tavistock Square *p.i.* (*LW*); see also Richard Kennedy, *A Boy at the Hogarth Press*

103 Rylands came to the Hogarth Press ... G. H. W. Rylands, *BBC/TV Omnibus*, 18 January 1970

103 "Thank God, Angus ..." G. H. W. Rylands to *VW*, n.d. [November/December 1924] (MH)

104 "we are trembling ..." *Mr Bennett and Mrs Brown*, p. 24

104 "those sleek, smooth novels ..." *ibid.*, p. 23

105 the "Old Man" ... *AWD*, p. 68, 17 October 1924

106 "I don't think I shall tell you ..." *VW to Jacques Raverat*, 4 September 1924

106 His reply ... *Jacques Raverat to VW*, n.d. [September 1924] (MH)

106 "Certainly" Virginia replied, *VW to Jacques Raverat*, 3 October 1924

107 "I like to please Jacques" *AWD* (*Berg*), 22 August 1922

107 "Your letters ..." *Jacques Raverat to VW*, n.d. [December 1924]

107 "Since I wrote ..." *AWD*, p. 72, 8 April 1925

107 "all over long ago" *Gwen Raverat to VW*, n.d. [early October 1924]

108 "you'll probably not like Will" *Katherine Cox to VW*, 1 August 1918 (MH)

108 "Never ... have I felt so much admired" *AWD* (*Berg*), 16 May 1925

CHAPTER FIVE

Page

109 "Many scenes ..." *AWD* (*Berg*), 4 September 1927

110 "Woke up perhaps at 3." *AWD* (*Berg*), 15 September 1926

111 "Virginia was in ..." *RF/VB*, 11 May 1926 (CH)

111 "I tremble and shiver ..." *AWD* (*Berg*), 6 May 1926

111 "The Woolves are ..." *CB/VB*, 19 February 1928 (CH)

111 "Virginia is still ..." *CB/VB*, 2 March 1928 (CH)

111 "Since February ..." *AWD* (*Berg*), 18 March 1928

Page

REFERENCES

Page

129 after taking their Singer . . . *p.i.* (*LW*)

130 . . . asked them the time. *p.i.* (*A. Davidson*); also *AWD* (*Berg*), 22 October 1927

131 "Yesterday morning . . ." *VW/VSW*, 9 October 1927 (Berg); also *AWD*, pp. 114 and 117, 18 September and 5 October 1927

132 materials which she noted . . . *AWD* (*Berg*), 23 January 1927

132 "Don't" he said . . . *AWD* (*Berg*), 18 September 1927

132 Maynard and Lydia . . . *VW/GLS, Letters*, p. 114, 3 September 1927; also *p.i.* (*QB*)

133 "Lovely little things" E. M. Forster, *Virginia Woolf*, p. 11

133 "I don't think" he said . . . *p.i.* (*EMF*)

133 . . . when he informed her, *AWD* (*Berg*), 23 January 1924

134 "Your article . . ." *EMF/VW*, 13 November 1927

135 "Dear Morgan, . . ." *VW/EMF*, 16 November 1927

136 "Often" she declared . . . *VW/QB*, 6 May 1928

136 "Clive (who smacked me . . .) *AWD* (*Berg*), 17 April 1928; also *AWD* (*Berg*), 21 April 1928

136 a contrite letter . . . *CB/VW*, 1 April 1928 (MH); also *VW/CB*, 21 April 1928

136 . . . Clive made fun of her hat. *AWD* (*Berg*), 30 June 1926

137 "that he has great fun . . ." *p.i.* (*QB*)

137 "a rotten speech" R. Hart-Davis, *Hugh Walpole*, 1952, p. 289

138 "Morgan was here . . ." *AWD* (*Berg*), 31 August 1928

139 "I am melancholy . . ." *VW/VSW*, n.d. [September 1928] (Berg)

139 ". . . I was going to thank you . . ." *VW to H. Nicolson*, 7 October 1928

139 "The great excitement," wrote Vanessa . . . *VB/RF*, 27 October 1928 (CH)

140 "Well there can be no doubt . . ." *p.i.* (*QB*)

CHAPTER SIX

Page

141 "The Woolves" Vanessa observed . . . *et seq.* *VB/RF*, 19 January 1929 (CH)

143 haul her like a sack *VW/VSW*, [28 January 1929] (Berg)

143 . . . the usual symptoms – *VW/VSW*, 7 February 1929 (Berg)

143 "I am writing . . ." *VW/QB*, 20 March 1929

143 "Perhaps I ought not . . ." *AWD*, p. 141, 28 March 1929

144 "If truth is not . . ." *A Room of One's Own*, p. 39

145 "subtle and subterranean glow" *ibid.*, p. 17

145 A mongoose . . . *VW/VSW*, 5 April 1929 (Berg); *VW/VB*, 7 April 1929 (Berg)

145 "We met an elephant . . ." *p.i.* (*QB*)

146 "She lives" said Clive . . . *CB/VB*, 7 July 1929 (CH)

146 "reckoning how many more times . . ." *AWD*, p. 141, 4 January 1929

146 "I like printing . . ." *VW to Hugh Walpole*, 16 July 1930

146 "What a born melancholic . . ." *AWD*, p. 143, 23 June 1929

146 "adders' tails . . ." *VW/VSW*, 28 October 1929 (Berg)

146 Ivy Compton-Burnett . . . R. Kennedy, *A Boy at the Hogarth Press*, pp. 68, 84; also *VW to E. Sackville-West*, 23 September 1929 (Berg)

147 "a low art . . ." *p.i.* (*Mrs Lyn Newman*)

147 "helter skelter random . . ." *AWD* (*Berg*), 5 August 1929

148 ". . . I must think of that book . . ." *AWD* (*Berg*), 19 August 1929

CHAPTER SEVEN

REFERENCES

Page
170 "I don't like old ladies . . ." *AWD* (*Berg*), 2 June 1932
170 "I rather think she's through . . ." *ES/VB*, 28 June 1934 (CH)
171 "You are a little like . . ." *ES/VB*, 30 December 1934 (CH)
171 "no sense of glory; . . ." *AWD*, p. 182, 11 July 1932
171 ". . . I'm full of ideas . . ." *VW to G. H. W. Rylands*, 22 November 1931
171 ". . . to take in everything . . ." *AWD*, p. 189, 2 November 1932
174 "I have always been a literary painter . . ." *W. R. Sickert to VW*, n.d.; also *AWD* (*Berg*), 17 December 1933
174 she, Virginia, was an angel . . . *VW/QB*, 8 March 1934
174 "the kick screams" *ES/VB*, 23 October 1934 (CH)
175 "Don't you sometimes . . ." *O. Morrell to VW*, 16 October 1934 (MH)
178 "And then," asked Maynard . . . *AWD* (*Berg*), 19 April 1934
178 "Our Germany" . . . *AWD*, p. 199, 28 April 1933; also B. Walter, *Themes and Variations*, 1947, p. 289
179 "I am trying to start . . ." *AWD* (*Berg*), 27 August 1934
179 "After three days' grind . . ." *AWD*, p. 222, 30 August 1934
179 "I don't think I have ever . . ." *AWD*, p. 223, 2 September 1934
179 "Roger died on Sunday." *AWD* (*Berg*), 12 September 1934

CHAPTER EIGHT

Page
180 "They played Bach . . ." *AWD* (*Berg*), 15 September 1934
180 "a horrid time" *VW/VSW*, 23 September 1934 (Berg)
181 "So my dear Roger, . . ." *VW/RF*, 18 May 1923 (MH)
181 "I could trace . . ." *VW/RF*, 21 February 1931 (MH)
182 "Have I the indomitable . . ." *AWD*, p. 253, 21 August 1935
182 ". . . she could deal with facts . . ." LW, *The Journey . . .*, p. 43
182 "How to deal with love . . ." *VW/VB*, 8 October 1938 (Berg)
182 "I hope you won't mind . . ." *VB/VW*, 14 October 1938 (MH)
183 Mirsky and Swinnerton . . . D. S. Mirsky, *The Intelligentsia of Great Britain*, 1935; F. Swinnerton, *The Georgian Literary Scene*, 1935
183 *Men without Art* . . . By Wyndham Lewis, 1934, chapter V
184 "tremendous and delightful fun" *AWD*, p. 228, 14 October 1934
184 a letter . . . to *The Spectator*, 2 November 1934. See *The Letters of Wyndham Lewis*, ed. W. K. Rose, 1963, pp. 222–225; and *AWD*, p. 231, 2 November 1934
184 "I don't say it . . ." *AWD*, p. 231, 2 November 1934
187 "like an enormous frog . . ." *p.i.* (QB)
187 her chief reaction was dismay . . . *VW to Julian Bell*, 1 December 1935
188 "Oh my dear Virginia . . ." *EMF/VW*, 6 June 1935
188 "I was pressed . . ." *VW/ES*, 3 August 1936 (Berg)
188 a fainting girl . . . *AWD* (*Berg*), 20 March 1936
190 a simple No. *AWD*, p. 249, 19 May 1936
190 "A specimen day" *AWD* (*Berg*), 5 November 1935
191 on the steps of the London Library, *AWD*, p. 243, 9 April 1935
192 "that particular vein" *AWD* (*Berg*), 6 July 1934; also *AWD*, pp. 298, 299, 240, 241
192 "I think I have . . ." *AWD* (*Berg*), 28 March 1935

REFERENCES

209 "For the first time for weeks . . ." *AWD (Berg)*, 12 July 1939
210 "last year's mad voice" *AWD (Berg)*, 30 August 1939

CHAPTER TEN

Page

211 it was 'they' . . . *AWD (Berg)*, 3 September 1939
211 "we shall be attended to" *AWD (Berg)*, 11 September 1939
212 T. S. Eliot wrote . . . *T. S. Eliot to VW*, 12 September 1939
212 "THE WAR BEGINS . . ." *AWD (Berg)*, 22 October 1939
212 Mrs Sidney Webb . . . *MH/A 20*
213 "an outsider" *AWD*, p. 322, 18 December 1939
214 "Oh it's a queer . . ." *AWD (Berg)*, 8 February 1940
214 a very severe criticism . . . *AWD*, p. 328, 20 March 1940
214 "It's *him* . . ." *AWD*, p. 328, 20 March 1940
214 "Since Julian died . . ." *VB/VW*, 13 March 1940 (MH)
215 "So my little moment . . ." *AWD*, p. 332, 13 May 1940
215 "I didn't want to be silent" *AWD (Berg)*, 20 May 1940
216 "Jews were hunted . . ." LW, *The Journey . . .*, p. 14
217 "I can't conceive . . ." *AWD*, p. 337, 22 [actually 27] June 1940
217 "They came very close . . ." *AWD*, p. 342, 16 August 1940
218 . . . heard Vita's voice . . . *VW/VSW* [30 August 1940] (Berg)
218 ". . . what touched . . ." *VW/ES*, 12 September 1940 (Berg)
219 *The Leaning Tower*. Published in *Folios of New Writing*, Autumn 1940; reprinted in *The Moment*, 1947
219 "Our ignorance . . ." *The Niece of an Earl* in *The Common Reader: Second Series*, p. 217
219 "The subject of her writing . . ." R. L. Chambers, *The Novels of VW*, Oliver & Boyd, 1947, p. 1
220 ". . . je me permets . . ." *J. E. Blanche to VW*, 18 September 1938 (MH)
220 He wrote to Virginia . . . *B. Nicolson to VW*, 6 and 19 August 1940 (MH); also *VW to B. Nicolson*, 13 and 24 August 1940
222 *Anon* . . . *MH/B 8a–d*; also *p.i.* (QB)
222 "I wish I were Queen Victoria" *VW/VSW*, 29 November 1940 (Berg)
223 "a life that rings . . ." *AWD*, p. 353, 29 September 1940
224 "a sop" to public opinion. *AWD (Berg)*, 7 November 1940
224 "and she sat back . . ." Elizabeth Bowen, *BBC/TV Omnibus*, 18 January 1970
225 she would like to write . . . *VW to O. Wilberforce*, n.d. [4 March 1941] (MH)
225 for the next five days . . . *O. Wilberforce to E. Robins*, 27 March 1941; also *ditto*, 28 February, 14, 20 and 28/29 March 1941 (MH)
226 at about 11.30 . . . *The Brighton Argus*, 19 April 1941; also *VB/VSW*, 29 April 1941 (Berg)
226 "the one experience . . ." *AWD (Berg)*, 23 November 1926

A SHORT BIBLIOGRAPHY

(English editions are published in London, American in New York,
unless otherwise indicated)

ANNAN, Noel Gilroy: *Leslie Stephen; his thought and character in relation to his time.*
MacGibbon & Kee, 1951; Cambridge, Mass.: Harvard University Press, 1952

BELL, Clive: *Old Friends: Personal Recollections.* Chatto & Windus, 1956; Harcourt
Brace Jovanovich, 1957

BELL, Julian (and others): *Julian Bell: Essays, Poems and Letters.* Edited by Quentin
Bell. Hogarth Press, 1938

BELL, Quentin: *Bloomsbury.* Weidenfeld & Nicolson, 1968; Basic Books, 1969

CARRINGTON, Dora: *Carrington: Letters and Extracts from her Diaries.* Edited by
David Garnett. Jonathan Cape, 1970

FORSTER, E. M.: *Virginia Woolf.* (The Rede Lecture.) Cambridge University Press,
1942; Harcourt Brace Jovanovich, 1942

FRY, Roger: *Letters of Roger Fry.* Edited by Denys Sutton. Chatto & Windus, 1972

GARNETT, David: *The Golden Echo.* Chatto & Windus, 1953; Harcourt Brace
Jovanovich, 1954

   The Flowers of the Forest. Chatto & Windus, 1955; Harcourt Brace Jovanovich,
1956

   The Familiar Faces. Chatto & Windus, 1962; Harcourt Brace Jovanovich, 1963

GRANT, Duncan: "Virginia Woolf" in *Horizon,* Volume III, no. 18, June 1941

HARROD, Roy: *The Life of John Maynard Keynes.* Macmillan, 1951; Harcourt
Brace Jovanovich, 1951

HASSALL, Christopher: *Rupert Brooke. A Biography.* Faber, 1964; Harcourt Brace
Jovanovich, 1964

HOLROYD, Michael: *Lytton Strachey. A Critical Biography.* Volume I, *The Unknown
Years.* 1967. Volume II, *The Years of Achievement.* 1968. Heinemann; Holt,
Rinehart & Winston, 1968

JOHNSTONE, J. K.: *The Bloomsbury Group.* Secker & Warburg, 1954; Noonday
Press, 1954

KENNEDY, Richard: *A Boy at the Hogarth Press.* Whittington Press, 1972

KEYNES, John Maynard: *Two Memoirs.* Hart-Davis, 1949; Augustus M. Kelley,
1949

KIRKPATRICK, B. J.: *A Bibliography of Virginia Woolf.* Second Edition, Revised.
Hart-Davis, 1967; Oxford University Press, 1968

LEHMANN, John: *The Whispering Gallery: Autobiography I.* Longmans, 1955; Harcourt Brace Jovanovich, 1955

   I am My Brother: Autobiography II. Longmans, 1960

MAITLAND, F. W.: *The Life and Letters of Leslie Stephen.* Duckworth, 1906; Detroit:
Gale Research, 1968

MANSFIELD, Katherine: *Journal of Katherine Mansfield.* Edited by J. Middleton
Murry. Constable, 1927; Alfred A. Knopf, 1927

   The Letters of Katherine Mansfield. Edited by J. Middleton Murry. 2 Volumes,
Constable, 1928; Alfred A. Knopf, 1929

MORRELL, Ottoline: *The Early Memoirs of Lady Ottoline Morrell.* Edited by Robert
Gathorne-Hardy. Faber, 1963

BIBLIOGRAPHY

NATHAN, Monique: *Virginia Woolf par elle-même*. Paris, Editions du Seuil, 1956

PIPPETT, Aileen: *The Moth and the Star. A Biography of Virginia Woolf*. Boston: Little, Brown, 1955

SACKVILLE-WEST, V.: *Pepita*. Hogarth Press, 1937; Doubleday, 1937

ST JOHN, Christopher: *Ethel Smyth, A Biography*. Longmans, Green, 1959

SPENDER, Stephen: *World within World*. Hamish Hamilton, 1951; Harcourt Brace Jovanovich, 1951

STANSKY, Peter and ABRAHAMS, William: *Journey to the Frontier. Julian Bell and John Cornford: their lives and the 1930's*. Constable, 1966; Boston: Little, Brown, 1966

STEPHEN, Adrian: *The "Dreadnought" Hoax*. Hogarth Press, 1936

STEPHEN, James: *The Memoirs of James Stephen. Written by Himself for the Use of His Children*. Edited by Merle M. Bevington. Hogarth Press, 1954

STEPHEN, Leslie: *The Life of Sir James Fitzjames Stephen, Bart, K.C.S.I. By his Brother*. Smith, Elder, 1895

STRACHEY, Lytton: *Lytton Strachey by Himself: A Self-Portrait*. Edited by Michael Holroyd. Heinemann, 1971; Holt, Rinehart & Winston, 1971

Letters, see WOOLF, Virginia and STRACHEY, Lytton

WOOLF, Leonard: *The Wise Virgins. A Story of Words, Opinions, and a Few Emotions*. Edward Arnold, 1914

Sowing: An Autobiography of the Years 1880–1904. Hogarth Press, 1960; Harcourt Brace Jovanovich, 1960

Growing: An Autobiography of the Years 1904–1911 Hogarth Press, 1961; Harcourt Brace Jovanovich, 1962

Beginning Again: An Autobiography of the Years 1911–1918. Hogarth Press, 1964; Harcourt Brace Jovanovich, 1964

Downhill all the Way: An Autobiography of the Years 1919–1939. Hogarth Press, 1967; Harcourt Brace Jovanovich, 1967

The Journey not the Arrival Matters: An Autobiography of the Years 1939–1969. Hogarth Press, 1969; Harcourt Brace Jovanovich, 1970

WOOLF, Virginia: for a complete bibliography the reader is referred to B. J. Kirkpatrick, *op. cit.* The following books by Virginia Woolf were all, with the exception of the first and fourth, published by the Hogarth Press in Richmond or London. Harcourt Brace Jovanovich published all but the second, third, seventh, fourteenth and seventeenth in New York, some in different years.

The Voyage Out. Duckworth, 1915

The Mark on the Wall. 1917

Kew Gardens. 1919

Night and Day. Duckworth, 1919

Monday or Tuesday. 1921

Jacob's Room. 1922

Mr Bennett and Mrs Brown. 1924

The Common Reader. 1925

Mrs Dalloway. 1925

To the Lighthouse. 1927

Orlando: A Biography. 1928

A Room of One's Own. 1929

The Waves. 1931

Letter to a Young Poet. 1932

The Common Reader: Second Series. 1932
Flush: A Biography. 1933
Walter Sickert: a Conversation. 1934
The Years. 1937
Three Guineas. 1938
Roger Fry: A Biography. 1940
Between the Acts. 1941
A Writer's Diary. Being Extracts from the Diary of Virginia Woolf, edited by Leonard Woolf. 1953

The following selections of essays and stories by Virginia Woolf were published posthumously by the Hogarth Press and by Harcourt Brace Jovanovich:

The Death of the Moth and Other Essays. 1942
A Haunted House and other Short Stories. 1943
The Moment and Other Essays. 1947
The Captain's Death Bed and Other Essays. 1950
Granite and Rainbow. 1958
Contemporary Writers. 1965
Collected Essays. 4 volumes, 1966-67

WOOLF, Virginia and STRACHEY, Lytton: *Virginia Woolf & Lytton Strachey: Letters.* Edited by Leonard Woolf and James Strachey. Hogarth Press/Chatto & Windus, 1956; Harcourt Brace Jovanovich, 1957

INDEX

This is not an exhaustive index.
(ref=referred to)

INDEX

31; in love, 91; buys *The Nation*, 92; pamphlet on Mr Churchill, 114 and n; marries, 114; foretells catastrophe, 161; foresees failure of Asham Cement works, 169; on the young, 177–8; likes *The Years*, 200; illness, 201; on *Three Guineas*, 205; unwonted pessimism, 209; ref: 9, 37, 68, 83n, 87, 140, 155, 204n, 221

Keyneses (Maynard and Lydia), 90, 130, 132, 154

King's College, Cambridge, 178

Kitchin, C. H. B., 113

Knole, 132

La Fontaine, Jean de 148

Lamb, Walter, a figure of fun, 22; penchant for royalty, 23

Lansbury, George, 187 and n

Lappin and Lapinova, 208

Lawrence, D. H., only contact with, 65; ref: 50, 105, 151, 162, 185

Leaning Tower, The, 219

Le Grys, Mrs, remembered in *The Years*, 23; ref: 21, 22, 25

Lehmann, John, career in the Hogarth Press, 158, 168, 201, 204; enthusiasm for *The Waves*, 162; ref: 171, 186, 224

Les Rochers, Brittany, 210

Letter to a Young Poet, A, 171

Lewis, Wyndham, on VW, 183, 184; ref: 63, 192

Liverpool University, offers doctorate to VW, 172n

Lloyd, Marie, 77

Loch Ness, Monster of, 206

London Library, 47, 191, 207, 224

London Magazine, The, 86

London Mercury, The, 72

London National Society for Women's Service, 156

Long Barn, Kent, 111, 117

Lopokova, Lydia, *see* Keynes, Lydia

Lubbock, Percy, 134

Lucas, F. L., 90

Lyons' Corner House, 170

Lytton Strachey, a Biography, 218n

Macaulay, Rose, disastrous dinner with, 120–1; ref: 185, 191

MacCarthy, Desmond, resolves to write a novel, 23; his character, 81–3; conversation at Roger Fry's funeral, 180; ref: 43, 59, 83n, 138, 182, 188, 215, 257

— Mary (Molly), 12, 17, 23, 28, 83n

MacColl, Mrs, 47

Mackenzie, Compton, 185

Maitland, Florence, *see* Shove, Florence

Manchester, 77

Manchester University, 172 and n

Mansfield, Katherine, *see* Murry, Katherine

Mark on the Wall, The, 42, 43 and n, 72, 133

Marshall, Marjorie (*née* Thomson, known as Joad), 93, 103, 113

Martin, Kingsley, 170, 192, 206, 211

Martini, Simone, 96

Massingham, H. W., 92

Matisse, Henri, 7

Mauron, Charles, 188, 204n

Maxse, Katherine (Kitty), 87

Mayer, Louie, formerly Everest, 176 and n, 222, 223

Mecklenburgh Square, No 37, 210, 212, 218

Medea, 105

Memoir Club, 83 and n, 217

Men Without Art, 183

Mill House, Tidmarsh, 78

Minna, Aunt, *see* Duckworth, Sarah Emily

INDEX

Wellesley, Lady Dorothy, 197

Well of Loneliness, The, 138, 139

Wells, H. G., criticised in *Mr Bennett and Mrs Brown*, 104, 105; VW's relationship with, 122; ref: 95, 111, 133, 185

Whitman, Walt, 190

Wilberforce, Octavia, 224, 225

Wise Virgins, The, 9 and n

Wissett Lodge, Suffolk, 31, 32, 41

Women's Co-operative Guild, 3, 19, 35, 36, 36n

Woolf family (mother, brothers and sisters of LW), 3, 9, 22, 35

— family (Leonard and Virginia— 'Woolfs' or 'Woolves') to Clifford's Inn, 7; consult Savage, 14; at Richmond, 22; settled at Asham, 17; to Cornwall, 19; to Northumberland, 20; attitude to neighbours, 33; plan to buy a press, 38; their economies, 38, 41; keep two servants, 56; take Higher Tregerthen, 65; at Monk's House, 71; experiment with Desmond MacCarthy, 83; *To Spain*, 93; their unity, 94; social life in July 1925, 113; meet the Nicolsons, 116; disastrous meeting with Rose Macaulay, 120–1; to visit America, 125; troubles with Hogarth Press, 130; plan to end Hogarth Press, 131; to Cassis, 136; decide to see few people, 149; intervene to protect a whore, 150–1; to Italy, 126, 189; visit to Carrington, 165–7; plan to leave Rodmell, 170; to Ireland, 177; to France, 200; to Scotland, 205; visit Freud, 209; to Brittany, 210; wartime visits to London, 212; ref: 37n, 51, 87, 153, 176

— Herbert, 46

— Mrs (mother of LW), meets VW,

3; not at wedding, 4; tedious, 155; death of, 209; ref: 38, 46, 161

— Leonard: I—*As a guardian of Virginia Woolf's health*: records of her condition, 12, 13, 14; at Holford, 15; her suicide attempt, 16; his own health suffers, 17, 18, 19; analysis not attempted, 19n; apparent cure, 20, 21; relapse, 24; removal to Hogarth House, 25; VW's antipathy to him in 1915, 26; near to despair, 26; care of VW in 1915/16, 29, 30; role as family dragon, 34–5; restrains VW's generous impulses, 64; opposed to leaving Richmond, 102; promptitude in crisis, 114; regulation of VW's conduct in Berlin, 141, 142, 143; exasperated by her attendance at public meeting, 156; comforts VW when hurt by adverse criticism, 184; restrains her attempts at controversy, 185; conduct in matter of German excursion, 189; misgivings concerning *The Years*, 195; calculated falsehood, 196; diary entries in 1941, 224; consults Dr Wilberforce, 224, 225; dismisses reporter at Monk's House, 253

II—*As a politician*: political formation, 3, 7, 10; renewed activities, 23 and n; work with Margaret Llewelyn Davies, 25; attitude to the war, 30, 46; forms 1917 Club, 48; formation of League of Nations, 61; candidacy, 75, 77; views on General Strike, 122; rebuke to Labour candidate, 163; Labour Party Conference, 187 and n; on Munich Settlement, 207; on the war, 211; joins Local Defence Volunteers, 215

III—*As a publisher*: conception of the Hogarth Press, 23, 38; *Publication*

INDEX

on the Wall, 42, 43; diary renewed, 44–6; sense of a change of style, 72; journalism, 72 and n; vivid experience in London, 73–4; advantage of being one's own publisher, 74; *The Common Reader* and *Mrs Dalloway* written concurrently, 98–100; *Mrs Dalloway*, 101, 105, 107; *The Common Reader*, 105, 108; on biographers, 109; *To the Lighthouse*, 105, 120, 121, 122, 123, 124, 127; reactions to *To the Lighthouse*, 127, 128–9; *The Waves*, 126, 148, 150, 151, 156, 157, 159, 160; *Orlando*, 131, 132 and n, 136, 138; *A Room of One's Own*, 144, 148, 149; *Flush*, 163, 171, 172, 174; attitude to the study of English Literature, 173 and n; *The Years*, 171–2, 176, 179, 182, 185, 189, 191, 194, 195, 196, 198, 199, 200, 201; *Walter Sickert: a Conversation*, 173, 174 and n; *Roger Fry*, 182–3, 183n, 194, 204, 206, 207, 208, 209, 214, 215, 216; *Three Guineas*, 191, 197, 198, 203, 204, 205, 208; *Between the Acts*, 205, 211, 222, 224; unpublished memoirs, 211; *Anon* (unpublished), 222. See also *Anon*, *Between the Acts*, *The Common Reader*, *Mrs Dalloway*, *Flush*, *Jacob's Room*, *Kew Gardens*, *The Mark on the Wall*, *Night and Day*, *Orlando*, *Roger Fry: A Biography*, *A Room of One's Own*, *Walter Sickert: a Conversation*, *Three Guineas*, *To the Lighthouse*, *An Unwritten Novel*, *The Voyage Out*, *The Waves*, *The Years*, etc.)

IV—*Literary friendships*: meeting with Katherine Mansfield, 37 and n; subsequent relationship, 69–71; views on the 'Underworld', 50; on *Ulysses*, 54; relationship to Lytton Strachey, 54–5, 163–4, 165 (*see also* Partridge); friendship with T. S. Eliot, 63, 86, 135; meets Wells, 122; and Hardy, 123; relationship with E. M. Forster, 132–5, 191; with Hugh Walpole, 137–8; with Ivy Compton Burnett, 146; with John Lehmann, 158. See also *Mr Bennett and Mrs Brown*; Eliot, T. S.; Forster, E. M.; Hogarth Press; Spender, Stephen; Strachey, Lytton; and *Other Personal Relationships*

V—*Other Personal Relationships*: with Leonard Woolf, 1, 4, 5, 9, 94, 139, 204 *et passim*; with Mrs Woolf (her mother-in-law), 3, 4, 155, 209; with Ottoline Morrell, 44, 209; views on 'cropheads', 49; relationship with Nelly Boxall, 58–9, 176; mischief-making and indiscretion, 59–60, 78–80; attitude to Clive Bell, 85, 137; to Lydia and Maynard Keynes, 90; to Berta Ruck, 91–2; to V. Sackville-West, 116–20, 183; to Philip Morrell, 129; to Ethel Smyth, 151–153, 159–60, 170; to Stephen Tomlin, 160–1, 197; to Roger Fry, 179, 180–1; Julian and Vanessa Bell, 201–3, 218; to Janet Case, 201; to Elizabeth Robins, 225. See also Anrep, H; Bell, C.; Bell, J.; Bell, V.; Boxall, N.; Colefax, Lady; Dickinson, V.; Duckworth, G.; Fry, R.; Grant, D.; Keynes, L.; Keynes, M.; MacCarthy, D.; MacCarthy, M.; Nicolson, V.; Smyth, E.; Stephen, A.; and *Literary Friendships*.

VI—*Public affairs*: accompanies LW to industrial areas, 10; on the armistice, 61–2; on the Webbs, 61; the post-war world, 76–7; General Strike, 122; Freedom of Speech, 138;

TITLES BY VIRGINIA WOOLF
AVAILABLE IN TRIAD/PANTHER BOOKS

THE VOYAGE OUT

Rachel Vinrace is twenty-four. She has been sheltered with
love, but is now ready to discover 'life', to take the voyage out.

Moving away from Richmond means a real journey, for
Rachel is going to travel to South America on her father's
steamer. She will, in the intimacy of shipboard life, discover
the fashionable world of Mrs Dalloway, the academic
arrogance of a Cambridge don and first love in the shape of
Terence Hewlet who wishes that women could be the same as
men . . .

This is Virginia Woolf's first novel. Written in a simple,
flowing way, it is immediately accessible, thoroughly delightful.
There are only hints of the radical innovations of her later
novels, but the preoccupations which were to appear and
reappear are already present. Even in this, her earliest work,
the true originality which is the mark of her genius is present
and wonderfully alive.

£1.95

NIGHT AND DAY

Night and Day, Virginia Woolf's second novel, is about love
and marriage. These are familiar themes but Virginia Woolf is
asking questions which are both stunningly unfamiliar and
brilliantly incisive. The extent to which she involves us in her
characters' search for answers makes this not only one of her
most accessible novels, but also one which is highly relevant
to modern, everyday life.

What, after all, do love and marriage mean to women – and
to men? Does marriage necessarily involve compromise and
insincerity? Can intellectual development survive the loss of
solitude?

These questions, and many others still hotly debated today,
are posed by Katherine, daughter of a literary family who must
pursue her passion for mathematics in secret; by Mary,
committed to poetry, truth and Women's Suffrage; by Ralph,
who wants to believe that love between equals is possible, and
by William who can accept nothing less than unwavering
devotion . . .

'There is no writer who can give the illusion of reality with
more certainty . . . a perfection of style which is at once solid
and ethereal'
The Spectator

£1.95

A ROOM OF ONE'S OWN

A Room of One's Own is for everyone who has ever wondered
why it is that women are largely absent from the history
books, unless they are queens, mothers or mistresses.

Imagine that William Shakespeare had a sister, as
wonderfully gifted as himself. 'But she was not sent to
school . . . had no chance of learning grammar and logic . . .
Before she was out of her teens was to be betrothed . . . she
cried out that marriage was hateful and was beaten by her
father . . . She took the road to London . . . stood at the
stage door; she wanted to act. Men laughed in her face . . . At
last Nick Greene the actor-manager took pity on her; she
found herself with child . . . and killed herself one winter's
night . . .' In 1928 Virginia Woolf read two papers to the
women students of Cambridge. She wished to share with them
the ideas that had led her to conclude 'A woman must have
money and a room of her own if she is to write fiction'. *A
Room of One's Own* is the result. It is feminism infused with
humour and subtlety, and optimism for what the liberated
mind can accomplish.

'How much of life, and literature, and good society, and
philosophy, is packed into these pages.'
Bernard Blackstone

£1.25

THE YEARS

A family story from a writer of genius

London. A rainy day in 1880. The Pargiter children sit in their cluttered Victorian drawing-room staring through the windows and waiting for their mother to die. Her death will set them free to live their lives as they please. Or so they imagine. But the Victorian age is also a long time dying, and the scars it leaves fade slowly.

This is the story of the Pargiter family from the 1880s to the 1930s, a period of immense and exciting change. For some, the causes of their youth become the conservatism of another era. For others the search goes on, for new experiences, for wider horizons.

The Years was, during Virginia Woolf's lifetime, her most popular work and it remains her most accessible. Written with sympathy, insight and lively wit, it explores the ways in which the forces of society oppress the individual spirit.

£1.50

MOMENTS OF BEING

'By far the most important book about Virginia Woolf, and to
a lesser extent about Bloomsbury in general, that has appeared
since her death'
Angus Wilson, *The Observer*

'Moments of being' is Virginia Woolf's description of those
luminous experiences which remain in the memory after the
chaff of everyday life has been discarded. This collection of
autobiographical pieces brilliantly captures those moments of
her childhood, the early days at Bloomsbury, her attitude to
the grand social world.

In *Reminiscences*, written at the age of twenty-five, Virginia
Woolf vividly describes life in the large Stephen household of
her girlhood. But it is in *A Sketch of the Past* that she displays
her literary talent to the full. It is a thoughtful, moving
excursion into the past which gives sparkling glimpses of the
author's inner life, where tensions and fears are never far from
the surface.

These writings, together with the short, incisive *Memoir Club
Contributions*, are of absorbing interest, not just for their fact
and comment, but for the variety of literary form and
experiment they reveal.

£1.95

A WRITER'S DIARY

'A work of the highest imaginative genius, with powers of
perception and description unexampled in our time'
Isaiah Berlin, *Sunday Times*

From 1915 until her death in 1941 Virginia Woolf kept a
regular diary. This volume, *A Writer's Dairy*, consists of
extracts, selected by her husband Leonard Woolf, which relate
to her work and life as a writer. They reveal the excitement
and passion behind her creative genius but also show clearly,
and often painfully, the anguish and frustration that marked
Virginia Woolf's search for perfection.

If the commentary on her own work is the basic ingredient of
this *Diary*, the mixture is delightfully spiced with the witty,
shrewd and highly personal portraits she draws of friends and
fellow artists.

£2.50

THE WORLD'S GREATEST NOVELISTS NOW AVAILABLE IN TRIAD/GRANADA PAPERBACKS

Virginia Woolf

Night and Day	£1.95	☐
Between the Acts	£1.25	☐
The Voyage Out	£1.95	☐
The Years	£1.50	☐
To the Lighthouse	£1.25	☐
The Waves	£1.50	☐
Mrs Dalloway	£1.25	☐
Jacob's Room	£1.50	☐
Orlando	£1.50	☐
A Room of One's Own	£1.25	☐
Books and Portraits (non-fiction)	£1.95	☐

Memoirs

Moments of Being	£1.95	☐
A Writer's Diary	£2.50	☐

Quentin Bell's biographies available in Paladin Books

Virginia Woolf 1882-1912	£1.95	☐
Virginia Woolf 1912-1941	£1.50	☐

All these books are available at your local bookshop or newsagent, or can be ordered direct from the publisher. Just tick the titles you want and fill in the form below.

Name _____

Address _____

_____

Write to Granada Cash Sales
PO Box 11, Falmouth, Cornwall TR10 9EN.

Please enclose remittance to the value of the cover price plus:

UK 45p for the first book, 20p for the second book plus 14p per copy for each additional book ordered to a maximum charge of £1.63.

BFPO and Eire 45p for the first book, 20p for the second book plus 14p per copy for the next 7 books, thereafter 8p per book.

Overseas 75p for the first book and 21p for each additional book.

Granada Publishing reserve the right to show new retail prices on covers, which may differ from those previously advertised in the text or elsewhere.

TF381